Foundations of the assumed business operations and strategy body of knowledge (*BOS*BOK)

An outline of shareable knowledge

Gary R Oliver

DARLINGTON PRESS

First published by Darlington Press 2012
Darlington Press is an imprint of SYDNEY UNIVERSITY PRESS

Reproduction and communication for other purposes

Sydney University Press
Fisher Library F03, University of Sydney
NSW 2006 Australia
Email: sup.info@sydney.edu.au

National Library of Australia Cataloguing-in-Publication entry

Author: Oliver, Gary R.

Title: Foundations of the assumed business operations and strategy body
            of knowledge (BOSBOK) : an outline of shareable knowledge / Gary R. Oliver.
ISBN: 9781921364211 (pbk.)
Notes: Includes bibliographical references and index.
Subjects: Business--Handbooks, manuals, etc.
            Management--Handbooks, manuals, etc.
Dewey Number:
            658.4

Citation by reference style

APA (Publication Manual of the American Psychological Association):
Oliver, G. R. (2012). *Foundations of the assumed business operations and strategy body of knowledge (BOSBOK): An outline of shareable knowledge*. Sydney, Australia: Darlington Press.

MLA (MLA Style Manual):
Oliver, Gary Robert. Foundations of the assumed business operations and strategy body of knowledge (*BOSBOK*): An outline of shareable knowledge. Sydney, Australia: Darlington Press, 2012.

Dedication

For my Mother and Father.

The manuscript for this book was prepared initially in Microsoft Word v2003 and then v2010 by the author before being transferred to Adobe InDesign CS4 and finalised in CS5.5. Composed in Minion Pro (10.5/13) and Avenir.

Layout and cover design by Miguel Yamin, University Publishing Service

Contents

List of figures

List of tables

Preface

This primer is the first description of the assumed business body of knowledge. It is assumed business knowledge because business expects that its employees have a broad understanding of business even if their role and responsibilities are junior. *Foundations of the Assumed Business Operations and Strategy Body of Knowledge* provides an overview of knowledge about issues, techniques and decisions. These are informed by my own experience as well as other subject matter experts. The benefit is personal (knowing or understanding), career (experience or rewards) or in success of the business.

I first noticed there was a de facto assumed body of business knowledge in the 1970's when changing jobs. I was busy learning specific organisation policies and intricate procedural details including various control forms such as timesheets. But my supervisor and colleagues were more concerned with what I said to clients and managers. I began to give attention to knowledge in the workplace and read widely in management. I began to realise assumed business knowledge permeated most roles and responsibilities and can determine success or failure on a corporate or personal level. Three incidents reinforced my interest in knowing more about assumed business knowledge.

- When offered a chance to tear up an existing contract worth $5M and tender for a replacement contract worth $10M, Bill Fox the General Manager had no hesitation. He claimed he already knew the tenderer's needs and competitor weaknesses and had a winning strategy. Three months later the entire organisation was shocked when they heard the tender was awarded to the holder of a minor small contract with the customer. Shortly afterwards a large number of employees lost their jobs. Many employees could not understand why this occurred. Looking back I am convinced it was an early lesson in the usefulness of an assumed business body of knowledge. It makes clear that having superior resources without attention to the recurrent themes of performance and value overlooks key factors that influence decision-making.

- Summoned to an 'emergency meeting' late on a Friday, Jo Goodfellow was told that her internal consulting function in the public service would be outsourced as part of a commercialisation policy introduced by the new CEO. Despite its low costs, she was told that an organisation specialising in consulting would be cheaper as its costs would be distributed over a larger customer base and there would be better selection of projects. The CEO overlooked the contextual knowledge of the business that the internal consultants possessed. In fact, the costs were higher because the external consultancy managers were influenced by incentives to find additional consulting assignments. The assumed business knowledge suggests that outsourcing decisions are typically made on either a favourable financial comparison or a reduction in employee numbers and can overlook financial costs incurred in other parts of the business and non-financial costs. The assumed business body of knowledge fosters an awareness of issues and challenges faced by an organisation even when there is no personal knowledge of the actions of managers.

- After a takeover, Agatha Oldhand an experienced retail store manager was replaced by a new employee promoted from sales assistant. Max Newman acted as a mouth-piece for the new owners who immediately instituted a policy of premium markup on most products. Some customers detected the markup but many did not. Employees were uncomfortable with the policy and devised many grounds for exceptions. Using assumed business knowledge encourages a multidimensional view which recognises the combination of position in the life cycle and the bias in heuristics which produce generalisations and simplistic explanations (e.g. new ideas from a new owner) which are the products of largely automatic and unconscious mental processes.

Reflecting on these and many other business events culminated in the quest to understand what knowledge might be overlooked, discounted or taken for granted. With the assistance from colleagues using the Delphi method discussed in the appendix it became clear that the assumed business body of knowledge appears to be composed of five elements: (1) it is theory grounded, that is it uses analytical frameworks which have a formal basis; (2) it is evidence based, that is, there is some support from actual examples of businesses; (3) it is practical and has practical implications on how to improve business; (4) it is skeptical, that is it questions and explores; and (5) it rejects a single path to business improvement. So the ability to juxtapose many facets and simultaneously synthesise them can reveal hidden relationships and characteristics of the particular business and the industry. The following chapters provide a framework to harness this capability.

I tried to write *Foundations of the Assumed Business Operations and Strategy Body of Knowledge* without burdening it with detail which the reader might not want. I created a drill-down layer of footnotes and glossary of terms and expressions to separate the detail and make them easier to read. I hope you will agree. The introduction takes up the question what is an assumed business body of knowledge and why is it important.

Introduction to the assumed business operations and strategy body of knowledge

A body of knowledge (BOK) is a set of knowledge within a profession or subject area which is generally agreed as both essential and personally known. There are many formal examples. 'The Project Management Body of Knowledge (*PM*BOK) is an inclusive term that refers to the sum of knowledge within the profession of project management.' (Project Management Institute 2000: 3). Others are less formal for example, business analysis (International Institute of Business Analysts & Brennan 2006/2009) and valuation (Pratt 2003). For philosophy, Baggini and Fosl (2003/2010) referred to the philosophical body of knowledge as tools. Some BOKs lead to credentialisation (e.g. various Microsoft product certifications). Most of these BOKs are quite narrow.

The assumed business body of knowledge (*BOSBOK*) is broader. It is more diffused than knowledge gained from professional studies or in developing specialised skills. For example, it is wider that a formal business degree (Stewart 2009: 6) because it draws concepts, theories and examples from the disciplines of economics, education, finance, health sciences, international politics, law, marketing, philosophy and psychology. There are also differences dependent upon regulatory requirements of a country (e.g. allowable tax deductions) and business custom and practice (e.g. commissions and bonuses). In many ways it resembles the body of knowledge that an accomplished surgeon possesses after completing coursework and practical residencies. The *BOSBOK* enables improvisation and compromise and may mitigate mistakes where negligence, hubris and incompetence may affect many not just a single patient.

A broad business BOK is appropriate for two reasons. First the key challenges and principal tools differ depending upon the position of the business in the business life cycle. Second the managerial decisions and judgements depend upon the adaptation of the business to the issues confronting it and the ways it leverages allocated resources. A business BOK goes beyond a single theory or a set of specific techniques to offer a holistic framework for understanding business activities. It is therefore a better approach than that proposed by authors who take a textbook approach to assembling management knowledge. It is also superior to the encyclopaedic approach where topics remain separate except for cross-referencing. It is a starting point, not a comprehensive digest of management ideas,[1] although commentary is provided throughout.[2] References allow key sources to be found if required.

Nowadays when a commercial perspective has to be balanced with social and environmental considerations, specialist views can be too narrow. Conversely considering all possible stakeholders may result in bureaucratic or managerial approaches. BOSBOK seeks simplicity and considers the different aspects of a transaction to produce a richer understanding of the situation and most likely, a better outcome. There are considerable similarities in national economies and their commercial legislation (e.g. income tax). So there will be similar business challenges, interactions with government authorities and pressures from stakeholders.

The BOSBOK is useful for helping people understand business. The history of business has shown that its drivers for short-term results often create outcomes which are detrimental for both business and society. The continuing impact of the 2008 global financial crisis makes the advantages of considering context clear. Individuals also gain an appreciation of a broad economic position, a commercial perspective, capacity for reflection and career development. Employees and contractors who consider the wider ramifications for their action are likely to introduce checks and balances which make risk clearer and outcomes more transparent within the business parameters.

The BOSBOK makes for better decisions. Studies of decision-making tend to indicate that awareness of more than a single theory or criterion makes for a better decision. Perfect information may not be possible but BOSBOK offers a more informed understanding of the situation. The BOSBOK fosters asking questions and the spirit of inquiry. Investors in Lehman Brothers did not ask questions of the board or senior management; it was left to a few observers to ask basic questions.

The BOSBOK accepts a multidimensional view of economics and business. In The Wealth of Nations, Adam Smith (1776/1999) echoed earlier writers who observed that the actions of individuals are regulated by self-interest, an ability to reason and by moral sentiments including sympathy. Smith recognised a market dynamic known as the 'invisible hand'– the response to actions by individuals and rival businesses produces struggles among individuals – may have socially beneficial advantages.[3] While an efficient division of labour involves

---

1 Readers requiring an exhaustive tick-the-box approach are referred to speciality titles. Simple checklists are available, for example see Wright, (1977/2005). There are templates e.g. for business plans (Abrahams & Barrow 2005/2008). Outlines of best practice are found in the international standards; see for example, the ISO 9000 series (International Standards Organisation). Guides for particular professional groups are readily available, see for example, CCH (2009); Marsden, (2006/2008). Descriptions of frameworks and techniques are summarised, see for example, Harding and Long, (1998). Only the essential considerations and important concerns are surfaced.

2 There is usually some information online in the Wikipedia. However, it has many shortcomings. Most of its entries hardly go beyond providing definitions. Most have a narrow focus. Most use convenient or non-specialised references. The introduction of editorial moderation will make only a marginal improvement since an entry may appear authoritative by its structure with references while making unbalanced or excessive claims.

3 The market advantages of monopolies tend to encourage mergers and takeovers within an industry (subject to regulation) or collusion between businesses (Geis 1976). Smith (1776/1999) argued that anti-competitive business behaviour was an instance of inadequate competition. Frank (2011) sees it as a problem of reward based on rank which can only be solved by acting collectively. (Frank also suggests taxing harmful behaviours to eliminate government debt). The monopoly inquiries of the 1950's in USA suggested it is a problem of inadequate profits (United States Senate, 1961).

assigning each worker to the job that best suits their skills in markets,[4] there is a role for government to enforce contracts, oversee justice, regulate banking, protect intellectual property and provide public goods such as infrastructure and national defence.[5] 'Business' is used throughout the book to describe a trade, profession or occupation, or an enterprise that conducts a commercial or industrial operation. Other terms are used depending upon the context. They are 'company' (Collins 2001, 2006), 'corporation' (Berle & Means 1932), 'enterprise' (Hansmann 1980), 'entity' (Marcus, Tanis & van Fenema 2000), 'firm' (Porter 1980; Williamson 1964) and 'organisation' (Florence 1933; Weber 1956/1968). International and national businesses are the primary focus.

The *BOSBOK* encourages the view that the capacity for reflection is a personal advantage. The modern business gives very little time to employees for traditional learning through observation or from organisational storytelling. The employee who develops a capacity for reflection has a means for personal growth. Time-poor employees have limited acquisition of knowledge from outside sources such as reports in the media. Business expects employees to reflect on aspects of the business which are remote from their particular responsibilities as well as their own role and responsibilities. Part of this expectation arises from the tenets of continuous improvement and part arises from the development of critical faculties. Assumed knowledge is also reflective and reflexive.

The *BOSBOK* is also a career planning tool. Broad business knowledge is integral to personal career development. Understanding from the *BOSBOK* can suggest new career avenues. The assumed business body of knowledge can itself contribute directly by showing new orientations and preparations. Since the assumed business body of knowledge is not discipline specific it offers the widest possible variety of viewpoints. Business expects employees to take responsibility for their own career development. Assumed business knowledge reveals the many opportunities for career development by making use of strengths. (It is always possible with personal hobbies and interests to improve brain functioning.) In some cases awareness of the assumed business knowledge will suggest career planning which uses those strengths (e.g. Martin Feil's career path from customs officer to industry commissioner). In the *Effective Executive,* Peter Drucker advocates concentrating on strengths and avoiding the challenges raised by weaknesses.

In developing the *BOSBOK* it became apparent to me that it can overcome the pitfalls from three mistaken beliefs about business: First the reliance on Aristotelian analysis. That is, the belief that a problem is simplified by subdividing it. Second, a Newtonian view of the universe. That is, the attempt to making predictions assuming forces act like the laws of motion. Third, the quest for savings and to achieve control. That is giving primacy to efficiency without

---

4 A markets view of capitalism is contrasted with mercantilism where government regulation of an economy is justified for the purpose of augmenting national power to overcome rival nations. It can be contrasted with laissez faire or unregulated economic affairs. Other alternatives include monopolies and guilds, which are either dominated by activities pursued by the government itself, or government regulated. The aim of these models is to ensure the creation of economic growth through increasing returns. The market advantages of monopolies tend to encourage mergers and takeovers within an industry (subject to regulation) or collusion between businesses (Geis 1976).

5 Of course governments are tempted to make policies which improve their re-election prospects rather than improve outcomes for clients of government services and regulations.

considering effectiveness. These frameworks are often used to explain the unexpected when what is needed is a multi-threaded approach where careful attention to the context becomes equally as important as resolving the situation.

BOSBOK goes beyond increasing the factors under consideration. It provides five intersecting dimensions which both enrich personal understanding and provide increased opportunities for communication. In these times when the expectations of customers are far higher and competition is much fiercer, the broader knowledge base for making business judgements that the *BOSBOK* gives is an alternative to short-lived management fads.

Structure of the book, chapters and topics within chapters

The structure of the book is depicted in Figure 1 below. Each of the five dimensions opens with a description of its context (or setting), the perspective (or point of view adopted) and its impact (or effect) on business. It also provides an introduction to the set chapters which it contains.

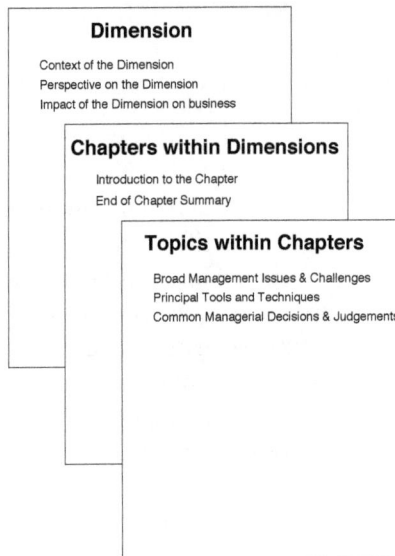

Dimension

Context of the Dimension
Perspective on the Dimension
Impact of the Dimension on business

Chapters within Dimensions

Introduction to the Chapter
End of Chapter Summary

Topics within Chapters

Broad Management Issues & Challenges
Principal Tools and Techniques
Common Managerial Decisions & Judgements

Figure 1. The structure of the assumed business body of knowledge with dimensions, chapters and topics

The *BOSBOK* detail is in each chapter. Each chapter comprises a number of Topics which are central to the assumed business body of knowledge. Each Topic also has a standard structure as follows. It opens with a short commentary. The backbone of each Topic is the triumvirate of management viewpoints (management issues and challenges, principal tools and techniques and managerial decisions). Management issues and challenges suggest the phenomena that may be encountered. Tools and techniques are the principal methods that could be used. Managerial decisions are the major questions to help formulate the decision. The managerial decisions and judgements are posed in the form of key questions. As with any matter, differences of opinion are bound to exist. The questions posed should be regarded as opening questions. The answers obtained should provoke additional questions. In general, about half a dozen points for each of the triumvirate are offered, although some Topics require a more extensive coverage.[6] The chapter then concludes with a summary.

Throughout the book two supplementary devices are used to keep each Topic brief. Footnotes are used throughout the book to amplify or comment on the main points.[7] They contain added information and supporting references to authors who advocate or criticise the view or provide examples. Definitions are removed from the text to avoid cumbersome interruptions and placed in a glossary of terms and expressions. The glossary is a guide to the vocabulary of management which is one of the five dimensions of the BOSBOK. It defines terms but more importantly identifies their relationships.

The reader is encouraged to explore those dimensions and select those chapters of interest to them. It is not necessary to read the chapters in their linear sequence. They stand alone. The vocabulary can be consulted to clarify terms and expressions.

Updates

Updates and supplements, including forms and templates, will also be posted on the book's website (www.sharing.info/bosbok.html).

Approach to assumed business knowledge

The approach prompts questions rather than presenting knowledge. The changing dynamic of business competition, the greater place of government in our lives and the diversity of opinion makes framing questions[8] a worthwhile skill. This approach encourages thinking about the point of knowledge in terms of elaboration and clarification, paraphrasing and synthesising, that is, making use of the knowledge.

The status of the BOSBOK is normative (or prescriptive) and positive (or descriptive). Normative views are used where there are clear indications on what is either a desirable or an unwise practice. These views are shaped by objectives, plans and analysis where a useful result or valuable outcome is sought. Positive views are used to indicate what theories are available, what beliefs are held, or what options might be considered. Much of the assumed business body of knowledge is contingent upon the situation rather than applying rules or following a recipe.

---

6 There is a small amount of redundancy across the topics and dimensions to ensure that different facets of assumed business knowledge are accorded proper attention.

7 Using footnotes is consistent with the publication style recommendation from the American Psychological Association (2009). The amplification and commentary with any supporting citations contribute a separate stream of value which can provide the reader with a supplement to the finished argument (Grafton 1997). The citing of literature is selective. In fact, the opinions that the cited literature represents were formed over time. In many cases there is widespread ignorance of both the primary sources and the processes by which those opinions were reached. Other aspects of style follow the Sydney University Press inhouse publication conventions.

8 Although Socrates as reported by Plato encouraged asking questions, Dewey (1934/1986: 331) advocated questioning to 'form … the independent habit of inquiry'. Dewey also saw questions as keeping a topic in development and review (Dewey 1933/1986: 332–33). Recent advocates of questions (e.g. Morgan & Saxton 1994/2006; Zwiers & Crawford 2011) confirm that questions foster critical thinking and content understanding.

1 The five dimensions of the assumed business operations and strategy body of knowledge

There are many descriptions available for understanding business. Selecting a single approach is unlikely to provide a rounded understanding. Multiple simultaneous dimensions, analytical frameworks, classifications or concepts must be used to decide what to do. They suggest the information that should be sought, assist formulating a range of options, weigh up the preferred course of action and manage its implementation.

Five business dimensions are useful to gain a rounded understanding.[1] The five dimensions are:

1. Position the business in one of the five stages of the business life cycle

2. Continuous and discontinuous adaptive behaviour to changing circumstances

3. Leverage available resources to improve performance

4. Recurrent themes supplements the initial three dimensions

5. The vocabulary of business knowledge.

Their relationship is shown as a lattice in Figure 2 on the next page.

---

1 Many other analytical frameworks exist including demographic, political, psychological and technological. The advantage of the above five dimensions is they readily organise the assumed business body of knowledge.

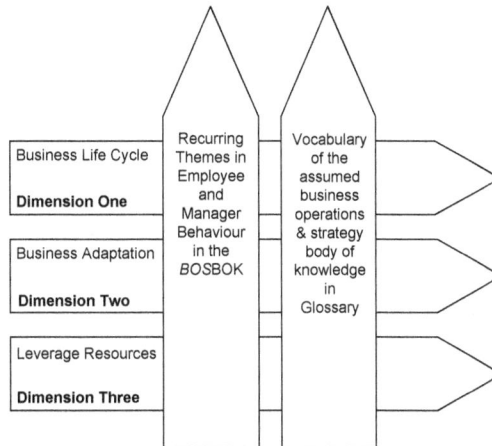

Figure 2. The lattice relationship of the five dimensions of the assumed business body of knowledge

1.1 DIMENSION ONE: Position the business in one of the five stages of the business life cycle

Life cycles are commonly defined for many different aspects of business. Cycles have been defined for acceptability/fashion (rubbish theory[2]), consumer products (product life cycle[3]), engineering projects (e.g. waterfall[4]) and quality of products and services (PDA[5]). The life cycle view of a business is based on the observation that a single business rarely survives for an extended period.

The five stages of the business life cycle suggests that a business passes through different stages of economic activity from its inception to its demise. The stages are an idealised, linear sequence. Business commences with its startup. This is discussed in Chapter 2. It is followed by growth or expansion domestically and often internationally. This is discussed

---

2 Rubbish theory suggests that product consumption moves through a cycle of fashionable to unfashionable but then may be rejuvenated and treasured (Thompson 1979).

3 It is used for (a) identifying the costs and revenues from the product over time and (b) framing strategy to manage the descriptions and properties of the product over different stages (Levitt 1965). The latter may also be termed product life cycle management. The product life cycle may also be responsible for the premature removal of products (Dhalla & Yuspeh 1976).

4 Many project cycles are in use. The original and basic cycle is known is usually described as a waterfall. A description and early criticism is by Royce (1970).

5 PDA is the Plan-Do-Act sequence (Shewhart 1939/1986; Deming 1982/1986). It has variants which include Plan-Do-Check-Act (PDCA) and Plan-Do-Study-Act (PDSA). It was originally intended to reduce tolerances in manufacturing to improve quality through consistency (Shewhart 1939/1986). Six sigma uses Define, Measure, Analyse, Improve and Control (DMAIC).

in Chapter 3. In maturity, sales revenue, market share and the available product or services are relatively stable. This is discussed in Chapter 4. Finally, in decline, the business is no longer sustainable in its current form unless a successful turnaround is completed. This is discussed in Chapter 5.

The continued existence of any particular business is unpredictable despite the sequential stages in the cycle.[6] Decline may occur earlier than the final stage. Turnaround may also occur before the final stage of decline if there are timely and substantial improvements to existing arrangements, growth in existing or new products or services and markets. In practice, turnaround issues are often similar to the issues associated with growth and turnaround is therefore placed in the same stage as growth. Turnaround may occur if there are timely and substantial improvements to existing arrangements, growth of existing products service and markets, or a strategic or operational turnaround. The common belief that moving into completely new markets with new products or services will mitigate decline is a high risk strategy.

1.2 DIMENSION TWO: Continuous and discontinuous adaptive behaviour to changing circumstances

Adaptive behaviour[7] describes the interaction between organised behaviour and their environment.[8] This is contingent upon history, the environment, customer preferences and revenue/funding flows. In practice adaptation involves structure, processes and boundaries.[9]

While adaptation implies a general fit between the business and its marketplace, there is also the matter of specific fit in relation to particular market segments and stakeholders and this is a central feature of the dynamics of business relationships. Adaptation may be reactive or proactive. A basic form of adaptation occurs when changing the structure and functions of the business. This is discussed in Chapter 6. A common form of adaptation is

---

6 There is a large literature on business fluctuations which are linked to economic growth, investment, employment and consumer demand (investment multiplier and accelerator). Schumpeter (1954) proposed a particular fluctuation may have three components: a long trend; a short or seasonal component; and an intermediate component. A long (major) cycle is 45–60 years (Kondratieff & Stolper 1935). The intermediate cycle is 7–11 years (Juglar 1862/1989). There are smaller fluctuations around 3–5 years (Kitchin 1923). All these have varying time cycles. Schumpeter considered these connected to innovations but excluded a 15–25 year cycle (Kuznets 1930). However, there are always random factors outside the combinations of cycles and subcycles (Burns & Mitchell 1946). These may be exacerbated where there are non-compensated errors (Pigou 1927), that is humans imitate one another's actions. There are also delays between economic action and its reporting. Pigou (1927) also emphasised amplitude over periodicity and identification.

7 This approach advocated by Alchian (1950) dispenses with profit maximisation and is used by Chambers, (1947/1986), Nelson and Winter (1982) and others including Toffler (1982). Other approaches include an evolutionary view using the business life cycle (OECD 1995) and the resource-based view (Barney 1991; Prahalad & Hamel 1991; Wernerfelt 1984).

8 Adaptation also has an interpersonal aspect using social exchange theory and trust theory as well as the familiar biological aspects.

9 While this draws on a specific form of business, the family business, the underlying theory is from the human relations and task-oriented business (Davis & Stern 1980). This avoids a sense of progressive adaptation allowing maladaption to also take place.

changing priorities to initiate new actions to respond to internal situations, external events and competitor actions. Existing priorities can be re-ranked or new priorities imposed. This is discussed in Chapter 7. Policies, controls and reviews allow operations to flexible accommodate change. This is discussed in Chapter 8. Personal power, authority, corruption and conflict are major determinants of business action. They have quite different effects on managers and employees. They can provide a rationale for action as well as create expectations which lead to conflict, pursuit of self interest and even betrayal. These are discussed in Chapter 9.

Adaptation changes the business in an evolutionary manner as well as by discontinuous interruptions. The burden of adaptation is often ignored by business in its quest for efficiency. The speed with which the change permeates the business depends upon the structure and agility of its resources.

1.3 DIMENSION THREE: Leverage available resources to improve performance

Resources, both tangible and intangible, must be carefully stewarded although this is difficult. One of the most important and least understood aspects of business is leveraging available resources. While economists use price[10] as the arbiter for the allocation of resources, this overlooks many other influences on the identification and allocation of resources.

There is a tendency to treat resources as objects overlooking that where humans are involved there is volition. This is discussed in Chapter 10. Another key resource is financial and non-financial information. Non-financial information often provides considerable supplementary understanding and background. It allows financial information to be qualified and situated in context. These are discussed in Chapter 11. Improving the tangible benefits from resources is not solely a quantitative matter although cost reduction measures remain a perennial favourite. Careful consideration of outsourcing products and services takes account of many outcomes, not only the short-term financial benefits. These are is discussed in Chapter 12.

Chapter 12 begins by noting there is general agreement that quality of the product or service is important although there are disagreements over which qualities are paramount in the product or service. Since the advent of knowledge management, there have been many instances of businesses turning to their employees for improvement and innovation although more recently this has shifted toward beneficial forms of training and credentialisation.

---

10 The economic theory of prices considers the actual and expected, current and forward prices of raw materials, finished products, services, labour. Before a resource is exhausted prices will rise, existing substitutes will be brought into more use, more efficient means to use the resources will be developed and new substitutes will also be developed. New and innovative products and services are generally priced well in excess of the cost of production to reward the human ingenuity and entrepreneurship associated with their production. Also in economics, price is distinguished from subjective value. Price is often used as an indicator of fairness when other details are hidden. However, the fact that there is no movement in price cannot be taken as an indicator of fairness since there can be changes in market capitalisation as well as subsequent movement in price as a delayed market response after additional information is considered.

Since cost reduction is usually a priority, wise capital investments in systems and technology offer an opportunity to avoid waste and failure. In many cases recognising the availability of resources and leveraging them to useful purposes can become a project in its own right. Some of the recurrent themes reveal how resources can be poorly utilised in adapting to change, or have their benefits miscalculated.

1.4 DIMENSION FOUR: Recurrent themes in employee and manager behaviour

Cutting across the three dimensions of life cycle, adaptation and resources are five recurrent themes: ethics, decision making, evaluating performance, value and improving business operations. The recurrent themes provide a set of considerations which can have consequences that are inefficient or ineffective when detail is overlooked.

Business behaviours are influenced by individual, peer and corporate morality or ethics. This is discussed in Chapter 13. Making a business decision or judgement often relies on a rational approach and using heuristics. This is discussed in Chapter 14. Evaluating productivity and profitability uses financial and non-financial information. This is discussed in Chapter 15. The quest for value in business is ably assisted by using Porter's value chain. This is discussed in Chapter 16. Automating business operations uses business cycles, business systems, business processes, workflow and data analyses. This is discussed in Chapter 17.

The recurrent themes are preoccupations that will be of concern to all managers and employees no matter where in the business life cycle the organisation is positioned, its adaptive behaviour and its resources. The recurrent themes guide behaviour and provide a set of considerations which can have consequences that are inefficient or ineffective when detail is overlooked. All four previous dimensions culminate in a vocabulary of assumed business knowledge.

1.5 DIMENSION FIVE: Vocabulary of assumed business knowledge

The fifth dimension is the vocabulary of assumed business knowledge. It is to be understood as an inconsistent set of terms and expressions with varying meanings which belong to families of terms and expressions, with synonyms and fashionable terms influenced by popular writings and the media coverage of authors.

Each industry and business develops its own terms and synonyms for existing terms and expressions which have currency based on the culture of the business, the industry and the discipline background of employees and managers. This is not necessarily identified in their discourse. So even specialist dictionaries as well as internet searches may only offer limited assistance. Moreover some dictionaries repeat the word to be defined in their definition so it is difficult to determine any practical meaning.

Business also has sayings, bon mots and maxims (e.g. 'The customer is always right'). Some are in conflict. (For example 'Do it right first time' and 'Practice makes perfect'). They depend for their success on sharing by employees, often in stories. They are not discussed as they are of secondary importance and do not add to assumed business knowledge.

DIMENSION ONE
POSITIONING THE BUSINESS IN ITS LIFE CYCLE

Context of the business life cycle

The business life cycle provides a convenient sequence of stages that a business may experience over time.[1] In many businesses the stages from startup to decline are clear. For example, the production and sale of analogue cameras is in terminal decline after popularity peaked in the 1970's with instant cameras. By subdividing the life cycle into stages, it is clear that success in an earlier stage does not guarantee survival in a later stages. For example, the initial success establishing railways in England did not ensure continued profitability.[2]

Perspective on the business life cycle

By considering the position of the business in the life cycle it is possible to anticipate a many characteristics and preoccupations of the business. For example, a growing business will be concerned with supporting its expanding products and services while a declining business will be concerned with using its capacity. Moreover, the stages are independent of whether it is run from home, from a secretarial service or from a formal office and in what industry and employment sector it falls.

Impact of the business life cycle

Understanding where a business fits on life cycle will help foresee upcoming challenges and frame decisions and judgements. Not every business will pass through each stage. Nor is it necessary for the stages to be experienced in the sequence of the life cycle.

---

1 The business cycle is distinguished from the economic cycle. The economic cycle is the periodic but irregular rise and fall of economic activity, measured by fluctuations in real GDP and other macroeconomic variables. Both the business cycle and the economic cycle are irregular and unpredictable. While the economic cycle may affect the business cycle, other factors such as owner competence, product or service viability and competition affect the cycle experienced by a particular business. Peaks and troughs in the economic cycle may not coincide with the profitability of a particular business.

2 Railways 'played a leading role in enlarging the investment market' but since shares were only partly paid there was considerable speculation (Perkin 1970: 178–79). Their decline was partly due to 'old and costly capital investment which had to be paid for out of current profits' leaving them vulnerable to new competitors and partly through attempts to solve this by 'econom[ising] in running costs' which meant labour costs (Perkin 1970: 287) .

Chapters in Dimension One (Business life cycle)

Four sequential stages are recognised in the business life cycle. They are:[3]

1. **Startup**   Establishing the full or part-time business and the assumption of continuity (discussed in Chapter 2)

2. **Growth**   Issues that arise from concerns with improving profitability (discussed in Chapter 3)

3. **Maturity**   Responding to reduced or stable revenue, profitability or erosion of market share (discussed in Chapter 4)

4. **Decline**   Issues that arise from cessation of the business activities (discussed in Chapter 5).

---

3 Many different numbers of stages are identified by different researchers. Those with six or seven stages (a) recognise as a separate stage the germination of the idea, (b) separate growth into growth and expansion and (c) separate decline from closure/exit. The additional stages do not increase understanding. 'Maturity' and 'decline' are preferred as they emphasise the opportunities for turnaround. Many features and themes from earlier stages continue to be relevant in later stages.

2 Startup: Establishing the full- or part-time business as a going concern

Startup covers inception or acquisition from the initial idea until the general purpose financial statements are produced for the first year. There any many reasons for establishing a full or part-time business. Its basis may be rational or irrational exuberance.[1] The effort may be based on experience or using first principles.[2]

Going concern or business continuity

When establishing a business the assumption is one of ensuring continuity. Many short term actions are attractive. Activities that have long-term adverse consequences are usually avoided. This may be due to the public nature of unpleasant consequences. For example, the loss of personal reputation where a business becomes insolvent. Or it may be due to the repercussions. For example, where there is knowledge that criminal prosecutions or substantial pecuniary penalties may be imposed.

Nevertheless, statistics suggest that the duration of many small and medium sized businesses is less than five to ten years.[3] In addition to the influence of the economic cycle, the owner or owner's family circumstances may change forcing business re-arrangements. Examples of these forces include acute competition in the shopping centre, human lifespan development or ill-health of the owner and the need to move with the business cycle into new products or services.

There are two notable examples where continuity is not an assumption. First, the organisations setup for a specific purpose (e.g. Sydney Olympics Authority for the year 2000 Olympics in Sydney Australia.). Second, fraudulent businesses (whether or not using the internet) are based on a limited period of exposure in which to collect confidential information and/or

---

1 Business literature as well as the social psychology literature has long recognised that emotions and biases affect judgement. Recent investigations propose that there is consistency in the operation of emotions and biases (Ariely 2008/2009; Sutherland 1992/2007).

2 According to Arisotle, the begining of enquiry is a problem or purpose. First principles are intuited or understood a priori but there is dialectic between inutition and reason or logic. Some of the first principles are peculiar to the discipline in question, such as definitions, while others are so general that they are common to all the disciplines. So the process is a mixture of rationalism and empiricism (Irwin 1990).

3 There are some differences between types of businesses. For example, the business duration of cafes and restaurants tends to be far shorter than chemists and professional services such as lawyers.

revenue. These often rely on Ponzi style judgment as to when incoming revenue funding is maximised against cash outflows to existing investors. For example, the Madoff Investment Securities Ponzi[4] scheme was unravelled when high investor withdrawals resulted in unexpected illiquidity.

E-business models for reach and richness

Since an e-businesses cannot rely on the public passing its store, its central goal is to find ways to attract and retain customers. Essentially this is the sales life cycle adapted and updated for the internet. Table 1 below identifies the major stages in an internet sales life cycle and provides a description of how the business translates its bricks and mortar approach to virtual contact with its prospective and established customers.[5]

Table 1. Major stages in the sales life cycle (traditional and e-business)

Traditional sales cycle	E-Business sales cycle	E-business objective
Search and identify suitable products and services	Attract	Online customers must be lured into the electronic marketplace. Websites should offer attractive virtual storefronts that will enhance the shopping experience. The pages and content of a website must be efficiently designed for ease of access, shopping and buying. There must be sufficient server power and telecommunications capacity for fast responses in searching and processing transactions.
	Inform	A website must provide an online customer with relevant information such as the product specification (including weight and size), accurate depiction of colour and supplementary information such as availability and the shipping cost and time.
Select and negotiate	Customise	A site should allow a customer to select exactly what he or she wants. Customers should be able to 'select colours and mix and match' product components to their own personal specifications.

Continued over page

---

4 A Ponzi scheme, named after its Italian devisor, relies on the revenue provided by new investors, promised high financial returns or dividends that are not available through traditional investments, to fund the periodic interest payments to the whole investor base (Ponzi 1937/2001). It is one of many forms of fraud that are widespread and often ingenious as shown by the wholesale petrol tax fraud described by Franzese (2009).

5 In order to properly forecast sales, the traditional sales cycle begins with the customer's perception of a product, or a perception of a need that the product might satisfy, evaluates and considers how long a sale will take to conclude and when and how often customers buy. An e-business sales cycle offers many opportunities to shorten it without relying on the personal selling skills of a sales person (Choi *et al.* 1997; Sterne 1997).

Traditional sales cycle	E-Business sales cycle	E-business objective
Purchase	Transact	The objective of any e-business website is to finalise the sale. This will depend upon the revenue model used (see Table 2 below).
	Pay	Customers must have an option to pay for products and services by cash (cheque), credit, debit, or using a third party (e.g. PayPal). Finalising the sale will depend upon the customer having confidence that all sensitive information from the transaction is secure from unauthorised use and will not be shared with other parties unrelated to the transaction (e.g. mailing list vendors).
-	Interact	Once a transaction is complete, post-sales support begins. Customers need to be kept up-to-date with progress on processing the transaction (order status updates) and allowed to rate the product or service purchased and the transaction. There may also be advice and problem resolution. Some advice can be handled through customer bulletin boards or forums. There may also be special interest groups to give customers with similar interests a feeling of belonging to a unique group. The business will also want to provide its online customers with exclusive offers and updates as incentives to return and buy. Such socialisation helps build customer loyalty and value
Deliver	Deliver	Reliable fulfilment and delivery systems are the key to customer satisfaction. It requires careful selection of suppliers and supply-chain management becomes critical.
After-sales service	Personalise	During each visit, the e-business should learn something about the customer to improve the next online interaction. This may include keeping a record of customer purchases, allowing a wish list to be maintained and providing details of similar products. The business should also analyse the data it captures so it can offer better products and services.

Ordinarily there is a trade-off between richness and reach so a business has to determine what kinds of richness it can add and how it will do so. However, e-business eliminates the trade-off so rich information can still have considerable reach (Evans & Wurster 1999). E-business opportunities framed around e-commerce business models and a revenue model need to take into account the impact on the businesses in the short and long-term.[6] Many businesses are unclear on how to pursue these business models particularly given the high costs and risk consequences if the initiative fails. Table 2 below subdivides e-business into e-commerce business models and revenue models.

Table 2. E-business models for e-commerce and revenue

E-Business models	Options	Description of service
E-commerce business models	Marketplace concentrators	Provide information about products and services from multiple providers allowing comparison shopping. Example: getprice.com.au
	Transaction brokers with some traditional delivery elements	A third party represents a manufacturer or reseller for specific products and services
	Content provider	Creates or allows access to content that it develops. Example: news.com.au
	Virtual storefront	For order placement and tracking with non-digital delivery through traditional means. Example: amazon.com
	Digital product delivery	Software, movies, music, books and other media are downloaded to the device which will play them. Example: itunes.com
	Electronic clearing house	Merchandise and surplus can be listed for sale. Example: ebay.com
Transaction model	Catalogue	Customers select products and services from a list
	Exchange	Customers buy and sell at negotiated prices
	Auction	Buyers bid on products and services
	Reverse auction	Sellers bid for the business of a buyer

Continued over page

6 The impact of the internet is a source of fundamental change to the business practice with the substitution of existing market arrangements by computer-aided buying and selling (Malone *et al.* (1989) so it is more than transaction processing, workflow automation and an aggregation of infrastructure and technology. It can simplify business processes, support electronic commerce, enable enterprise-wide communications and collaboration with its stakeholders. For an extensive discussion see Weill and Vitale (2001) although the differential success that business have had using the same business model suggest that many aspects of internet models remain uncertain.

E-Business models	Options	Description of service
Revenue models	Customer payment includes a profit margin	The sale generates a profit similar to a bricks and mortar store (a mark-up)
	Customer fees or commissions on sales or transactions	A charge is calculated (e.g. based on the value of transaction). May be in addition to margin.
	Supplier sale earns revenue	The e-business receives its payment from the supplier of the product or service (e.g. royalty)
	Supplier commission	The e-business receives a commission from the supplier when the product or service is sold (e.g. giving a brand preference in sales)
	Supplier contracts	The e-business negotiates payments when sales reach specified levels (e.g. rebates)
	Supplier fees	The e-business receives a payment for allowing the supplier to be associated with them (e.g. place an advertising banner on a webpage).

Topics in the startup stage of the business life cycle

Starting a business is a major decision requiring careful planning and execution with careful monitoring of progress. There are five programs of activity in startup:

1. Express and pursue the initial strategy
2. Crucial role played by the owner or founder
3. Determine the marketing, advertising, promotion and brand position
4. Establish and foster external relationships
5. Adopt a taxation planning viewpoint.

2.1 Express and pursue the initial strategy

At the outset the business establishes its initial priorities, scale of operations and its preferred methods of competition.[7]

---

7 Even popular biographies of charismatic business executives with a 'get rich quickly' goal advocate considerable preparatory effort (e.g. Belfort 2007), that is, strategy.

The broad management issues and challenges in expressing and pursuing the initial strategy include:

- Determining the broad strategic direction and offering the products or services that will satisfy perceived needs and wants of the buyers and using selected channels to reach them[8]
- The extent to which the strategy is expressed in a formal document or is held in the mind of the owner
- The extent to which competitors are perceived as active rivals
- Obtaining funding[9]
- Translating the strategy into a business plan[10]
- Finding time to review the business plan annually.[11]

The principal tools and techniques commonly utilised to express and pursue the initial strategy[12] include:

- Matching the experience and skills of the owner to the business opportunity
- A vision statement[13]
- A mission statement[14]
- The five P's or 7 S's of strategy[15]
- A fully articulated budget
- A SWOT analysis[16]

---

8 The combination of technical, social and economic change expanding into personal and social life impacts customers of businesses economically and psychologically. Attempts to extrapolate a future out of those trends may be inaccurate (e.g. Toffler 1970) but can indicate some problems that business will face.

9 Many small businesses are funded by the owner (e.g. from superannuation or other sources). See Chapter 3 (Growth: Issues that arise from seeking improved profitability) for discussion of flexible and balanced financing.

10 Best practice dictates that the rationale for establishing a business is a written business plan. It may be short and simple or comprehensive. As a minimum it envisions the next twelve months (anchored to a calendar or financial year) and contains milestones for a longer horizon (three or five years). The business plan may be shaped by the owner or influenced by stakeholders who provide equity, loans and products/services. Consequently there is no specific format and detail for the business plan.

11 Although there are wide variations in how it is structured, the business plan usually covers in detail (1) the products or services provided (2) the customer value proposition and (3) the cash flows.

12 Often management obtains assistance from consultants to 'give a second opinion'.

13 A vision statement encapsulates the future for the business aligned with the values and culture of the business. Often the vision statement is not labelled as such. For example at Hewlett-Packard this management outlook is known as 'The HP Way' (Packard 1995; Yuen 2007).

14 Examples of mission statements are provided by Foster (1993) and Abrahams (2007). The mission statement encapsulates the essence of the business as endorsed by the board and CEO. A new CEO is therefore likely to either endorse or change the mission statement.

15 There are two implementations or formulations of strategy (Mintzberg & Quinn 1991). The five P's are: plan, ploy, pattern, position and perspective. The seven S's are: structure, strategy, systems, superordinate goals, skills, style and staff. Mintzberg and Quinn (1991) argue against a single definition of strategy.

16 The SWOT analysis is the usual starting point for strategy (Johnson, Scholes & Whittington 1984/2005).

- A resource analysis[17]
- An external environment factor analysis[18]
- An industry analysis using the five forces.[19] Consider:
  - Competition among rivals[20]
  - Power of buyers
  - Power of suppliers
  - Threats to new entrants
  - Availability of substitutes.
- Matching strategy and structure to position in the supply flow[21]
- Determine strategic direction that is the generic competitive strategy[22] (See Figure 3).

Competitive advantage

		Lower cost based on operational efficiency and effectiveness	Differentiation based on focusing on the market
Competitive scope (Target)	Broad	Cost leadership	Differentiation
	Narrow	Cost focus	Focused differentiation

Figure 3. Generic competitive strategies recommended by Porter (1980)

---

17 Resources are the scarce potential value to the business. They may become capabilities (including value-creating core competencies). Resources are considered in terms of usage (allocation, combination, stretching resources to get more out of them (e.g. best practice and reuse) and their performance. Resources vary across different products or services and in more than one business unit.

18 There are many different factor descriptions. The set recommended is PESTEL (sometimes rearranged as PESTLE) meaning the Political, Economic, Social, Technological, Environmental and Legal factors (Johnson Scholes & Whittington 1984/2005). There are earlier variations known as PEST and STEP (Social, Technical Economic and Political). It allows diverse macro economic factors such as weak consumer spending, impact of weather to be identified.

19 In an update of a 1979 article Porter (1979/2008) proposes that the five forces to allow managers to consider competition that might emanate from other than the direct and known competitors by considering the underlying drivers of profitability.

20 Small business has to compete with other small businesses but also big business and the red tape of governments at all levels. The increasing role of independents in parliament tempts vote buying, either through the government offering enticements to independents to support legislation, or through businesses offering enticements to independents who lobby in their interests. The increasing role of independents may also encourage governments to be risk averse for fear of losing the support of independents. It is unclear what impact this will have on business and consumer confidence.

21 A vertical integration strategy should consider the supply stages (raw materials, primary manufacture, fabricator, product producer, consumer marketer and retailer) and determine its centre of gravity between the upstream and downstream stages (Galbraith & Kazanjian 1987).

22 Generic strategy is expressed as either low cost leadership or differentiation from its competitors (Porter 1980). Trying to do both will result in being 'stuck in the middle' (Porter 1980). The market where the generic strategy is applied may be broad or narrow (niche).

The managerial decisions and judgements in expressing and pursuing the initial strategy include:

- What should be the business profile? Consider:
  - What is the intended employer sector?[23]
    - Large
    - Medium
    - Small.
  - In what of the four commonly recognised industry sectors will the business will operate?[24]
    - Manufacturing (e.g. cabinet makers, petroleum refiners and steel makers)
    - Merchandising (e.g. grocers, milliners, supermarkets and toy stores)
    - Resources (e.g. the mining of iron ore)
    - Service[25] (entertainment, hospitality and transport).
  - What is the profit motivation?
    - For profit
    - Not-for-profit.[26]
  - What will be the ownership sector?
    - Private
    - Public
    - Mutual (Co-operative, association, or friendly society).
  - What will be the business presence?
    - 'Bricks and mortar'
    - Online (or virtual)

---

23 Small scale businesses require a location, small stock and simple supporting technology. Examples include the corner store and the café or takeaway store. They dominate the local retail trade and the supply of household services. Medium size businesses may be either be medium scale businesses serving large populations or a chain of small trading businesses. Examples include the multi-location business and the large shop with several departments. They cater to specialised demand. Large scale businesses depend upon an assured demand that can justify high initial outlays of capital investment with long-term return. Examples include industrial operations in mining, consumables, durables and service centres in a branch network. A criterion is provided by Florence (1933) which considers transactions, contingent reserves and capacity (or multiples).

24 An industry sector should not be confused with an ownership sector, an employer sector, or an economic development sector. An employer sector is small, medium or large. The ownership sectors are: nonprofit, private and public. The economic development sectors are: primary, secondary and tertiary; these are part of the three sector hypothesis introduced by Fisher (1935) and developed by Clark (1940/1951).

25 The prevalence of some service businesses to also sell products to increase the revenue should not be overlooked. For example, the personal hairdresser who uses the grooming relationship to sell 'professional quality' shampoos, conditioners, hair brushes etc to their clients. Another example is the artist or band which makes tour merchandise available in the foyer before and after their show. Harley-Davidson has developed a major merchandising business to accompany its core motorcycle business.

26 Not-for-profit enterprises may place themselves at a disadvantage if they attempt to be business-like (Collins 2006).

- o A combination of 'bricks and mortar' and online.
  - What is the appropriate legal entity?[27]
    - o Sole trader
    - o Partnership
    - o Proprietary company
    - o Limited company
    - o No-liability company[28]
    - o Trust.
  - What industry categorisation is used?[29]
- What is the context of the business? Consider:
  - What is the macro, (general or institutional) environment?
  - What is the micro (or industry) competitive environment?
  - Do barriers exist which make for easy or difficult entry and exit?[30]
  - To what extent are industry competitors likely to be active rivals?
  - What substitute product or services constitute a threat or opportunity?
  - Does the strategy rely on the law of plenitude?
  - What alternative channels of supply constitute a threat?
  - What is the stability of the industry?[31]
- To what extent does the industry ably represent itself to government, suppliers and the public through representative bodies?

---

27 It is optimal to set up in the correct structure at the outset because transfer of businesses and real estate incurs substantial stamp duty and legal expenses and negate serious tax timing issues, such as the small business CGT concessions available to an individual selling a business after being in operation for 15 years.

28 In Australia, mining companies are not entitled to calls on the unpaid issue price of share and shareholders are not liable to pay calls on unpaid shares.

29 There are many different categorisations which usually depend upon the business or authority collecting statistical or other data from the business. They can be characterised as broad and detailed. An examples of a broad categorisation from the Australian Bureau of Statistics is the Australian and New Zealand Standard Industrial Classification (ANZSIC, 2006/2008) comprising: A = Agriculture, Forestry and Fishing; B = Mining; C = Manufacturing; D = Electricity, Gas and Water Supply; E = Construction; F = Wholesale Trade; G = Retail Trade; H = Accommodation, Cafes and Restaurants; I = Transport and Storage; J = Communication Services; K = Finance and Insurance; L = Property and Business Services; M = Government Administration and Defence; N = Education; O = Health and Community Services; P = Cultural and Recreational Services; and Q = Personal and Other Services. Ratings businesses such as Dun and Bradstreet also have their own industry classifications.

30 The magnitude of returns in an industry depends upon the strength of market entry and exit barriers (Porter 1980). These change over time owing to changes in intellectual property (e.g. expiry of patents), developing capabilities within the business and the formation of strategic alliances. The barriers include available, knowledge or government approval. For example, there are many barriers which make setting up as a new bank difficult. But there are very few barriers which prevent setting up a new café. Some barriers may not be apparent until the setup of the business is under way.

31 The stability of the industry is affected by the number of businesses in it and whether it is easy for existing businesses to exit and new businesses to enter it.

In summary, there is a tension between establishing or maintaining existing operations and taking advantage of emerging situations.

2.2 Crucial role played by the owner or founder

The experience, skills and passions of the owner of the business play a crucial role in shaping the business and in determining its success.[32]

The broad management issues and challenges that arise from the crucial role of the owner or founder include:

- Giving sufficient attention to anticipate and respond to the direction the business is taking
- Clarity of the values and aspirations of the owner or founder
- The availability of funds (e.g. using funds provided by their superannuation payout or property sale)
- Adopting a different life style
- Making a quick profit
- A preference for being their own boss (that is, self-employment).

The principal tools and techniques used by the owner or founder to understand the business include:[33]

- A business plan covering sales strategy
- A fully articulated budget
- Cash flow projections.

The managerial decisions and judgements of the owner/founder (sometimes acting on recommendations advised by others) initially will include:

- Where funds should be obtained?
- What costs and obligations are appropriate for equity and borrowings?
- What should be the initial products or services that the business offers?
- Where should the business be located?

---

32 Mokyr (2009) suggests that entrepreneurship, trade and business depended a great deal on what key players knew and believed and how those beliefs affected their economic behaviour. For example, the Filofax diary and organiser business managed by Grace Scurr was bombed in World War 2. The building and all records were destroyed. Scurr had meticulously kept customer details up-to-date in her own Filofax and was able to resume business (Sinclair 1988: 2–3). Wiener (2004) traces the decline to an industrial ethos in which the aesthetics of industry which were critical of manufacturing and mechanised agriculture replaced the moral concerns of earlier generations.

33 Some of this knowledge may also be held by the owner or founder in her or his head owing to their day-to-day involvement in the business.

- Should items be purchased (asset) or leased?
- What are the priorities for sales and marketing?[34]

In summary, the owner's or equity holder's values and aspirations are crucial in shaping the business priorities.

2.3 Determine the marketing, advertising, promotion and brand position

The marketing, advertising, promotion and brand position is itself part of the business strategy. It aims to stimulate sales directly[35] and create a brand image[36] for the business.

The broad management issues and challenges concerning marketing, advertising, promotion and brand position include:

- The need to attract customers and the preferred customer profile
- The methods to gain maximum exposure of products and services
- The unique value proposition for the customer[37]
- The budget for marketing, advertising and promotion
- The budget for marketing, advertising and promotion of competitors
- The expected return in terms of improved sales volume, margin and profit
- The customer perception of the product.[38]

---

34 Products and services that are high-tech should be marketed differently to other industries. The chasm theory (Moore 1991/2002) argues that the Technology Adoption Life Cycle should differentiate between the early adopters of a technology and the mainstream market. Hence marketing to the groups might have to be different. A similar point is made by Shapiro and Varian (1998).

35 This claim was part of the justification used by Ogilvy Mather. In a post-television but pre-internet tutorial on slogans, brands and copyrighting (Ogilvy 1983: 1) it was the opening paragraph. The book also underlines the importance of having and using research.

36 The advantage of achieving a recognisable brand may include: (1) Greater willingness to sample or purchase the product or service; (2) A greater likelihood in choosing the product or service over a competitor; (3) A willingness to pay a higher price; (4) A willingness to switch other purchases to a product or service related to the brand; (4) Reduced time taken to finalise sale of the product or service; (6) increased reluctance to switch to competitor offerings after price increases; and (7) Less willingness to sample or purchase competitor products or services.

37 The unique value or selling proposition is the benefits the customer receives. 'A product is sold to satisfy a certain need.' (Goldmann 1958/1971: 16); for example furniture is the product but the need or idea is comfort. After releasing a book with a similar customer needs approach (Girard 1977) he championed marketing the self (Girard 1979: 29–31) as 'we're all salespeople' (p 16).

38 For example, Japanese cars were able to penetrate the USA market owing to their lower price and smaller size but the perception also that the Japanese made better quality cars (Halberstam 1986). Japanese cars may have had a market share exceeding 30% in the 1970's if it had not voluntarily capped its exports.

The principal tools and techniques commonly utilised in marketing, advertising, promotion and brand position include:

- Using survey, analysis and focus group techniques[39]
- Determining the market[40]
- Development of a brand image[41]
- Test marketing[42]
- Use of customer advisory panels and pilot programs
- Connection between a category and the brand[43]
- Association of the brand with community activities or charities.

The managerial decisions and judgements involved in marketing, advertising, promotion and brand position include:

- How does the marketing, advertising, promotion and brand strategy support the business strategy?
- Are marketing, advertising, promotion and brand positioning being tailored for market segments?
- What is the short-term financial cost and benefit to the business?
- What are the aspirations for the brand image and how will they be attained?
- What will be the priority in product or services advertised or promoted?
- Are major businesses who are customers being leveraged?
- What value proposition is most valuable to our customers?
- How can the brand be leveraged?

In summary, marketing has short and long-term objectives. Where a cost leadership strategy is adopted, comparison with competitor cost bases are essential. Where a differentiated

---

39 For an introduction to survey design highlighting the key questions and describing many of the issues and pitfalls, see Krosnick and Fabrigar (1997).

40 Essential market information includes: (1) Determining the measure to be used; (2) Alternative ways of segmenting the market with the goal of giving the business leverage; (3) An estimate of the current size and potential for growth of each market segment served; (4) A reliable estimate of the market share the business has in each market segment; (5) An estimate of the value of the potential growth for the business in terms of product offered and the augmented services; (6) The main strengths and weaknesses where action would significantly improve customer perceptions; and (7) Knowledge of the most and least profitable products and customer groups for the business. Poor definition of the market may lead to incorrectly understanding the market and therefore pursuing unproductive marketing and advertising (Levitt 1960).

41 Product choices may be partly evolutionary in the sense that choices are rooted in the desire to advertise our personality and attract friends and partners (Miller 2009).

42 The account of an early pioneer (Hopkins 1923/1966) in selling mundane products by direct marketing guided Ogilvy Mather (Ogilvy 1983).

43 Perception is primarily the connection of a category (e.g. chic, luxury, prestige) with a brand (e.g. Apple, Mercedes Benz, Rolex) so that each category leads to a brand provided the brand is not contaminated by multiple, contradictory messages (Reis 2009).

strategy is adopted advertising campaigns must enhance the value of the product or service perceived by the customer.

2.4 Establish and foster external relationships

There are many external relationships essential to the business. They go beyond any list of stakeholders, political connections, mentors and confidants.

The broad management issues and challenges concerning external relationships include:

- The need to retain existing relationships
- The need to pursue new relationships
- The need to establish relationships with stakeholders[44]
- Preferences for formal or informal relationships.

The principal tools and techniques to establish and foster external relationships include:

- Shareholder agreement and buy-sell agreement
- Stakeholder identification[45]
- The formation of or joining industry associations[46]
- The use of lobbyists to meet with politicians and departmental heads to put the case for a development proposal
- Establishing a presence in the community[47]
- Hosting social occasions.[48]

The managerial decisions and judgements to establish and foster external relationships include:

- How will capabilities and core competencies be protected?[49]
- What is the likely financial and non-financial cost and benefit to the business?

---

44 A stakeholder theory comprises attitudes, structures and practices (Freeman 1984) but the 'concepts stakeholder, stakeholder model, stakeholder management and stakeholder theory are explained and used by various authors in very different ways and supported (or critiqued) with diverse and often contradictory evidence and arguments' (Donaldson & Preston 1995: 66).

45 A competitor is not a stakeholder.

46 Competitors may form an association to represent their industry. The industry association may also lobby the government concerning regulation of the industry and the effects of government taxes and charges on the industry.

47 This may be done through support for local community groups such as sporting clubs, charities or providing assistance to schools. The support may take the form of donations and/or supply of products at discount or no cost.

48 The golf day is a popular event with many suppliers and customers.

49 Prahalad and Hamel (1991) propose core competency to identify the unique and difficult to imitate characteristics of the business.

- What are the stakeholder expectations of financial or non-financial benefit (or yield or payoff)?
- Is the business in a position to accommodate the demands and obligations from stakeholders?
- Is the business maintaining favourable brand awareness for itself?
- Should the business join industry and other associations[50] to promote its interests?
- What community involvement should the business seek?

In summary, there is usually competition among rivals for these relationships. Managing relationships needs to consider the impact on all stakeholders, rivals and its own strategic objectives.

2.5 Adopt a taxation planning viewpoint

The pervasiveness of taxation across business activities makes a tax-aware viewpoint essential. This means the dominant purpose must always be pursuit of a genuine commercial strategy not avoidance of tax.

The broad management issues and challenges concerning taxation planning include:

- Being aware of the taxation implications of financial and non-financial activities prior to executing them
- Linking tax benefits to worthwhile business initiatives
- Being able to document compliance with all taxation.[51]

The principal tools and techniques for taxation planning include:

- Taxation planning over a one, three and five year horizon
- Obtaining taxation rulings
- Ensuring that all proposals include calculations of the tax position
- Preparing budgets which identify the tax effect of managerial decisions prior to approval being given by management
- Preparing capital budgets which identify the after-tax basis of discounted cash flows for investments over more than one period to enable management to make an informed decision to approve, defer or reject.

---

50 Associations are not considered to be stakeholders.

51 Tax legislation covers tax on personal income tax, tax on fringe benefits provided to an employee by a business (e.g. motor vehicle) tax on the increased worth of an asset (e.g. the capital gain on property) and tax on expenditure on products and services consumed (e.g. meal served at a restaurant).

The managerial decisions and judgements concerning taxation planning include:

- What will be the basis for tax reporting?
- What are the arrangements to ensure incentives offered by the government can be realised?[52]
- What are the arrangements to ensure the business has lodged taxation returns and reports by the due date?
- What are the arrangements to ensure that the business is able to pay its tax charges by the due date?

In summary, it is important that the business plans its tax position in light of the concessions offered by government from time to time and the obligations imposed by amendments to taxation legislation and rulings issued by the tax department.

Chapter summary

Startup occurs through the motivation of the owner or promoter of the business. The owner oversees implementation of the initial strategy even if it is poorly expressed. In some cases tax planning occurs from the outset; otherwise it becomes apparent when the tax return is prepared. Depending upon the success of the business, the marketing, advertising and promotion arrangements may be finetuned or entirely revised. The stage lasts until the owner or Board recognise the need for growth.

---

52 Tax allowances include depreciation available as a deduction in most years (at predictable rates) and investment concessions offered at particular times.

3 Growth: Issues that arise from seeking improved profitability

Growth includes the initial growth any and any secondary expansion. Initial growth is focused on the defined customer base and establishing a market presence. Secondary expansion is establishing new markets and distribution channels. Where growth involves increased volume it can lead to economies of scale owing to increased consumption of raw materials or components. Pursuing growth and the consequences of growth may necessitate a new structure and new methods of coordination. Changes in aggregate sales are approximate indicators of growth.[1]

Implications for growth

A strategy for business growth should ensure that the business is able to fund the growth and overcome any perceptions by the regulator that fewer businesses will have the effect of lessening competition[2] . In any case, there may be limits to expansion by acquisition as either the marketplace has shrunk and targets are no longer available, or the targets do not offer an attractive payback.[3]

Unplanned growth may have repercussions. Since it relies on an increase in the number of major customers as well as increased volume of sales to customers any customer dissatisfaction must be detected. Dissatisfaction may be due to insufficient inventory or delays in service. Where production or inventory results in poor quality products there may be delays in detecting warranty claims or changed customer buying preferences. Growth may place excessive demands on employees which result in a decline in employee morale.

Topics in the growth stage of the business life cycle

Growing the business requires prolonged execution of a strategy which itself requires fine tuning as it is accomplished stage by stage. There are five programs of activity in growth:

1. Formulate a viable growth strategy
2. Balance debt and equity (Flexible internal and external financing)

---

1 Sales revenue may be used as a basis of percentage analysis since it is a compound of selling price and unit cost but the figures must be interpreted with care (Chambers 1947/1986: 248).

2 For example, the four pillars Australian banking policy prevents the four Australian banks from acquiring one of their number.

3 For example, there are few takeovers occurring among the major software businesses as they share markets.

3. Coordinate diversified business units

4. Acquire and allocate scarce resources among the business units

5. Align manager's and employee's interests to the owner's interests.

Attention to these programs goes a long way toward ensuring the sustainable growth of the business.

3.1 Formulate a viable growth strategy

A decision to pursue growth requires a restatement of the business strategy based on understanding what the previous formal or informal strategy has accomplished.[4]

The broad management issues and challenges that the owner will consider for a viable growth strategy include:

- The preferred form of growth. Consider:
  - Taking market share from existing incumbents[5]
  - Expanding the market for existing products or services[6]
  - Increasing the number and types of products or services offered[7]
  - Acquisition of existing competitors or business segments provided funds are available.[8]
- Whether the business can 'learn' from competitors or other businesses[9]
- The extent to which the business is reliant on growth.

---

4 The initial strategy may not have been formalised as a plan or have emerged as a product of various exigent circumstances (Mintzberg & Waters 1985). While looking outward is common, building a corporate perspective on the future is frequently overlooked (Hamel & Prahalad 1996: 4). Napoleoni (2010) suggests that the evolution of terrorism has stages which follow conventional economic principles with commercial financing (including seigniorage) being a significant issue.

5 Where this depends upon planning approval for developments the authorisation may be clouded by political elections, independent advisory committee deliberations and public protest. In such cases claims of substantial local employment and long-term economic contribution may be challenged by claims concerning impact on the urban context, public amenity and environmental sustainability.

6 This may be increasing market share or finding new markets. The relationship between profitability and market share was identified from regression analysis (Buzzell 2004). Finding new markets requires locating new customers with similar needs. For example, a business that produces furniture for classrooms may increase its sales by selling to universities and private education colleges.

7 For example, a business that produces bread can expand into cakes and biscuits.

8 For example, in 2003 Oracle began with the acquisition of PeopleSoft, a competitor to its Oracle Financials software suite. Then in 2009 Oracle made an offer for Sun Systems. Sun has products in hardware server, operating systems and networking services which enable Oracle to grow through vertical integration.

9 Peters and Waterman (1982) provide a variety of 'success stories' in different sectors. This approach has been critiqued as poor methodology (Collins 2001, 2006). Another critique contends that exceptional businesses bring about their own downfall (Miller 1992). It is also likely that some businesses are simply buoyed up and down by the economic cycle and thus their success was not a reward for exceptional business acumen.

- The preferred operational arrangements for growth. Consider:
  - Incorporation[10]
  - Subsidiary[11]
  - Franchising[12]
  - Exporting[13] products or services based on the size of the export market and barriers to entry
  - Using e-commerce to trade via the internet
  - Expansion of the scale of existing operations[14]
  - Expansion through opening additional branches[15]
  - Acquisition by takeover[16]
  - Acquisition by merger[17]
  - Joint venture.[18]

- Whether to integrate both people and systems to obtain added value[19]

---

10 Changing the legal configuration of the business (for example, from a sole trader to a proprietary company).

11 A subsidiary introduces new a legal configuration with additional administration.

12 The advantage of detailed systems, training and a well-known brand or trading name have to be offset against the controls imposed by the franchisor ostensibly to protect the brand or trading name. Unscrupulous franchisors may have poor territory and product definitions which may diminish the profit potential. The legal contract including the initial and ongoing fees and the arrangements for relinquishing the franchise should be closely scrutinised.

13 The risks and responsibilities of buyer and seller will determine the terms under which products are transported (e.g. free on board, cost insurance and freight, cost and freight), the arrangements for duty and taxes at the incoming port and arrangements for customs clearance and release to the importer. Additionally the product may need to be certified, customised or tested to meet local laws or standards and be supported by brochures and manuals in the local language.

14 The simplest form of growth is increasing the production and revenues from existing products or services. Substantial growth in the existing business usually requires substantial investment (e.g. to build a new factory or to open a large number of sales branches). Expansion may introduce step-level costs if systems and capacity are already at the maximum level but if not then its costs should be less than acquisition.

15 While a branch in a domestic business can be structured legally within it, overseas it may be regarded as a separate legal entity.

16 A takeover may provide additional revenue, access to a brand, new geographic markets, complementary products or services, specialist skills, licences, or advanced technology. Usually the high cost of takeovers requires external financing. Many difficulties are underestimated including the time management spent overseeing the acquired business and integrating business support functions such as accounting, information systems, procurement, legal services and human resources. Consequences of the takeover may include job losses, loss of customers, additional capital investment and discovery of hidden liabilities in the target business. If there are differences in the culture of the two businesses then management may need to spend additional time meshing the two businesses.

17 A merger will have similar difficulties to a takeover. Since the merger often promises equal standing there is often more risk associated with it when employees, customers and suppliers find that more far reaching changes have adverse effects on them. The merger will require management to spend time overseeing the acquired business and integrating business support and meshing the cultures of the separate businesses.

18 Since it is not a separate legal entity the joint venturers need to carefully structure the joint venture. Typically a joint venture is framed around a project. The advantage of being able to share resources and risks makes it common in manufacturing, mining, property development, research and development and resources. For example, to expand into an overseas market, a local business contributes its local knowledge and the overseas business contributes its expertise and skills.

19 Whether it is new and old employees or different business systems, integration is often costly and time consuming. For example, Ford Motor company allowed Aston Martin to continue largely unintegrated with it. While this allows easy divestment, it also leaves potential savings unrealised. Obtaining value from growth may also be difficult where

- The preference for domestic or overseas expansion
- The investment preferences in automation versus human resources
- Taxation implications.

The principal tools and techniques to formulate a viable growth strategy include:

- Ensuring a general perspective on growth. Consider:
  - Revision of the previously expressed vision and mission statements
  - A new fully articulated budget
  - The relationship between a merger and acquisition strategy and share price performance
  - An up-to-date analysis of strengths, weaknesses, opportunities and threats (SWOT) associated with expansion
  - An up-to-date analysis of resources
  - An up-to-date industry analysis
  - A review of strategic direction (low cost leadership or differentiation from its competitors)
  - An up-to-date re-assessment of the route to strategic advantage.[20]

- Obtaining an international perspective on growth. Consider:
  - Predicting international business patterns using interacting forces[21]
  - Considering the attributes which determine the competitive advantage of the nation for a specified industry.[22]

The managerial decisions and judgements for a viable growth strategy include:

- What should be the growth or turnaround strategy? Consider:
  - What are the advantages of expansion over other options?[23]

---

systems have no overlapping features or where it becomes apparent that substantial investments are essential for future products. For example, Ford made substantial investments in engine technology for Land Rover and Range Rover cars which then benefited the new buyer in the tender process who was Tata Motors of India.

20 A business should compete in four ways: by using new products, by being creative, on relative superiority exploiting competitor weaknesses or by maximising benefits to the end-user (Ohmae 1982). 'Head-on' competition is often unwise.

21 Conditioning variables affect opportunities for competitive advantage, motivation variables influence competitive strategy and control variables are associated with incentives and controls (Robock & Simmonds 1977/1989).

22 Competitive advantage is a relative advantage (Ricardo 1817). The four specific attributes are firm strategy, structure and rivalry, factor conditions, demand conditions and related supporting industries (Porter 1990). They may be applied to a business unit or an industry. Other forms of strategy derive from war (von Clausewitz 1832/1908; Sun, 6BC/1996) and games (Lai 2004).

23 Expansion is also known as 'organic growth'. It involves opening new branches within the existing business framework domestically or overseas. Alternatives include changing the legal configuration, franchising, takeovers, mergers and joint ventures.

- – What is the relationship between a merger and acquisition strategy and share price performance?
- – What is the most appropriate option for raising funds?[24]
- – Is a growth strategy sustainable?
- – What is the level of working capital necessary to support the strategy?
- – What are the risks associated with executing the strategy?
- – What will be the consequences for personal ownership and control?

- Should there be an international growth strategy? Consider:
  - – What is the most appropriate legal configuration based on restrictions on foreign ownership?
  - – Is proximity to the new market important?
  - – Are established or historical trade links in the new market important?
  - – How will the relevant commercial, employment and trade laws and regulations affect business operations?
  - – What will be the likely influence of cultural customs and protocols on business etiquette and operations?

In summary, a growth strategy requires a coordinated effort. This is best achieved through formal plans which can be made available to significant stakeholders (e.g. lenders) or which can be reworked into prescribed document formats (e.g. prospectus). A review of the documents should provide preliminary answers to the many of the issues raised above.

3.2 Balance debt and equity (Flexible internal and external financing)

The business may choose to obtain its capital[25] from debt or equity or a mix of both.[26] Debt leaves the business exposed to demands for repayment by nervous or exigent creditors, which may in turn follow from its bank tightening its lending or from monetary policy. Equity is affected by investor perception of the new share issue and dilution.

The broad management issues and challenges that arise from balancing debt and equity include:

- Establishing the priorities for additional investment. Consider:

---

24 See the next Topic for details of funding.

25 An early discussion (Fisher 1896) points out the difficulty of the concept of capital with its many misconceptions.

26 Borrowings and equity have commercial risks which are evaluated on the capacity to pay based on other constraints and the security offered.

- Finding likely sources of funding[27]
- Purchasing the additional raw materials or inventory to support the required levels necessitated by growth
- Employing additional full-time, part-time or casual employees
- Purchasing or leasing larger or additional premises
- Financing additional amounts of trade receivables[28] where sales occur on credit
- Acquiring new technology
- Purchasing or leasing equipment to increase production capacity.

- Determining appropriate types of finance. Consider:
  - Equity:
    - o Initial public offering (IPO)[29]
    - o Private and personal funds leading to capitalisation of shareholder loans[30]
    - o Retained earnings
    - o Venture capital[31]
    - o Public subscription.[32]
  - Debt financing:
    - o Short-term (e.g. Commercial bills[33])
    - o Medium-term (e.g. notes)
    - o Long-term (e.g. bonds)
    - o Securities[34]

---

27 There are many nonwestern forms of funding. The Grameen Bank provided micro loans in Bangladesh based on guarantees of those known to the recipient of the loan (Yunus 1999/2007). Muslim Sharia (Shari'a) law forbids the payment of interest so General Electric created Islamic bonds (or Sukuk) based on a revenue stream from aircraft leases (Slater & Haywood 2009).

28 Where the creditor is the government there is little risk of default although it is quite likely there will be a delay in payment. Walker (2009a: 196) observes that this may be due to financial management practices within the government authority or agency and annual reports may include performance reports on making payments.

29 Although a set price for shares is common, the alternative is to set a range for the share price so the investor market interested can bid and rebid during the offer period (bookbuild).

30 Some assurance will be sought that funds will not be extracted at short notice or in difficult economic times that jeopardises the financial viability of the business.

31 A higher interest rate of return is payable to compensate the investor for high risk or lack of security. Venture capital is usually sought at start up, expansion or management buyout when other sources of finance are not available. The investor gains equity, a seat on the board of directors and usually expects to sellout once the business is attractive to other buyers and shareholders.

32 Legislation requires the registration and issue of a disclosure document describing the offer unless an exemption is granted. Some of the consequences of poor legislative control for investors are described in Sinclair (2003/2004). The example of the Beatles songs as an income stream is described by Southall and Perry (2006).

33 Commercial bills are issued at a discount and are credited to the customer account at the face value (excluding interest payable). They are priced according to the market. There are rollover charges on maturity.

34 The issue of government securities and bonds usually is regulated by the Loan Council (1993).

- o Bank overdraft[35]
- o Term loans from financiers[36]
- o Trade finance[37]
- o Fixed asset financing
- o Inventory finance[38]
- o Factoring[39] of inventory or accounts receivable
- o Inventory and floor-plan[40] financing using short and medium term loans
- o Promissory notes
- o Debentures and other securities
- o Property mortgages
- o Leasing[41] including sale and leaseback arrangements
- o Leveraged leasing and other forms of consortium finance
- o Hire purchase agreements[42]
- o Offshore finance.[43]
- – Other funding approaches. Consider:
  - o Obtain extended credit from suppliers
  - o Seek subsidies and rebates from suppliers.

---

35 The financier charges interest on the outstanding balance and an annual or line fee for making the overdraft available. The line fee is usually a percentage of the limit regardless of its actual use. The overdraft is repayable on demand so it may be withdrawn at any time or particular cheques may be dishonoured.

36 A term loan from 3 months to ten years is mostly used for asset purchases usually secured by a mortgage over property. It is usually only repayable on demand when triggered by a default clause.

37 Trade finance for importers and exporters is provided in many forms including letters of credit, guaranteeing letters, preshipment financing, post-shipment financing, acceptance and discounting of trade bills of exchange and financing of the costs of shipment. Since there are many risks (credit, country exchange control, buyer refusal) associated with foreign exchange it is important to be sure that the buyer will make payment by the due date by ensuring the products comply with the contract of sale.

38 Finished goods inventory or work-in-process may be used as collateral to borrow monies. Usually costs are high owing to both high interest rates and the need for audit assurance. It can provide finance for a business whose assets are already encumbered.

39 Usually 80% of the value of the accounts receivable can be factored but this can be higher where there is a long-term relationship between the business and the financier. An establishment fee and a monthly administration fee are also payable. Since the customer is aware that payment has to be made to the factoring company it may create a stigma in the mind of the customer disinclining them toward giving the business any future orders.

40 The global financial crisis highlighted the use of floor-plan financing loans provided to motor vehicle dealers for the new (and used) vehicles in their showrooms and on their premises awaiting sale.

41 Any asset may be leased subject to approval of the lessor. To simplify administration many lessors create a master lease agreement which specifies the class of asset which may be leased. New assets may be leased by adding a schedule to the master lease agreement.

42 The advantage is that the security is in the form of the asset itself so other aspects of the business are unaffected. The disadvantage is that costs usually exceed those for a term loan. A finance lease or short-term loan may be equally or more advantageous.

43 Where the borrowing is in a foreign currency then there is a risk of an unfavourable movement in the exchange rate. A hedge using foreign assets or forward rate agreements may be appropriate or covered by the expected repayment of sales to be earned in the foreign currency.

- – Seek subsidies, special purpose and tied grants and funding allocations:
  - o Direct subsidies are provided for many public services including transport and health care
  - o Fulfil community service obligations.
- – Internal funds:
  - o Retained earnings
  - o Additional revenue windfalls
  - o Savings from cost reduction program.

- Determining the priorities for financing. Consider:
  - – Startup or expansion
  - – Working capital
  - – Fixed asset financing.

- Determining suitable providers of finance. Consider:
  - – Banks[44] who have a commercial or business division
  - – Merchant banks and financiers who operate in niche markets
  - – Suppliers who will negotiate extended payment terms often associated with expectations of future sales
  - – The ability to recover debts from debtors
  - – The willingness of the market to subscribe to share a new share issue or existing share buyback to the desired level
  - – Government trade authorities.

- General financing issues. Consider:
  - – Pricing financial instruments such as stocks to take into account price variation[45]
  - – The fees associated with obtaining finance
  - – The market interest in capital raising via debt and equity
  - – The willingness of creditors to fund borrowings to the desired level
  - – The margin on sales and the sales value compared to the costs associated with generating the sales
  - – The resulting position of the business if it is successful in obtaining borrowing or capital change

---

44 Banks regard business loans as high risk (particularly at times of economic stress) and demand real estate security. This will prevent the use of that real estate as security in future. The use of loans for business acquisition is regarded as an even greater risk. Some segments and industries are regarded more favourably owing to their protected status in the market and the certainty of their cash flow to service the loan. For example, liquor outlets and newsagencies.

45 A model of price variation is provided by Black Scholes (1973). There are a many variants of the original Black–Scholes model.

- The prevailing and predicted economic conditions
- The opinion of the market on the financial prognosis for the business.

The principal tools and techniques for balancing debt and equity include:

- A loan criteria for borrowing from lenders. Consider:
  - Financial forecasts where the business plan and strategy is converted into cash flow projections[46]
  - Financial measures such as debt to equity ratio and the current (quick) ratio
  - Non-financial measures such as market sentiment toward the business.

- A securities criteria for a change in equity. Consider:
  - The form of share (e.g. ordinary or preferential)
  - The conferring of voting versus dividend distribution rights
  - The costs of the prospectus, advertising, underwriting and incidentals
  - The pricing of the share.

The managerial decisions and judgements that arise from balancing debt and equity include:

- Borrowing involves repayment and security. Consider:
  - What will be the interest rate?
  - What is the period for repayment?
  - What is the risk that repayments cannot be made and borrowing covenants are breached?[47]
  - Can the lender pass the loan to another party without consent or notification to the borrower?
  - Does the loan vest any ownership with the lender?
  - What will be the effect of the taking this loan on seeking further borrowings?

- An equity change involves ownership change and possibly the payment of dividends. Consider:
  - What will be the type of share offered?
  - What will be the aggregate increase in equity and overall position?
  - What will be the level of dividend and effect on existing dividends?
  - What will be the impact on the price of existing shares?[48]

---

46 All business plans and financial forecasts should be rooted in systematic studies of the market to avoid over-optimism.

47 Covenant ratios on banking facilities often involve three measures: net debt to equity (gearing), net debt to EBITDA and EBITDA to net interest (interest cover ratio). Reasons may include reduced sales, profits or collections. Businesses that breach a covenant by a small ratio may later claim it was through management information systems 'oversight' or through holding waivers from banks.

48 The dilution of the proportion of interests of existing shareholders may be offset by benefits from prior profits or by preceding the new issue with a bonus for existing shareholders.

In summary, the planning for financial flexibility by using debt and equity should be integrated with the broad strategy. Once completed there should also be monitoring to ensure borrowings can be repaid as and when due and any equity changes.

3.3 Coordinate diversified business units

A business unit is a unit within a business which is distinguishable from other business units because it is responsible for different products, customer segments[49] or customer territories (that is, different meaningful external markets). There are many different rationales for identifying business units including the Strategic Business Unit (SBU)[50] and the Cash Generating Unit (CGU).[51] No matter how they are legally and hierarchically structured, large companies are composed of separate businesses. The business units themselves may be known as divisions, subsidiaries or companies. There may be one or more divisions, subsidiaries or companies that operate under the control of a head office.

The broad management issues and challenges that arise from coordinating diversified business units include:

- Diversification approach
- Coordination of the business units
- Decision-making prerogatives and autonomy
- Expected level of performance or return on investment
- Overall business life cycle position of the business unit.

The principal tools and techniques to coordinate diversified business units include:

- A fully articulated annual budget
- Capital investment approval controls[52]
- Diversification grid[53]
- Internal control reports
- Audits

---

49 The expression 'segment' is often used in financial statements. A segment is then a convenient way of grouping financial data for a set of related businesses in a format that disguises the precise performance of divisions or subsidiaries.

50 'Strategic Business Unit' may owe its origin to usage in General Electric, USA.

51 A Cash Generating Unit is relevant to financial statements in which issues of impairment testing and goodwill arise.

52 In a centralised structure all decisions are made at head office. This will require the head office to be provided with sufficient supporting documentation to enable them to make the decision. Insufficient documentation will lead to rejection of the proposal. In a decentralised structure the head office makes policy while allowing the divisions, subsidiaries or companies to operate semi-autonomously. Divisions, subsidiaries or companies are measured by their achievement of preset budgetary targets.

53 The diversification grid (Salter & Weinhold 1979) can identify related and complementary diversification to harness strengths or overcome weaknesses. Related diversification may reduce unit costs and improve margins.

- Business strategy coordination meetings.[54]

The managerial decisions and judgements that arise from coordinating diversified business units include:

- Will it be easy to separate the functions of the business unit if it needs to be sold?
- Has the strategic acquisition and divestment initiatives been authorised?
- Have capital investment initiatives been authorised?
- What arrangements have been made for the selection and replacement of senior executives?
- How can a portfolio of projects and investments be achieved that will be strategically advantageous for the business?
- Do different business units coordinate their efforts with customers and suppliers that they have in common?
- How can managers help negotiate the tensions between the need for short-run results and long-term building of the business?

In summary, management conducts strategic planning in relation to products, channels and markets using the Strategic Business Units as the primary focus for measurement.

3.4 Acquire and allocate scarce resources among the business units

The acquisition and allocation of scarce resources is a vexing problem for most businesses. There are many competing claims for scarce resources using credible arguments.

The broad management issues and challenges for acquisition and allocation of scarce resources include:

- The estimation of adequate (e.g. numbers) and appropriate (e.g. skills) resources
- Ensuring availability or development of needed resources
- Determining sourcing (make versus buy).[55]

---

54 Even in a decentralised structure there is likely to be some interdependence between divisions, subsidiaries or companies. For example, division 'A' may produce a product that is used as an input by division 'B'. This raises the problem of transfer pricing.

55 The procurement of resources externally via procurement, contacts and alliances is both a tactical and strategic issue (Pfeffer & Salancik 1978). Resource Dependence Theory often influences the divisional structure of organisations, selection of board members, recruitment of employees, production strategies, contract arrangements, preferred external organisational alliances and perceived power and interdependence between organisations (e.g. Hayward & Boeker 1998). Resource Dependence Theory is similar to Transaction Cost Theory (Commons, 1931; Coase 1937, 1960; Williamson 1981) and Institutional Theory (Selznick 1948).

The principal tools and techniques to acquire and allocate scarce business resources include:

- Determining the value of information[56]

- Pricing

- Project management

- Resource combination analyses

- The Boston Consulting Group (BCG) Matrix[57] is primarily used to analyse the product portfolio and allocate resources consistent with strategy. It uses four quadrants to indicate the status of the portfolio and corresponding recommended resource allocations as shown in Figure 4 below.

Competitive position

		High relative market share	Low relative market share
Prospects For Growth	High industry growth	**Stars** (Potentially tomorrow's cash cows) (Action: Support with additional resources)	**Wildcat** (Potentially an emerging star) (Action: Consider resourcing)
	Low industry growth	**Cash cow** (Harvest from mature activities) (Action: Support to maintain)	**Dog** (Weak competitive position and prospects) (Action: Withdraw resources)

Figure 4. Boston Consulting Group (BCG) portfolio matrix showing four quadrants and the action appropriate to each quadrant

The managerial decisions and judgements affecting the acquisition and allocation of scarce resources include:

- Will current resources be retained at the existing levels?

- How will new resources be acquired or developed for short and long-term needs?

- How will new resources be allocated against competing projects with similar payback or rate of return?

- How will resources be costed and priced?

- How will resources be leveraged consistent with the business strategy?

In summary, the usual approach is to use an economic analysis which seeks to maximise output considering diminishing returns. However, a strategic view considers the products or services offered by the business and their position in the product life cycle.

---

56 One method of determining the value of information is to identify challenges to management with regard to the concept, the object and the method of measurement (Hubbard 2007: 19).

57 The BCG matrix identifies stars, question marks, cash cows and dogs (Henderson 1984).

3.5 Align manager's and employee's interests to the owner's interests

As the owner becomes too busy to carry out all the important business functions they hire additional managers to supervise the employees.[58] There is a separation[59] of owner and employee/manager interests and the in the risk that managers and employees will not share the owners' passion for the business and may not be prepared to work as diligently.[60]

The broad management issues and challenges in aligning manager/employee interests to owner interests include:

- Whether changes in the size of the business will force an increase in the number of employees and managers
- The preferred approach to obtaining additional labour[61]
- Employing trainees and junior employees who can be easily supervised
- Considering incentives targeted at particular behaviour such as finalising sales or making higher value sales through selling combinations of products
- Promising a career in the business leading to a senior management position or offering future shares in the business
- Recruiting employees as a 'cadet' or as an 'intern' with responsibility to remain with the business to give it the benefit of their knowledge.

The principal tools and techniques for aligning manager/employee interests to owner interests include:

- Investors requiring managers to provide them with general purpose financial statements disclosing the financial and non-financial health of the business
- Changing decision-making from a single individual to a committee
- In a centralised business, decision-making is retained by senior management
- In a decentralised business, devolving decision-making throughout the business

---

58 In USA, Berle and Means (1932) separated ownership (meaning transferable shares) from control of active property (meaning the plant, machines and other items). In a small business, it is likely that the owner will work with some immediate and extended family members and this may be less apparent.

59 Many investors are not present during the day-to-day activities of the business. The managers act as agents for the owners. This is referred to as the agency problem or principal-agent problem (Eisenhardt 1989).

60 Increasingly, businesses use a hybrid form of structure with some decisions delegated to divisions or branches and others retained centrally. The recent financial crisis has resulted in close scrutiny of all cash flows and capital formation being centralised. Some aspects of centralisation-decentralisation are also affected by decisions to form alliances or outsource business functions.

61 Additional human resources may be obtained by hiring additional full-time employees, or by increasing the use of casual or part-time employees, or by using the services of contractors who work in the business, using consultants or by engaging contractors who work outside the business (e.g. from home).

- Using an employment contract that includes post-employment restrictive covenants on the activities that an employee or manager may undertake when their employment ends for any reason.[62]

The managerial decisions and judgements for aligning manager/employee interests to owner interests include:

- What should be the format and frequency of reports made available to owners?
- Should there be payment of piece rates or commissions?
- Should profit sharing be introduced?
- Should performance measures (such as management by objectives or using the financial statements) be adopted?

In summary, the inspection of operations is no longer as popular or practical as it previously was for investors. The growth and geographical spread of the business and the recruitment of additional managers introduces a hierarchy of management. Accountability tends to be achieved through the use of information.

Chapter summary

Growth is only successful if there is a plan to manage the stresses that result from demands on employees, finance and products or services. A viable growth strategy considers all three. Additional financing is required to support working capital and finance acquisitions, mergers or expansion. Generally growth involves acquiring additional business units or subdividing existing business units introducing problems of coordination and allocation of resources between the business units. Once the growth stage is complete the business enters its maturity stage.

---

62 An employee should remain loyal to their employer. There are restrictions on the use of the former employer's property or information is prohibited. Encouraging disloyalty or breaching these restrictions may give the former employer grounds for a successful legal action. Enforcement of a restrictive covenant depends upon being able to demonstrate that it protects a legitimate business interest and that it is no wider than necessary to protect that interest. Typically the clauses would prevent the employee from soliciting business from defined customers they had dealt with, dealing with those customers, poaching employees and operating in a defined geographical area.

4 Maturity: Eroded or stable revenue, profitability, or market share

As the business experiences the end of growth there may also be some reductions in sales and reduced revenue, profitability or erosion of market share. The business comes under increasing pressure to respond.[1] Although the tendency is to take little action and 'see what happens', eventually decisive action is necessary. So this chapter may also be read as an introduction to heighten awareness on prudent actions to pre-empt sliding into business difficulties.

Maturity as complacency

Business difficulties may arise from external forces or internal factors. Frequently a business does not appreciate the severity and immediacy of events in the environment. For example, in 2008 most businesses were not aware of the growing global financial crisis.[2] Some pressures are also internally generated. A business may undertake product redesign or rebranding and offend its customers. For example, Kraft introduced a cream cheese softened vegemite in Australia branded iSnack 2.0 which was an unpopular name and within a month changed it to Cheesybite. Other internally created pressures include diminution or variation of quality. In many cases there is little warning to business[3] as it tends to have an individual customer view rather than a broad[4] customer view.

---

1 Another view of the threat to growth and the maturity of markets is provided by Levitt (1960) who argues that many industries endanger their future by 'improperly defining their purposes' (p 46). One of the examples provided is the Hollywood motion picture industry which saw television as a threat instead of an expansion of the entertainment business. Levitt (1960: 46) refers to managers of such businesses lacking the 'same managerial imaginativeness and audacity that made them great'.

2 Apart from the difficulty in specifying legislation that would be effective in protecting investors, the power of Wall Street and financial institutions more generally, to out manoeuvre and rebut analyses has generally proven formidable (Seligman 1982/2003). Also see the accounting history by Chatov (1975) on the power of dominant business interests to allow flexibility in the definition of generally accepted accounting principles. The report from United States Congress (2011) may reveal the banking excesses although the time available may limit its findings.

3 This may be a tipping point (Gladwell 2000/2001; Granovetter 1978; Schelling 1971) where ideas, behaviours and new products suddenly spread in a population similar to the spread of a contagious disease. Gladwell (2000/2001) imported the term from epidemiology where a virus can reach critical mass and becomes an epidemic epidemic.

4 Surowiecki (2004) suggests that the aggregation of information from individuals is superior to both individual and expert judgement. However, creating such an aggregation is both difficult and infrequently done.

Appearance and reality in the maturity stage of the business life cycle

A common mistake is equating the visible signs of difficulty as the root cause. This can often lead to action being directed at fixing things which may be peripheral to the difficulty. Many business difficulties require multiple actions in a staged and progressively evaluated sequence. Frequently a social complexity approach is appropriate[5] when a plan to resuscitate the entire business proves difficult to frame.

Boundary between maturity and decline

If a business encounters a loss of revenue then it will need to respond quickly otherwise it will magnify the effect of its losses. At all times it is essential to determine whether the loss of revenue is short-term or medium-term. In some cases the urgency of the response will determine whether the business survives. The business may respond in four ways (which are not mutually exclusive): (1) Undertake additional advertising and promotion; (2) Reduce investment in inventory; (3) Reduce production; or (4) Delay production.

There may be operational constraints[6] that limit the response of the business and a reduction in revenue may also be the result of non-payment or partial payment by customers.[7] These may necessitate a turnaround discussed in Chapter 2 as part of growth or preparing to cease business which is discussed in Chapter 5 (Decline: Issues that arise from turnaround or cessation of business activities).

Topics in the maturity stage of the business life cycle

Maturity in the business can produce reduced revenue, reduced profitability, erosion of market share all of which require attention. There are five programs of activity in maturity:

1. Strategic refocusing on core markets, products and services

2. Restrain internal expenditure including procurement

3. Delay or defer new investment and renegotiating existing investment arrangements

4. Make beneficial changes to ownership

5. Recognise threats to employment and employee security.

---

5 Complexity approaches can be computational, biological or social. See Oliver and Snowden (2005) for a discussion and the preference for using a social complexity approach. A complexity approach accepts that benefits may arise from disorder (Abrahamson & Freedman 2006).

6 These may include operating leverage such as limits to the overdraft, obligations to the lender concerning repayment where it is exceeded; and employee awards which limit or prevent disruptions to production. One view of constraints emphasises that removing one constraint highlights another formerly hidden constraint (Goldratt 1999). Goldratt and Cox (1984/2004) collaborated on a fictional business novel using theory of constraints to improve manufacturing operations and overall profitability.

7 There is the potential for bad debts which have to be written-off.

4.1 Strategic refocusing on core markets, products and services

Refocusing on core markets[8] and products is the most direct method of improving revenue and reducing costs. Businesses are susceptible to diluting their presence in multiple markets and offering an increasing range of products and services. Usually there are sound grounds for this proliferation, for example, penetrating new markets or launching new or complementary products. Once a contraction occurs in a market or competition reduces profitability, the need to understand the core markets and products become apparent.

The broad management issues and challenges concerning strategic refocusing on core markets and products and services include:

- Avoiding being misled by temporary manias and mass action[9]
- Establishing the products and markets which should be closed
- Identifying the consequences for markets or products affected by closure
- Developing an appropriate response for adverse customer reactions to products being 'orphaned'
- Making collections from customers who no longer have any ongoing relationship with the business
- Maintaining cordial relations with suppliers whose volume of sales is now substantially reduced
- Ensuring that making these changes does not provide an opening for a new or existing competitor that will affect the remaining markets and products.[10]

The principal tools and techniques to strategically refocus on core markets and products or services include:

- Cost reduction or containment
- Financial engineering techniques[11]
- Credit controls

---

8 'Stick to the knitting' or doing what it does best is one of the Peters and Waterman (1982) eight attributes of excellence. However, Porter and Siggelkow (2008) mount a case for considering the sets of activities whose interaction effects are contextual, because these activities are more difficult to imitate.

9 Speculation with the commodities such as tulip bulbs in 1624 suggests errors in pricing and mistaken needs for a product (Mackay 1841/1980). Irrational behaviour is easily repeated in a crowd which may even ignore advice on a soundly based strategy.

10 For example, IBM is no longer in the laptop product or market. Its Thinkpad brand has been sold to Lenovo based in China despite the advantage it gained for IBM in large businesses by conveying the impressions of innovation and reliability.

11 Porsche was the most profitable and successful independent car marker in the period 2000–2009 owing to income earned from the increased price of share options in Volkswagen (VW) that Porsche bought under its CEO Wedelin Wiedeking with the objective of taking control of VW. The global financial crisis prompted banks to seek collateral and the situation backfired and Porsche became the tenth brand owned by VW.

- Improving the timing and content of financial reports including cash flow and non-financial reports to enable timely monitoring of the effects of the changed strategy
- Ensuring that commissions are adjusted so they are consistent with the new strategy
- Reviewing the inventory level order points and economic order qualities for the raw materials for the products which are now expected to drive profitability[12]
- Reviewing the billing methods particularly where it is for work-in-progress or work performed under a contract.[13]

The managerial decisions and judgements to strategically refocus on core markets and products and services include:

- What will be a realistic timetable for products and market contraction?
- What will be the costs of leaving markets and eliminating products?
- Have appropriate employees been identified to maintain contact with customers and suppliers affected by the change?
- What will be the policy on progressive or regular billing under contracts?
- What actions concerning suppliers and customers will increase cash flow?
- What are the likely responses by competitors to the new market and product focus?
- What is the follow-on strategy to anticipate changes in the market and introduce later generation products?

In summary, refocusing on core markets and products has the advantage of bringing the business back to the area where its strengths and competencies should be maximised. In doing so it may be able to better assess how those strengths and competencies can be leveraged for not only overcoming current difficulties and setting a strategy for growth and future prosperity.

4.2 Restrain internal expenditure including procurement

Containing internal expenditure conserves internal cash flow. Changes in expenditure and procurement are made for different purposes. They may have a cost containment emphasis to gain leverage from existing supplier relationships. Alternatively they may be the basis for a 'clean slate' approach with the intention of making substantial improvements even if existing arrangements have to be terminated.

---

12 Ordering increased quantities of raw materials may also affect the previous lead times or prompt consideration of Just-in-Time production methods. Advanced manufacturing methods may change the batch size (Milgrom & Roberts 1990).

13 Where existing contracts cannot be amended, there need to be methods which ensure that any new contracts specify regular billing during the contract.

The broad management issues and challenges from restraining internal expenditure include:

- Signalling to employees the need for economy[14]
- Establishing a relationship between new priorities and improved cashflow
- Ensuring a comparable cost base to competitors
- Determining the saleable inventory[15]
- Taking advantage of linkages to streamline the supply chain[16]
- Ensuring the supply relationship remains abreast of technology and product innovations.

The principal tools and techniques to restrain internal expenditure include:

- Changing arrangements for non-trade items. Consider:
  - Limiting the office cash float by issuing eligible managers with credit cards[17] in the name of the business
  - Transferring petty cash claims to a credit card in the name of the business (with appropriate controls over the allowable types of purchases)
  - Issuing petrol cards to cover petrol/diesel/gas and oil purchases
  - Issuing taxi vouchers to travel by taxi[18]
  - Placing sundry purchases within the normal purchasing ambit
  - Placing the purchase of morning and afternoon tea items within the normal purchasing ambit
  - Making bulk purchases of stationery
  - Transferring other purchases to a reimbursement system tied to payment of the employee's wages.
- Insurance may reduce the financial impact of some events
- There may be business contingency plans which anticipate the consequences of the event and provide counter measures or actions which mitigate the seriousness of the event

---

14 Examples include asking employees to justify their employment, reduce their cost base and working to the common goal of business survival. There may be opportunities to use the data already held on customers to offer additional services. For example a recruitment business may offer skills training and workshops for the unemployed.

15 Taking steps to avoid obsolete inventory is often overlooked. The business processes that lead to the procurement of the inventory in the first place need to be understood. If it was ordered as part of a planned advertising campaign then controls are needed to better match the expected success of the advertising campaign with timing of inventory deliveries.

16 This can include (a) reducing the number of vendors, (b) increasing the number of components that are common between different products. Both have risks which can only be offset by both formidable design standards and highly evolved quality management processes. A known problem is the fact that customer demand is rarely stable and this leads to the Forrester Effect (Forrester 1958) within the supply chain.

17 The provider of the credit card would be selected on the basis that it can provide (a) reliable details with an audit trail to support the expenditure, (b) suitable individual summary reports for both employee expenditure for a period and of expenditure for a period and (c) business unit summary reports.

18 Two sequences of vouchers may be necessary: (a) one set to cover travel costs borne by the business unit or department and (b) one set to cover expenditure which must be reimbursed or recharged to other departmental cost centres.

- The ability to keep the public and the media informed about the causes of the event and the remedial actions being undertaken is often vital in ensuring continued viability of the business
- Renegotiating contract arrangements with suppliers (perhaps involving changes to discount levels, frequency of supply and reduced volume in orders)
- Seeking alternative (cheaper) products and services
- Undertaking joint cost containment reviews.

The managerial decisions and judgements that arise from restraining internal expenditure include:

- Is there evidence that the negotiated arrangements with suppliers are well below market, industry cost curve or current circumstances?
- Have all costs and revenues for an event or a defined period been accurately identified?
- Will customers place their orders with a competitor?
- In an emergency can expenditure be controlled?
- Will the existing relationship with a supplier (where preferential treatment is obtained) be affected?
- Will the existing relationship with a customer (where preferential treatment is given) be affected?

In summary, changes in expenditure and procurement may be instigated for many reasons. They may be driven by cost reduction considerations or from implementing quality management programs. Some suppliers may offer products or services which are more attractive than the incumbent.

4.3 Delay or defer new investment and renegotiate existing investment arrangements

Changes to investment involve delaying or deferring investment and renegotiating existing investment arrangements. In situations where there are only a small number of lenders then this may present added difficulties culminating in higher costs.

The broad management issues and challenges that arise from delaying, deferring or renegotiating investments include:

- Whether existing programs of work and contractual obligations can be deferred or cancelled without excessive penalties

- Whether there will be detrimental consequences to morale from delaying expected benefits and entitlements
- Whether there will be unfavourable public perceptions arising from deferral of publicly announced initiatives
- Whether there will be sufficient funds available (under acceptable terms and conditions) to finance any initiatives regarded as essential.

The principal tools and techniques to manage delaying, deferring or renegotiating investments include:

- Using Altman's Z score model[19] or gambler's ruin[20] to predict financial distress
- Implementing an investment 'freeze'
- Introducing higher hurdle rates for return on investment used in investment proposals
- Seeking cheaper sources of funding.

The managerial decisions and judgements that arise from delaying, deferring or renegotiating investments include:

- Are the actions proposed sufficient for the horizon of the difficult times?
- Are there any legislative implications from deferring expenditure?
- Will cheaper sources of funds be reliable?

In summary, since investment directly affects the business it is essential to obtain monies at favourable rates for the term of the loan (medium or long-term). This occurs by taking into account both confidence in the financial viability of the business and the economic environment.

4.4 Make beneficial changes to ownership

Changes to ownership may arise for many reasons. They include changes in the economy, the repercussions from failure of other businesses, a hostile takeover, failure to secure financing, the injection of new capital, retirement of the owner or strategic disposal (e.g. owing to a favourable offer).

---

19 A result of less than 1.81 indicates forthcoming distress. A result of between 1.81 and 2.99 indicates uncertainty and above 2.99 little chance of distress. The relevant period for the measures is two years (Altman 1968, 2000).

20 Wilcox (1976) suggests using the fundamental risk parameters of net liquidation value and the processes that affect it. It depends upon predicting when creditors are likely to assert their rights.

The broad management issues and challenges that arise from beneficial changes to ownership include:

- Selecting the preferred type of ownership change. Consider:
  - Seeking new owners and relinquishing control usually by transferring ownership where the business is privately owned[21]
  - Allowing the other existing owners to run the business and maintaining passive involvement[22]
  - Passing the business on to family members[23]
  - Appointing a professional manager
  - Using the public trading of shares (stock) to change ownership[24]
  - Privatisation of government activities.[25]

- Maintaining goodwill
- Capability to continue trading without disruption
- Transfer of tacit knowledge built up over time
- Preserving the confidence of employees
- Successfully transitioning to the priorities of the new owners.

The principal tools and techniques to manage beneficial changes to ownership include:

- Succession planning where family members are involved
- Preliminary due diligence. Consider:
  - For a listed business, the evaluation of share price[26]
  - For an unlisted business, its acquisition value.

- A formal takeover process. Consider:
  - Acquisition of shares beneath the limit of a declared takeover

---

21 Typically a transfer of ownership occurs as part of selling the business. The sale price will be negotiated for assets, goodwill and often the inventory and the right to fulfil uncompleted orders.

22 This will entail continuing exposure to liability. It may result in friction in a family business where the former owner believes that new policies or directions conflict with the business that s/he nurtured and controlled over a long period. This may be exacerbated where customers or suppliers still have contact with the former owner.

23 The capability of family members to run a small business is not necessarily assured by some of them possessing commercial qualifications since it is their management capabilities which are paramount.

24 There may be restrictions on this stated in the constitution of the company. There may be a restriction on the maximum proportion of shares one entity can hold. For example a co-operative may wish to limit the power exercised by any single member. Some companies have adopted a 'poison pill' to defend themselves against a hostile takeover.

25 Privatisation may take the form of sale, outsourcing or franchising (Walker & Con Walker 2000/2006: 26, 31).

26 Where the companies are both listed information on their financial positions is summarised for share holders in an offer statement. However, there may be differences due to cosmetic accounting and legitimate different combinations of interpretation of standards (Chambers 1947/1986: 265). Wechsberg (1968) provides some examples of how this may arise.

- – Soliciting a formal takeover offer[27]
- – Assessment and decision by a government regulator where it meets review criteria
- – Further negotiations[28]
- – Acceptance leading to finalisation.[29]

- Post-change of ownership. Consider:
  - – Situation audits
  - – Facilitation workshops
  - – Communication workshops
  - – Strategic retreats
  - – Third-party consultancy interventions
  - – Leadership from the former senior management (if they have credibility with the employees).

The managerial decisions and judgements that arise from beneficial changes to ownership include:

- When will be the date of effect of new ownership?
- What announcements will be made to employees in the transition period and following the change of ownership?
- What obligations to employees, suppliers and customers will be carried forward and what ones will be revised?
- What notification will be made to the general public?
- What will be announced as areas for investigation and possible change?

In summary, changes to ownership are difficult to predict and the ensuing changes depend upon the style of management and hierarchical structure preferred by the new owner. Whether any benefits are realised 'turns on the vigour and ingenuity applied to the conduct of the augmented business' (Chambers 1947/1986: 267).

---

27 The consideration may be stated as a cash sum, a rate of securities (shares) in the offer or a company to be formed, or some combination of the two.

28 Where publicly listed companies are involved, an initial offer may be followed by a counter offer by another company. The initial offer may also choose to increase or vary their offer. The target may also mount defensive actions. For example they may issue bonus shares or grant an additional dividend. Press coverage may draw attention to the offer and lead to reactions by the target company and the offer.

29 For cases where the amount paid exceeds the value of actual items, the difference is treated as goodwill. Any such offer with its premium is 'little different from any other prospective project. Its exploration is an exercise in project appraisal' (Chambers 1947/1986: 267).

4.5 Recognise threats to employment & employee security

Threats to employment and employee security may arise from both a change in the number of employees required for reduced volume of production or service as well as from considering external substitutes. The threats may be exacerbated by employee emotions including trauma.[30]

The broad management issues and challenges that arise from threats to employment and employee security include:

- The likelihood that key employees leave giving little notice with repercussions on the viability of the business[31]
- Creating a sense of survivor syndrome
- Whether there are contractual obligations with employees or their employee associations (guilds or unions)
- Whether there are legislative provisions which specify minimum benefits and entitlements
- Whether there will be unfavourable publicity
- Whether there will be sufficient funds available (under acceptable terms and conditions) to fund retrenchments and superannuation payouts.

The principal tools and techniques to manage threats to employment and employee security include:

- Using employment formulas to determine the numbers of employees in proportion to workload
- Using casual and part-time employees to increase employee flexibility
- Using economic forecasting to predict when demand[32] is likely to increase so that finished product or services can be available
- Bringing forward early retirement programs
- Closing unprofitable operations.

---

30 A sense of trauma may arise from witnessing unexpected retrenchments. The personal nature of trauma makes its recognition and resolution difficult. For summaries of the Mitchell (1983) and Dyregrov (1989) stress debriefing model see Parkinson (1997).

31 For example, advertising employees carry most of their knowledge in their head. In the advertising business there very few assets that remain in the building overnight since the creativity resides in the employees.

32 Two issues related to demand should be remembered: (1) demand and supply using the simple graphs introduced by Marshall (1890/1920) are helpful but must also consider elasticity; and (2) price and production theory of the firm 'serves only to explain and predict effects of mass behaviour' (Machlup 1967: 6). 'What an individual firm does, or a few firms do, may be subject to different considerations' (Katona 1967: 147).

The managerial decisions and judgements that arise from threats to employment and employee security include:

- What is an appropriate number of employees for the foreseeable future?
- Will employee benefit and entitlement funds be viable with reduced membership?
- What will be the financial effects of retrenchment reported in the financial statements?
- How can unfavourable publicity be avoided?
- What is the likely effect on the morale of existing employees?

In summary, employment and employee security are affected by reduced revenues and profitability. A reduction in the workforce is often the first resort of management when short-term return to profitability is paramount.

Chapter summary

In maturity many issues arise from erosion of revenue, profitability or market share. The existing strategy is usually refocused on core markets and products or services. Typically there are changes in expenditure including procurement and investment. It may be necessary to also change ownership in part or wholly. Reduced demand for products and services is a threat to employment and employee security. When handled well the business is rejuvenated and reverts to a new growth stage otherwise further decline will occur with the options of takeover or closure.

5 Decline: Issues that arise from turnaround or cessation of business activities

In decline[1] the business must either turnaround, cease its business or accept a takeover.

Exploring the possibility of turnaround (recovery or revival)

Turnaround requires greater strategic and operational effort than would normal operations. Since employees and suppliers will be aware of the difficulties of the business this must be taken into account when executing the turnaround.

Events leading to cessation of business

There are many reasons for ceasing business. The two primary reasons are retirement of the owner and business failure. While many businesses encounter difficulties and then recover if there is sufficient time, some financial difficulties are insurmountable. Some personal factors may also contribute. Business failure may also be due to particular managers and their propensities for erroneous judgement[2] or poor management. The major issue is how long the business can survive a negative cash flow. These are related and once they reach a serious position, remediation is usually precluded. Thus failure may be prompted by reasons directly due to the business or outside the control of the business.

Avenues for ceasing business

There are many avenues leading to business cessation. The most common actions are: takeover (absorption); merger (amalgamation); rationalisation of products, brands or product

---

1 A business may experience a one-off internal or external event which disrupts revenue. For example, an external disruption would be the cessation of supply of electricity. An internal disruption would be an employee strike. One-off events lead to the loss of revenue but generally are not responsible for decline unless risk has been improperly assessed. For example, insurance cover for the business has not been obtained or kept up-to-date.

2 There are many cases where boards and senior management may correctly foresee problems and opportunities however either their strategic choice or their implementation is flawed. Examples include Harley-Davidson in 2002 which foresaw an economic downturn but which by 2008 required them to take a substantial investment from Warren Buffet. In the 1990's Burns Philp Limited sold its diversified businesses to switch its strategy to yeasts which destroyed most of the shareholder value.

groups;[3] a re-organisation of a divisional or departmental structure;[4] an inability to sell the business and its stock as a going concern; or the inability to pay debts or continue trading leading to administration, liquidation or bankruptcy.

Topics in the decline stage of the business life cycle

Decline in the business may be evident by poorer results or there may be mixed signals so it is unclear. There are five programs of activity in decline:

1. Recognise proximate signs of distress and possibility of a turnaround

2. Explore and finalise the sale of the business

3. Wind up the business either voluntarily or under direction

4. Human consequences of an orderly closure

5. Disposal of assets, items and intellectual property, the retention of business records and preservation of historical artefacts.

5.1 Recognise the proximate signs of distress and possibility of a turnaround

There are financial and non-financial signs of distress so turnaround may occur in any of the stages of the business life cycle. Some signs of distress may be associated with growth or maturity so turnaround is also highlighted in both these stages. It is discussed in decline because once in decline the need for turnaround is acute and it is likely that resources will be limited owing to insufficient profit and reserves.[5] Turnaround depends upon circumstances and careful assessment is required to ensure the attempt has the best chance of success.

The broad management issues and challenges that arise from proximate signs of distress and possibility of a turnaround include:

- Recognise the proximate signs of distress. Consider:
  - Financial factors:
    - o Inability to produce cash flow and earn profits
    - o Under-capitalisation including reliance on debt

---

3 In 2009 the Fosters group in Australia wound back its substantial wine business by selling many of its vineyards (used to produce grapes in-house) and its under-performing brands. In addition (Speedy 2009: 26), some under-performing brands, such as Kaiser-Stuhl, were simply withdrawn.

4 These are also known as restructuring or rationalisation. Unfortunately senior managers feel the need to make an announcement about reorganisation (often to gain publicity and improve the share price of a publicly listed company) without making clear the new arrangements. Social psychology suggests this is likely to affect morale and encourage employees to seek employment elsewhere.

5 The findings from Schendel, Patton & Riggs (1976) suggest that a downturn occurs when two major events are coupled. For example a downturn in the economy combined with either inefficient operations or an inappropriate strategy vis-à-vis competitors (p 10).

- o Allowing increased liabilities with debtors and inventories
- o There is no market for the assets
- o Over-gearing and a poor borrowing strategy[6]
- o Inability to satisfy creditors.
  - – Non-financial factors:
    - o Retirement of the owner[7]
    - o Depletion of raw materials necessary to accomplish the process[8]
    - o Invention or discovery of new processes that supersede existing processes[9]
    - o Availability of cheaper products obtained overseas[10]
    - o Recognition by the individual businesses that their separate capacity and reserves exceed what a single business would require
    - o Over trading
    - o Loss of advantage gained from competitors combining different competitive advantage or value
    - o Potential gains made by competitors from vertical integration or horizontal integration
    - o Effects of illegal or unethical business practices[11]
    - o The expected advantages of takeover, merger or joint venture may not be realised.[12]
- • Ensuring the Board and senior management is appraised of the situation[13]
- • Conducting a review of the stage of evolution and competitive structure of the industry
- • Determining the causes of the current business malaise

---

6 Often there is a mismatch between long -and short-term debt with short term borrowing being used to fund assets which have a long-term life.

7 This is likely where the business is small and closely tied to the involvement and unique knowledge of the owner.

8 For example, coal mining around Sydney ceased when extraction became too difficult and too expensive.

9 For example rubber plantations in Malaysia were made obsolete by synthetic rubber which could be manufactured in a factory local to the tyre manufacturer.

10 For example, many manufacturers have relocated to China, Indonesia, Vietnam and Thailand. Even manufacturers of prestige products such as Wedgwood pottery manufacture their bone china in China.

11 For example, the prestigious accounting and audit firm Arthur Andersen was convicted by a federal jury of obstruction of justice concerning Enron. Although Enron had wrapped financial contracts around cash flows to comply with FAS 125 probably guided by a former Arthur Andersen executive (Salter 2008: 117–18) and had refused to approve a transaction without clarification (Salter 2008: 168) its own actions were its undoing (Salter 2008: 9). The GAAP principle of transactions having a 'true business purpose' goes beyond the auditor providing comfort on the accounting aspects of a transaction.

12 For example, intangible advantages may prove incompatible in aggregate.

13 The increasing independence of boards may result in reduced intimacy with the business and industry issues (Olson & van Bever 2008: *xi*). The Board should therefore ensure the business has a strategy and that resources are being allocated to support it.

- Determine whether attention is required to strategy or operations[14]
- Marshalling sufficient resources.

The principal tools and techniques to recognise the proximate signs of distress and possibility of a turnaround include:

- Operational related techniques. Consider:
  - Controlling short-term costs compared to major competitors
  - Understanding break-even points
  - Maximising the revenue generating potential of existing products
  - Establishing close ties with major customers to retain and extend their business revenues
  - Protection of the resources that the business will need in order to implement its long-term strategy.
- Strategy related techniques. Consider:
  - Identifying what provides value to the business
  - Completing fast sales of unwanted assets to maximise their revenue
  - Assessing current and future production (or service) capacity needs
  - Raising additional finance (see 3.2 Balance debt and equity).

The managerial decisions and judgements that arise from recognising the proximate signs of distress and possibility of a turnaround include:

- What are the appropriate strategic responses? Consider:
  - Will change to the structure of the business (for example, integration, diversification or disinvestment) improve operations?
  - Will replacement of top management bring new ideas that can save the business?[15]
- What are the appropriate operational responses? Consider:
  - Should there be investment in new infrastructure?
  - Should there be revitalisation of business functions?
  - Should there be improvements in efficiency?
- Would a combined approach (strategic and operational responses) be more appropriate?
- What short-term (immediate) actions are essential?
- What stakeholders should be involved and when should they be contacted?

---

14 Turnaround partly depends on whether the problems are strategic or operational. Strategic causes require strategic responses and operational causes require operational responses (Hofer 1988).

15 Peter Drucker considers the decisions on hiring managers to be among the most important decisions that a business can make.

In summary, turnaround involves making an initial judgement on likely success, addressing a range of priorities and making trade-offs between short-term versus long-term actions.

5.2 Explore and finalise the sale of the business

Many businesses have a loyal customer base and well established products and services which would be attractive to competitors. A competitor may be interested in purchasing another business to expand its operations, remove a competitor and acquire its customers or to acquire knowledge about the processes and systems used by the business.

The broad management issues and challenges that arise from exploring and finalising the sale of the business include:

- The viability of the market to sustain operations in the future
- The discovery of interested parties and the likelihood of acceptable offers
- Sufficient cash or cash flow to enable continued operation pending the sale[16]
- Ensuring detailed financial records are available to substantiate the claimed performance of the business in the years prior to the sale
- Ensuring the business operations are protected so they are available to the new owner[17]
- Valuing[18] the business taking into consideration the market
- Documenting operations[19] so it is available for due diligence
- Details of employee skills, delegations, training, roles and responsibilities[20]
- The ability to continue managing the business during the sale period where there may be distractions or insufficient time left for attention to the business
- Ensuring there is a realistic budget and sufficient funds to cover costs for any business refurbishment, preparation of documentation, promotion to prospective buyers and agents, for professional advisers

---

16 This may be exacerbated if the revenues are cyclical, seasonal, or dependent upon the outcome of events (e.g. which team wins a grand final match).

17 The relevant assets will include plant and equipment, premises (freehold/leasehold), brands, patents, trademarks and key contracts with suppliers and customers.

18 The methods of valuation include (1) earnings (profits and cash flow), (2) market-based, (3) asset-based and (4) rule of thumb. Earning methods use historical or estimated future earnings at either a capitalisation or discounted cash flow rate adjusted for depreciation, amortisation, borrowings and income tax expense. Market based methods use a price/earnings ratio or multiple applied to earnings. Asset-based methods value the only the assets and ignore goodwill or other intangibles. Rules of thumb include gross revenue, but in general earnings or price/earnings ratio are the most common. Where the business is a private company comparisons may be made with comparable listed businesses discounted for its smaller size and private ownership.

19 Documentation provides evidence the business is well-run as well as giving the new owner confidence to make an offer. Documentation will usually cover budgets and forecasts, audited financial statements, policies and procedures and up-to-date descriptions of key operations and their record-keeping systems and taxation returns lodged.

20 Where the knowledge of employees is significant then their intention to remain may also be an issue. This may be assuaged by evidence of previous low turnover.

- Selecting appropriate currently qualified professional advisors (accountant, lawyer, valuer) and intermediaries (real estate agent and broker)[21] for the jurisdiction and agreeing rates or commissions

- Identifying potential buyers[22] and notifying them of the opportunity.[23]

The principal tools and techniques to explore and finalise the sale of the business include:

- The preparation of a marketing and selling plan for the business well in advance of seeking interested parties will ensure nothing is overlooked which reduces the selling price or delays the sale. It is also essential that caution is exercised where competitors express interest as they may express interest solely to gain information about the business and its competitive advantage[24]

- Financial measures such as net present value and sensitivity analyses and valuation techniques[25]

- Non-financial measures including the effect on competitors, suppliers and customers

- Wider considerations including national competition policy, infrastructure capabilities and social welfare issues.

The managerial decisions and judgements for exploring and finalising the sale of the business include:

- What is the seller's point of view? Consider:
  - Is it intended to sell the business as a going concern?
  - Are other alternatives to selling the trading business more attractive?
    - o Would a partial sale of the business be advantageous?
    - o Should it merge with another business?
    - o Is there time to consider a partnership or joint venture?
    - o Should a professional manager be appointed to take charge of managing the business?
    - o Would franchising be viable?

---

21 It is usually unwise for the seller and the buyer to use the same professional advisors (accountant, lawyer, valuer, real estate agent and broker). The potential for a conflict of interest (professional independence) usually suggests use of different individuals as well as different businesses (companies). Even within broad accounting responsibilities it may be appropriate to engage different accounting businesses based on their specialisation. The arrangements for liaison between professional advisers will also require attention.

22 Buyers may include local and overseas competitors, investment businesses, or managers/employees.

23 Notification may occur through general advertisements in the press, use of trade media, direct mail and personally approaching potential buyers.

24 Competitors will already have a substantial knowledge of the industry and the business and therefore may devalue its goodwill.

25 Valuation may be based on many different criteria. See Glossary for three examples. In any case, investors may overreact to bad news or anticipate economic events with the result that valuations may change through decline, rebound or volatility of perceived crisis and opportunity.

      o Is there time to seek new funds?

      o Is it possible to reduce the number of hours worked each week/month by employees?

– Is it possible to take any short-term action to improve the performance of the business by increasing revenue and reducing costs?

– Is it desirable to sell as an entire unit or is it better to break the business into parts?

– What is the package of information[26] provided to prospective purchasers and what additional detailed information may be made available?[27]

– Is there a timetable with a deadline for the sale or closure to be completed?

– Will offers be solicited through tender, expressions of interest, auction or an open ended process?

– Is the valuation sufficiently realistic to elicit offers at that level?

– Is the market supportive of this kind of business activity and this particular business endeavour?

– Does the equity holder wish to remain in the business or in the industry in any capacity?[28]

– Does the contract adequately express the terms of the sale?

      o What is the deposit and payment of the balance of the purchase price?[29]

      o What land, buildings, plant and equipment are included and excluded?

      o What are the details of trading stock including work-in-progress?

      o What is the status of debts owing by trade debtors?

      o What are the arrangements for leave and superannuation of employees?

      o What are the rights in intellectual property, royalties and licences?

      o What is the consideration for goodwill concerning business name and clients/customers, contracts?

---

26 The package may contain the key features of the business, a history of the business, reasons for its sale, a business plan, a summary of assets and liabilities, details of leases, financial statements with history, income tax returns, consumption tax returns, commentary on strategy, potential for growth, organisation charts, job descriptions, any potential contingent liabilities, any imminent investments or expenditures, budgets and forecasts for current and future years. These should be prepared and vetted by professional advisors to ensure there are no misleading statements or inducements that may allow rescinding the sale contract or damages to be claimed by the purchaser.

27 This will usually be detailed information and schedules such as: a detailed list of assets and liabilities, aged debtors listing, aged creditors listing, lease contracts, customer contracts, supplier contracts, other contracts, schedules of plant and depreciation, schedules of asset and inventory valuation, employment contracts, details of trademarks, details of licences, details of inventory and valuation, schedules of depreciation and amortisation and warranties and indemnities.

28 The purchaser may wish to insert in the contract restrictions on competitive trading.

29 There may also be earn outs which depend upon future events and conditions being achieved. For example, sums may be payable upon availability of audited statements for the current financial year.

- o Is any restraint of trade[30] imposed on the vendor, directors and selected employees?

- o What are the arrangements for consumption tax and capital gains in the sale?

- o Is there any expectation of confidentiality required in a separate confidentiality agreement?

- What is the buyer's point of view? Consider:

  - Is the business is sound?

    - o Does it have consistent profitability over a long period?

    - o Is the business efficiently run?

    - o Are records accurate?

    - o Does the business have a reputation for quality products and services including delivery and after-sales support?

    - o Does the business have a reasonable market share based on key competitors and competitor products and services?

    - o What are the tangible and intangible assets?

    - o What are the financial projections?

    - o Are the production and distribution processes sustainable?

  - Will the business continue with its current structure and remuneration arrangements?

    - o How are the employees organised and managed?[31]

    - o What is the remuneration and other benefits or incentives for employees?[32]

    - o Are key employees likely to remain?[33]

  - Will the business require minimal or additional attention?

    - o How much effort is required to run the business on a day-to-day basis?

    - o Are there particular seasonal peaks and troughs?

  - Are there taxation and profit considerations?

    - o Are there accumulated tax losses?

    - o Are there balances in the franking account?

  - Are there any product or service liabilities?

    - o Are there warranties?

---

30 Restraints of trade include engaging in competing business activities, assisting a competitor, acting for clients of the business being sold, disclosure of non-public information and enticing or interfering with existing employees of the business being sold

31 Organisation charts, employee descriptions will supplement the operational manuals and policies and procedures.

32 The advice of a professional advisor should be sought as there may be privacy issues associated with releasing information naming employees.

33 To ensure the continuity of operations may necessitate formal contracts or incentives being offered to key employees.

     o Are there indemnities?

   – Is there a need for transitional arrangements?

     o Should there be a period where new and existing owner sit side by side?

     o Will sufficient understanding have been obtained by the handover date?

In summary, the sale or closure is not a matter exclusively for the vendor as other parties determine if one or more viable offers will be made. In some cases, closure is a simpler step owing to the immediacy that it offers and the certainty that it brings.

5.3 Wind up the business voluntarily or under direction

Once the possibility of sale is exhausted then the options for winding up the business have to be considered. Management will usually attempt to prevent this from occurring but they may be blocked by creditors determined to establish the financial position of the business and obtain the payments due to them.

The broad management issues and challenges that arise from winding up include:

- Where the initiative originates and what form of action is proposed

- The issue of personal versus business (company)[34] insolvency

- The certainty over insolvency[35] and the consequences of trading while insolvent.

- Making the effort to stave off winding-up or restructuring which may be instigated by the business itself, creditors or other parties. Consider:

  - Taking action by realising cash utilising assets (e.g. sale) or equity (e.g. capital raising)

  - Entering into compromises, arrangements or reconstructions to improve the chance of survival and reduce any detrimental effects to creditors

  - Entering into a deed of arrangement to allow continued trading with a moratorium on debts, restructure creditor claims and share capital (debt for equity reconstruction), or reconstruct the business via a capital injection, merger, sale or other restructure.

---

34 Usually the solvency of individuals and businesses is treated under separate legislation although there are similarities between them. The terminology varies by jurisdiction. In many cases bankruptcy is applied to individuals and liquidation is applied to businesses.

35 Insolvency has two senses: (1) a global sense where in the balance sheet liabilities exceeds assets and (2) a cash flow sense where a debtor cannot pay debts as and when they fall due owing to illiquidity. Generally, it is an offence to authorise or consent to a company incurring a debt if there were at the time reasonable grounds to expect the company would not be able to pay them as and when they fell due.

- Entering into voluntary administration to allow the business to continue trading with the appointment of an official administrator[36] (instigated by the business, creditors or liquidator) for a limited period.
- The consequences of proceeding with liquidation[37] to ensure a just distribution of the assets of the business and payment of creditors as far as is practicable by winding up. Consider:
  - Schemes of arrangement which allow a compromise or moratorium to creditor rights for allowing the business to continue trading[38]
  - Voluntary administration to allow the business to continue trading
  - Voluntary liquidation where there is urgency to freeze the position of the business in relation to its creditors or other interested parties
  - Provisional appointment of a liquidator to safeguard the assets of the business preventing their dissipation or removal pending the court making an order to wind-up the business
  - Court liquidation[39] sought by an interested party which may be against the wishes of owners/managers and majority shareholders
  - Having the business taken over owing to a charge over the assets[40] using a receiver.[41]
- Obtaining the services of a receiver. Consider:
  - Using a private receiver appointed under the terms of the security
  - Using a court appointed receiver.

The principal tools and techniques available during winding up include:

- Preparation of financial statements of the same kind as a business that is a going concern

---

36 The administrator is responsible for providing an up-to-date report on the affairs of the business and convening a meeting of the creditors and to enable creditors to assess the financial position of the business. An administrator may be appointed even when liquidation appears inevitable.

37 The liquidator may either terminate the business activities on liquidation or authorise the business to carry on activities for a foreseeable period to ensure a beneficial winding up. The decision is usually based on which will be most advantageous. Once a liquidator is appointed, the directors of the business will have their powers lapse. Once a liquidator applies to a court for release and dissolution of the business the court liquidation is finalised.

38 A scheme of arrangement may also be finalised after a business has been placed in provisional liquidation, liquidation or receivership given the exposure of officers to personal liability if the business is on the borderline of insolvency and it continues trade.

39 A court may presume insolvency where the business has not complied with a statutory demand or an order of the court remains unsatisfied.

40 This may arise through a lending institution or other creditor obtaining charge such as a fixed or floating charge, a registered mortgage debenture, a deed or a contract containing a charge clause. The clause will then specify that if the business defaults in making payments or exceeds levels of specified ratios that the creditor may enter into possession of the assets or the business either directly through a receiver or by appointing an agent. Upon appointment of a receiver, the directors of the business are obliged to report the affairs of the business to the receiver.

41 The receiver may either continue to trade or close the business depending upon the benefits of completing work-in-process, the possibility of sale of the business or the possibility of return to profitability allowing satisfying of the debt. This may entail replacement of the receiver with an administrator or the execution of a deed of arrangement to ensure repayments resume to the lending institution.

- Corporate legislation which specifies the order of precedence for distribution of monies[42]
- Demonstration of proof of debt by creditor[43]
- Recovery of property and monies[44]
- Providing information to creditors and conducting creditor meetings (by the liquidator)
- Remuneration of an administrator or liquidator
- Corporate legislation which specifies offences for officers of the business knowingly giving information that is false or misleading in material particulars.[45]

The managerial decisions and judgements that arise from winding up include:

- Can the thorough pursuit of economies and the ruthless elimination of efficiencies provide an immediate turnaround and permit survival?
- Is it likely that the business will be prevented from trading by creditors?
- Is the latest accurate financial information disseminated promptly to stakeholders?[46]
- What will be the cost of litigation to the business if irregularities or misdemeanours are suspected and there is an inquiry or a trial?
- Is there a likelihood of damage to personal reputation or disbarment as a director if an adverse finding is made (also considering litigation may be delayed and protracted)?
- What is the likelihood of accomplishing a sale or obtaining a capital injection on favourable terms?

In summary, lack of profitability and inability to pay debts make winding up likely. In some cases quick action to improve trading or sell assets may sufficiently improve cash flow. Creditors may bring actions or the business may voluntarily seek winding up.

---

42 In many cases the taxation authority receives preference over creditors and employees are lowly ranked.

43 The proof of debt application must be supported by adequate evidence. When presented to the liquidator the liquidator has a time limit to respond and the creditor has a right of appeal if it is rejected.

44 Transactions completed prior to liquidation which had the effect of preferring a creditor or disposing of business property may be set aside. The types of antecedent transactions may include conveyance, transfer or disposition of property, giving a charge, making a guarantee, making a payment, incurring an obligation, releasing or waiving a debt and receiving a loan. In addition, unfair preferences, uncommercial transactions and unreasonable payments are included.

45 Both Australian and international examples are provided in Clarke, Dean and Oliver (1997/2003) and Clarke and Dean (2007).

46 Accounts, reports and financial statements should be free from any false or misleading statements. Nevertheless, they may be erroneous. The business may defend itself on the grounds that it provides general purpose information and it is the responsibility of the user to assess it. The role of the external auditor in providing endorsement of financial statements is ambiguous. In some cases the external auditor has been found to have been exonerated and in other cases found culpable according to Clarke, Dean and Oliver (1997/2003) and Clarke and Dean (2007).

5.4 Human consequences of an orderly closure

The consequences of closure[47] are felt differently by the individuals depending upon their career ambitions, their expectations for the business and their ability to make acceptable alternative arrangements.

The broad management issues and challenges that arise from the human consequences of an orderly closure include:

- Retrenchment and redundancy of employees
- Funding of employee entitlements (e.g. wages, long service leave and superannuation)
- Redeployment of employees to other divisions within the business or to another business in the case of a takeover
- Advising customers of the non-ability to continue supplying their needs (assuming an orderly shutdown of the business
- Advising suppliers of the non-ability to continue supplying their needs (assuming an orderly shutdown of the business.

The principal tools and techniques to manage the human consequences of an orderly closure include:

- Voluntary redundancy offers[48] with payments to compensate for loss of job and payout of superannuation entitlements (where the business has funds to make these payments)
- Project management of the shutdown, relocation, transfer or merger
- Counselling
- Facilitation and communication
- Outplacement services
- Work-life balance seminars.

The managerial decisions and judgements that arise from the human consequences of an orderly closure include:

- What is the date for the closure?
- What are suitable arrangements and rates for redundancy and retrenchment?
- How will work-in-process be completed?

In summary, the human consequences of an orderly closure will involve sensitivity to the employees affected both by remaining if the employee numbers are reduced and being retrenched. The tendency of businesses to release bad news ahead of festive events (e.g.

---

47 Where the closure is imposed then there may be little or notice to employees. In some cases, employees may not receive any of their monetary entitlements owing to the deep insolvency involved.

48 These are often embodied in enterprise agreements or awards.

Christmas) adds to employee stress levels as well as making it difficult to find alternative employment. There are fewer and fewer employers and managers who display sensitivity and therefore employees and their family often shoulder the burden of closure both economically and psychologically.

5.5 Disposal of assets, items and intellectual property, the retention of business records and preservation of historical artefacts

Usually there are assets and items owned by the business with some remaining value for which market value needs to be determined. In an orderly closure these will be handled by the business over an extended time period to obtain the best price. Where the closure is imposed then the liquidator may wish to realise cash as soon as possible. This may involve using an auction sale method. There is national and state legislation on the retention of records which cover private enterprise, government departments and state corporations.

The broad management issues and challenges concerning disposal of assets, items, intellectual property, business records and historical artefacts include:

- What are the arrangements for disposal of assets, items and intellectual property? Consider:
  - Sale of raw materials, work in process and finished products (inventory)
  - Sale of equipment where these are owned (assets)
  - Sale of premises and fixtures and fittings where these are owned (assets)
  - The sales and promotion arrangements such as advertising and the web site
  - The business name
  - The status of intellectual property and any royalty earning capabilities.
- What are the arrangements for retention of records? Consider:
  - Identifying the records that have legal retention requirements
  - Determining where records will be stored and the likely duration of that storage
  - Preserving the records in a manner that will prevent decay during the required retention period
  - Labelling the records to allow comprehensive search and easy retrieval of the target records
  - Managing the retention of records that have different retention periods under record keeping legislation.
- What are the arrangements for historical artefacts? Consider:
  - Relationship to the history and evolution of the business

- Potential for enhancing reputation or brand image.

The principal tools and techniques to manage disposal of assets, items, intellectual property, business records and historical artefacts include:

- For disposal of assets, items and intellectual property, consider:
  - Abandonment
  - Relocation to other Strategic Business Units
  - Auctions to sell individual assets, items and intellectual property
  - Auctions of batches of assets, items and intellectual property (e.g. premises and fittings)
  - Tenders to sell assets, items and intellectual property
  - Transfer of ownership at negligible cost.
- For retention of records, consider:
  - Electronic storage including text or image scanning, microfiche and database storage of digital images
  - Indexing and cataloguing document management systems
  - Powerful search capabilities[49]
  - Use of special non-deteriorating papers
  - Use of temperature and light controlled display and storage environments[50]
  - The production of duplicates that can be used as working copies.
- For historical artefacts, consider:
  - Heritage and conservation orders and similar preservation requirements
  - Use of speciality archiving or preservation services
  - Commissioning descriptions of historical significance.

The managerial decisions and judgements that arise from disposal of assets, items, intellectual property, business records and historical artefacts include:

- What are the arrangements for disposal of assets, items, and intellectual property? Consider:
  - Is there a comprehensive list of assets and items available?
  - How will market value be established?
  - Will employees be allowed to purchase any assets, items and intellectual property?
  - What forms of payment for purchase will be accepted?

---

49 Most simple searches rely on using a search of the entire text search or a keyword. Powerful searches allow combinations of user selected words (tags) and separate the organisation of the items from their storage arrangement (Weinberger 2007/2008: 64–128).

50 For example, where documents are made of materials likely to deteriorate or where paintings are affected by light or humidity.

- What are the arrangements for retention of records? Consider:
  - What items of the business have historical value and ought to be offered to organisations whose interest is in their preservation?
  - What records are intrinsically valuable and require secure storage?
  - What records are fragile and require special storage arrangements?
  - What records must be filed (lodged) to comply with statutory and other obligations?
- What are the arrangements for historical artefacts? Consider:
  - Is there documentation which should accompany the artefact?
  - Do the artefacts require special transport or storage arrangements (e.g. security, lighting, temperature, humidity)?
  - Are there benefits in gifting to a suitable custodian?

In summary, closure involves the disposal of assets and the filing and retention of records. Disposal of items uses the benefits exceed costs heuristic except where there is materiality in the assets. Retention of records uses the criteria of compliance and historical value. Ensuring compliance with obligations and archiving allows the information to be available for the future. The future requirements for information may be for social, economic or political history.

Chapter summary

Decline in the business may be arrested and the business may re-enter a stage of turnaround or all attempts may be unsuccessful. A sale of the business may be contemplated by public notification or by directly approaching prospective buyers. Where this option is either unsuccessful or unavailable the remaining option is closure by winding up. There are many human consequences of closure particularly where it occurs with little notice to the employees and their families. Disposal of assets, items and intellectual property, then follows. It is desirable that there is retention of the basic records for legal purposes. Where the business has historical significance it is desirable that other records are also retained. They may be handed to an archiving authority (for example a museum or library) or given to a community history preservation society. This completes the review of the business cycle. All the stages involve continuous adaptive responses to circumstances and these are now considered.

DIMENSION TWO
CONTINUOUS & DISCONTINUOUS ADAPTIVE BEHAVIOUR TO CIRCUMSTANCES

Context of adaptive behaviour

An adaptive response is arguably one of the most distinguishing characteristics of business although the continuity of the business day-to-day often makes it difficult to recognise the presence of change. Adaptation is not used in a biological sense: human genetic constituents therefore only partially determine behaviour. A business is composed of autonomous individuals with roles, identities and personal ambitions.

Perspective on adaptive behaviour

Four differing views of adaptation are prominent. First, change is continuous and brings about existence with the metaphor of stepping in the river[1] (Heraclitus 1979). Second, the evolutionary approach featuring survival of the fittest (Spencer 1864; Darwin 1859/1869; Alchian 1950; Nelson & Winter 1982; Dosi, Malerba & Teece 2003). Third, the view of continuous improvement which is one of the responsibilities of management (Deming 1982/1986). Finally, a discontinuous or complex approach where the interaction between the intricate arrangements of parts results in unpredictable consequences (Holland 1998).[2]

---

1 Heraclitus (of Ephesus, presumably now coastal Turkey) was a pre-Socratic Greek philosopher whose philosophy is preserved only in fragments. The exact quote is 'No man ever steps in the same river twice, for it's not the same river and he's not the same man.'

2 This introduces several related concepts including coevolution where adaption to change occurs to both the business and its environment.

Impact of adaptive behaviour

The impact of adaptive behaviour is seen in the many responses of employees and managers. They include (1) doing nothing;[3] (2) reorganisation;[4] (3) apathy or disinterest; (4) employee resistance; and (5) making unreasonable demands which show little regard for employees. The tendency to use performance incentives and measures may exacerbate the mechanistic features of business. On the other hand, some employees and managers recognise the meaning provided by work and take a caring or people-centred approach to their peers and subordinates.

Another kind of response is planning to achieve a fit. The outcome of a decade long research project to investigate how IT could be aligned with organisation strategy produced the MIT90s model.[5] Although its value as a fit or alignment guide for IT is debatable,[6] it does have utility when considering adaptive behaviour. In part it is due to its antecedents, namely Chandler (1962) and the Leavitt diamond (Leavitt 1974: 263–64). They proposed that an organisation redesigns itself by focusing on management processes, structure, strategies, people and tasks, to meet the demands of such external forces as technology and changing markets. Figure 5 on the next page depicts the MIT90s model. There is interaction among the factors, as well as interaction with external forces. The five factors are: (1) Strategy is the general mode of doing business in pursuit of the objectives of the organisation; (2) Structure is the way that the organisation is partitioned and the way the partitions interrelate; (3) Management processes are the standardised sequences of activities that organisations adopt in order to undertake the tasks they perform regularly; (4) Technology refers to the information and communications technologies that can be applied to facilitate business processes; and (5) Individuals and roles are concerned with people within the organisation, the tasks they undertake and the education and training they require for performing their functions.

---

3 Kodak (Eastman Kodak) enjoyed high market share and high revenue for many years. They found it difficult to recognise that the film imaging market had declined and the business had to compete with low margin products in a capital intensive industry where legacy investments were of little value. On a financial analysis the fully amortised legacy investments have relatively high economic returns while the economic return from alternatives are comparatively unattractive. Kodak did not act to divert its resources to emergent and disruptive products.

4 A well-known quote is: 'We trained hard, but it seemed that every time we were beginning to form up into teams we would be reorganised. Presumably the plans for our employment were being changed. I was to learn later in life that, perhaps because we are so good at organising, we tend as a nation to meet any new situation by reorganising; and a wonderful method it can be for creating the illusion of progress while producing confusion, inefficiency and demoralization.' It is usually attributed to Gaius Petronius Arbiter (Titus Petronius Niger) AD 66. In fact it is far more recent, Brown (1978) pinpoints that it first appeared in an article by Ogburn (1957) in Harpers Magazine.

5 The MIT90s model is named after 'The Management in the 1990s Research Programme' which was a major research program conducted between 1984 and 1990 at MIT Sloan School of Management. The major objective of the program was 'To help managers throughout the world understand the kinds of impact IT will have on business missions, organizational structures and operating practices'. (Scott-Morton 1991: 6). The major finding was that there were fundamental changes occurring in the way work is done (Scott-Morton 1991: 11). The manifestations for this included the integration of business functions at all levels, shifts in the competitive climate in many industries, new strategic opportunities and changes in management and organisational structure. The challenge identified for management was to lead their organisation through the transformation (Scott–Morton 1991: 21).

6 The strategic alignment process in practice (Luftman 1996) found three of the forces (management processes; structure; and individuals and their roles) to be critical to any organisational transformation. However the relationship with technology is inconclusive.

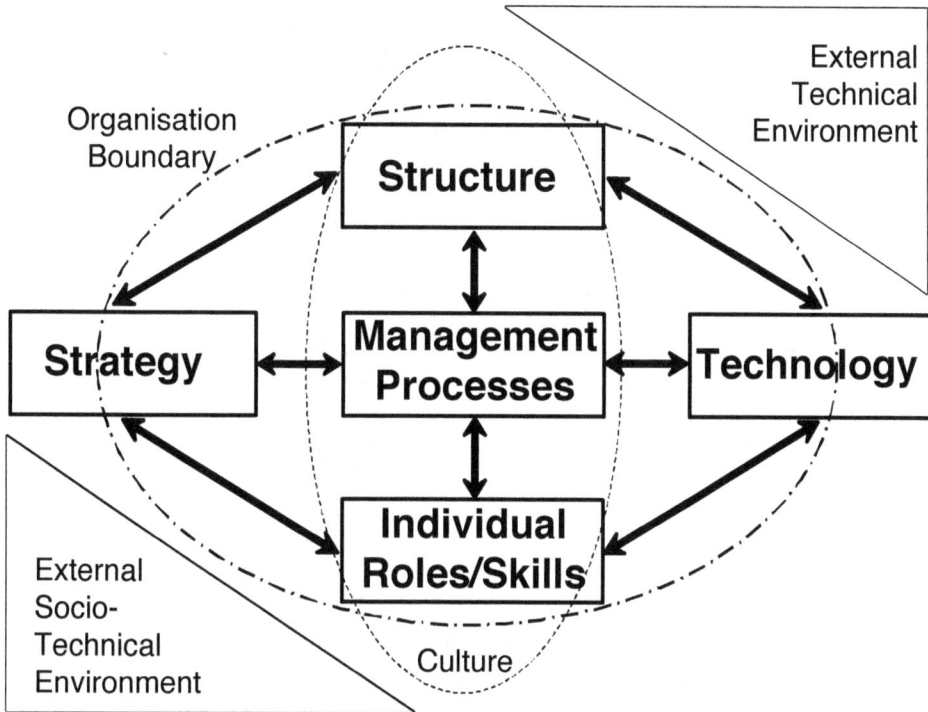

Figure 5. MIT90s model

Chapters in Dimension Two (Adaptive behaviour)

There are four forms of adaptation within the business which influence its assumed business knowledge. They are:

1. Adjust the organisation structure and business functions as the rationale for the existence of the business changes (discussed in Chapter 6)

2. Use sensemaking to understand phenomena and reassess priorities (discussed in Chapter 7)

3. Use policies, controls and reviews to bring flexibility to operations (discussed in Chapter 8)

4. Personal power, authority, corruption and conflict (discussed in Chapter 9).

6 Adjust the organisation structure and business functions as the rationale for the existence of the business changes

Usually the CEO determines the business functions and structure. The CEO will then usually empower managers reporting to her or him to determine the structure of the business units that they manage on the basis that they (the managers appointed) are held accountable for achievement of goals. In some cases if the CEO is recruited or promoted on the basis of improving business, they may be able to impose a structure across the business as part of their mandate or as part of their negotiated terms of engagement.

In circumstances where the industry or the business is struggling, or if improved performance is required, the advice of consultants may be sought. The CEO and senior managers may, in these circumstances, amend the structure of the business to the blueprint recommended by the consultants. In some advisory engagements, the brief of the consultants may be to complete the changes to the business structure, determining who to retain, who to retrench and who to recruit. This kind of human resources engagement will include determining job descriptions, performance measures and evaluation and career services for those employees who are retrenched.

In those cases where an equity holder or lender has substantial control over the business, they too may determine the business structure.

Topics in adjusting the organisation structure and business functions for adaptation

The integration of these five elements of business functions and structure goes a long way toward ensuring the viability of the business:

1. Optimise the legal configuration
2. Allocate and name the business functions

3. Arrange the organisational structure of the business

4. Allocate roles (positions), responsibilities and ensure accountabilities

5. Determine the best arrangements for employee cooperation and supervision.

6.1 Optimise the legal configuration

Many considerations determine the optimal legal configuration. The financial circumstances of the owner at the time the business was instigated, taxation considerations and funding are three primary determinants. The growth of most business prompts reconsideration, particularly when the business has more than one major contributor to profit. For example, Harvey Norman obtains its income from property leases, importation and distribution revenue and retail sales.

The broad management issues and challenges associated with the optimal legal configuration include:

- The most beneficial form of legal configuration

- The extent of benefit or protection afforded to the owners

- Whether the existing tax status of entities and their assets may be affected when changing the legal configuration.

The principal tools and techniques for an optimal legal configuration include:

- The legal status established for the business (sole proprietor, partnership, one person proprietary company, multiple party proprietary company, limited company)

- Some forms of legal status (e.g. co-operatives) offer options for production or marketing or both

- Some forms of legal status (e.g. trusts) offer additional advantages such as taxation benefits

- Whether to adopt an advisory board if the business does not have a company structure[1]

- Joint venture (although it may also be treated as a partnership)

- Service entities.[2]

The managerial decisions and judgements concerning optimal legal configuration include:

- What foreseeable events might occur which may require an alternate legal configuration?

---

1 An advisory board is a small group of trusted advisors who are not directors, that meets in much the same manner as a board of directors would to review the progress of the business. It provides guidance and advice, assists in solving problems, provides contacts and business introductions that may prove useful. The members of the board can include accountants, strategic advisor and subject matter experts. The frequency of meetings and the items discussed vary widely from business to business.

2 Typically the service entity is linked to an associated entity and enables the associated business to protect its assets while providing it with administrative, employment or other services.

- How robust is the current legal configuration against shareholder takeover actions?
- How robust is the current legal configuration against shareholder class actions?
- How robust is the current legal configuration against substantial employee fraud?[3]

In summary, there is considerable detail attached to the legal configuration of a business. This is particularly the case where it forms a part of a group of companies. This may necessitate the involvement of more than one specialist (such as Accountant, Lawyer, Tax Advisor and Finance) in company structuring.

6.2 Allocate and name the business functions

The business performs activities which are referred to as business functions. A business function may change. The change may be in the substance of the function. For example, quality control has changed from inspection to assurance. The change may also be in the way a business function is accomplished. For example, e-business allows virtual activities and electronic linking of employees working from home.

The broad management issues and challenges for allocating and naming business functions[4] include:

- Determining the core or essential business functions and additional business functions. Consider:
  - Sales
  - Marketing
  - Procurement
  - Production[5] if in the a manufacturing sector
  - Distribution.[6]
- Determine the essential additional business functions. Consider
  - Accounting
  - Tax
  - Legal matters.

---

3 Types of fraud are grouped into management and employee fraud by Rezaee (2002: 3). Employee fraud includes embezzlement, breach of fiduciary duty, theft and illegal acts.

4 Several major businesses provide exemplars as to how to manage business functions. One detailed description is provided by General Motors (Sloan 1963/1990). In the foreword Drucker states he believes Sloan wrote it to counter Drucker's earlier commentary (Drucker 1946/1972).

5 The scale of manufacturing production creates scope for many different production techniques. A small manufacturing plant lacks the market power to organise its suppliers. A large-scale business such as Toyota was able to create a unique production system (Ohno 1988) which was copied throughout the world.

6 For example, Dell used to undercut its rivals on price by selling personal computers directly to business and consumers. It now sells through retailers to broaden its appeal to a wider market.

- Determining which business functions will be in-house and which will be outsourced[7]
- Determining which functions will be allocated to ambiguous activities.[8]

The principal tools and techniques for allocating and naming business functions include:

- Specialisation[9]
- Generalisation
- Using the conventional business functions names prominent in the industry
- Gathering together similar functions under one person or group (e.g. office administration)
- Outsourcing selected business functions or services
- Using an organisation chart to depict the business functions in an easy to read visual layout.[10] A simple example is provided in Figure 6 below.

```
          ┌─────────────────────┐
          │  Board of Directors │
          └──────────┬──────────┘
                     │
          ┌──────────┴───────────┐
          │ Chief Executive Officer │
          └──────────┬───────────┘
        ┌──────┬─────┴─────┬────────┐
    ┌───────┐ ┌─────┐ ┌─────────┐ ┌───────────┐
    │Production│ │Sales│ │Marketing│ │Procurement│
    └───────┘ └─────┘ └─────────┘ └───────────┘
```

Figure 6. Organisation chart showing major business functions

The managerial decisions and judgements concerning allocation and naming of the business functions[11] include:

- What additional business functions arise through the need to operate competently? Consider:
    - Is a dedicated function for product design necessary?
    - Should there be a dedicated advertising function?
    - Is there sufficient workload for dedicated in-house legal advice?

---

7 It is unusual to outsource the core functions. However, there are examples such as Nike Corporation keeping in-house only its product design function.

8 Although most activities can be unambiguously allocated to functions some remain contentious. For example, where does web site overall design and content lie? It can be assigned to Information Technology or to Marketing.

9 In a large business there is likely to be a separate department known as purchasing and a separate department for sales.

10 These arrangements may change over time or in response to incidents that directly affect the business or that are observed by the business.

11 A more generic grouping is described as 'front counter' and 'back-office'

- – Is there sufficient workload for dedicated human resources function including payroll?
- – Should there be a dedicated investment function including treasury dealing?
- – Should there be a dedicated function for market research?
- – Should there be a dedicated function for public (or media) relations?
- – Should there be a dedicated function for taxation advice, taxation planning and completing taxation returns?

- • What additional business functions are necessary for environmental concerns and social networking?[12] Consider:
  - – Is it necessary to have a separate function for environmental compliance and reporting?
  - – Is it necessary to have a separate function for product feedback and commentary related to the business, its brands or use of its products and services?[13]

- • Does the allocation of business functions serve the overall objectives of the business? Consider:
  - – What is the relationship between business functions and business units?[14]
  - – What is the relationship between business functions and systems?[15]
  - – Should any business functions be outsourced?
  - – Which business functions can be handled by seeking specific advice for a particular problem?
  - – Which business functions are best handled by an experienced manager of another business function?
  - – How can business functions be reconfigured to eliminate resource consuming activities which do not contribute to customer value?[16]

---

12 The motivation for the majority of individuals becoming involved is clearly not money (since very few are paid). Malone et al. (2009) suggest that online operations should be aware of what drives people to become involved in sharing information and provide examples from Amazon, Linux and YouTube.

13 For example, Amazon.com initially allowed the public to make comments offering their opinion on the books it sold. In 1999, Amazon introduced a wish list feature to allow people to share lists of their favourite products and make recommendations about individual products.

14 Business functions typically correspond with business units. For example the business function of procurement is assigned to the purchasing department. Many business functions may be the responsibility of a single business unit. For example, manufacturing, engineering and research and development may all be assigned to the production department. Some business functions may be outsourced. For example, the information technology function may be outsourced to a specialist vendor who provides the hardware, software and support services to end-users.

15 A business function may not correspond with the systems in the business. For example, a small corner store has no defined marketing department. A home business may only undertake sales when the owner has time and the need for new customers. A business function may also change. For example, the quality control function has changed from inspection to assurance.

16 The use of information should contribute value to business processes (Taylor 1982). Ideally business processes are identified at their lowest discrete or 'primitive' level (DeMarco 1978/1979).

In summary, while it is convenient to recognise each business function as a separate department in the business this is not essential. There are many examples where one person performs many different functions or where one department is responsible for many different functions.

6.3 Arrange the organisational structure of the business

There are many influences over the organisational structure of the business. Uncertainty in the environment is a key to understanding organisational structure since an organisation structure attempts to bring control and predictability to both its operations and relationship with the environment.[17]

The broad management issues and challenges of organisational structure[18] that management can consider include:

- The levels (layers or hierarchy) of the business[19]
- The influence of managerial action[20]
- The social psychology and sociology of reporting hierarchies where there are groups.

The principal tools and techniques to determine the organisational structure of the business include:

- Formalising authority through delegations
- Assigning employees at varying levels or grades in the business
- Allocating employees to common teams or work groups[21]
- Creating virtual teams (communities of practice)
- Allowing employees to form working groups that extend beyond the boundaries of the business.

---

17 Theories of structure usually rely on situational or external variables. Thompson, (1967/2003) emphasises the need to separate the actions of individuals from the overall responses of the organisation.

18 This assumes the principle that structure follows strategy (Chandler 1962).

19 Three levels (strategic, tactical and operational) are traditionally identified. Strategic is the upper-most group of managers who set and monitor the strategic direction of the business. Tactical is 'middle management' who is responsible for translating broad strategy into specific routines and initiatives. Operational is responsible for the day to day transactions.

20 Managerial action has been responsible for administrative coordination becoming more efficient than market coordination (Chandler 1977). Two by-products of the ascendancy of managers are (1) a preference for policies of growth trends rather than maximisation of current profit and (2) large enterprises which offer careers for professionals owing to their size and influence in their sector of the economy.

21 Formerly, individuals may be assembled from different business functions to work on a project owing to their expertise or their interest.

The managerial decisions and judgements concerning the organisational structure include:

- How many levels (layers) of management are appropriate?
- What proportion of operational, tactical and strategic employees is appropriate?
- What are the consequences for entitlements?[22]

In summary, as a work group or team develops its own identity it may be able to overcome business unit inertia or power blocs that would delay or prevent new or changed arrangements.

6.4 Allocate roles (positions), responsibilities and ensure accountabilities

Once a business has more than one employee there is a need to assign roles (also known as job titles or position titles) with responsibilities and accountabilities.[23]

The broad management issues and challenges in allocating roles, responsibilities and ensuring accountabilities include.[24]

- Ensuring a balance between those who undertake the core activities ('Line' employees) and those who support them ('Staff' employees)
- Ensuring a balance between those who support customers (front line employees) and those who support them (back office employees)
- The allocation and naming of the position titles and their responsibilities.[25] Consider:
  - Chief Executive Officer ('CEO') or equivalent (e.g. Managing Director or General Manager)
  - Chief Financial Officer ('CFO')
  - Sales[26] Director
- A business is in the manufacturing sector will the additional function of Manufacturing Director.[27]

---

22 Examples of entitlements include motor vehicle luxury level, class and frequency of travel and reimbursement of incidental expenses.

23 An early broad view of the division of work and structure of roles, responsibilities and accountabilities was provided by Fayol (1916/1949). Also see Brodie (1967) for an assessment. Another view is expressed by Follett (1941).

24 These roles may change over time or in response to incidents that directly affect the business or that are observed by the business. For example within sales, servicing existing customers is often separated from generating new business.

25 The functions of the executive included formulating organisational aims, establishing and maintaining communications and securing the services of other executives according to Barnard (1938).

26 The sales function may also include the marketing function. The Sales Director may instead be known as the Marketing Director.

27 The manufacturing or production function may also include engineering. It is a matter of preference whether these titles have the word 'director' first or last.

The principal tools and techniques to allocate roles, responsibilities and accountabilities include:

- Management by objectives[28] ('MBO')
- Balanced ScoreCard[29] ('BSC')
- Setting budgets (or their equivalent such as sales targets)[30]
- Using internal controls (see Chapter 8)
- Setting specific overall numeric limits.[31]

An organisation chart depicts the job titles (also known as position titles) in an easy to read visual layout. A simple example is provided in Figure 7 below for the upper management level of a business.

```
                        ┌─────────────────────┐
                        │  Board of Directors  │
                        └──────────┬──────────┘
                                   │
                        ┌─────────────────────────┐
                        │ Chief Executive Officer  │
                        └───────────┬─────────────┘
        ┌──────────┬──────────┬──────────┬──────────┐
   ┌─────────┐ ┌─────────┐ ┌──────────┐ ┌──────────┐ ┌──────────┐
   │ Sales   │ │Marketing│ │Procurement│ │Distribution│ │Production│
   │ Director│ │ Director│ │ Director │ │ Director │ │ Director │
   └────┬────┘ └────┬────┘ └────┬─────┘ └────┬─────┘ └────┬─────┘
   ┌─────────┐ ┌─────────┐ ┌──────────┐ ┌──────────┐ ┌──────────┐
   │Territory│ │ Product │ │  Tender  │ │ Logistics│ │ Factory  │
   │ Manager │ │ Manager │ │ Manager  │ │ Manager  │ │Supervisor│
   └────┬────┘ └────┬────┘ └────┬─────┘ └────┬─────┘ └────┬─────┘
   ┌─────────┐ ┌─────────┐ ┌──────────┐ ┌──────────┐ ┌──────────┐
   │ Sales   │ │ Market  │ │Purchasing│ │ Warehouse│ │ Factory  │
   │Represent│ │ Analysts│ │  Clerks  │ │  Clerks  │ │  Hands   │
   │ atives  │ │         │ │          │ │          │ │          │
   └─────────┘ └─────────┘ └──────────┘ └──────────┘ └──────────┘
```

Figure 7. Organisation chart showing major business roles (positions)

The managerial decisions and judgements concerning allocation and naming of the business functions include:

- What are the conditions for managerial accountability?[32]
- What roles and responsibilities will be identified?
- What position titles will be allowed?

---

28 For a discussion of management by objectives see Drucker (1964) and Reddin (1971).

29 There have been many attempts to link strategy to performance. For example PIMS links profitability and market share (Buzzell & Gale 1987; Buzzell 2004). There are many discussions of the balanced scorecard. For the original statements see Kaplan and Norton (1992) for the short article and (1996) for the monograph.

30 Budgets are a suitable control for profit and cost centres. For a discussion of the case against the master budget, see Hope and Fraser (2003).

31 Examples include the number of employees and their salary levels or position grades; this is known as an establishment ceiling or headcount.

32 Many positions tiled 'manager' are not according to Jaques (1976); he suggests a manager needs to have rights concerning (1) membership of the group, (2) differentially reward performance and (3) allocation of work among the group.

- What measures of performance will be adopted to focus behaviour and provide rewards?

In summary, allocation and approval of roles and titles is usually the prerogative of the general manager who determines the upper management structure. The upper managers then determine the roles (position titles), responsibilities and accountabilities of lower level employees.

6.5 Determine the best arrangements for employee cooperation and supervision

Cooperation between employees and supervision of employees is necessary to achieve business goals and may take considerable time to achieve and take a form different to that which administratively might be pursued.[33]

The broad management issues and challenges concerning employee cooperation and supervision include:

- Determining the role of the Board of directors and senior management[34]
- Retaining the confidence of employees
- Balancing supervision with motivation[35]
- Allocating ad hoc tasks and responsibilities to employees
- Monitoring the performance of employees.[36]

The principal tools and techniques for employee cooperation and supervision include:

- The number of levels or layers of employees in the business hierarchy
- The relationship of the operational units to the head office.[37] Consider:
  - Centralisation versus decentralisation
  - The type of responsibility centre (cost, profit or investment)
- The type of management style or supervision necessary. Consider:
  - 'Command and control' or an autocratic or authoritarian style
  - Paternalistic

---

33 An example is The Royal Society (UK) discussed by Lomas (2002/2009) who explains why Robert Boyle was admitted but Thomas Hobbes was not. This has been echoed with regard to science by the physicist de Solla Price (1963/1986: 56) which has developed many 'invisible colleges' of tacit knowledge.

34 The Board together with senior management are often referred to as 'top management'.

35 According to Buckingham and Coffman (1999: 32) 'people leave managers, not companies'. Of course, when people leave they take their knowledge, experience and contacts with them, usually straight to the competition.

36 There are many targets which can be used to measure performance. Common targets are agreed objectives, sales budgets, cost reduction budgets, programs of work, project goals, or a combination of them.

37 Chapter 14 (Evaluating performance with financial and non-financial information) argues that these factors are crucial in selecting the performance evaluation approach.

- Democratic
- Laissez-faire or participative style.[38]
- The extent of micromanaging[39]
- Arranging employees into a reporting structure to assist supervision[40]
- Span of control is the number of subordinates (employees) that can be supervised by a supervisor
- The span of control and number of levels determine the lines of communication.

The managerial decisions and judgements concerning employee cooperation and supervision include:

- What theory does management hold of the employee's approach to work?[41]
- How do managers manage the consequences of difficult decisions?[42]
- What reliance is placed on the tacit knowledge of employees?
- How complex are the business processes and standards of service?

In summary, employee cooperation and supervision is paramount where the business is organised in business functions and employees are assigned roles and responsibilities. It is inevitable that there will be gaps and ambiguities in responsibilities as well as weaknesses in controls.

Chapter summary

The business continuously adapts to circumstances under which it operates. The legal configuration of the business is least liable to change owing to the costs of doing so. Frequent changes of structure, functions, grouping of functions and responsibilities are therefore more common. These paper changes of lines of reporting may also be accompanied by replacement of the employees performing the functions.[43] The most vexatious aspect is determining the best arrangements for employee cooperation and supervision. Despite the somewhat formulaic recommendations in the management literature it is clear that obtaining cooperation depends upon trust. Usually this is built over time, starting from discrete alliances. Further internal responses arise from external events and competitor actions.

---

38 Decision-making may be vested in the group if there is a semi-autonomous work group. In their review, Cohen and Bailey (1997) suggest that effectiveness is influenced also by task, processes and group traits.

39 This is where the manager involves themselves directly in the detail of what employees are doing instead of being concerned with resources, quality and results.

40 The number of distinct layers in a business may lead to it having a hierarchical or flattened management structure.

41 For example, Douglas McGregor's Theory X and Theory Y suggest that employees are productively engaged when they have satisfying work (McGregor 1960).

42 Examples include pursuing innovation, entry into new markets, retreat from long standing activities and retrenchment or dismissal of valued or longstanding employees.

43 The author once witnessed a senior manager receiving a bonus on Wednesday for outstanding performance who was then retrenched on the next Friday after the new General Manager preferred different managerial characteristics.

7 Use sensemaking to understand phenomena and reassess priorities

There are many unpredictable external events (e.g. the actions of competitors and customers) which are so unpredictable and puzzling that the conventional logic of reasoning makes it difficult to work out what is going on or what it all means.[1] There are also many internal incidents (e.g. systems breakdown) which demand attention. Making sense of the phenomena is the prerequisite to reassessing priorities and ensuring an effective and timely response with appropriate economy and efficiency.

Sensemaking[2] is useful where the actions of others and observed events may be difficult to understand with the existing knowledge or mental models. It goes beyond simply taking multiple perspectives (e.g. the six hats suggested by De Bono, 1986/1999). Sensemaking creates a context based upon education, training, past experiences, skills and cognitive capabilities and preferences. It assembles many vague and disparate fragments of information which themselves may be incoherent or contradictory for consideration. It may produce informal hypotheses about the situation (relevant objectives, its constraints, the influential factors and precedents) as well as inferences about future outcomes (generalisations, implications, feasibility and desirability of different courses of action and forecasts of success and failure).

Sensemaking is often assisted by hearing or knowing anecdotes, micro narratives, and stories told by employees about what they have observed or heard. In most cases, a micro narrative is sufficient and is more effective that an elaborate story constructed with a plot and characterisations similar to the features of fiction.[3] Indeed this can be counterproductive.[4] However,

---

1 Weick (1995: 34–35) observes 'In a dynamic, competitive, changing environment, illusions of accuracy are short-lived and they fall apart without warning ... because those data are flaws in unrecognisable ways they lead to non-adaptive action.'

2 Sensemaking uses concepts from psychology, neurophysiology and decision-making. It can be traced to the concepts of assimilation and accommodation in Piaget's (1966/1969: 5, 6) theory of cognitive development, Weick's (1988) interest in situations which create bewilderment and Dervin's (1992) approach to research.

3 Business (and life) is more complex, more involving and more dramatic than a linear sequence of events with a turning point, crisis or conversion. Its complexity makes to difficult to predict or recognise a turning point, crisis or conversion. Their importance is their brevity and the lesson learnt.

4 There is a strong tendency to account for many aspects of life (including business decisions, careers, life events and social relationships) that determine the ensuring years in terms of character flaws, 'make or break' moments and lack of control. This can be counterproductive because psychology informs us that we are more likely to select and reframe the facts to fit the demands of the narrative. Adopting this kind of thinking can create significant problems for employees by placing paralysing pressure on themselves or who promoting despondency and ennui if they feel they have missed a mjor opportunity. It is desirable to recognise that other opportunites may arise. For a discussion of stories and narrative in business from a social complexity perspective, see Oliver and Snowden (2005).

it is essential that a micro narrative is produced in the context of the experience[5] and it is the sensemaker who determines its salient features[6] irrespective of any stated meaning.

Topics in using sensemaking for adaptation

Sensemaking is a combination of individual human thinking and social functioning driven by cues and plausibility and is considered as five acts of attention and interpretation:

1. Scan the internal and external environment to understand their impact on the business

2. Revise financial projections based on circumstances

3. Assess competitor actions and changing customer demands

4. Protect supply arrangements

5. Control costs and cost structures.

7.1 Scan the internal and external environment to understand their impact on the business

Changes in the external environment impact the business and the business affects the environment.[7]

The broad management issues and challenges in understanding the impact of the environment on the business include:

- Understanding the political standing and campaign policies[8] of parties. Consider:

  - Economic budgeting, monetary policy, interest rates[9] and debt

  - National security including defence spending, regional strategic alliances (e.g. ANZUS treaty), overseas troop commitments and domestic security (counter terrorism)

---

5 A number of popular forms of narrative are rejected (Oliver & Snowden 2005). These include: (1) those produced in response to a demand for an appreciation of a situation; (2) those where a moderator or facilitator interprets the meaning of the narrative; and (3) those where the story tellers are instructed to frame the story around a plot using literary devices.

6 If there is any reason for the micro narrative to be captured, this may be done formally though meta tags or by simply appending comments to their story as told (or recorded).

7 The report of the United Nations commission chaired by Brundtland (1987) advocates a cautious approach to the future and economic growth sufficient for basic human needs. This approach overlooks the ingenuity of humans to overcome challenges and creates unwarranted anxiety. Schnaars (1989) discusses some of the errors made when forecasts overlook the possibility of technological change.

8 These policies may not necessarily be reported in the mainstream media let alone be scrutinised thoroughly by them. Nor may they necessarily be clearly stated by the party itself. Some policies may not be clear until the party finds itself with political influence or seeks to claim a political mandate.

9 The less the public sector places demands on the building and construction industries, the less likely there is to be pressure on interest rates, wages demands notwithstanding. 1980 Cabinet submission by Treasurer John Howard quoted by Stone (2011).

- International (foreign) policy (including United Nations Security Council veto powers and economic sanctions and the role and power of other international organisations (e.g. International Monetary Fund, World Bank and World Trade Organisation)
- Likelihood that there may be a green whiskers outcome[10]
- Foreign relations (e.g. with major trading partners including Japan)
- Taxation (including level of income tax thresholds, applicability of fringe benefits tax, application of carbon and resource taxes)
- Export controls or prohibitions (e.g. coal, livestock, woodchips from native forests, uranium)
- Population levels by age group, skill and immigration, migration eligibility and refugee processing arrangements
- Education funding, access and payment
- Communications including broadband, wireless and satellite
- Infrastructure funding and contract administration
- Urban planning, home affordability, population density, transport congestion and suburban amenity.

- Rapid changes in the local or international economy that may affect customer purchasing power or attractiveness of the product
- Changes introduced by the government that may change the cost structure of the product or service
- Perceived threats or actual incident in the community may reduce the attractiveness of the product
- Accept there are different investment perspectives[11]
- Opportunities to acquire a competitor business or the competitor's product
- Opportunities to divest a business or a product at a favourable price.

The principal tools and techniques to understand the impact of the environment on the business include:

- Using the available economic statistics[12]

---

10 A 'green whiskers' project may result from (1) poor coordination among diferent government policy making bodies; (2) ignorance through failing to perceive the inconsistencies and their costs; (3) attempting to both appease stakeholders with different objectives (e.g. promoting development and preventing any disruption or loss to those who live in the vicinity of the development). In testimony for the Subcommittee on Urban Growth of the Committee on Banking and Currency, U.S. House of Representatives, 7 October 1970, Forrester (1971–1972: 5) stated that 'in many instances it emerges that the known policies [often of the business itself] describe a system which actually causes the troubles.

11 Investment perspectives vary. For example, the developer, the owner-occupier and the investor view property investments quite differently. Livermore, (1940) is an illuminating example of an investor.

12 The difficulty with obtaining up-to-date information on financial and non-financial business information including economic and financial measures, competitive intelligence and specific industries is the long publishing process and the

- Reading reputable business newspapers, magazines and journals
- Analyses of the market[13]
- Five forces analysis of the industry structure[14]
- Using a theory of the business[15]
- Using Affinity Diagramming to synthesize large amounts of data
- Attending industry and professional conferences and seminars
- The use of consultants to provide specialist advice.

The managerial decisions and judgements concerning the impact of the environment on the business include:

- What will ensure fore warnings about changes in the external environment?
- What action needs to be taken to represent concerns and interests to government and regulatory authorities?
- What options exist for responding to changes in the external environment that assure the viability of the business?

In summary, the resulting managerial decisions will influence both short term performance and long-term strategy.

7.2 Revise financial projections based on circumstances

Financial projections which reflect cash flows, profitability and balance sheet are important for all businesses because they serve as a basis for evaluating whether the business is succeeding in attaining its objectives. These projections are not regarded as rigid. Rather they are a goal – their attainment or not are considered in the light of what transpires in the economy and the industry.

---

frequency with which important new sources appear. Some attempts to keep pace cease after a few editions (e.g. Daniels 1976/1993). For this reason the recommended approach is to consider the economic indicators. For details of useful economic indicators see the titles by Carnes and Slifer (1991), Frumkin (1955/2005), Tainer (1993/2006) or Yamarone (2004/2007). Useful economic indicators include GNP, employment/unemployment, retail sales, housing starts/building permits, consumer price index, business inventories and capital investment. Industry associations can usually be located by using an internet search engine. A specialised subscription service can be used to find articles describing competitor intelligence.

13 As noted in Topic 2.1 the most common method of macro or institutional analysis uses PESTEL.

14 As noted in Topic 2.1 the most common method of industry analysis uses five forces (Porter 1980). The effect of the five forces varies depending upon the strength of the business, the characteristics of the sector and the type of products or services provided.

15 In the theory of the business, Drucker (1994) writes 'The root cause of nearly every [business failure] is not that things are being done poorly. It is not even that the wrong things are being done. Indeed, in most cases, the right things are being done – but fruitlessly. What accounts for this apparent paradox? The assumptions on which the organisation has been built and is being run no longer fit reality.'

The broad management issues and challenges that arise in revising financial projections include:

- The internal capacity to achieve projected levels of sales
- The extent to which the business is dependent on external factors including suppliers.

The principal tools and techniques for making and revising financial projections include:

- Manual and automated systems. Consider:
  - Pencil and paper analytical worksheets
  - General productivity software applications (electronic spreadsheets)
  - Specialist software applications (e.g. Hyperion)
  - Modules from Enterprise Resource Planning (ERP) software suites (e.g.SAP, Oracle Financials).
- General purpose reports.[16] Consider:
  - Cash flow statements[17]
  - Profit and loss report[18]
  - The balance sheet.[19]

The managerial decisions and judgements involved in considering financial projections include:

- What is the extent to which the financial projections can be relied upon?[20]
- What is the extent to which financial projections are comprehensive?
- Will high, stable returns be achieved?
- How adequate are systems[21] and controls in providing accurate information?
- What special purpose reports are available to resolve management doubts or uncertainties?

In summary, using the set of financial projections to ensure adequate financing of the business is a key responsibility of senior management. In most cases a mix of financing is used.

---

16 These three general purpose reports are prepared at periods appropriate to the business (daily, weekly, monthly, quarterly, six monthly and annually) and use a format appropriate to the business. In addition, an alternate format will allow comparison with summary budgets again with content appropriate to the business. The capacity to prepare such documents has increased dramatically with advances in technology.

17 These should be a part of the financial reporting routine. The frequency will depend upon the severity of the situation or the speed at which action needs to be taken. Many businesses prepare cash flows on a daily basis.

18 This measures the success of the business as the outcome of meeting sales revenue targets and controlling expenses.

19 This provides insights into the capital structure of the business.

20 Spreadsheets typically contain errors and many are serious (Panko 1998/2008).

21 System is not synonymous with information technology. A system may be entirely manual or paper-based.

7.3 Assess competitor actions and changing customer demands

Awareness of competitor actions particularly in price changes and increased market share is the first step in determining a response. In many countries both the initial action by a competitor as well as any response by other businesses may be subject to restrictive trade practices legislation.[22] Awareness of competitor actions and changing customer demands are central to the survival of the business

The broad management issues and challenges concerning competitor actions and changing customer demands include:

- Having a sufficiently broad view of the market[23]
- Having a sufficient information about the business[24]
- Setting the price at a sufficient level to cover costs and fund future development of new products
- Considering whether products should continue to be stocked or manufactured
- Ensuring that products coming to the end of their product life cycle[25] will be replaced by new products which are equally attractive to customers
- Setting the price to be competitive with alternate products that will be considered by customers
- Developing a suitable advertising and promotion plan to ensure that potential customers are aware of a new product or service
- Ensuring that claims about a product or service do not contravene consumer legislation
- Determining whether regulatory authorities will take action for predatory pricing or unfair competition.

The principal tools and techniques for assessing competitor actions and changing customer demands include:

- Cost-Volume-Profit (CVP) analysis
- Pricing analysis[26]

---

22 These restrictions attempt to prevent collusion and enforce high penalties once it is admitted or proven.

23 This is a matter of strategy since an error in the scope of the market may have catastrophic consequences in the short and medium terms (Levitt 1960).

24 The extent to which a business relies on information instead of observation determines competitive advantage (Porter & Miller 1985).

25 The product and its market can be considered using Ansoff's box (Ansoff 1965) and the product life cycle (Wright 1974).

26 There has been limited disclosure by governments of their pricing policies and pricing adjustment policies. Walker (2009a: 193) notes that governments often use agencies to review or recommend prices. There are many increases which either precede or are higher than official consumer price index price rises.

- Target costing[27]
- Investment analysis using discounted cash flows[28]
- Activity Based Costing (ABC)
- Strategic cost management[29]
- Customer and Supplier Profitability assessment
- Investment in new equipment or systems to change the cost structure of processes.

The managerial decisions and judgements concerning assessing competitor actions and changing customer demands include:

- What will be the cost of acquiring new customers?
- What are the benefits of retaining unprofitable customers?[30]
- What product(s) or service(s) will be discontinued?
- Can a customer relationship be re-engineered to make it more profitable?
- Can the pricing structure be made more favourable?[31]
- What product(s) or service(s) will be pushed over other products or services?[32]
- Will competitors be acquired (as a takeover or as a merger)?
- What advertising and product promotion campaigns will be authorised?
- What will be the level of discounting (in the short or medium term)?
- Will distributors, retailers and buyers be offered rebates?

In summary, responding to competitor actions must not only be considered from the internal perspective but also from the perspective of external regulators domestically and overseas.

---

27 This approach shifts cost management so it starts before the product is produced (Hiromoto 1988). For this reason it is usually linked with value engineering (Cooper & Slagmulder 1997).

28 The calculation of Net Present Value (NPV) and Internal Rate of Return (IRR) are preferable to simple payback calculations of the number of years taken for a project to repay its investment. Criticisms of DCF and NPV often are based on point estimates rather than ranges. However, sensitivity analyses can provide best, average and worst estimates where assumptions and factors are subjective or cannot be reliably or consistently measured.

29 The dangers of ABC lie in the areas of overhead costs and a product line that is differentiated by complexity. The true margins of different products are masked and cross-subsidisation of unprofitable products may easily occur (Shank & Govindarajan 1993).

30 The non-financial benefits from some customers may be their value as a reference site or the halo effect that they provide. This may assist the entry into new markets or retention of other customers.

31 The aim may be to change customer behaviour or recapture some of the costs incurred in serving the customer at the level of attention they demand.

32 This may also take the form of product groups (or service groups) being 'pushed' over other product groups (or service groups).

7.4 Protect supply arrangements

It is important to ensure continuity of supply as failure creates opportunities for competitors to poach customers.

The broad management issues and challenges that arise from protecting supply arrangements include:

- The potential for stock-outs of regularly stocked items
- Inability to place back orders for products desired by customers
- Late delivery of inventory
- Delivery of inventory at times that are inconvenient to the business
- Damage to or contamination of perishable items
- Viability of transfer pricing arrangements.[33]

The principal tools and techniques for protecting supply arrangements include:

- Making supply contracts with the supplier which nominate the dates and times for deliveries
- Developing closer alliances with the supplier
- Nominating contractual penalties for late or non-supply
- Providing on-site facilities for the supplier
- Placing a person at the supplier to oversee deliveries
- Creating supply relationships with a second supplier
- Bringing the component or raw material in-house to reduce dependence on suppliers.

The managerial decisions and judgements for protecting supply arrangements include:

- Are the techniques of lean manufacturing suitable for adoption?
- Is the supplier/distributor agreeable to exclusive arrangements?
- Can the frequency and volume of procurement and sales be changed?
- Can direct customer service responsibilities be imposed on the supplier?
- Can incentives be provided?
- Should alliances be formed with other businesses?

---

33 Where there are international related party dealings many issues such as the use and acceptance of profit methods, the standards of comparability and the effect of losses arise. Comparability may use a Transactional Net Margin Method or a Comparable Uncontrolled Price (subject to case law). Other commercial issues may also be relevant including competition, management and employee performance.

- Should the product cease to be stocked?[34]
- Can the product or service be delivered or bundled in a different manner?

In summary, there are many options available for sourcing and delivery. Responding to challenges in costs and supply arrangements often requires quick action maintain an acceptable cost structure and to secure supply.

7.5 Control costs and cost structures

It is important to control costs as fluctuations in pricing can create opportunities for competitors to poach customers. Many businesses take a short-term view of costs. That is, when profits or margins are reduced, either employee working hours are reduced or the employe head count is reduced. Understanding costs begins by combining cost behaviour with cost assignment[35] to understand how costs change as production or sales vary. Figure 8 below shows the combination results in six cost classifications.

		Cost Assignment	
		Direct (Traceable)	Indirect (Assigned)
Cost Behaviour Pattern	Fixed	Cost Object: Direct & Fixed Within the Relevant Range	Cost Object: Indirect & Fixed Within the Relevant Range
	Fixed Step and/or Mixed	Cost Object: Direct with partly Fixed and partly Variable	Cost Object: Indirect with partly Fixed and partly Variable
	Variable	Cost Object: Direct & Variable	Cost Object: Indirect & Variable

Figure 8. Combination cost behaviour and cost assignment results in six classifications for costs.

---

34 Since stocks and flows have different units they cannot be meaningfully compared, equated, added, or subtracted. However, it is valid to take ratios of stocks and flows, or multiply or divide them.

35 The higher the point of view in the business the more costs can be considered direct so the cost asignment is somewhat relative. For this reason there is often an emphasis on whether the cost is controllable or noncontrollable.

The broad management issues and challenges that arise from control over costs and cost structures[36] include:

- An increase in the wholesale or retail selling price may change the selling price relative to competitor products or services. Consider:
  - Increases which affect the cost or availability of raw materials[37]
  - Increases in the cost of labour.[38]
- An increase in the wholesale or retail selling price may reduce the profit margin.

The principal tools and techniques for control over costs[39] and cost structures include:

- Using the cost combination[40]
- Economies of scale
- Break-even analysis[41]
- Ensuring only relevant costs are considered
- Variance analysis[42]
- Using 'Just-in-Time (JIT)' supply techniques
- Use of lean production methods[43]
- Analysis of industry cost levels and competitor costs
- Recruit former employees of competitors
- Recruit qualified graduates with recent specialisations in the target business areas
- Use data from published studies to evaluate productivity and profitability.

The managerial decisions and judgements for control over costs and cost structures include:

- Can the frequency and volume of procurement and sales be changed?
- Can additional customer service be provided?

---

36 Some of these costs may be differential or Ricardian rents which require consideration of the wider productive factors.

37 This may make the price of the product or service unfavourable compared to products or services offered by competitors.

38 This may also make substitute products more attractive.

39 Costs are often conveniently reported as costs per unit or unit costs (or average costs) but this overlooks the influence of the relevant range of fixed costs.

40 Factors affecting the assignment of costs include (1) the materiality of the particular cost; (2) whether details of the cost can be readily collected; and (3) whether acticivites have been designed with reference to an exclusive cost object such as a specific job or a particular customer.

41 A marginal costing technique identifies the relationship between total costs, total revenues and profits to sales volume.

42 Variances are unfavourable if the results are worse than planned as this decreases operating income. A favourable variance is better performance than planned. Standard costing should ideally minimise variances, allow rapid investigation of variances and attribution for the variance to the appropriate responsibility centre (Bromwich 1980).

43 Toyota was one of the pioneers of lean manufacturing (Womack, Jones & Roos 2007).

- Can incentives be provided?
- Are variances being properly investigated?
- Should alliances be formed with other businesses?
- Can internal costs be reduced through streamlining (efficiencies) or changing the value of the item (effectiveness)?
- Should the product cease to be produced or stocked?

In summary, the many methods used to calculate costs mean that suppliers will be able to take advantage of opportunities to improve their margins. Responding to challenges in costs often requires quick action maintain an acceptable cost structure.

Chapter summary

The internal responses to external events and competitor actions may be slow or quick. effective or ineffective. There must be constant scanning for changes in the external environment and skilful interpretation to understand their impact on the business. Stories or narratives are an important part of scanning and sensemaking.[44] This usually leads to making new financial projections based on current circumstances. Competitor actions in pricing and expanding market share can be countered by a variety of responses tailored to the sales territory, product and customer base. Similarly, arrangements to protect supply are essential and where these are inadequate additional arrangements can be enacted. Finally, control over costs is a frequent resort for unexpected or short term shortfalls in finances. Further adaptive responses arise through the power of policies, controls and reviews in operations.

---

44 In recent years there has been the rediscovery of storytelling and the use of anecdotes to share knowledge. When used without directions as to topic, timing and message conveyed these are effective means of conveying knowledge. (Oliver and Snowden 2005).

8 Use policies, controls and reviews to bring flexibility to operations

Policies, controls and reviews all serve to bring flexibility to operations by anticipating common and exceptional situations. They should assist employees in their work. The increased regulation of business leads to a high reliance on business policies, controls and reviews. Flexibility can also be assisted by the use of technology. The efficiency and effectiveness of policies, controls and reviews has a substantial effect on operations.

Relationship between administration and operations

The relationship between administration and operations usually takes one of two forms. It is common for administration to be an afterthought to functions and activities. This form of administrative support then grows by perceived need and the initiative of the employees' performing the functions. If they are busy (e.g. with customer activities) then administration is likely to be fragmented. Administration may also be regarded as an overhead. In this case it is allocated to a separate employee who has sole responsibility for it and they may be regarded as secondary to operations. The general criterion for administration is efficiency. That is, the least amount of administration and the simpler the better.

Topics in using policies, controls and reviews for adaptation

Flexibility is a hallmark of a successful business. Using policies can improve efficiency and simplify customer interactions. Controls and reviews can assess the effectiveness of policies and practices in the business with five avenues of activity:

1. Develop corporate policies, standard operating procedures and ensure adherence
2. Enable reliable controls that correspond to business goals and risks
3. Monitor employee performance and development
4. Minimise administration and overhead
5. Periodically review the economy, efficiency and effectiveness of systems and processes.

8.1 Develop corporate policies, standard operating procedures and ensure adherence

Corporate policies and standard operating procedures may range over a wide variety of business phenomena. They allow the business to adapt to changing circumstances.[1] The volume of corporate policies and the ways in which they are documented and communicated are influenced by the size of the business and the day-to-day involvement of senior managers.

The broad management issues and challenges associated with corporate policies and standard operating procedures include:

- The extent to which policies and procedures can be easily consulted[2]
- The ease with which policies and procedures can be read and understood
- The difficulty in keeping policies and procedures up-to-date
- The difficulty in ensuring coverage of key areas[3]
- The overhead in having to maintain policies and procedures in different languages where there is a global or international presence
- The potential embarrassment in having the kind of policy and procedures failures found in politics.[4]

The principal tools and techniques to develop and ensure adherence to corporate policies and standard operating procedures include:

- Empowering employees through explanation of policies and procedures
- Technologies to keep policies and procedures up-to-date and make them available to employees
- Communication mechanisms which ensure that employees are aware a policy and procedure exists on some aspect of business
- Internal controls and (internal and external) audit functions which provide a measure of independent assessment on how effectively policies and procedures are being observed

---

1 Corporate policies are a mechanism that facilitates the business adapting to unpredictable events (Toffler 1982).

2 Some organisations prefer to have little written on the grounds that costly mistakes in judgement may be easily made; instead they encourage consultation with colleagues, supervisors and managers.

3 Often it is not recognised that policies are essential for consistency. Examples of consistency in customer-related policies include: return of products or refunds for services billed; warranty periods and arrangements; and acceptance of a special order from a customer. The policies themselves are informed by the culture of the business in they way in which they are formulated and interpreted.

4 Typical government reactions to policy failure include praising the effort of people involved in dealing with the consequences of the policy failure, announcing an inquiry, expressing outrage at the occurrence of the event, blaming the timing as unfortunate, threatening legal action and transferring blame to the architects or instigators.

- The business culture which suggests whether the policies and procedures need to be followed and the consequences of ignoring them
- The events in the environment and in the business which prompt additional or revised policies and procedures.

The managerial decisions and judgements that arise from development of and adherence to corporate policies and standard operating procedures include:

- Does a global or international presence make it difficult to have uniform policies and procedures?
- Do policies allow latitude for first offences but not repeat offences?
- What will result where there is a policy or procedure vacuum and a situation which cannot be foreseen occurs?

In summary, the influence of corporate policies and standard operating procedures is such that they act as a form of coordination and training when used successfully.

8.2 Enable reliable controls that correspond to business goals and risks

Ensuring there are reliable controls operating throughout the business is an essential accompaniment to proper financial management. Such controls should correspond to business goals, risk and uncertainty.[5]

The broad management issues and challenges concerning reliable controls include:

- Preparing and keeping up-to-date supporting documentation.[6] Consider:
  - Organisation charts and position duty statements
  - Making available consolidated manual of finance and accounting policies:
    - Credit control
    - Asset recognition
    - Purchases
    - Payment process[7]
    - Sales
    - Inventory.

5 Following Knight (1957/2006) a distinction is made between risk (randomness with knowable probabilities) and uncertainty (randomness with unknowable probabilities).

6 Training will be an essential accompaniment to the issue of manuals.

7 The Sarbanes-Oxley Act (United States) specifies a number of payment controls including cheques and the use of purchasing cards (Schaeffer 2006).

- – Share registry, dividend distribution and shareholder report procedures
- – Systems documentation.
- Implementing general financial controls. Consider:
  - – Preparation and use a of a reliable chart of accounts
  - – Maintenance of an up-to-date asset register
  - – Authorisation of journal entries accompanied by supporting vouchers completed according to the accounting manual.
- Implementing specific controls over cash and cash equivalents. Consider:
  - – Segregation of duties[8]
  - – Security of cash and cheques received leading to same day banking
  - – Ensuring daily balancing of cash register takings and the float
  - – Ensuring daily balancing of takings with sales receipts
  - – Sweeping funds from separate bank accounts into a central account[9]
  - – Placing surplus funds on the overnight money market to earn interest
  - – Security over blank cheque printing and blank cheque storage
  - – Restrictions over authorisations provided to the bank including cheque signatories.[10]
- Implementing specific controls over sales. Consider:
  - – Review before acceptance of customer orders for non-stock inventory
  - – Approval of any variations to standard terms including discounts before a sale is concluded
  - – Credit check of customer before allowing despatch of product.
- Implementing specific controls over inventory. Consider:
  - – Ensuring products are removed from inventory supported by a sales document
  - – Addressing lead-time planning and supply chain issues to overcome late supply
  - – Adopting on-time delivery where Just-in-Time production is used
  - – Identifying fast and slow moving inventory[11]
  - – Identifying inventory locations[12]
  - – Reducing the inventory holdings to avoid obsolescence or damage

---

8 A traditional segregation is custody of an asset, record keeping for the asset and authorisation for its use. This may be difficult in small businesses where one person performs many business functions.

9 Apart from minimising the overdraft this acts as a check on the level of funds and usage of the subordinate accounts.

10 For example, requiring that all cheques require two signatories and that there must be an accompanying authorisation document (McMillan 2006).

11 It is usual to classify the inventory line items into three categories 'A', 'B' and 'C'. The ABC analysis is used to identify three separate management and control approaches for inventory line items.

12 This is essential where the same line item is kept in more than one place or where customers have access to the inventory and may move it to an incorrect location.

- – Periodic count of physical inventory with comparison to book records
- – Authorising and returning to inventory returned products.
- Implementing specific controls over debtors. Consider:
  - – Providing statements of indebtedness
  - – Performing regular bank reconciliations and investigating discrepancies
  - – Ensuring adjustments to the customer account are authorised
  - – Ensuring write-offs are authorised
  - – Reviewing the aged debtor listing each period.
- Implementing specific controls over purchases. Consider:
  - – Storage of items in assigned locations
  - – Product from the supplier is checked upon arrival
  - – Allocation to a job is tracked
  - – Reconciliation of supplier invoices to product receipts.
- Implementing specific controls over employees. Consider:
  - – Making an assessment of the main areas of employee fraud or theft
  - – Verification of employee background before offering employment
  - – Authorisation of loadings, overtime and any additional bonuses
  - – Payment on proof of attendance or work performed
  - – The ways in which employee, supervisor and manager misbehaviour can be prevented
  - – The ways in which employee, supervisor and manager misbehaviour can be detected.

The principal tools and techniques for reliable controls include:

- The use of evaluation templates such as the Control Matrix[13]
- Ensuring that the benefits from establishing and retaining controls exceed their costs of operation
- Producing aged debtor reports which show indebtedness in relation to customer invoices and days outstanding
- Setting collection targets for collection of outstanding customer debts
- Using specialist agencies to collect customer debts
- The investigation of breakdowns in controls and the evaluation of the need for modification or supplementation of existing controls

---

13 The Control Matrix lists the control goals of the business processes horizontally and the various control plans vertically.

- The responsibility on managers to review their systems and make continuous improvement[14]

- Periodic internal audits against a checklist to detect weaknesses or breaches and provide an independent opinion of the operations

- External audits to provide an outside opinion of the operations

- Making a specific term of reference to include controls in all systems projects[15]

- The use of procedures to deal with late payments.[16]

The managerial decisions and judgements concerning reliability of controls include:

- Are there suitable controls over receipt of payments such as cash and cheques?

- Are there suitable controls over valuable[17] inventory and assets?

- Are there suitable controls over purchasing?[18]

- Are there suitable controls over the dollar amount of products or services that a customer is able to charge to their account?

- Do adequate controls exist over the physical assets of the business that ensure that business resources are used for its advantage and not for employee personal gain?

- Do adequate controls exist over record keeping ensure that there is an authentic record of transactions?

- Is there sufficient segregation of duties ensure that it is difficult to alter records or if there is an alteration then it can be readily detected?

- Is there adequate overlap between different controls covering the same activities to increase the chance of detection of unusual or ingenious frauds?

- What is the likelihood that fraud or theft can be promptly detected?

- What are the likely levels of losses arising from fraud or theft?

- What controls exist to specify and ensure the quality of the products to be supplied?

- Do the controls operate in a timely manner to allow appropriate remedial action to be initiated to minimise losses?

In summary, the creation of controls (in conjunction with internal and external audit) should ideally prevent fraud and theft. Where this is not possible they should enable easy and

---

14 As systems evolve in response to minor changes in operations or are adapted by employees new to a position the reliability of the control may be diminished. Weaknesses may emerge which can be exploited by the employee herself or himself, or by an observant peer.

15 The project may be either: (a) the redevelopment, replacement, redesign or modification of an existing system, or (b) the introduction of a new system.

16 Common procedures include: issuing monthly statements showing aged balances of indebtedness, stopping purchases on credit, making contact with the customer and initiating legal action for recovery of the debt.

17 High value portable inventory (for example, gold watches) may be kept in a locked security room.

18 For example, a disgruntled but still employed employee may be able order (without the knowledge of their supervisor) a semi-useless product from a supplier as revenge for being given notice.

quick detection to prevent incurring high losses of monetary value or business reputation and brand image. Controls should be selectively implemented and be distinguished from internal performance systems and processes.

8.3 Monitor employee performance and development

Monitoring employee performance depends upon agreement over both targets and the course of action where there are disruptions to their achievement. In most cases performance is reviewed periodically. The review may also include agreed development targets and the provision of enabling resources.

The broad management issues and challenges that arise from monitoring and analysing employee performance and development include:

- Ensuring employee performance is reviewed. Consider:
  - The scope of the performance review (e.g. full-time employees, part-time employees, casual employees, contractors)
  - The frequency of the review (e.g. monthly, annually)
  - Allowing sufficient time to monitor internal performance
  - Actions of the competitor may requiring matching or counter-measures
  - Management may perceive gaps in reporting and need to commission ad-hoc or new routine reports to provide them with the required data.
- Assessing the results from a review. Consider:
  - Understanding the importance of targets and feedback on systems and processes[19]
  - Understanding the dysfunctional effects of information on behaviour[20]
  - Differentiating between routine and exceptions processes and systems
  - Detecting trends which are favourable and unfavourable
  - Performance in particular products or sales territories may be poor
  - Reports may show poor performance and management must enquire why whether action has been taken to identify the cause and commence remedial action.

---

19 The principles of cybernetic or control systems have been thoroughly discussed by Weiner (1948), Ashby (1956), Boulding (1956) and Beer (1959).

20 Dysfunctional behaviour is often the unintended consequence of setting performance targets and measures (Ridgway 1956) that use single (Blau 1955), multiple or composite criteria. The use of the ratchet principle (Roethlisberger & Dickson 1939; Berliner, 1957), where higher performance targets (or quotas) are introduced and become the new standard, is a means of continually raising output. However, it can result in tacit agreement among employees to actively resist performing to the higher standard needed to reach higher performance targets.

The principal tools and techniques for monitoring and analysing employee performance and development include:

- Comparing (financial) budgets with actual performance
- Comparing non-financial goals and targets with actual performance
- Comparing actual performance with reported industry benchmarks
- Commissioning spot checks and reviews
- Using internal controls to identify problem areas
- Using variances to identify potential difficulties (subject to investigation and verification).

The managerial decisions and judgements in monitoring and analysing employee performance and development include:

- Should there be an inspection of work to ensure it conforms to quality standards?[21]
- Do the implementation and control of strategies support employee creativity and initiative?[22]
- Is an extensive review warranted?
- What corrective action needs to be taken in the short term?
- Does the current strategy needs reconsidering?
- Are the current measurement techniques sufficiently informative?
- Are the processes and systems adequate?

In summary, monitoring employee performance is fraught with difficulties and ambiguities. It is desirable to use a mix of measures when reaching conclusions about poor performance and selecting the course of action proposed for rectification. It is also important to provide employees with development opportunities so they sharpen existing skills and acquire new capabilities as the world of business is not static.

8.4 Minimise administration and overhead

Administration and overhead typically arises for reasons of compliance owing to external imposition.[23] There is an inherent tendency for administration to grow without being able to

---

21 This has been partly replaced by quality assurance with the task being performed according to pre-defined processes and standards.

22 There is often a tension between the vision of the business and the management controls utilised. One approach is to use traditional controls as well as customer/market driven controls and employee empowerment controls. Four levers of control (beliefs, boundary systems, diagnostic and interactive controls systems) are proposed by Simons (1995).

23 Adam Smith (1759/2007) refers to over-regulation through the efforts of the 'Man of Zeal' who 'is apt to be very wise in his own conceit and is often enamoured with the supposed beauty of his own ideal plan of government that he cannot suffer the smallest deviation from any part of it.'

demonstrate any intrinsic benefits to the business[24] and this can be facilitated by uncritical management endorsement. Administrative growth occurs usually because an administrator's salary, perquisites of office, public reputation and power tend to be related to the size of the budget they control.[25]

The broad management issues and challenges that arise from minimising administration and overhead include:

- Ensuring employee job descriptions focus on key goals not the minutiae
- Preventing the proliferation of desirable or superficial requirements when managers have budget funding, spare employee time, or unchecked power
- Allowing sufficient time to formulate policies that integrate administration
- Allowing sufficient time to formulate design systems that integrate administration
- Avoiding using breakdowns in systems or controls to justify the imposition of additional policies which require additional systems or controls.

The principal tools and techniques for minimising administration and overhead include:

- Zero budgeting
- Allocating selected tasks outside the business (e.g. to customers and suppliers)
- Using forms to capture all essential data[26]
- Using a single integrated database to facilitate the re-use of data
- Brevity and clarity in written documents[27]
- Careful design of systems to avoid partial, duplication and shadow systems.

The managerial decisions and judgements to minimise administration and overhead include:

- Is information being sought which is not used?
- Is the cost of searching, collecting and storing information understood?[28]

---

24 Many examples of the unchecked growth of administration were provided in the 1950's and 1970's. See for example Townsend (1970/2007) writing about his experiences at Avis. Parkinson's Law is that work expands to fill the time available (Parkinson 1958). A humorous example was provided in 'The Compassionate Society' (Episode 1 series 2) of the 'Yes Minister' television series (Jay & Lynn 1981) which featured St Edwards Hospital which had been open for 15 months with over 500 administrators, no patients and no medical staff.

25 In an early discussion of administrator's preoccupation with their total budget (Niskansen 1968) concluded that 'In the demand-constrained output region, a bureau's only concern about costs is to assure that they exhaust the obtainable budget.' The solutions offered included: (a) introducing competition; (b) changing incentives of managers; and (c) contracting provision to profit seeking businesses. A more comprehensive examination (Niskansen 1970) needs revision as it was written prior to the internet.

26 Forms design is basic organisation and methods. However the skills of logical sequencing and providing sufficient space on the layout (e.g. Longman 1967: 170) appear to have been displaced by data normalisation techniques (Date 1975/1999).

27 There are many style guides for written expression. For British English there is Gowers (1948/1986), written originally for officials. For American English, there is Strunk and White (1918/1999), written originally for college students.

28 Since the internet allows collection of information at minimal cost, there is a motivation to always ask for more without considering the cost imposed on the information provider. This is known as a negative externality which is not

- What performance measures will balance operations and administration?[29]
- Is there empire building and favouritism[30] and if so, how can it be prevented?
- How can employee attitudes which enshrine unwieldy policies and processes be changed?
- Is this an expenditure proposal which satisfies desirable or superficial requirements when essential requirements remain unfulfilled?
- Are employee suggestions that reduce the administrative load valued?[31]
- Are managers responsible for ensuring they champion lean operations?[32]

Minimising administration and overhead requires both a vigilant senior management and diligent managers. In a decentralised business, the availability of budget/funding, spare employee time allows the growth of administration even when there are performance incentives.

8.5 Periodically review the economy, efficiency and effectiveness of systems and processes

Reviewing the economy, efficiency and effectiveness of systems and processes provides both assurance of performance and identifies capabilities for improvement.[33]

The broad management issues and challenges that arise from reviewing the economy, efficiency and effectiveness of systems and processes include:

- Establish what information is available and at what cost[34]

---

efficiently controlled by prices. Pigou (1920) argued that negative externalities should be offset by a tax, while positive externalities should be offset by a subsidy. This analysis remains relevant despite Coase (1960) showing that taxes and subsidies are not necessary if the parties in the transaction can bargain over it.

29 Targets may exist in the form of management by objectives, key performance indicators or the balanced scorecard (Kaplan & Norton 2004).

30 The tendency for administrators to increase is partly due to their competence in making a business case and partly due to their ability to point out operational deficiencies.

31 Suggestions typically relate to customers, product or service quality as well as cooperating with other employees or businesses.

32 There is considerable scope for transforming a business using lean thinking to eliminate waste along entire value streams, instead of at isolated points to create processes that need less human effort, less space, less capital and less time to make products or deliver services (Womack & Jones 2003). This may lead to the replacement of some annual activities with ones which occur every second or third year.

33 When a business has an opportunity to undertake a comprehensive review it is often surprised by the number of matters to which attention must be simultaneously given. In some cases, attention is given to these matters when there is a review of operations or viability. For many businesses attention is imposed by external and internal deadlines. For example, end of month deadlines, tax (e.g. GST, Income, Capital Gains) reporting deadlines, contract/tender deadlines, recruitment interview schedules and accounting cutoff dates. Reminders often are provided through membership of professional societies (e.g. accounting bodies) or business groups (e.g. chambers of commerce).

34 The tendency to conduct reviews without regard to previous investigations and findings may doom the review from the start. It may create an expectation that nothing useful will follow and reduce the engagement by participants, particularly if the review is structured to gather information, analyse it and release it as a final report. This is the typical

- Establishing and agreeing the cost of common or support services to each business function or clientele[35]

- Reasons for increased costs particularly if they are not experienced by competitors

- Determining the opportunities to achieve a presence in new markets, increased market penetration, or protect existing markets

- For systems, determining the scope of the system and interfaces to other systems[36]

- The extent to which the results of these reviews will consider internal controls and internal audit plans

- The extent to which the results of these reviews will consider external audit findings

- The need to accept inefficiencies to foster growth, change or preparedness to overcome unforeseen difficulties[37]

- Whether the focus of the review should be the improvement of existing processes or the better integration of systems via their interfaces to better use existing data

- The kind of review necessary (e.g. diagnosis[38], feasibility, implementation)

- Whether any findings will require in-depth investigation or act as a gateway to allow the next stage to proceed.

The principal tools and techniques for reviewing the economy, efficiency and effectiveness of systems and processes include:

- Use of efficiency-based investigative methods[39]

- Analyses that use only tangible financial measures

- Analyses that take into account intangible measures

- Investigating production or administrative constraints[40]

---

government inquiry mode. Initially Boisot (1987: 56) uses the extent of codification and diffusion as lenses to explore the implications. Later Boisot (1995) added abstraction/concreteness as a third dimension.

35 The capacity of a government to continue to deliver services depends upon funding from taxes and appropriation levels in the budget. The accurate and timely projection of needs and changes in demographics depend upon the availability of suitable information, the suitability of the infrastructure and the recognition of the need by managers in the relevant public authorities or agencies.

36 Forrester (1958: 40) emphasises the system does not lie in the paperwork or the procedures but in the 'interrelationships between all the company operations'. This view results in investigating the characteristics of the system. Mistaken views investigate the characteristics of individual parts.

37 The traditional cost reduction approach of increasing efficiency assumes that both cost and time can be simultaneously controlled. Where they are both dependent variables this is working with two mutually exclusive goals (DeMarco 2001: 43–44). DeMarco (2001: 18–19) asserts there is also a 15% penalty when switching between tasks and argues for the worth of middle management 3–6, 80–85).

38 The Kepner-Tregoe method for isolating problems involves a situation appraisal, determination of the root cause of a problem, identifying and weighting options and further investigation of the best alternative. A problem is a deviation with an unknown cause that requires action (Kepner & Tregoe 1965).

39 These include studies of work including time taken for tasks (e.g. Taylor, 1911), the availability of items for the next stage of the process (Ohno 1988) and the analysis of production operations (e.g. Goldratt 1999).

40 The theory of constraints (Goldratt 1999) points to the futility of thinking a problem has been solved when there are multiple constraints some of which are not revealed until others have been removed. A fictional account of improving manufacturing operations and overall profitability is provided by Goldratt and Cox (1984/2004).

- Using benchmarks that are either publicly available or which are based on published data
- Agreeing Service Level Agreements (SLAs)
- Agreeing Service Delivery Outcomes (SDOs)
- Using sensitivity analyses[41]
- Creating ratios and rates from internal historical data to determine whether there has been relative improvement or deterioration in performance[42]
- Comparing levels of performance against standards.[43]

In some cases, risk assessments and internal control systems may be provide additional sources of data.

The managerial decisions and judgements in reviewing the economy, efficiency and effectiveness of systems and processes include:

- Is this a matter to be decided 'solely on the figures'?[44]
- Is the evidence sufficiently clear to enable decisive action to be taken?
- Are the likely outcomes from the change specified in detail in the report?
- Is it desirable to adopt a phased approach?
- Has there been consultation with all relevant stakeholders?
- Are the recommended new arrangements sustainable?

In summary, reviewing the economy, efficiency and effectiveness of systems and processes is consumes both time and effort. It is necessary to be meticulous in selecting the tools and technique and rigorous in critically evaluating the findings and recommendations.[45]

---

41 The use of sensitivity analyses may give a false sense of reliability (Taleb 2007) owing to the power law, or more definitively, may confuse randomness with known probability with randomness with unknowable probabilities (Knight, 1957/2006).

42 Although simple ratios and rates are easy to calculate (e.g. number of warranty claims per year) the objective should be to calculate comparative rates (e.g. number of warranty claims per 100,000 kilometres).

43 These measures will only be meaningful where they relate to business goals or standards which reflect customer expectations (e.g. time a customer has to wait 'on hold' in a telephone queue at a customer enquiry call centre).

44 Doing so may result in a decision which has repercussions for the business. For example, the figures may suggest the loss of a customer has only a small revenue loss. However, this lacks the context that the customer's actions are watched by other businesses in the same sector that then make the same decisions. Some decisions such as outsourcing should not be based on the figures as there are far more important strategic considerations (Langford-Smith 2000).

45 A critical review is essential where consultants have been used since their report may overlook assumptions and practices which are not apparent to them. The diffusion of management knowledge by consultants has an authority (Bloomfield & Best 1992) which makes questioning difficult (Schon, 1983), particularly if they are among the management gurus (Huczynski 1993). The use of consultants with limited business experience using the methodology of the particular consulting company and techniques learnt in master of business administration awards has been remarked by several commentators (e.g. Whiteley 1984). Many of these actions are reinforced in management books which emphasise unobtrusive control (Perrow 1986) that is, leadership and management (Fursten 1999: 98) and ignore the contribution of other factors such as products.

Chapter summary

It is important that the business has a rounded approach to operations since there are frequently unexpected difficulties which can distract managers. Using policies, controls and reviews to bring flexibility to operations is achieved through establishing a range of corporate policies which embody measures for adherence. In addition, controls should operate to provide an independent assessment. Controls should be distinguished from monitoring the internal performance systems and processes. Administration and overhead should be minimised. The economy, efficiency and effectiveness of systems and processes should be periodically reviewed. All these involve retaining the support of at least three stakeholders: customers, employees and suppliers.[46] The final area of adaptation is the use of ethical principles and standards to make judgements and encourage others to behave ethically.

---

46 The satisficing approach is therefore frequently adopted by business.

9 Personal power, authority, corruption and conflict

In business, personal power refers to the ability, opportunity or right to make a decision or carry out an action that involves others;[1] it includes a person's influence, their own behaviour and their treatment of others. The exercise of personal power may not be based on personal strength or energy; force, influence or taking a role. While many views of power have a leadership orientation, there are also many which consider the influence that the person has on others around them. It is necessary always to have a multidimensional[2] view of power and this is the basis for the assumed business body of knowledge discussed below. It suggests that any situation will always involve more than one form of power although only one form may be apparent.[3] There is a connection between power and corruption expressed in the aphorism power corrupts and absolute power corrupts absolutely.

Conflict is apparent in organisations both as a direct and symbolic form. In the direct form it involves antagonistic encounters. In its symbolic form it is represented as both ideas and attitudes that are in opposition as an emotional and intellectual struggle. A conflict often involves power although it is convenient to consider them separately as well as together.

Topics in power, authority, corruption and conflict for adaptation

Personal power, authority, corruption and conflict are multidimensional. Power, authority and conflict are most apparent to the employees in their activities and interpersonal relations in the business. Corruption, conflict and subversion may surface or remain concealed depending upon the culture of the organisation. There are five aspects:

1. Personal power and authority
2. Corruption and concealment

---

1 Under this rational choice framework it is usual to differentiate between outcome power (power to bring about outcomes) and social power (changing the incentives that encourage others to bring about outcomes). The social power may take the form of coercion. In relationships, power has five bases: positional (legitimate power), referent (loyalty and attraction), expert (skills and the need for them), reward (conferral and degree of reward) and coercive (negative influences) (French & Raven 1959).

2 There is a connection between power and authority which is often separated by the use of definitions. Weber used domination rather than authority to obedience of commands (Weber 1956/1968) to consider the sources of authority (rational, traditional and charismatic). Alternatively, power exists in relationships between people which may be strategically exercised (Lukes 1974; Machiavelli 1958/1989) also shown by Foucault (1977/1980) in a combination of empirical insights and normative confusion. Lukes (1974) suggested three criteria (1) observational decision-making with subjective interests, (2) the first dimension with the addition of covert behaviour, (3) the other dimensions expanded to include latent power; Lukes also recognises that power includes agenda-setting.

3 This may be through consensual power in a similar manner to the concept of hegemony (Gramsci 1971).

3. Payment for influence or favouritism

4. Conflict as ordinary human behaviour in organisations

5. Subversive actions.

9.1 Personal power and authority

In the modern organisation there is personal power and authority in terms of both the formal organisation and the informal organisation.[4] Personal power involves personal traits and dispositions as well as influence and the capability for enforcement. Some views of power and authority are rooted in the legitimacy of its authority while many sociological views recognise the characteristics of the individual in gaining acquiescence from other individuals.[5] The difficulty with simple definitions of power lies in the myriad manifestations of power in organisations. In many cases power is closely aligned with information and the asymmetry of the information held or available.

The broad management issues and challenges that arise from the authority of personal power and authority include:

- The acquisition of power
- The assumption of power
- The ex officio exercise of power
- The relinquishment of power.

The principal tools and techniques for personal power and authority include:

- The formal exercise of power under delegations
- The use of power associated with roles and identities[6]
- The conferral of power by directors

---

4 The power may be vested in an individual and formally expressed as delegations of authority. Or it may depend upon the expertise and personal relationships that one individual has with other individuals. Other views of power are proposed by Foucault (1977/1980) who uses tacit consent and Giddens (1979, 1984) who uses structuration. Haugaard (1997) provides a useful critique of power and knowledge while Collins (1990: 462) regards Foucault's attempt as that of an amateur. Cialdini (1984/2008) provides a broader conception of power taking into account the animal and human psychology of commitment, reciprocity, affection, proof and social authority. Resource Dependency Theory (Pfeffer & Salancik 1978) also posits that power is the relational, situational and potentially mutual relationship between organisations.

5 The identification of three personal power roles (compensatory, condign and conditioned) draws on Galbraith (1983a) who drew on Weber (1956/1968) and sources (personality or leadership, property or wealth and organisation). Galbraith (1983b) comments that he takes a 'more reserved view of countervailing power' than he did in his earlier writings.

6 A notable example is provided by Owen (2011). Under the authority of its CEO in the 1970's Courtaulds who had pioneered a major new industry (synthetic fibres), pursued a flawed twin strategy of vertical integration which left it vulnerable to cheaper Chinese fabrics and diversification. The authority of its CEO was unquestioned and when he retired the resulting period of economic turbulence overturned the power he had gathered to the role of CEO.

- Psychopath behaviour (in some instances)[7]
- The sharing of power in a committee or group
- The taking of power in ambiguous or disaster situations where there is a vacuum.

The managerial decisions and judgements associated with personal power and authority include:

- What level of judgement and personal responsibility will be encouraged?[8]
- What should be the formal specification of powers both in day-to-day activities and non-routine events?
- Will the association with notable personalities and celebrities to add to personal esteem?[9]
- What is the extent to which decisions can be made without reference to others either before or after the fact?
- What kinds of decisions can be made in the absence of guidelines or protocols?
- Will decisions have to be documented and justified?
- Will decisions be transparent or need to be communicated so they are known?
- What is the likelihood decisions will be acted upon without being questioned?

In summary, the exercise of personal power and authority depends upon how it is conferred and whether it has to be made available for examination. This latter point is also associated with whether there is a delay between the making of the decision and its execution.

9.2 Corruption and concealment

Since the time of Al Capone in Chicago, the presence of criminal activity in business has been apparent.[10] The power that is associated with corruption has two aspects for a assumed business body of knowledge. The first is the insidious nature of corruption. Television and

---

7 The myth that a psych path conceals a hero is rejected by Hare (1999) who contrasts their charm with their motive for pleasure and calculating rationality with an inability to treat others as thinking, feeling human beings. He discusses a Psychopathy Checklist but it is a clinical instrument not intended for use by lay persons.

8 Philosophically authority (Latin '*auctoritas*') and governing are associated with leadership. Authority refers to the power and influence that come from being trusted and respected for their capcity to initiate and lead. The failure of much leadership is not authority but the capability to face uncertainty and judge what needs to be done and exercise discretion. Judgement requires tacit knowledge aquired from experience and what Aristotle called the virue of *phronesis*, or practical wisdom gained by experience and engagement with the world around us and not by using a formula. There are many who see authority as something to be restrained and controlled, particularly through using pre-specified rules so there is a juridification of everyday life discouraging the taking of responsibility, the use of discretion and the making of judgement calls. So there is less judgement and risk-taking. Each employee must determine the view of authority embodied in the culture of their business.

9 Sociologist C. Wright Mills (1956) suggested that the interests of the leaders of the military, corporate and political elements of society are interwoven.

10 Modern crime combines high technology, global links and a billion-dollar turnover. An Australian example describes outlawed motorcycle gangs, powerful Asian crime syndicates and government agencies (McKenzie, 2012).

movies provide numerous plots (e.g. Internal Affairs released in 1990 starring Richard Gere) which describe the gradual and imperceptible development of corruption through simultaneously cunning and treacherous yet deceptively innocent actions. In some case it can be following what is believed to be an acceptable procedure. In other cases it can be a novice following a recommended approach recommended by peers. In yet other cases it is a breakdown of independence between the regulator and those regulated.[11] The second aspect of power is the action to maintain power.[12]

The broad management issues and challenges that arise from corruption and concealment include:

- The concealment of personal power through its execution *ex officio*
- Links with high political and judicial office[13]
- Confused media reporting which does not make clear the criminal purposes and behaviours of corporate and social identities[14]
- Links with gambling[15]
- Poor or reluctant investigative inquiries
- The scope for corruption to occur through losing objectivity and independence
- The allocation of many tasks to a single employee (or consultant/contractor)
- The lack of oversight in exploring recommendations for decisions often due to time pressures
- The inadequate controls and checks in operational activities which result in practices which have loopholes visible only to the employees that carry them out
- The flexibility that employees have in carrying out their duties which permit shortcuts or elimination of recording and checking tasks[16]
- The gradual reduction of random checks and audits (both internal and external).

---

11 The example of local government is of particular importance owing to its development, zoning and planning powers which allow for large profits to be made over a short time for relatively minor investments.

12 This can include the selective nature of enforcement, or the control over political or economic institutions, as well as the financial crimes of tax evasion, copyright infringement, counterfeiting of products and cyber warfare, human trafficking and drug smuggling (OECD 2002).

13 A well-written criminal history of any city will illustrate many examples. In the case of Sydney NSW, the key reference book is Whitton (1985).

14 In many cases this is due to the laws of libel combined with the lack of successful criminal prosecution which result in an unblemished record and concealed conspiratorial action.

15 A criminal history also involves gambling. The key books on the power of gambling are Hickie (1985) and Con Walker (2009). Hickie (1985) shows that many people are caught in the web of organised crime because criminal control of illegal casinos provides them with a major cash flow.

16 It is acknowledged that cost pressures from management are often responsible for a reduction in internal controls and this sends a signal to employees that management is more concerned with monetary savings than maintenance of proper controls. Many instances of corruption have an unprosecuted senior manager who was unconcerned about such matters because their priority was making short-term savings, often to secure their annual bonus.

The principal tools and techniques for considering corruption and concealment include:

- Assistance which will taint the recipient and render them powerless in future circumstances where either the favour has to be repaid or where silence or inaction is the price of the return of the earlier favour
- Informants[17] who are sufficiently close to the collection and dissemination of information to be able to both report on the availability of new information as well as the proposed actions under consideration
- Murder to protect the knowledgeable financiers, legal representatives and distributors and those higher up the chain of a criminal network[18]
- Social penetration of the judicial, political and audit functions which permit social encounters that will discount and dissuade any attempt to conduct investigations
- The ability to mislead and misconstrue facts and circumstances may also lead to the casting of doubt on honest employees which in turn affect the behaviour and attitudes of their peers
- Clear descriptions of processes and actions to be taken where an employee feels they facing a potential borderline corruption situation
- Clear corporate policies that corruption will not be tolerated
- Training in vulnerable situations for both new and long-term employees
- Use of corruption cases with competitors to illustrate the behaviour expected by senior and middle managers
- Use of business tender losses as illustrations of refusal to engage in corrupt behaviour and
- Vigorous investigation of suspected cases of corruption.

The managerial decisions and judgements associated with corruption and concealment include:

- Is there a presence of organised crime?[19]
- Will there be recruitment, promotion or rewarding of individuals sympathetic to the values and practices of those in charge of operations or particular resources?

---

17 Informants may be willing accomplices (e.g. professionals, recruits from the workforce), tricked into informing, or be providing helpful information in what they believe to be good faith. Should the group discover the informant there is both the possibility of hostility and punishment Marx 1974).

18 In a twist worthy of a thriller, the investigators from homicide will find it difficult to find the murderer or the instigator of the murder because the killer is a former homicide investigator with inside knowledge of investigatory techniques (Jiggens 2009).

19 Various approaches can be used which will depend upon the definitions adopted. Albanese (2008) recommends considering illicit markets rather than groups.

- Will the use of resources (including cash and cash reserves) on activities and infra-structure benefit the administrators either directly or indirectly?[20]

- Is there the possibility that rumours based on criminal say-so about several illegal activities printed and such hearsay is subsequently quoted as evidence?

- What will happen if none of these allegations are ever proven?[21]

- Is it possible to select persons with a suitable public demeanour or appearance of probity for political administrative appointments?[22]

- Will the granting of indemnities and the payments of rewards for admitting the details of corrupt behaviour or implicating others, reduce the credibility of the process?

- Will there be appointment of individuals as payback although the individuals appointed may be representative of a faction or group so there is not necessarily any direct reward?

- Will the appointment of favourable or predictable chair persons for enquiries, inves-tigations and commissions ensure that an agreed result is obtained?

In summary, there is usually a considerable delay between corrupt behaviour occurring and it coming to light.[23] Even then it is likely that many instances will be either uncorroborated or overturned on appeal. The use of a Royal Commission, the availability of embargoed public documents, or the publication of memories suppressed during the author's lifetime can often be the only avenues to suggest the extent of corruption.[24]

---

20 The most notable example is expenditure on offices, fit out and amenities enjoyed by the administrators themselves. For example, NSW club gaming industry is a multi-billion dollar business with big clubs operating more poker machines than many casinos, but not subject to the same scrutiny as casinos. The gaming revenues of clubs are primarily spent on management, capital works and subsidised sales of food and alcohol (Con Walker 2009).

21 Even though they are often repeated.

22 McCoy (1980) suggests power and corruption must of necessity involve publicly elected figures. In some cases they may be aware they are dupes of a corrupt colleague, friend or third-party.

23 The long delay between corruption and exposure means that employees are likely to take the view that either they will not be caught in the act or that they will subsequently be far removed so as to avoid being tainted by it. Accounts from some Wall Street financiers actions before and during the global financial crisis seems to confirm this implication (see for example, McDonald 2009).

24 It is acknowledged that the press in a democratic country may often be the precursor to such disclosures. However, the freedom of the press to publish such damaging accusations or evidence has been limited by requirement for sources to be identified and the high penalties if a court case occurs and is lost by the newspaper. The case of *Private Eye* magazine (UK) is instructive; they lost many cases in the 1980s and paid damages; in some they appear to have been subsequently vindicated but it did not result in return of their damages. In 2009 *Private Eye* was successful in allowing rulings by the Law Society to be publicised.

9.3 Payment for influence or favouritism

The result of corruption is payment for influence or favouritism.[25] Usually it takes the form of gifts, financial payments and bribes. These may begin with special discounts (e.g. cheap purchases), minor gifts (e.g. from incumbent suppliers) and indirect payments (e.g. being taken to lunch). They also include behaviours introduced by colleagues as acceptable. The borderline nature of such activities is due to the fact that they arise from the carrying out of normal job functions in a non-corrupt way.

The broad management issues and challenges that arise from the payment for influence or favouritism include:

- The likelihood that a sophisticated corruptor will commence with innocent, minor and borderline payments to obtain influence or benefits
- The probability that payments will be made away from the office where they are unlikely to be observed
- The possibility that payments will take the form of cash rather than objects to make the transaction less visible
- The sophistication of monetary payments which can result in bills being paid or payments on loan accounts which obviate the need for intermediate transfers
- The possibility that precautionary payments can be made well ahead of time simply to establish loyalty
- The use of domestic and offshore companies that specialise in handling payments
- The continued operation of private (or secretive) banking institutions and tax havens.

The principal tools and techniques for identifying and addressing payment for influence or favouritism include:

- Ensuring the pre-decision process involves several employees
- Ensuring decisions are made by more than a single person
- Ensuring there are clearly documented reasons for decisions about selection and financial terms and operational conditions
- Establishing a mechanism to evaluate recommendations against a criteria which has multiple factors
- Establishing a mechanism to allow periodic review of performance of arrangements or advice against the criteria used for the original decision
- Comparing internal arrangements with competitors

---

25 The effect of liking the persuader and having external social proof that others are doing likewise are powerful persuaders (Cialdini 2001).

- Being aware that influence and payment will be undisclosed and giving an opportunity for employees to raise any concerns they have including about becoming embroiled in receiving payments (or making payments).

The managerial decisions and judgements associated with authority include:

- When an investigation will be triggered?
- What kind of investigation will occur?
- To whom will the report from the investigation be forwarded?
- What criteria will be used by the recipient of a report when considering further detailed investigation and/or disciplining of employees found to be in breach of corporate policy?
- Under what circumstances will the employee be referred to the authorities for own investigation and prosecution?
- What encouragement will be given to employees to bring forward information that implicates themselves or others in borderline or major corruption?
- What obligation is there to inform shareholders?
- What information will be made public?

In summary, a policy on payments for influence and favouritism is more likely to make employees sensitive to the organisation's stand on corruption. There must, of course, be consistency with the behaviour of senior management and their policies. Processes must ensure that senior management is sufficiently in touch with frontline operational employee actions to avoid findings which will later prove an embarrassment. The example of the *News of the World* phone hacking and other behaviours suggests that there is no substitute for all levels of management to communicate and for expenses to be stated accurately and rigorously checked.

9.4 Conflict as ordinary human behaviour in organisations

Conflict may be an emotional or physical struggle or quite frequently a combination of the two. It may be open opposition or a subtle obstruction. Many aspects of conflict are also tests of power. This is not only the case in employer-employee industrial negotiations but also management-employee interactions. While traditional management views tend to regard management as holding the power this overlooks the subtle stratagems that employees may engage in on a selective basis. Examples include disclosure of management plans to customers ('We changed supplier and now have double the profit on this widget now') as well as suggestions ('You can buy the same product from the new store opposite for half price this week'). In this way conflict and power become intertwined and the distinction between advantage and disadvantage for the employee become blurred. A psychological view of conflict recognises many points of view and many triggers for the conflict. In some cases conflict is difficult to resolve even with the best intentions. This may be the result of long-standing and strongly harboured resentment. Or it may be a sound expression of loss of position or income. It may be exacerbated where there are many individuals of the same opinion and where a strong counter measure is enacted which is perceived as strong-handed. One of the major areas of conflict is the ways in which employee contributions are valued. While some contributions are ascribed to self-promotion by the employee, others are acknowledged through prior perceptions of the manager. This may arise from the manager's own perception of the employee, or more likely, from opinions conveyed by the manager by colleagues whose opinion they value. This is a psychological phenomenon only partially understood although the cognitive biases which support it are well-known.

The broad management issues and challenges[26] that arise from conflict in the workplace include:

- Distinguishing conflict for personal gain from conflict between different groups
- Disruption to work (e.g. manufacturing, receiving products, despatching products, providing services)
- Loss of income from the non-productivity of business infrastructure
- Loss of reputation particularly if supply is disrupted to customers
- The ability to resolve disputes quickly
- The future impact on the business if a conflict is settled in ways that limit the flexibility of management or create employee benefits with high fixed costs
- Establishing a history of credible conflict resolution
- Impact on the economy in the short and long-term
- The myriad of ways in which conflict can manifest and the possibility that in combination they may have as much symbolic aspects as substance
- To recognise the many types of cognitive bias that influence decisions at an unconscious or subconscious level
- To have the view that conflict may not be resolvable, that is, that it may continue to be present
- To recognise the different kinds of conflict (e.g. overuse of resources, remuneration, working conditions and organisational standards) and the need for different approaches.

The principal tools and techniques for managing conflict include:

- Providing early opportunities to notify conflict in a non-inflammatory manner

---

26 Simmel (1904) emphasises that harmony and disharmony are essential to the formation of society and this can include antagonism. He writes (p 507) '[t]here must be agreement in order to struggle and the struggle occurs under reciprocal recognition of norms and rules.' This suggests that there is room for debate over the conclusions drawn from the facts (p 513).

- Agreeing on a neutral, trustworthy and readily available person or body who will hear the grievance
- Ensuring the person or body hearing the grievance is capable of suggesting creative and productive remedies
- Having a criteria on whether other parties (e.g. customers, suppliers, other employees) will be affected by the conflict
- Ensuring that other parties will be given timely warnings that conflict is immanent
- Use of government conflict resolution statutory bodies.
- Private mechanisms for allowing power plays to occur (e.g. having meetings at which power behaviours can be expressed)
- Public mechanisms for displaying conflicts with power (e.g. ensuring attention)
- Using ritual for expression of conflict
- Considering temporary power reversals (e.g. role exchange)
- Using a third party as mediator.

The managerial decisions and judgements associated with managing conflict include:

- Is a speedy resolution preferable to a prolonged conflict?
- Does the conflict have its basis solely in power?
- Is the conflict a mask for an underlying, more serious conflict?
- Whether to escalate a situation or attempt to contain it?
- Does the conflict lend itself to a resolution that both parties will find acceptable?
- What is the nature of the power that each party possesses or believes they possess?
- What is the likely reaction of the party that potentially will lose the conflict?
- Is the conflict likely to enhance or diminish the party's stock of power?
- Is there likely to be a transfer of power among the individuals within any particular party or group?
- What are both parties likely to consider an acceptable settlement?
- What is likely to be the impact on the business in terms of share price, customer loyalty and competitor response?
- Whether the conflict is an intractable problem and therefore it cannot be resolved?
- Will introducing a third party into the negotiations help or hinder reaching a settlement?
- What a settlement is likely to mean in future conflicts?

In summary, a view of conflict as an ordinary element of organisational life is most likely to result in a set of practices which seek to accept it as a part of the business. It would be a mistake to have a view that it could or should be resolved and ended. The nature of social relations and economic advantage and disadvantage makes for readily available conditions for conflict. Instead of seeing it as incompatible or irreconcilable, it is more productive to see it as a continuous dialogue in which understanding and meaning are as important as particular negotiation points, while trying to understand the conditions for conflict and exercise of power.

9.5 Subversive actions

The term subversive does not have an agreed definition. Subversive actions are directed toward accomplishing objectives by either taking action directly or by influencing, dominating or displacing individuals (or groups). Their essential characteristic is to thwart or defeat the current arrangements. While originally applied to military and national concerns it has become a feature of industrial relations and individual employees in the workplace. It may include non-violent protest, surreptitious and unpredictable activities which are not outright overt sabotage or espionage.

The broad management issues and challenges that arise from subversive actions include:

- Dealing with informal groups[27]
- Ensuring that employees and contractors (or casual employees) are made to feel part of the organisation
- Being able to distinguish between random[28] process failures and subversive actions
- Identifying changes in attitudes of existing employees
- Having a plan to respond to apparent subversive actions in a positive and non-threatening manner.

The principal tools and techniques for preventing and handling subversive actions include:

- Being open with information about the organisation
- Providing opportunities for employees to be involved in decision-making
- Ensuring that participation in committees is open to all and is shared among all employees
- Valuing employee expertise and specialised knowledge
- Taking an interest in seeming failures, oversights and omissions.

---

27 Social psychology suggests that compared to individuals, groups are both more aggressive and more competitive owing to their competition for resources and social rewards (Sherif et al. 1954/1961). The experiment is noteworthy because it suggests that superordinate goals (goals that requires more than one group to achieve the goal) reduce conflict significantly more effectively than other strategies (e.g. communication, contact).

28 Human cognitive dispositions are inclined to reject interpreting an event as random. Events can be rejected as random when they are subject to chance. Events can be taken as random when they have an interdependence. The examples of Long-Term Capital Management and Lehman Brothers are cases of the interdependence of events. In any period, the distribution of a set of returns from superannuation/mutual fund managers is some outperformers, some under performers with most bunched around the middle. On the other hand, the comparison over two discrete periods is usually utter chaos. See Mandelbrot (2004) and Mlodinow (2009) for a discussion and more examples.

The managerial decisions and judgements concerning subversive actions include:

- What distance is there between senior management and employees?
- What is the morale of employees at different levels in and different groups?
- What views do employees hold of management and current and recent major organisational initiatives?
- What opportunities exist for employees to make their views known without suffering retribution?
- What kinds of employee initiatives are being stifled?[29]
- What kinds of decisions cause the most angst among employees?
- What are long-standing grievances are being overlooked?

In summary, subversive actions are more likely to be associated with poor opinions of management. This may be the result of either new managers being appointed or existing managers making unpopular decisions. Some western management theory gives prominence to communication and persuasion. It is clear from many industrial disputes that both employees and customers are likely to regard expenditure in these areas as evidence of waste and incompetence. This is then likely to produce further subversive behaviour. The long history of human relations studies[30] makes clear that there is no substitute for taking an interest in the actual tasks performed by employees and the conditions under which they work.

Chapter summary

The exercise of power has potential for conflict. Many management approaches regard conflict as something to be removed when it becomes apparent. Early management and economic writers regard the disruption that occurs with conflict as part of the inevitable management landscape which from time to time requires the attention of management. The aspects of power which tend to be overlooked are in the areas of corruption. Although an emphasis on ethical principles and standards to make judgements and encouraging others to behave ethically is important, the borderline nature of some corruption suggests that other approaches should be considered including role-play tasks and examples from both inside the company and competitors. The poor record in bringing prosecutions and success in convictions has encouraged employees to take the view that the chance of punishment is small.

---

29 This may result in individuals secretly pursuing innovation that is later embraced either by senior management when they recognise the value of an idea they had dismissed (e.g. Abrahamson 1991), or by management at the organisation that subsequently hires the employee.

30 The Hawthorne experiments (Mayo 1945/1975) show both the advantage of attention and arranging work in small teams of about six people; they also show that employees are motivated by the psychological conditions more than the physical conditions. The studies also showed that employers needed to consider prior life experience, conditions at home and the social aspects of work.

DIMENSION THREE
LEVERAGE AVAILABLE RESOURCES TO IMPROVE PERFORMANCE

Context of leveraging available resources

Traditionally resources are divided into tangible and intangible resources. Tangible resources are physical or economic in their nature. Intangible resources include reputation,[1] technological and human resources.[2] There are three forms of resources. Resources are converted into capabilities by the existence of routines[3] which identify and harness them. Those capabilities which are central to competitive advantage and profitability are core competencies.[4] Figure 9 below shows the hierarchical relationship between the different forms of resources.

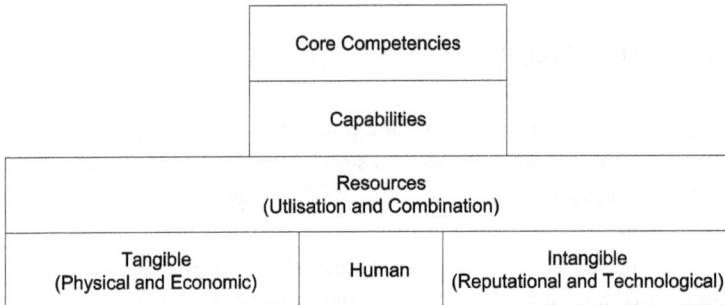

Core Competencies		
Capabilities		
Resources (Utlisation and Combination)		
Tangible (Physical and Economic)	Human	Intangible (Reputational and Technological)

Figure 9. Hierarchical relationship between the different forms of resources.

---

1 For example, Coca Cola and McDonalds rely on their worldwide reputation to attract customers.

2 Human resources are also known as intellectual capital (Edvinsson & Malone 1997) or human capital (Smith 1776/1999: Book 2; Becker 1964/1994). It is used to emphasise that more than just knowledge is involved. It includes competencies (or abilities), skills and personality attributes embodied in the ability to perform labour.

3 Initial operating arrangements either evolve into routines which are maintained by word-of-mouth or are formalised by signs, notes and checklists. Often this occurs in a haphazard manner, stimulated by particular incidents and suggestions.

4 Businesses who recognise their core competencies will take steps to protect them by making it difficult for competitors to understand and imitate them (Prahalad & Hamel 1990).

Most resources are internal to the business. However, resources can also be viewed at the industry and country level.[5] More recently, resources have been viewed jointly between companies.[6]

Perspective on leveraging available resources

The perspective for understanding resources is centred on their inter-related nature. It is difficult to isolate one or two aspects of the business for attention. For example, a decision to target a different customer segment requires employee training to improve understanding of the presale and postsale needs of that customer group as well as monitoring to determine whether the decision is successful in the short and medium term. To gain competitive advantage from resources depends upon the resources and competitors described in Table 3 below.

Table 3. Factors in gaining competitive advantage from resources

Resource Profile	Factor in competitive advantage
Available resources leveraged and deployed	Chance possession of suitable capabilities with initial demand for them.
	The possession of resources that are valued and rare.
Competitor resources marshalled	Competitors possess inferior resources, capabilities and core competencies.
Industry competition and evolution	Limited competition allowing an early dominance.
	The general dynamism of the industry environment.

One reading of this resource profile table is that three uses for resources can be distinguished: (1) Resources potential for competitive advantage;[7] (2) Resources for gaining competitive advantage; and (3) Resources for sustaining competitive advantage.[8]

Impact of leveraging available resources

The impact of resources varies among stakeholders and depends upon their sustainability. Employees will be concerned with the adequacy of the resources available to them. The

---

5 Porter (1990) expanded his competitive advantage framework to countries to explain the prevalence of strong businesses in the same industry.

6 The increasing use of outsourcing and willingness of businesses to form alliances makes it necessary to consider interorganisational (inter-firm) analyses of competitive advantage (Dyer & Singh 1990).

7 Many features of the Apple Computer originated with Xerox which did not regard their intangible resources as valuable (Davenport & Prusak 1998/2000).

8 The success ascribed to some businesses may therefore not be due to foresight and wise strategic implementation but may be the result of trial and error success or simple luck (Alchian 1950). After asking Microsoft to produce the BASIC language for its IBM PC, IBM then asked Microsoft for an operating system. Microsoft acquired the Quick and Dirty Operating System written by Tim Paterson of Seattle Computer Products and redeveloped it for the IBM PC at the same time retaining licensing rights.

imposition of temporary freezes in resources (e.g. capital expenditure, or recruitment) can be managed if there is a buffer in resources, if work can be delayed or deferred, or if there is a downturn in demand. Eventually a restriction on resources transfers advantage to competitors unless the savings improve market share. Financial institutions are concerned with the productive use of resources and preserving the security of resources in case the loan cannot be repaid by the due date. A loan agreement usually specifies performance thresholds and the means by which they can be verified. The risk that resources can be claimed by other stakeholders is also assessed. Investors usually give attention to resources since the literature of investment advice has moved beyond a simple cyclical view that share prices reflect economic circumstances (e.g. Burns & Mitchell 1946) or are random (Cootner, 1964). They recommend a strategy of diversification (e.g. Templeton, 2008) based on the fundamental intrinsic value[9] of the business, (e.g. Graham & Dodd 1951) considering the integrity of the business, (Fisher 1958/1996) which Buffet extended in his letters to Berkshire Hathaway shareholders (Buffet & Cunningham 2001) and to considering the calibre of the senior management.[10]

Sustaining competitive advantage will depend upon the extent to which resources can be successfully utilised. Resource position barriers can make it difficult to imitate a resource or to substitute an acceptable equivalent. Competitive advantage is eroded over time through resource obsolescence and imitation by rivals. In general, four resource position barriers can sustain competitive advantage: (1) substitutability: (2) ease of appropriability; (3) degree to which a resource is replicable (or imitable); and (4) durability. Resources which are context-specific owing to their embeddedness in a business are likely to sustain competitive advantage. It may be difficult for competitors as well as the business itself to determine exactly what makes the business successful.[11]

Chapters in Dimension Three (Leverage available resources)

There are three aspects to leveraging available resources to improve business performance. They are:

1. Benefit from the intangible resources of employee ability and expertise (discussed in Chapter 10)

2. Recognise information as a resource (discussed in Chapter 11)

3. Improve the tangible benefits from resources (discussed in Chapter 12).

---

9 As measured by the total cash dividends from a business for its remaining life discounted to present value. This crucial but difficult to calculate sum is another example of a non-GAAP measurement that is preferred to cash flow or profitability.

10 The efficient market hypothesis (Bachelier in Cooter 1964) claims that the prices of traded assets reflect all past and currently available public information and thus consistent achievement of returns in excess of the average is unlikely. The debate among proponents and critics leads to favouring of either value or growth shares.

11 Apparent transparency may also produce causal ambiguity which misleads competitors. The core competency of Honda in combustion engines and power train technology shows in its cars, motor cycles, outdoor mobile tools and power hand tools, may be read as the product of developmental history, business relationships, formula one racing experience or a myriad of other factors.

10 Benefit from the intangible resources of employee ability and expertise

The intangible resources of employee ability and experience are often an untapped potential. Ability (or competence) includes both the skills to accomplish specific work tasks and fulfil work responsibilities as well as the general abilities expected of an employee. Expertise is part of know-how and involves applying knowledge to new circumstances. While they are separately identified they are intermingled and interact. They are also subject to the influence of emotions and groups.

Overcoming gaps in resources

In some cases there are programs to assist employees where they lack specific abilities. For example, a person lacking motor abilities can be exceptionally competent handling animals when provided with a mobility aid.

Relationship between resources, routines and controls

One of the means for dealing with variation and uncertainty is the application of rules or principles to situations. Where it becomes commonplace to follow a rule these may be termed norms or conventions of the business. Routines that are embedded within groups of employees result in better utilisation of resources.

Topics in benefiting from employee ability

When operating or establishing a business there are five resources which should always present. They are:

1. Provide leadership
2. Encourage broadly based fiscal responsibility with a cash focus
3. Undertake thorough risk/benefit assessment of strategy and operations
4. Fostering creativity and innovation
5. Recognise emerging situations and intractable problems.

The efficiency and effectiveness of this resource base goes a long way toward ensuring the viability of the business.

10.1 Provide leadership

Leadership is the role of guiding the business forward. Some businesses vest the leadership in the Chief Executive Officer while others vest it in a committee of senior management.

The broad management issues and challenges concerning leadership that management can consider include:

- Leadership is assumed to include having people skills that will motivate employees to ensure that they are fully committed to the objectives of the business
- The leader is expected to be successful at communicating and persuading stakeholders (including employees) as to the potential capabilities of the business
- At difficult times the actions and statements by leader usually determine the chances of success owing to the attention that they receive
- More recently the actions and statements by the leader are regarded as setting the moral and social responsibility tone of the business ('tone at the top').

The principal tools and techniques for leadership include:

- Determining the number of direct reports (that is, the number of executives with day to day reporting responsibility to the CEO)
- The extent to which past executive behaviour is replicated or abandoned
- The ways and means of staying in touch with employees, customers and the community. This includes the established technique of MBWA (Management by Walking About)
- The ways and means for conveying policy and strategy.

The managerial decisions and judgements concerning leadership include:

- What is the morale within the business?
- What is employee perception of the leader (master of the situation or motivated by survival)?
- What are the ways in which change is viewed and pursued?

In summary, senior management and Boards are selected on their potential to provide leadership and retained for the business benefits resulting from their leadership.

10.2 Encourage broadly based fiscal responsibility with a cash focus

Broadly based fiscal responsibility focused on cash flow is essential to business survival.

The broad management issues and challenges for fiscal responsibility include:[1]

- Reacting to a financial emergency[2]
- Complying with reporting deadlines and standards
- Choosing a range of financial reports with different frequencies and levels of detail in order to obtain a rounded view of its financial performance
- Satisfying borrowing and debt covenants[3]
- For publicly listed companies, being aware of analyst and shareholder expectations on earnings and yields.

The principal tools and techniques for fiscal responsibility include:

- A suitable Chart of Accounts (which categorises similar expenditure along more than one dimension)[4]
- Open book management[5]
- Working capital management[6]
- Availability of a variety of financial reports at different time frequencies[7] summarising key business activities and cash flows
- Obtaining reports from third parties including bank deposits, borrowings and financing
- Preparation of regular customer and supplier reconciliations

---

1 These are important in all businesses because it is difficult to predict when business circumstances will become difficult or when it can take advantage of opportunities that have emerged.

2 An early resource-based view was provided by Donaldson (1969: 72) who set out a proforma for considering the financial mobility of business resources for three time horizons (one quarter, one year and three years to avoid reliance on a key resource (e.g. cash reserves or short-term borrowings).

3 It is wise to have advice on such matters as the legal standing of personally guaranteed securities and the warning or notice given where the lender proposes to take any action (including mortgagee sale).When the business secures funding with stringent conditions precautionary care is essential to avoid triggering intervention by the lender. Similar prudence is essential where assets are leased.

4 Descriptions of how to construct charts of account are now rare. Early discussions are provided in Kester (1917/1939: 660–69) and Tornborgh (1943: 26–51). Gordon and Shillinglaw (1951/1964: 162–64, 534–40) point out that in addition to the account classification the responsibility centre should be identified.

5 Open book management is aimed at job security through sharing financial information before making decisions. Stack writes (1994: 8) that 70% of the job is manufacturing and 30% is learning. Learning creates a common understanding of the financial statements (Case 1995: xvii). This may be linked to using items in the financial statement as targets which determine the bonuses for groups or teams (Stack 1994: 8).

6 While accountants devote considerable effort to the discussion of working capital management (see for example Marsden 2009: 408–25) its elements (inventory, debtors, creditors and cash) require separate dissection and management.

7 The usual time frequencies include daily, weekly, monthly, quarterly, six monthly and annually.

- Conducting a number of financial analyses notably the comprehensive set of DuPont analyses[8] (see Chapter 15)
- Specific analyses may also be made, including ageing of customer liabilities, most profitable customer, customers with the highest sales volume, high volume products and slow moving products
- Physical verification of the inventory including work-in-process.

The managerial decisions and judgements concerning fiscal responsibility include:

- What is not reported?[9]
- Is the business currently solvent?
- Is the business a viable going concern?
- Should trading continue?
- Can sales be increased at times when they are low?
- Will changes to customer payment terms accelerate their payments?
- Should new terms be negotiated with suppliers?
- Can inventory levels be reduced through improved stock control?
- Should additional financing be sought based on cash flow forecasts?
- Should additional capital be injected into the business?
- Should sales be declined or postponed where they will create financial stress?

In summary, fiscal responsibility extends beyond relying on financial data to measure the viability of the business. Fiscal discipline with a cash focus is vital. Improving the cash position cannot be left to senior management or the finance team. It is something which should involve all employees. In tough times the fiscally responsible business stands the best chance of survival.

10.3 Undertake a thorough risk/benefit assessment of strategy and operations

Risk assessment is an essential accompaniment to proper financial management. Managing risk is a competitive weapon in two respects. It allows the business to do what others cannot because the risk is better managed in strategy, operations and support activities such as changing technologies. It also focuses attention of the adequacy and realisation of benefits. Figure

---

8 DuPont financial ratio analyses were pioneered by DuPont de Nemours and Co. in the 1920s for its own use by F. Donaldson Brown (1885–1965), later its Treasurer. They integrated a number of separate financial ratios from the balance sheet and the income statement. They were also used at General Motors.

9 Discussed by Walker (2011) for the public sector with regard to the application of acounting standards as well as build, own and operate arrangements.

10 below provides a matrix where benefits and risk can be assessed. The cells are populated with the conclusions that might be reached, for example using the criteria of profitability, market dominance, reputation. A matrix of this style de-emphasises the tendency to see risk as wholly disagreeable and makes clear the trade-off between risk and benefit to the business.

Potential benefit to the business	Potential risk to the business	
	High	Low
High	Cautiously examine	Identify and develop
Low	Avoid	Re-define

Figure 10. Risk/benefit matrix showing possible actions

The broad management issues and challenges concerning assessment of risk include:

- Taking a broad and balanced view of uncertainty and fortune[10]
- Ensuring that directors and senior management have a thorough understanding of the risks and opportunities in the industry and the business
- The trade-off between risk and reward in the various business activities[11]
- Establishing the current point in the business cycle and whether there is a forthcoming inflection in the curve of the business cycle
- The kinds of failure which have substantially impacted the business in the past or that have affected its competitors[12]
- The need for specific disaster recovery plans for functions such as information systems and technology[13]
- The impact of failure owing to natural disasters
- The impact of failures by suppliers. Consider:
  - Suppliers providing raw materials too late
  - Penalties having to be paid to customers for late delivery.[14]

---

10 A lack of information certainty is often associated with maintaining an apocalyptic perspective and worst-case precautionary thinking leading to premodern anxieties of hidden forces instead of taking responsibility for destiny. The dramatisation of events for entertainment should not be confused with either poor planning (including balance of probabilities and risk assessment or inability to anticipate outcomes) or incompetent action. Long before the enlightenment, Petrarch (1366/1991) proposed humanity should control actively its destiny.

11 The reference for a risk free return is provided by the current short-term rate and long-term rate for guaranteed government bonds.

12 Fortune and Peters (1995) suggest some difficulties in the approach that advocates learning from failure.

13 With the outsourcing of information systems and technology this cannot be made contractually the responsibility of the vendor. The business must also specify the nature of the services it requires in the event of a disaster and the response time and quality for services that are provided.

14 Both Airbus Industries and Boeing have paid substantial penalties to their customers for the late delivery of aircraft (the Airbus 380 and Boeing 787 respectively). Working capital is then also greater than it should otherwise be.

- The likelihood that customer orders will be cancelled or delivery delayed without the customer incurring any additional costs[15]
- The areas of the business in which a coincidence of failures or a sequence of failures would have catastrophic consequences.

The principal tools and techniques for assessment of risk include:

- Conducting a general risk assessment. Consider:
  - Documenting risks in all functions of the business
  - Periodically reviewing all risks
  - Determining where to focus risk management attention to obtain improved business performance
  - Having insurance or other mitigating plans to ensure continuity of the business with minimal disruption.
- Testing the effectiveness of plans for risk management. Consider:
  - Whether the proposed responses are workable[16]
  - Whether there suitable and sufficient resources will be preserved and available to ensure continuity of the business
- Exploring financial risks.[17] Consider:
  - Exposure to interest rate changes using gap analysis, duration analysis and value at risk
  - Exposure to foreign exchange changes
  - Exposure to commodity price changes.
- Using internal controls to support operational risks. Consider:
  - Ensuring compliance with applicable legislation and licences
  - Ensure reliability of reporting of financial and non-financial information
  - Assurance of the economy, efficiency and effectiveness of operations
  - Providing directors and senior managers with independent evidence on the operations of the business.
- Ensuring basic controls operate for routine transactions. Consider:
  - Whether transactions are valid or authorised
  - Whether the transaction is recorded accurately and in the correct period

---

15 The order or contract may specify progress payments are to be made by the customer for work-in-process. The absence of such arrangements will further increase the level of working capital.

16 This will include verifying with customers and suppliers that the documented arrangements are acceptable to them. Frequently this is overlooked or the full implications of the disruption are not explained to suppliers and customers resulting in endorsement of the plan and then subsequent complaints that it is unacceptable.

17 This involves matching the use of funds to their source. For example, short-term sources fund current assets and seasonal or cyclical working capital while long-term sources fund non-current assets.

- – Whether the physical products or services associated with the transaction are properly handled.
- Creating limited redundancy[18]
- Designing, implementing and documenting internal controls with sufficient strength and reliability which can be assessed by the auditor
- Responding to recommendations by the auditor on improvements to internal controls.[19]

The managerial decisions and judgements concerning assessment of risk include:

- What is the likelihood of incurring high losses of business reputation?
- What is the likelihood of incurring substantial damage to brand image?
- What are the likely levels of losses arising from fraud or theft?
- What is the protection and obligations[20] stated in formal contracts with suppliers?
- Is there sufficient investigation of credit risk before opening an account allowing a customer to charge purchase products or services to their account?
- What arrangements exist to obtain the most favourable price for raw material or inventory?[21]
- What arrangements exist for finalising a new contract before the existing contract expires?
- What is the likelihood that a contract may be prematurely terminated?[22]

In summary, the assessment of risk requires assessment of both the likelihood of an event occurring and the severity of its impact on the business. These should be documented across the business and be reviewed periodically to ensure that where assessed risks have changed there is an acceptable response plan.

---

18 Redundancy may be necessary to avoid loss of revenue. For example, anticipating mechanical breakdown or software malfunction will result in installing more than one ticket dispensing machine.

19 The response will identify for each of the auditor's recommendations whether it is accepted, accepted in part or rejected. The basis for a rejection may be that it does not have an impact on the true and fair presentation of the financial statement of the business, that costs will exceed benefits, or that the claimed problem is addressed through other controls.

20 These may be aimed at ensuring that supply is assured and specify that it will occur at agreed intervals, be triggered by specific events (e.g.minimum stock levels) or on nominated delivery dates.

21 It may be necessary to create an inventory forecasting system for those products that can be forecast for a 1 month or longer period. This may create an opportunity to issue a tender and asking other suppliers to bid for the contract.

22 There may also be clauses in the contract which provide for termination of the contract when its terms are not fulfilled.

10.4 Foster creativity and innovation

Innovation refers to an improvement in a product or process.[23] The improvement may be incremental or major.

The broad management issues and challenges that arise for creativity and innovation[24] include:

- Assessing the extent of government funding or concessions for research and development (R&D)[25]

- Determining whether innovation in the industry is punctuated equilibrium or continuous change[26]

- Relying on external innovation or creating its own innovation[27]

- Overcoming the high costs of gaining relevant knowledge[28]

- Having sufficient financial foresight (that is, budgeting cash flows and planning for capital investment)

- Avoiding overcapitalisation

- Recognising the balance between autonomous entrepreneurship and strategy[29]

- Having an understanding of the market[30] and the entrepreneurship appropriate to it

---

23 It is usual to differentiate between an invention and an economic innovation. An invention is a discovery, which is making manifest a new form, composition or process. An innovation is the commercialisation of an idea. It may refer to either the process itself or any output from the process. An innovation may therefore utilise an invention.

24 Drucker (1985/1994) suggests that innovative opportunity exists where there are unexpected successes or unexpected failures within an industry, incongruities and demographics. This means that there are entrepreneurial opportunities even in declining industries.

25 Two schools of thought take opposing positions. Baumol (2002) considers innovation essential in market economies with competition stimulating research while Romer (1990) uses an argument of public good to support government funding of research. Innovation may create technologies and management techniques that transforms markets and sustains an initial competitive advantage according to a study of large enterprises by Chandler (1990). Tax concessions may redirect R&D away from activities with a higher return (Hall & van Reenen 2000).

26 Since both kinds of change rely on product innovation (Burgelman 1991) the apparent oscillation between stability and change (Abernathy & Utterback 1978) may overlook rapid and continuous change that is part of the culture of the business (Brown & Eisenhardt 1997).

27 Dell formerly relied on Intel and Microsoft to provide it with innovation; in consequence it invested less than 1% of revenues in research and development. Dell now allows customers to customise the design of their desktop or laptop and introduces features to make it stand out as innovative.

28 In science the high cost may be associated with both basic research as well as technological application of knowledge (e.g.Lynn 1991; information is more likely to be pooled among leading researchers (e.g.Hippel 1991) rather than bartered or bought (Merton 1942/1973).

29 This may be more apparent in diversified businesses where strategy needs to be malleable (Burgelman 1983).

30 Christensen (1997/2003) cautions against placing high emphasis on satisfying the current needs of customers. It diverts a company from adapting or adopting new products that will meet the unstated or future needs of customers. Technologies that disrupt or redefine the competition in markets are not as good as currently available products but which have the advantages of simplicity, and convenience at an inexpensive price. This can disrupt or redefine competition in markets by appealing either to new customers or to existing customers who do not demand the existing level of features or performance. In contrast, a sustaining innovation targets demanding, high-end customers offering better incremental or breakthrough performance (Christensen, 1997).

- Balancing discipline and rigor with creativity and freedom[31] to pursue innovation
- Identifying appropriate sources of innovation[32]
- Ensuring there is a market for the innovation[33]
- Ensuring an appropriate legal structure and control over any resulting products[34]
- Having a suitable underlying invention or technology
- Ensuring strategic fit.

The principal tools and techniques[35] for creativity and innovation include:

- Allowing time for creative opportunities
- Obtaining expert input on innovation[36]
- Pressure to innovate with limited resources[37]
- The s curve of diffusion of innovations[38]
- Experimentation and prototyping
- Providing creativity and brainstorming opportunities separate from the routine of the business[39]
- Appreciating the forms of technology improvement[40]

---

31 Brown (2009) argues that design thinkers rely on rigorous observation of how spaces are used and how objects and services occupy them. They seek to discover patterns and to synthesise new ideas. Design thinking is a method in which genius, in the end, is not required

32 For example, end-users develop innovation for their own purposes. Hippel (1994) argues that end-user innovation is both of critical importance and often overlooked.

33 The popular Hewlett-Packard laser printer was a failure on the first attempt (HP 2680) after five years development. The third attempt (HP2686A, later retitled as LaserJet) was an unexpected success.

34 Patents may be used as a competitive weapon to (a) increase the costs of competitors through licensing fees to secure a price advantage and/or (b) to distract competitors and reduce customer confidence by slowing down the momentum competitors have with their new products through legal challenge. Copyright and royalties may affect the creators of artistic works. John Lennon and Paul McCartney lacked creative control and intellectual property over record and publishing royalties and sheet music sales for their Beatles songs (Southall & Perry 2006: 17, 33).

35 Techniques from the innovator's toolkit such as workshops, user observations of the systems that they work with, prototyping, role playing, storytelling, scenario building and brainstorming assist in building an innovation capability but are rarely sufficient by themselves to generate innovation (Brown 2009). Similarly the addition of organisational anthropologists, a chief innovation officer or slogans are unlikely to be more than short-term band-aids.

36 Under Leo Fender, the Fender Musical Instrument Company developed the electric bass and created solid body electric guitars (Telecaster, Stratocaster, Mustang and Jaguar). The common approach with them all was that the design was refined on the basis of expert players using the instruments.

37 Innovation with limited resources may occur with individuals or teams. An example of a team innovation involved the need to fix the carbon dioxide filters (scrubbers) using only the materials available on Apollo 13. It was tested by the engineers at Mission Control before the astronauts built the filter the engineers designed (Kranz 2000/2001; Lovell 1994/2000).

38 An s-curve is a Cartesian mapping of the growth of revenue or productivity against time. It recognises that new products have a product lifecycle but it also implies there will be successive s-curves and that a large number of products fail to produce normal returns (Rogers 1962/2003).

39 This has been described as a 'skunk works.' The term skunk works was first introduced during World War 2 by engineers at Lockheed Martin Corporation, who were tasked with building a fighter jet for the United States Government (Rich & Janos 1994).

40 These include miniaturisation (e.g.mobile phone), improved display/presentation (e.g.flat panel television) and increased output quality (e.g.digital camera).

- Scope for merchandising.[41]

The managerial decisions and judgements for creativity and innovation include:

- What will foster an innovation culture? Consider:
  - Does the culture of the business support innovation?
  - How can a greater proportion of employees be involved in innovation?[42]
  - How can we empower employees to innovate?
  - Is safety being compromised?[43]
- What will facilitate specific innovation? Consider:
  - What independent knowledge confirms the anticipated demand?
  - What are the risks compared with simply exploiting an established demand?

In summary, innovation contributes to business growth. It is achieved through processes with targets, funding, resources and accountability. It occurs in a culture where opportunities generate value earning products and services.

10.5 Recognise emerging situations and intractable problems

Some problems emerge slowly and almost imperceptibly and are frequently ignored until action becomes unavoidable. Some problems are given attention but remain unresolved either through incorrect identification, inadequate resourcing, poor project management or a lack of wholehearted commitment from senior managers. In many cases problem solving is improved where there is diversity in the group.[44]

The broad management issues and challenges in recognising emerging situations and intractable problems include:

---

41 The tension between merchandising and protecting an image was recognised by Brian Epstein who licensed the Beatles (Southall & Perry 2006: 34–35.) setting an example followed in entertainment. For example George Lucas brokered a lesser payment for directing Star Wars in return for wholly owned licensing rights for merchandising (Lewis 2003/2007).

42 One approach is to create a project team or task force (Waterman, 1990/1992: 16). It may be populated with employees or external advisors. The team is empowered to work quickly, trust each other and approach senior management to obtain answers.

43 A number of safety issues arose with the design of the Boeing 747. A strongly conservative risk approach was adopted (Sutter & Spenser YEAR? 128, 130–31) characterised by plain speaking (p 115) and commitment to sound argument (p 127).

44 Investigations by Page (2007) suggested that groups with members with the best individual ability were frequently outperformed by a random and therefore diverse group. He makes claims that greater identity diversity in groups produces benenfits 'not every time, not in every context' (p xxii) but where it is relevant to the conditions (p xxiii).

- Establishing the salience of the situation[45]
- Establishing the initial state of a situation
- Establishing the characteristics of the problem
- Determining whether the problem is new or intractable[46]
- Agreeing the goal to be reached[47]
- Identifying relevant assumptions
- Identifying relevant prior knowledge
- Categorising the problem appropriately.[48]

The principal tools and techniques for recognising emerging situations and intractable problems[49] include:

- Root cause analysis[50]
- Five 'whys'[51]
- Statistical process control charts
- Fault tree analysis
- Ishikawa or fishbone diagram
- Pareto analysis
- Social complexity.[52]

The managerial decisions and judgements in recognising emerging situations and intractable problems include:

- What will be the terms of reference for investigating the problem or opportunity?
- What is the type and number of resources to be allocated to prepare preliminary findings?
- What time is allowed in which to undertake and report findings?

---

45 The need for action and the likely consequences if action is postponed or the issue is ignored may be clear to operational employees but dismissed by their manager. The consequences are discussed in Chapter 4 (Maturity: Responding to reduced revenue, profitability or erosion of market share).

46 An intractable problem is one which is resistant to resolution. This may be because it has multiple causes and not all have been resolved, or it may be that it has been rekindled by unaddressed factors.

47 The exact nature of the goal may be unclear or the path to the goal may be unclear (Robertson 2001: 4–5).

48 This refers not only to strategic or operational but also to the kind of threat or opportunity it presents.

49 The way in which a problem is represented often depends upon the form or description provided when initially encountered. Robertson (2001: 74) suggests five ways out of this kind of impasse. They are: (1) focusing on a different aspect of the problem; (2) looking at extreme conditions; (3) using an analogy; (4) viewing the problem differently; or (5) relaxing constraints that appear to be part of the problem.

50 There are many discussions of root-cause analysis. Kepner-Tregoe (1965) situate it in a broader framework.

51 The objective is to (a) avoid assumptions (b) overcome errors in logic and (c) trace the causal chain in direct increments from symptoms to root cause, (d) to reveal the nature of the problem as well as its solution.

52 A social complexity approach avoids a linear analysis and considers the emergent properties of the situation (Oliver & Snowden 2005).

- What form the report should take?
- Who will receive copies of the report?[53]
- Has there been consultation with all relevant stakeholders?
- Are the recommendations for new arrangements sustainable?

In summary, timely problem recognition which is poorly actioned may lead to a poor analysis. The problem may have been previously recognised but the action taken did not resolve it. The process for recognising a problem should also capture sufficient characteristics to ensure that there are clear tests to establish whether it has been reduced or removed as well as to detect any recurrence.

Chapter summary

There are many ways in which the business benefits from the intangible resources of employee ability and judgement. The ability of employees to recognise and respond to the qualities of a leader is a key factor in the success of the business. Throughout the business everyone needs to exercise fiscal responsibility with a cash focus. The uncertainty of business demands the ability to conduct a competent risk assessment of strategy and operations. New products and services are dependent upon expertise and innovation. Finally, the changing business environment requires recognition of any emerging situations and intractable problems. The ability and judgement of employees in these areas relies on information as a resource.

---

53 While the terms of reference may make clear to whom the report should be addressed, there is usually a wider audience which includes the stakeholdes and those responsible for the implementation of the approved recommendation.

11 Recognise information as a resource

Business can use information as a resource. For ease of comprehension the terms 'data', 'information' and 'knowledge' are used interchangeably[1] in this chapter.

Forms of financial and non-financial information

There are many forms of financial and non-financial information. Traditional pen and paper manifestations of information remain common. These may take the form of public documents or private notes including annotations, marginal marks and other forms of evidence left by readers which lead to the construction of new or additional meanings (Jackson 2005: 141–49). Various file formats (e.g.proprietary word processor, proprietary spreadsheet, database, 'ASCII' text, mark-up language) exist. These software applications can also produce text, graphical and multimedia output in both hard copy and electronic formats.

Use of technologies

The popularity of digital technologies (for example, e-mail, messaging via mobile phone) has replaced some traditional forms of communication including face-to-face interaction, meetings, workshops and small group gatherings. Improvements in networking and connectivity have facilitated communication within the business and between the business and other stakeholders.

Misrepresentation and misinformation

There is considerable debate concerning the adequacy of legislative protection and sanctions for misrepresentation and misinformation. Clear examples of failure have occurred with leveraged borrowing schemes, consumer investment schemes and some major public companies. There are many factors involved including high rates of return, excessive asset valuations and natural disasters. While new and formidable legislation is often introduced (e.g. Sarbanes-Oxley Act in USA) there is little abatement of failure and fraud. It is arguable that more legislation simply provides more loopholes and more scope for business failure and fraud.[2]

---

1 The paper by Repo (1989) makes clear that there can be no single definition of information and knowledge since giving primacy to different characteristics results in economists, accounting researchers and management scientists assessing the value of information differently. Zuboff (1988) provides one of the earliest discussions of the information realm of the business being distinct from observation through physical completion of processes.

2 More legislation increases the likelihood of ambiguity until cases clarify the legislation and any conflicts with other legislation. The amplification of legislation by regulations introduces new opportunities to avoid compliance or comply with the letter but not the spirit of the legislation. Proponents of this position include Clarke, Dean and Oliver (1997/2003) and Clarke and Dean (2007) and Salter (2008). Chambers (1947/1986: 273) also comments that 'It is curious that only at

Topics in recognising information as a resource

Recognising information as a resource has five Topics:

1. Measure resources using financial and non-financial information
2. Report on financial and non-financial performance using a hierarchy
3. Interlink business processes and systems using their dual function
4. Use information to comply with regulations and standards
5. High reliance on communication within the business and between the business and its stakeholders.

11.1 Measure resources using financial and non-financial information

Business uses many forms of measurement. Most measures are predetermined because they are part of a system using digital technologies record transactions and business events. Both the financial and non-financial resources of the business[3] are measured. Investment criteria are not always possible.

The broad management issues and challenges that arise from measuring resources using financial and non-financial information include:

- The assumption that users will know what to measure and that the information will be available in a recordable format

- Having a suitable mix of financial and non-financial measures of success to evaluate how a business is performing[4]

- Ensuring the intangibles[5] are contributors to the annual plan and strategic intent

- Having sufficient lead indicators to get forewarning of impending problems so timely action can be taken[6]

- Selecting a manageable set of items to be counted or measured.[7]

---

the point where the interests of creditors are seriously at hazard are the financial statements of firms ... consistent with the money valuations that ... [are] ... appropriate.'

3 While accountants prepare much of the information they are not the prime users of accounting reports (except where they have a responsibility to handle compliance issues).

4 Profitability is a measure of success not a goal in its own right (Drucker 1974; 2001/2005).

5 The popular championing of intangibles is scrutinised by Walker (2009b) who concludes that it may distract readers from information which affects market standing.

6 The option of using external indicators is often overlooked although they may suggest opportunities to satisfy customers with current and new products or services.

7 The basic questions (Breadmore 1971: 54) are (1a) What to measure? (2c) How to measure? and (3a) When to stop measuring? However the second question may be expanded to create a broader framework by some additional questions including (1b) Why is it important, (2a) What is already known? (2b) What are the consequences of being wrong? (2c)

The principal tools and techniques to measure resources using financial and non-financial information include:

- Adopting traditional financial measures. Consider:
  - Direct financial outcome measures such as revenue and profitability
  - Investment criteria[8]
  - Customer focused financial measures.
- Focus on intangible measures. Consider:
  - Delivery lead time
  - Service response time
  - Employee morale.
- Use comparative measures. Consider:
  - Position (for example, rank position) summary figures
  - Variation[9] in measures including:
    - Trends monitored over time in terms of dollar or unit terms and percentage movement
    - Comparison of actual results to targets in terms of forecast and previous corresponding period
    - Ratios and indices which restate figures as proportions or using a base amount as a reference.[10]

The managerial decisions and judgements that arise from measuring resources using financial and non-financial information include:

- What will be measured?[11]
- What form of performance measurement will be used? Consider:
  - Are KPI's (Key Performance Indicators) appropriate?
  - Are CSF's (Critical Success Factors) appropriate?
  - Do Service Delivery Outcomes exist?

What is the cost of measurement? (2d) What are the critical observations for different options? and (2e) How can errors be avoided (Hubbard 2007)?

8 The evaluation of stocks can consider well-known four factors: (1) price to earnings, (2) price to free cash flow, (3) price to net tangible assets, that is price to book and (4) gross yield. Lynch (1989/2000) comments on the institutional investor and mutual funds and how small investors can take advantage of what information they possess to uncover investment opportunities by researching before investing.

9 Variability could be expressed according to the formula: (Maximum value less minimum value) divided by the mean value.

10 For financial analyses this is the common sizing approach. For other analyses it involves restating items reported as a percentage of a specific item chosen as the base amount.

11 The items selected for measurement signal to employees what is valued and develop an organisation culture that in turn affects operations.

      – Will a Balanced ScoreCard (BSC)[12] be informative?

      – Can stories or anecdotes[13] be used?

- Are there likely to be irreconcilable conflicts between different measures?
- When will reviews be scheduled to ensure the selected measures remain representative and useful?

In summary, measuring resources using financial and non-financial information management depends upon careful planning and selection of items to measure. A variety of measurement techniques are available. The next Topic deals with arranging the measures in a hierarchy.

11.2 Report on financial and non-financial performance using a hierarchy

The objective of reporting is to provide up-to-date and reliable information to authorised recipients. Reporting on financial and non-financial performance should use a hierarchy to ensure consistency across the business[14] with reference to its strategic intent.[15] The hierarchy will extend horizontally as well as vertically to avoid redundant overlapping reporting.

The broad management issues and challenges for reporting on financial and non-financial performance include:

- Providing compensation or incentives that do not produce dysfunctional behaviour[16]
- Considering the quality of the underlying data on which reports rely[17]
- Deciding the manner in which external reports will be produced. Consider:

---

12 The Balanced Scorecard (Kaplan & Norton 2004) requires a causal relationship between a perspective and the next higher perspective. This may be difficult both to select and to verify.

13 There is a strong tendency to account for many aspects of life (such as business decisions, careers, life events and social relationships) in terms of 'make or break' moments that determine the ensuring years. This can be counterproductive because psychology informs us that we are more likely to select and reframe the facts to fit the demands of the narrative. A narrative or story allows a separation between KPI's and client feedback so it is difficult to manipulate the results.

14 Integration of the measures is essential (Allen 1982).

15 Strategic intent is intended to create a dynamic strategy. It is designed to overcome a static approach to competition brought about by considering strategic fit and competitive advantage and techniques such as portfolio planning and industry analysis which are readily decoded by competitors. Strategic intent results in the setting of medium-term challenges to focus employee effort (Hamel & Prahalad 1989).

16 Employees may come to depend on the increased income resulting from compensation or incentives and manipulate their behaviour to ensure the expected revenue is earned (Austin 1996; Hofstede 1968/2003; Ridgway 1956).

17 Data is a resource. Frequently it cannot be readily integrated (Brackett 2000: 3). There is also a drift to its quality being poor (Brackett 2000: 11). The data itself may be a problem. Redman (1996: 27–29) suggests that 'it is rarely practical to improve all data at once' (p 28) and the rate of data creating and replacement (p 29) of its turnover are often a guide. There is also the possibility of deficiencies in the structure of the data/database. Olsen (2003: 212) finds that attempts to improve performance may have led to changes in the structure or functionality.

- The use of financial information to convey the impact of activities and processes on the 'bottom line'[18]

- Using non-financial information to supplement financial information[19]

- Deciding the level of detail concerning products or services in reports.[20]

- Deciding the internal reports to be made available to the Board and senior management. Consider:

  - Performance and productivity reports

  - Proposals concerning investments

  - Evaluation reports on the benefits achieved from investments in projects

  - Status reports.

- Allowing the production of tactical management reports as part of reporting from systems. Consider:

  - Input reports[21]

  - Status reports[22]

  - Detailed productivity and variance reports.

- For any new report. Consider:

  - Purpose

  - Timeliness of the information it contains

  - Frequency of issue:

    o Periodic reports to provide information for internal users

    o Periodic reports to meet external reporting deadlines

    o Ad hoc reports on specified topics.[23]

  - Whether to make available aggregated or consolidation reports[24]

---

18 Financial performance measures may promote short-term behaviour as they focus on outcomes or measure what has already happened. They are lag indicators that are influenced by accounting choices.

19 Non-financial performance measures capture other important aspects of organisational functioning (e.g. innovation). They provide a more complete view. In addition, they can be used as lead indicators of future financial performance. However their development may be ad hoc and unfocused using data which is unreliable. Where there is a range of possible measures it can be difficult to select the key measures which are the drivers of future performance.

20 Usually individual product line items are aggregated one level higher into product groups. If there are considerable products and product groups they too may be aggregated a further level into product supergroups. The sales volume or dollar amounts may then be conveniently summarised. For example, sales by product group such as all passenger cars.

21 For example, the attendance summary of employees present during a shift.

22 These include production shift reports for a factory and the quantity of finished products held in a warehouse.

23 Ad-hoc or special purpose reports fulfil information requests which cannot be anticipated. They may require special collection of data or re-analysis of data that have already been collected. For example, the vehicles sold where customers have requested applying decals by the factory or by the dealer.

24 These reports contain a variety of data aggregated owing to the period. For example, total dollar sales summarised for each business unit for the month of January 2009.

- Whether to create exception reports[25]
- Whether there is a need for benchmarking against competitor or industry data.

The principal tools and techniques for reporting on financial and non-financial performance include:

- Non-financial measures including customer satisfaction, repeat business of customers (customer loyalty); and long-term favourable contractual arrangements with customers
- Measures which are rewards for achievement or exceeding sales objectives[26]
- Employee morale fluctuates at different times[27]
- Employee turnover
- Hard copy and screen-based reports. Consider:
  - Assistance in interpreting reports[28]
  - Seeking corroborating information
  - Seeking supplementary information
  - Using external sources of information which may be less precise.

The managerial decisions and judgements for reporting on financial and non-financial performance include:

- When will strategy for products or services, customers and suppliers be reviewed?
- What budgeted levels of revenue and expense are expected?[29]
- Do managers consider that the costs reported for their responsibility centre are fair and reasonable?
- What to do with unprofitable customers?
- Whether incentives should be offered to reward achievement of goals?
- How will standards be set to the 'right' level so they motivate without being too hard or too easy to achieve?
- What proportion of profit should be retained for growth and for business continuity?

---

25 These are desirable when events occur outside routine parameters. They show unusual or unexpected outcomes. For example, access made between midnight and 6 am into a high value inventory area.

26 These include payment of commissions to sales employees; payment of bonuses to employees based on achievement of targets; and payment of incentives to employees for exhibiting appropriate behaviour.

27 Morale is affected by actions such as disciplining of an employee, retrenchment and renegotiation of employee conditions.

28 Cognitive limitations affect the interpretation of information (Miller 1956). Using graphical displays (e.g. charts and graphs) may be helpful. Situating figures within tables that encompass several time periods may allow trends to be more easily discerned.

29 It will usually cover the next twelve month period in detail. This should be reasonably accurate. It will also specify the following two years in summary. This will be a best 'guess-timate'. This is a static budget and it has to be flexed to take into account actual levels of sales and production.

- What proportion of profit should be returned to stakeholders for risking their investment?
- What operational changes are necessary?[30]
- What actions are necessary to retain and attract customers?

In summary, a hierarchy of financial and non-financial measures are used to compare performance against the annual plan and strategic intent and selected variances are investigated. In some cases a decision has to be made or a judgement reached for which there is insufficient information or for which the information is uncertain.[31] In those cases management will have assured itself that it has made reasonable effort.

11.3 Interlink business processes and systems using their dual function

Interlinked[32] business processes and systems may have many unappreciated effects on the business since they can inhibit information sharing or result in separate sources of authoritative information that are apparently contradictory. A business process has a dual function: it is the centre of operations events, that is physical outcomes and generates information events.[33]

The broad management issues and challenges that arise from interlinked business processes and systems with dual functions include:

- Recognising where increased working capital arises from poor linkages. Consider:
  - Increased in accounts receivables
  - Additional inventory held through either increased safety stock or non-use of purchases
  - Production that incurs overtime and higher than budgeted other expenses.
- Insufficient recognition of increased customer demand for products and services
- Additional raw materials or merchandise will have to be sourced and suppliers may force increased costs on the business for these unplanned purchases or for expediting delivery to the business to meet production schedules

---

30 These may include: the level and number of employees based on sales or work programs; the likelihood of achieving sales targets and the extent of control over expenses.

31 Examples of the options may be considered to improve our state of knowledge or reduce the error of an estimate include using (1) Fermi questions for market estimates (Fermi 1965; Fermi 1995; Weinstein & Adam 2008), (2) confidence intervals to calibrate personal judgement, (3) sensitivity analyses to avoid using averages and (4) broad estimates as a starting point. The effort depends upon the size and frequency of the decision.

32 These linkages and the process sequences may change over time or in response to incidents that directly affect the business or that are observed by the business.

33 Since a physical event contains a virtual event there is the tendency for the physical event to become the focus of attention.

- There will be an increase in after-sales support and perhaps an increase in product warranty claims.

The principal tools and techniques to analyse and design the interlinking of business processes and systems with dual functions include:

- Data flow modelling
- Entity relationship analysis
- Unified modelling language (UML) analysis
- Flow charting
- Value chain analysis (see Chapter 16).

The managerial decisions and judgements that arise from interlinked business processes and systems with dual functions include:

- Are information flows being filtered, diverted or suppressed?
- Are costs understood in terms of the business context (strategy, product life cycle, supplier relationships and customer relationships)?
- What is the profitability of products?
- What is the profitability of customers?
- Is the way in which direct and indirect costs are attached to business processes optimal?
- Should production or merchandising of selected products or services be abandoned?
- Is the source of defects or faults being attributed to the correct originating process?

In summary, interlinked business processes may be closely or poorly coupled. The value chain (Porter 1985/1998, 1987) offers a useful means of assessing the coupling and the value obtained by the business.[34]

11.4 Use information to comply with regulations and standards

All businesses are required to comply with applicable international, country specific legislation and state, province or territory regulations and standards. Much of the time of directors and senior management is consumed by compliance work.[35]

Using information for the production of compliance reports which are mandatory under legislation and distribution to an external authority is one form of compliance. Income-tax

---

34 The alternative is devising entirely new processes (Hammer 1990; Hammer & Champy 1993/2001).

35 Discussion in the press often confuses the role of directors to pursue business initiatives with the responsibility of directors to ensure compliance with a myriad of regulations and standards.

returns are a common example. Information may itself be an evidentiary record. E-mail is a common example.

The broad management issues and challenges that centre on compliance[36] with regulations and standards include:

- The many obligations of financial legislation.[37] Consider:
  - Registration for taxation purposes
  - Eligibility and deductions relating to the income tax law and the consumption tax law
  - Reporting deadlines and the penalties if judged to have infringed the legislation
  - There are also specific disclosure requirements for public companies (listed on the stock exchange).

- Another compliance area is the responsibility of senior management for the safe working conditions of the employees:
  - There are occupational health and safety requirements that an employer must observe[38]
  - There are obligations for ensuring employees are trained to operate machines
  - Even in offices employers are responsible for providing a safe working environment[39]
  - There are obligations for reporting and investigating accidents in the workplace.

- Businesses must also comply with standards which may have the weight of legislative sanctions. Consider:
  - Accounting and auditing standards
  - Quality control standards.

- Employee health and security protective legislation. Consider:
  - Remuneration and benefits may be prescribed as part of the 'Basic Wage' or specific industry awards
  - The same awards may also stipulate arrangements for disciplinary action
  - The employment conditions for employees may also include grievance handling and appeal arrangements[40]
  - Procedures that management must follow to retrench or dismiss an employee.

---

36 The amount of regulation is often referred to 'red tape'.

37 Since legislation often changes in response to instances of serious business failure, changes in the financial information that will need to be reported can often be anticipated.

38 For example, an office-based business must ensure its employees have a safe working environment (chairs, desks, cabinets and cupboards etc). In the construction industry directors are liable for employee safety as a criminal offence.

39 For example electrical appliances and extension cords must be tested to confirm they are not dangerous.

40 Some of the major areas where business has been found to have treated employees poorly are in the areas of male-female discrimination, bullying and sexual harassment. For example, professional firms are the subject of ongoing litigation in this area.

- Registration, licences or permits for the business itself. Consider:
  - Adopting a business or trading name to help customers recognise the business
  - An internet domain name.
- Regulations specific to particular industries. Consider:
  - Hygiene in the preparation of food and purity (non-adulteration) in serving food
  - Training in the responsible service of beer and alcoholic spirits
  - Inspection of the road worthiness of vehicles using public roads
  - Permits to transport inflammable or hazardous solids or liquids permits.

The principal tools and techniques for compliance with regulations and standards include:

- Designing internal controls to facilitate observance of authorised processes
- Arranging for internal and external audits of key processes, responsibilities and programs of work
- Introducing computer based information systems to force employees to observe the desired processes
- Using the services of consultants to document approved processes and systems
- Using the services of consultants to provide an assurance that the documented approved processes and systems are being observed.

The managerial decisions and judgements concerning compliance with regulations and standards include:

- Who will sign off as responsible for complying with government legislation (statute and regulations), standards and licencing?
- Are all licences current?
- Does the business comply with new or revised obligations under legislation, standards or licences?

In summary, there are a wide range of matters requiring compliance. Often there are specific statutory penalties for the business and its officers (senior management) for breaches of the law. In some cases individuals may also be subject to criminal penalties. A court finding may be followed by disciplinary actions by the professional associations if the person is a member.

11.5 High reliance on communication within the business and between the business and its stakeholders

The modern business is highly reliant on various forms of communication.[41] Factors leading to this reliance include decentralisation of the business, geographical dispersal of stakeholders, differences in time zones, the reducing cost of technology-based communications and the expectation of status reports or feedback.

There are many forms of communication. Much of the financial and non-financial information (e.g. tables,[42] charts,[43] and multimedia graphics) are asynchronous. Recent social networking (e.g. Facebook, Twitter and blogs) are also asynchronous.

The broad management issues and challenges that arise from a high reliance on communication include:

- The assumption that communications will be available when wanted and fully operative
- The balance between formal communication by management and use of informal communication[44] by employees
- Deciding the manner in which external reports will be disseminated
- Deciding the internal reports to be made available to the Board and senior management
- Allowing the production of tactical management reports as part of reporting from systems
- Ensuring adequate attention is given to the content of communication[45]
- Determining whether information has been filtered, or concealed
- Determining whether information is given a public relations spin.[46]

The principal tools and techniques to deal with a high reliance on communication include:

- Selection of devices that use standard protocols and that are compatible

---

41 The justifiable scepticism of each new form of communication may partly depend upon which form is considered culturally superior at the time (Baron 2009: 45–46). The succession of technologies (writing, the telegraph, telephone, typewriter and computer) all had their detractors.

42 Tables permit quantitiative data to be set out in an easy-to-read manner which also facilitates comparison. How to present data in tabular form is discussed by Rosenberg (1968).

43 A chart or graphic visually depicts data in order to give a more profound understanding. Early discussion is Zeisel (1985). A more recent treatment is Tufte (1983/2001).

44 The formal organisation is planned by management (Blau & Schoenherr 1971). Informal organisation involves ad hoc actual behaviour (Katz 1965: 208).

45 Cherry (1957/1966: 279–80) refers to the cocktail party problem. It is the ability listen and to follow a particular speaker while simultaneously giving attention to other separate conversations.

46 Spin is making unfavourable information as favourable as possible. This may be done by media advisors, public relations advisors or the media itself. Examples can be found after googling 'airline disasters', 'oil spills' and 'taxation'.

- Security techniques to prevent business information being accessed or read by unauthorised individuals[47]
- Three modes of content communication. Consider:
  - Business case (or proposal)
  - Feasibility
  - Program evaluation.
- Three layout modes for communication. Consider:
  - Memos (memoranda)
  - Reports
  - Presentations.
- Technology for communication. Consider:
  - Hardcopy
  - Softcopy.
- Meetings that are conducted according to best practice precepts. Consider:
  - Have a written agenda distributed before the meeting so that participants can come prepared[48]
  - Be short (maximum of one hour)
  - Identify the persons responsible for action, the expected action and the deadline during the conduct of the meeting so those responsible can raise any issues
  - Document minutes of the meeting[49]
  - Distribute the minutes very soon after the meeting.
- Multiple means to access reports[50]
- Use of anecdotes and micro narratives in conjunction with sensemaking.[51]

The managerial decisions and judgements that arise from reliance on communication include:

- What will be communicated?
- Should a meeting be used to serve other than communication needs?[52]

---

47 This may include passwords or equivalent, encryption of data or not storing data on mobile devices.

48 The agenda will list the items in priority order and provide any supporting documents.

49 One form of minutes includes: (a) the points discussed, (b) responsibilities and (c) deadlines. Minutes should be distributed promptly after the meeting.

50 This may include the use of laptop computers, personal digital assistant devices and smartphones.

51 The aim is not to rework an anecdote or micro narrative to give it the kind of into a plot that would be acceptable in a Hollywood movie production. This leads to plots centred around one of seven themes (1) Rags to riches; (2) Overcoming the monster; (3) The quest; (4) A voyage and return; (5) Comedy; (6) Tragedy; and (7) Rebirth (Brooker 2004). These are dramatic devices and stories in business should be far simpler, shorter and less structured.

52 Some represent 'power plays' between attendees competing for senior management attention or organisational resources. Some are held to announce already reached decisions.

In summary, communication depends upon accurate and timely information reports and communication. In some cases a decision has to be made or a judgement reached for which there is insufficient information or for which the information is uncertain.[53] In those cases management will have assured itself that it has made reasonable effort.

Chapter summary

Recognising information as a resource begins by measuring resources using financial and non-financial information. It also involves reporting on financial and non-financial performance using a hierarchy. The interlinking of information between business processes and systems can avoid many unwanted discrepancies and errors. Information can demonstrate compliance with regulations and standards. Finally there is a high reliance on communication within the business and between the business and other stakeholders. Resources are not simply inert objects and it is often desirable to improve their tangible benefits.

---

53 Examples of the options may be considered to improve our state of knowledge or reduce the error of an estimate include using (1) Fermi questions for market estimates (Fermi 1965; Fermi 1995; Weinstein & Adam 2008), (2) confidence intervals to calibrate personal judgement, (3) sensitivity analyses to avoid using averages and (4) broad estimates as a starting point. The effort depends upon the size and frequency of the decision.

12 Improve the tangible benefits from resources

Improving the profitability and productivity of resources is an ongoing preoccupation of business. No single approach or method is likely to be perennially successful. Some proven methods including value analysis and value chain analysis have emphasised the importance of providing products and services that are highly regarded by customers. However, this always makes clear to competitors avenues they can pursue. So there is an ongoing need to measure value[1] and improve the value obtained from both existing resources within the business and external resources used by the business.

Value added resources

The worth of the accumulated knowledge of employees, technologies, employee capabilities and customer relationships is not an economic transaction and is therefore excluded from the general ledger. The value of resources is best reflected in what it contributes to the capacity of people to deliver to customers the products and services that they value.

Topics in improving the tangible benefits from resources

Value can be improved via efficiency and effectiveness in five areas:

1. Improve the quality of products and services
2. Encourage organisational learning and knowledge development
3. Identify beneficial forms of skill training and credentialisation
4. Carefully consider outsourcing products and services
5. Obtain commercial advice from legal services and conduct litigation cautiously.

12.1 Improve the quality of products and services

Quality management seeks to improve the quality of products and services using process and statistical methods.[2] Quality management is related to mass production and the inter-

---

1 Value is distinguished from business valuation, corporate values and ethical values. Value is equated to profit in value chain analysis (Porter 1985/1998).

2 There is no single approach that represents quality management (Garvin 1988). It has evolved from the statistical approach of Deming (1982/1986), the 'breakthrough' standard of Juran (1964/1995), the zero defect goal (Halpin 1966)

changeability of components (parts) but is a separate avenue of productivity and competitive advantage.[3] It is the antithesis of a kludge.

The broad management issues and challenges that arise from improving the quality of products and services include:

- Providing the kind of leadership[4] that is compatible with improving the quality of products and services
- Fostering a business culture and climate where innovation is valued
- Allowing sufficient time to implement, gain acceptance and stabilise new practices
- Improving customer satisfaction ratings
- Extending the approaches used in manufacturing into service sectors and into areas such as sales, marketing and customer service.

The principal tools and techniques to improve the quality of products and services include:

- Replacement of inspections with assurance of quality processes
- Use of standards including the ISO 9000 series (Quality management)[5]
- Placing emphasis on doing the job correctly first time to avoid scrap and rework costs
- Differentiating between variation due to the system itself and variation introduced by meddling with the system
- Achieving continuous improvement in quality
- Recognising the need to undertake education and self-improvement of employees.

The managerial decisions and judgements that arise from improving the quality of products and services include:

- How should individual and group performance goals be revised to take into consideration continuous improvement?
- Has sufficient time been allowed for changed practices to become accepted and routine?
- Is there is sufficient statistical knowledge to be able to use applied statistical process control methods and interpret their results?
- Do employees and managers support the improvement of processes?

---

and the whole of business (total quality management) approach of Feigenbaum (1951/2004).

3 Quality management promotes continuous improvement. This contrasts with the business process re-engineering approach which recommends starting afresh (Hammer 1990; Hammer & Champy 1993/2001). Clearly wholesale replacement of existing processes entails a higher risk.

4 Deming (1982/1986: 23–24; 24–96) advanced the 14 points to alert management to its responsibilities at a time when it was common for management to transfer responsibilities for quality to the employees.

5 There may be local issues or supplements to the series of ISO 9000 standards (International Organisation for Standardisation, 2000). There is also considerable commentary including model process descriptions based on the standard sold as services by consultancy firms as well as published.

In summary, quality management provides an important foundation for a business to improve its business processes, interactions with customers and to remove variation in the materials used as inputs to its processes.

12.2 Encourage organisational learning and knowledge development

Encouraging organisational learning[6] and knowledge management[7] are two approaches to improve the competitive position of the business. Many earlier initiatives did not recognise the incomplete nature of knowledge as well as the decay of its usefulness.

The broad management issues and challenges that arise from organisational learning and knowledge development include:

- Short, medium and long-term development of knowledge
- Short, medium and long-term retention of knowledge
- The knowledge needed and potential sources
- Learning from mistakes[8]
- The changing or evolving state of knowledge on processes, practices and theory[9]
- The use of knowledge in fostering creativity
- The use of knowledge in encouraging innovation
- Viewing the sharing of knowledge as a market within the business[10]
- Some formal knowledge based systems have sought to prompt their contributors for updates and verification, however they are often ignored
- The ease with which knowledge created in one part of the business is made available in other parts of the business as and when needed.

---

6 Organisational learning uses learning processes to transform the business for the benefit of stakeholders (Dixon 1994/1999: 6). It differentiates between single and double-loop learning (Bateson 1972: 253, 284; Argyris & Schon 1978). Bateson (1972: 293) also refers to third-order (known as Learning III) which is a corrective change in response.

7 A major driver of organisational learning and knowledge management is the recognition that knowledge is personal (Polanyi 1966/1983). Information and knowledge are frequently treated as objects which are similar to products or commodities (Buckland 1991). It is also overlooked that knowledge cannot be conscripted from the individual (Oliver & Snowden 2005).

8 Some mistakes are so catastrophic as to terminate the business. The example of Nick Leeson and Barings Bank is well-known. The excessive printing of Star Wars books from Dorling Kindersley is less well-known. The overstock was of the order of 13 million books (Davis 2009: 298–300). The business was then bought by Pearson.

9 A major problem is the widespread conflation of knowledge and information (McNeely & Wolverton 2008: 272, also 269). This appears to be a distinction between personal information resident within an individual organised by judgment, experience and rules and legitimated knowledge although the book is silent on the author's descriptions. McNeely and Wolverton (2008: xxi) also show the legitimation role of various institutions (library, monastery, university, correspondence, disciplines and the laboratory) in the discontinuous history of the pursuit of knowledge.

10 Viewing the market for knowledge within a business also raises its political uses (Prusak & Cohen 1997/1998).

The principal tools and techniques to encourage organisational learning and knowledge development include:[11]

- Considering 'stocks' and 'flows' of knowledge
- Providing 'yellow pages' directories of skills and knowledge
- Encouraging communities of practice for interest groups
- Providing formal coaching sessions
- Providing formal mentoring arrangements
- Making sponsorship connections outside the business
- Encouraging professional development
- Organisational learning and knowledge management initiatives to make tacit knowledge explicit through using databases, information repositories and descriptions of procedures
- Codifying expert decision-making rules to allow decisions to be made by non-experts
- Engineering social interactions to permit disclosure of information held by a restricted number of employees[12]
- Social interaction through third party websites (e.g. 'Facebook')
- Social interaction messaging (e.g. 'Twitter')
- Promulgating opinion through 'blogs' and feedback web pages.

The managerial decisions and judgements that arise from organisational learning and knowledge development include:

- How is the tacit[13] knowledge of individuals to be made available to the business?
- What is the contribution of experts?[14]
- Should information be obtained from more than one source to gain an appreciation of the breadth of views and range of possible alternatives than can be considered?
- Will knowledge management assist in overcoming barriers to organisational change?[15]
- What is the possibility for reuse and repurposing of knowledge?
- What is the value of knowledge to the business?[16]

---

11 Organisational learning and knowledge management has also been embraced by human resources functions to provide new forms of training and assistance to employees. Generally these take the form of individual assistance. Although there are also activities which place employees in ad hoc or work group teams to foster organisational learning.

12 For example, recognition can be gained by sponsoring the activities of social clubs.

13 Tacit knowledge may even be difficult for the individual possessing it to surface (Polanyi 1966/1983).

14 Many experts work in industries that are knowledge-intensive (Alvesson 2004).

15 This view proposes that there is a strong link between knowledge and action (Argyris 1993).

16 Information about quality is harder and more costly to obtain than information about price as it involves information through experience instead of by search (Nelson 1970, 1974). Another view is provided by Akerlof (1970) who considers how asymmetric knowledge can be overcome.

In summary, the outcomes from organisational learning and knowledge management are generally that the business has greater success in the marketplace than it would have without the use of the additional knowledge. The future and form of social media is unclear.[17] It is assumed that the costs associated with the re-purposing of the knowledge are outweighed by either the benefits derived from it or savings gained.

12.3 Identify beneficial forms of skill training and credentialisation

There is an increasing trend toward both training and credentialisation (certification). In many cases higher education studies are associated with professional qualifications (e.g. accountant, financial planner; lawyer, nurse). In other cases, training and certification are achieved through trade courses (e.g. electrician) or short courses (e.g. hospitality employees such as bar attendants and waiters).

The broad management issues and challenges that arise from training and credentialisation include:

- Whether reducing hours/days/weeks worked by employees is preferable to retrenchment with the consequent loss of skills and knowledge
- Whether there will be suitably skilled employees available on the job market
- Whether there is a potential loss of skills and experience through employees retiring
- Whether there is a potential loss of skills or experience through employees switching to other employers or other jobs
- Whether employees' qualifications and skills remain sufficiently up-to-date.

The principal tools and techniques to identify beneficial forms of training and credentialisation include:

- Apprenticeships
- Internships
- Reimbursement of fees for completed units of study
- Conducting in-house courses and workshops
- Using industry accredited bodies.

---

17 Many of these social media represent new forms of traditional media (e.g. newsletters, broadcasts). The incidental and personal nature of their content makes them attractive to visitors particularly if the visitor does not have to disclose their identity. The extent to which such activities contribute to organisational learning and knowledge management differs depending upon the industry and culture of the organisation.

The managerial decisions and judgements that arise from training and credentialisation include:

- Is there a need for on-the-job training of employees on how to perform tasks?
- Will the business have the appropriate mix of skills and experience in future periods?
- Is it better to engage employees who possess the qualifications?
- Should the business facilitate the acquisition of suitable qualifications by existing employees?
- Is it more practical to conduct essential courses in-house?
- What incentives should be offered to employees to gain new or updated qualifications?
- Will employees undertaking work-related studies be allowed time off during business hours to attend classes or to study?

In summary, training and credentialisation offer useful knowledge to the business. However, the business must be able to take advantage of the knowledge and in many cases this involves developing a culture where ideas learnt from studies and training can be trialled without detrimental effects on the business.

12.4 Carefully consider outsourcing products and services

Outsourcing is a major decision for any business. Outsourcing differs from a make versus buy decision because it is a long-term strategic decision rather than a tactical decision. As such it is difficult and costly to reverse. It is also an area where partisan, subversive or corrupt conduct, and conduct which can discredit the profession is apt to occur. There are now businesses which specialise in many services which formerly were operated in-house. They include design (e.g. motor vehicle design houses such as Pininfarina), distribution and warehousing, technology management (e.g. IBM Services) and cleaning. Generally the rationale for outsourcing rests on reducing the number of employees or being able to better budget and reduce costs. Outsourcing successes are well publicised but the failures are less evident. .

The broad management issues and challenges that arise from considering outsourcing products and services include:

- Determining who are the target suppliers of outsourced products and services
- Knowing exactly the value of the in-house product or service to the business and its customers
- Having an accurate estimate of costs and benefits of the in-house product or service beyond those recorded in an accounting system
- Understanding the importance of quality in the product or service to the customer

- Understanding the importance of quality in the product or service to the customer
- Considering whether strategic alliances or long-term relationships with suppliers which share resources and activities will be beneficial
- Assessing whether the benefits of outsourcing substantially outweigh its disadvantages[18]
- Recognising the loyalty and understanding that the staff providing the product or service have of the business.

The principal tools and techniques for considering in considering outsourcing products and services include:

- Establishing a clear business case including the feasibility of contracting and managing the outsourced product or service and an analysis of the skills and capabilities
- A cost benefit analysis to determine the financial basis for the decision based on relevant costs[19]
- Clear specification of the product or service to be outsourced with clear standards and tolerances
- Managing the processes and systems
- Building informal controls and trust
- Attention to the terms of the contract or agreement
- Establishing communication channels
- Performance monitoring.[20]

The managerial decisions and judgements associated with outsourcing products and services include

- What are the opportunity costs?[21]
- Has a clear business case been established?
- Do qualitative[22] and long-term factors inform the outsourcing decision?
- Is there likely to be a loss of vital skills and knowledge?

---

18 The benefits can include: (1) Access to specialised skills; (2) Accelerated time-to-market, particularly of new products or services; (3) An ability to focus on core competencies; and (4) Potential cost savings. The disadvantages can include: (1) The 'hollowing out' of the business; (2) A loss of skills, knowledge and expertise; (3) The loss of control; and (4) unrealised savings and perhaps increased costs.

19 For relevant costs, the total revenues and total costs should be used, not their per-unit equivalents and not all variable costs are relevant and not all fixed costs are irrelevant. Costs should also be classified as avoidable and unavoidable for a comprehensive analysis. Some cost savings may be due to changing supplier arrangements (e.g. just in time purchasing) and can be obtained by refining existing arrangements. Supplier costs will include: (1) The price paid for the product or service; (2) The cost of supplier related activities. For example, (1) costs of purchasing; (2) costs of holding inventory; (3) costs of poor quality; (4) costs of delivery failure; and (5) costs of managing the relationship.

20 The Supplier Performance Index (Carr & Itner 1992) is a useful measure.

21 For example, the loss of profits from using existing capacity to make the product or service.

22 Non-quantitative factors may be extremely important in an evaluation process, yet do not show up directly in calculations. Examples include: (1) ability to meet quality requirements; (2) reputation of the supplier; (3) effect on employee morale; (4) logistics such as distance to supplier.

- Is the supplier able to guarantee dependability of supply?
- Is the supplier able to guarantee quality of product or service?
- Is the supplier amenable to changes in delivery quantities and delivery schedules?
- Does the supplier respect confidential information?
- Will the supplier provide 'open book' accounting?
- Does the supplier remain financially stable?
- Can core competencies be protected?
- Is the outsource provider likely to become a future competitor?
- Will competitors be able to benefit from the outsourcing?

In summary, there are many reasons for selecting to outsource products or services. For example the outsourced business may possess expertise, or have an up-to-date investment in infrastructure. The criteria for outsourcing should be both financial and non-financial. Many businesses that have outsourced have returned to an in-house function at the end of the contract because the profit margin of the outsourced business was an unacceptably high premium.

12.5 Obtain commercial advice from legal services and conduct litigation cautiously

Ensuring legal services provide commercial advice is the principal underlying legal services. A comprehensive investigation and assessment of case law is of little value if it cannot be translated into practical action. Using litigation is something to be considered carefully. Not only does it require an assessment of the chances of a favourable judgement but it also requires calculation of the costs and benefits of delays in the judgement and the likelihood that it may not be finalised until all levels of appeal have been tried.

The broad management issues and challenges that arise from obtaining commercial advice from legal services and conducting litigation cautiously include:

- Finding a suitable law firm and ensuring legal work is done by persons with sufficient experience and suitable expertise in the chosen law firm
- Whether the legal firm has had arrangements with competitors
- Arranging appropriate text in contracts to ensure adequate protection for the business before they are signed and finalised. Consider:
  - Engagement of third parties to complete deliverables for the business (e.g. software development and installation)

- – Terms and conditions used when finalising a cash sale and a sale which involves an account receivable[23]
- – Credit application terms and conditions (but the approval is handled by the Accounts Receivable Manager)
- – Employment contracts.
- Whether to respond to correspondence with a legal approach or as a public relations exercise
- Determining what should be the balance between parties in terms of the provisions of any legal agreement
- Whether in litigation the party with the largest budget will win.

The principal tools and techniques for obtaining commercial advice from legal services and conducting litigation include:

- Specifying performance criteria and objectives as a criteria for the engagement
- Whether to place the legal firm on a retainer to preclude competitors from using them if their services are outstanding
- Obtaining both a quote and specific details of the proposed services
- Ensuring changes (visible for example as track changes) in any contractual documentation are reviewed by an operational manager to ensure appropriateness and viability
- Ensuring selection and veto of the employees from the legal firm involved with the business
- Specifying review checkpoints and agreed actions in the event of dissatisfaction with the quality of the services or progress with the engagement.

The managerial decisions and judgements that arise from obtaining commercial advice from legal services and conducting litigation include:

- How will it determine the acceptability of legal professionals for particular engagements (given the employee turnover in legal firms)?
- How will it budget for the cost of legal advice and where appropriate representation in court with solicitors and barristers?
- Will it provide lay legal training to employees? Consider:
  - – What should be the type, frequency and length of training on illegal sales practices?
  - – What should be the type, frequency and length of training on collusion between competitors?[24]

---

23 The actual sale is completed by a sales employee.

24 The human motives behind collusion include its apparent cultural normality in the organisation, direction from senior management and assurances by senior management (Geis 1976).

- – What should be the type, frequency and length of training on occupational health and safety codes of practice?
    - – What should be the type, frequency and length of training on employment and human resources compliance?
- How will the business stay informed of changes in legislation[25] that affect it? Consider:
    - – Who will be responsible for accounting standards which have the force of law?
    - – Who will be responsible for company/corporation law?
    - – Who will be responsible for consumer protection?
    - – How will directors' and officers' obligations be kept up to date so their insurance covers them?
    - – Who will be responsible for export/import laws?
    - – Who will be responsible for human resources and employment?
    - – Who will be responsible for intellectual property?
    - – Who will be responsible for product liability and warranties?
    - – Who will be responsible for takeover and stock exchange listing rules?
- Whether to place legal services in house or outsource them?
- How to deal with overseas jurisdictions where trading takes place?

In summary, legal services and using litigation can be very expensive. It is easy to engage legal services or commence litigation without appreciating the cost and added delay that it can introduce. For this reason obtaining commercial legal advice which recognises that the business must continue trading and in most cases, retain its existing business relationships should be emphasised.

Chapter summary

Businesses take many steps to improve the value of their resources. There are many factors involved and particular businesses give different weights to them. The recognition of the value of employees has encouraged organisational learning and knowledge development and identified beneficial forms of training and credentialisation. Financial and non-financial information is a unique resource as it enables the interlinking of business processes and communication about them. There is further scope to improve the tangible benefits obtained from resources in terms of products and services. An alternative is to obtain the product or service through outsourcing. One of the major advances shown by the Japanese after World War 2 was through using information to improve the quality of products and services. Information is also used in performance evaluation and improving business processes. These are discussed in the next dimension as recurrent themes.

---

25 This includes both statutes agreed by the government and regulations to the statute made administratively.

DIMENSION FOUR
RECURRING THEMES IN EMPLOYEE BEHAVIOUR

Context of recurring themes in behaviour

Although there are separate dimensions for the business life cycle, adaptation and leveraging resources, they are an incomplete description of the assumed business operations and strategy body of knowledge. Cutting across them is a set of recurring themes. They involve both scanning as well as investigating.

Perspective on recurring themes in behaviour

The recurring themes are a general set of competencies and they may be enacted with varying degrees of attention. This dimension recognises the potential for some problems or issue to occur despite well managed efforts in the three dimensions and in the recurrent themes. There are always unexpected events and unforeseen consequences. The combination of events and chance may produced outcomes which are difficult to manage.

A problem may be addressed but reappear. The recurrence may be due to lack of sufficiently comprehensive analysis or the poor attention to the solution. Frequently observers of the business as well as its employees and managers adopt or reject a tool or technique without considering the merits of its use.

In some cases, difficulties are due to an irrationally held personal belief or giving in to pressure to provide a 'quick answer'. In other cases it indicates a strong pragmatic belief that the decision will not be improved by additional investigation or information. The skills and experience associated with the recurrent themes make working with them a lifelong learning project. Previous experience or a proven methodology does not guarantee success as there are always nuances and variations which give unique features to the situation.

Impact of recurring themes in behaviour

The recurring themes in behaviour are part of an ongoing need for close attention to operations and strategy. No matter what is going on in the business, it depends upon employees and managers appreciating the significance of ethics, decision making, productivity, profitability, value and automation to the business. While concerns about productivity and profitability are common, it does not always mean that attention is sufficient or well directed. In many cases, resolving a problem requires a combination of approaches with sensitive implementation.

A recurrence may also indicate an intractable problem. An intractable problem is likely to resist successful resolution as well as harbour new components which necessitate a different approach. They require a longer and more intensive analysis but their reappearance may lead to them being mistaken as readily soluble. They will require a major new initiative which can deal with their emergent properties.

Chapters in Dimension Four
(Recurring themes in employee behaviour)

The earlier dimensions are supplemented with four recurring themes in the assumed business knowledge which affect all employees and managers. They are :

1. Use ethical principles and standards to alter behaviour and encourage others to behave ethically (discussed in Chapter 13)

2. Improve the conceptualisation, reasoning, business judgement and decision-making of managers and employees (discussed in Chapter 14)

3. Evaluate productivity and profitability with financial and related non-financial information (discussed in Chapter 15)

4. Pursue a quest for value in business operations and strategy (discussed in Chapter 16)

5. Automate transactions and decision support using business system, business process, workflow and data analyses (discussed in Chapter 17).

13 Use ethical principles and standards to alter behaviour and encourage others to behave ethically

Ethics is a branch of philosophy. It is concerned with making judgments about intention (motivation) and actions (behaviour), what is right and wrong, just and unjust, or proper and improper. Ethical judgements are normative not descriptive. Descriptive theory explains how things are (e.g. this text is black). Normative (or prescriptive) theory tells us how things ought to be for example, people ought to be honest. Ethics is about what ought to be, not what is.

Ethics has been discussed in civilisations since the Egyptians (approximately 1700 BC), by Confucius (approximately 500 BC), in the Bible (approximately 950–539 BC), by Socrates (approximately 469–399 BC) and by Aristotle (approximately 384–322 BC).

Early references to ethics in business are found throughout the world and through history. A selective selection of examples include Tao Zhu Gong 500 BC, Assistant to the Emperor of Yue, whose 2nd Business Principle stated 'Treating people with respect will gain one wide acceptance and improve the business'. In the Koran, Surah Cattle, 6: 149 (612–632 AD) stated 'Give just weight and full measure'. It is embodied in the Buddhist ideas of karmic justice (the 'law' that good deeds will be rewarded with happy results while evil deeds will entail suffering for the one who does them). It is stated in the Christian dual commandment to love God and to love thy neighbour (Matthew 22: 37–39).

Trends in business that influence ethics

There are a number of industry trends which influence business ethics. The major industry trends and their impact on ethics are shown in Table 4 on the next page.

Table 4. Major industry trends and their impact on ethics

Major Industry Trend	Impact on Ethics
Wider choice of supplier	Many different customs and cultural values in a global marketplace
Considerable cost and price pressures	Temptation to make savings or gain market share in the short-term
Reduced customer loyalty	Likelihood that customers will switch suppliers without warning
Changes in product consumption or popularity	Customer tastes change without warning

Forms of unethical behaviour in business

Unethical behaviour in business can take many different forms. Unethical behaviour in business can take many different forms. It can apply to the treatment of others, for example, allowing harm to occur (e.g. to employees, stakeholders, or the environment). It can be taking a financial benefit (or avoiding a loss). It can be the concealment of knowledge (or only partial disclosure). It can be requiring participation in events or circumstances (by creating a non-consensual obligation). It can be the re-purposing of resources intended for a particular activity or group. It may also be the cloaking of private interests in public purposes.

Consequences of a drift in ethical behaviour

Ethical drift may occur because it can be rationalised.[1] There are three consequences of ethical drift:[2] (1) the recognition that there may be business pressures which have personal consequences where the stance is unpopular; (2) the recognition that there may be cultural pressures toward business duplicity or personal gain that may also extend to coercion; and (3) the recognition that dominant problems for businesses operating internationally are bribes, gifts, unearned commissions and corruption.

Financial performance incentives may encourage unethical behaviour (Schweiter & Douma, 2002) by maximising short-term pecuniary interests. The payment of bonuses, before profit is

---

1 For example, at Enron there were many errors in pricing on which it claimed were due to its overseas expansion (Salter 2008: 31–45. Many of the popular accounts on Enron do not reference their sources and are not used although their findings support lapses in ethical behaviour at Enron.

2 Salter (2008: 136–45) claims that up to 1997 in its gas trading business, subsequently widened to energy trading, Enron did not intend to deceive shareholders. The creation of partnerships as off-balance sheet entities to achieve cash-flows which then were subject to additional conditions by the financing bank appears to be the drift into unethical and subsequently illegal actions by senior managers (Salter 2008: 3, 303, 381). Thus 'many allegedly fraudulent practices … were actually close calls from a legal point of view.' (Salter 2008: 303). The reasoning for this statement is that 'accounting and tax rules are … subject to multiple interpretations beyond those envisaged by lawmakers' (Salter 2008: 381). For an example of how many interpretations are possible see Walker and Oliver (2005).

realised, may be acceptable where there is a culture of honesty and the bonus can be rescinded. For example, at Enron, according to Salter (2008: 284–86) neither of these occurred.

Characteristics of systems and processes that facilitate ethical behaviour

Systems and processes that facilitate ethical behaviour have the characteristics identified in Table 5. The characteristics are grouped around three major facilitators to highlight the broad approach to ethics which recent business events suggest is essential.

Table 5. Characteristics of systems and processes that facilitate ethical behaviour

Major facilitator	System or process characteristic
Corporate policies	Oriented toward the pre-defined outcomes
	Transparency (openness)
	There is adequate time to perform the task
Processes and practices	There is a systematic process for information gathering
	There are clearly stated decision criteria
	The expected (deliverables) are clearly identified or specified
	Use of a review process as decision making progresses to confirm acceptability
	There is recognition that there are benefits from considering 'lessons learnt'
Employee motives and skills	Acceptable qualifications held by and formally allocated roles for decision makers
	There is recognition that making an ethical decision is often difficult
	Incentives do not encourage unethical behaviour

The number of characteristics suggest that employees and managers will need support to make ethical decisions as the ethical decision can be clouded by the pressures of circumstances and an apparent equivocality.

Relationship between law (lawfulness) and morality (ethics)

Changes in law tend to reflect changes in society and what society takes to be right and wrong. In any case, laws do not cover all modes of moral behaviour. For example, there are a number of behaviours which are, generally, unregulated including lying, breaking promises; and breach of trust.

The relationship between law and ethics is difficult since the two generally operate in different domains.[3]

Topics in using ethical principles and standards to alter behaviour

The use of ethical principles and standards is apparent in five ways:

1. Recognise employees bring different ethical moralities to work

2. Recognise an ethical dilemma

3. Resolve any legal aspects of an ethical dilemma

4. Seek assistance to ensure a timely ethical decision

5. Consider making information public.

13.1 Recognise employees bring different ethical moralities to work

In general, employees and managers express an ethical morality (or ethical stance). There are usually three options: (1) ethical relativism; (2) ethical absolutism; or (3) ethical nihilism. Mostly a position of ethical relativism or ethical absolutism is adopted which are underpinned by one of four main ethical theories:[4] (1) consequence-based (considers just the result); (2) obligation-based (deontology or duty); (3) social contract-based (around the rights of individuals or social groups); or (4) the aretaic turn (requires a person to possess a virtuous character). Each of these four ethical theories has sub-categories or variants with its own characteristics.

The broad management issues and challenges from recognising different ethical moralities include:

- Identifying the ethical moralities that operate both in the business and in the wider society

- Recognising any practical conflicts between the ethical moralities that operate.

---

3 Since the law specifies the minimum acceptable behaviour, being found innocent of a charge still leaves open making an ethical judgement of the person's actions. For example, an action may be judged as not corrupt in law but a contravention of the ethical code of a business and therefore an ethical lapse.

4 Although a common criterion is considering the consequences (Bentham 1789/1996, 1983) there are other criterion. They include obligation (Kant, 1948/2005) which has no regard to the consequences and aretaic (that is, dealing with character and virtue) advocated by Aristotle (ND/2002), Hume (1777/1975) and Macintyre (1991). An important consideration with ethics is intent (Etzioni 1988). Deontological theories of ethics align closest with the legal functions of senior managers.

The principal tools and techniques from recognising different moralities include:

- Seeking out ethical codes advanced by professions
- Recognising implicit ethical codes in literature and the arts
- Adopting a reflective stance[5] to recognise the ethical position and appraise ethical moralities
- Being transparent about the resolution of any practical conflicts between the ethical moralities
- Encouraging others to be aware of their own ethical position and behaviour.

The managerial decisions and judgements from recognising different ethical moralities include:

- Is the preferred ethical morality expressed in policies?
- What is an appropriate tone and content of the communication of the preferred ethical morality to employees?

In summary, recognising ethical moralities avoids ambush from competing ethical moralities discarded without consideration. Typically ethical moralities are not recognised, and different policies in the business often embody different ethical moralities which later manifest themselves as problems.

13.2 Recognise an ethical dilemma

An ethical dilemma arises because there is more than a single possible course of action. These different actions may be either acceptable or justified for many reasons such as (1) right and wrong is not governed by laws;[6] (2) there are sound arguments for and against the action; (3) codes of conduct may be non-specific; (4) it is acceptable that decisions are made at the individual employee level without reference to management; or (5) personal gain may not involve financial rewards.

The broad management issues and challenges that involve recognising an ethical dilemma include:

- There are many nuances on an ethical dilemma[7]

---

5 Reflection or self-reflection was promoted by Socrates as a means of reviewing the knowledge supposedly possessed. It has been promoted in education as a method for learning (Brookfield 1995) and reframed for business using three tasks: insight, critique and transformative redefinition (Alvesson & Deetz 2000: 16–20, 140–46).

6 With regard to accounting there has been a major shift. For example, Dickson (1913/1918: 240) comments: 'The public accountant's responsibility in respect of his certificates [of the truth and fairness of the financial statements] is largely moral and only to a small extent legal.'

7 Ethical principles or values are statements of human obligations or duties that are generally accepted and are the expression of normative ethical systems. Ethical principles are not contingent upon cultural features such as tradition, religion, or law.

- There may be difficulty in finding acceptable alternatives
- There may be missing data which is unavailable
- Personal involvement and self-interest are present[8]
- Difficulty in persuading others on the appropriate action.[9]

The principal tools and techniques to recognise an ethical dilemma include:

- Following a process for resolving the dilemma. An example is the sequence:

  1. State ethical dilemma in terms of the alternatives
  2. State the ethical approach used
  3. Clarify what is the ethical outcome
  4. Weighing up the options to reach the preferred option
  5. Giving a clear reason for the decision.

- Adopting a reflective stance to examine the situation and avoid ethical drift.

The managerial decisions and judgements for recognising an ethical dilemma include:

- Is it covered by a legal obligation?
- Do the benefits outweigh costs?
- Is this a standard of action for others?
- Is this acceptable to my family and friends?
- Would I be prepared to allow the same thing to happen to me?
- Does an independent opinion confirm my intended action?

In summary, recognising an ethical dilemma ensures early awareness of the possible repercussions. There is the added advantage that any subsequent actions are taken in light of that awareness. This may include seeking assistance.

---

8 Research among bank employees (Luyendijk forthcoming) suggests that this is partly due to letting their lifestyle grow with their premium remuneration (for generic or specific skills) and partly due to the high salaries and enhanced severance payment arrangements which effectively buy their silence.

9 The circumstances surrounding the Challenger space shuttle disaster highlight that it is not the availability of information but dynamics involving many individuals which is the problem (Kramer 1992).

13.3 Resolve any legal aspects of an ethical dilemma

Ethics do not arise if there is legislation that specifies or governs conduct.[10] Ethics arises where the legislation is falls in a grey area for conduct.[11] There are four areas: (1) the legislation is silent; (2) the case law is fragmented; (3) a remedy is difficult to enforce; or (4) evidence is difficult to obtain.

The broad management issues and challenges associated with any legal aspects of an ethical dilemma include:

- Whether it is a grey area between the domains of law and morality
- Whether voluntary compliance a factor
- Whether the action will have adverse consequences
- Whether the reputation of the business is jeopardised.

The principal tools and techniques associated with any legal aspects of an ethical dilemma include:

- Obtaining a legal opinion
- Assessing the intent and conduct against existing policies
- Assessing the intent and conduct against broader community and society standards
- Considering what might follow in a long range timeframe if the course of action is pursued.

The managerial decisions and judgements associated with any legal aspects of an ethical dilemma include:

- What penalties exist?
- Are the penalties a deterrent?[12]
- Is any legal 'loophole' likely to be perceived as such?
- What effect will the proposed conduct have in the short-term and long-term?

---

10 The exception is where some people will consider an illegal action to be morally justified. For example, there have been laws of apartheid, prohibiting women from voting or inter-racial couples from marrying which have been challenged.

11 In some cases the border is unclear. In those cases, continually engaging in borderline activities is likely to become ethical if later acts become more extreme.

12 Where the penalties are not a deterrent people choose to behave illegally and, if caught, pay a fine. There is some evidence that penalties encourage making a commercial decision, that is, a decision which focuses of gain (profits or benefits). The reliance on voluntary compliance generally produces better behaviour as it encourages a personal ethically responsible decision (in which decision-making departs from the optimal economic choice). This distinction was first drawn experimentally where Tenbrunsel and Messick (2001) introduced small penalties. Of course, there are many situations where there are sanctions (consequences) for a personal ethical choice only if caught (e.g. the penalty for being caught cheating in tests and examinations).

In summary, it is not possible to settle moral questions by settling the legal questions. Law is subject to moral scrutiny. The question 'Do laws provide moral guidance?' does not have a single or simple answer. Laws codify some customs, norms and values and in so doing may provide some broad moral guidance. Where this occurs they represent a trade-off between individual freedom and welfare protection. However laws may also reflect vested interests.

13.4 Seek assistance to ensure a timely ethical decision

Ethical decisions should be made promptly. Delay in notifying unethical behaviour introduces additional ethical considerations. In general, an immediate response is most appropriate to ensure that an ethical stance is conveyed in a timely an unambiguous manner. A delayed response may be seen to be orchestrated for personal advantage.

Seeking assistance to make an ethical decision occurs in two ways. First by following the guidelines stated in ethical codes of conduct. Second, through directly sharing the circumstances with another person to obtain their opinion.

The broad management issues and challenges that arise when a person seeks assistance to make an ethical decision include:

- The circumstances may make it difficult to confide in another person
- Ethics is one of several values[13] in professional settings which may be in conflict
- The self-regulation of many professional groups involve systems and processes that may preclude an unofficial enquiry or advice
- Some business code operates at the level of individual business with the result that competing businesses may have different codes
- Different professions have different codes.[14]

The principal tools and techniques to seek assistance to make an ethical decision include:

- Considering similar ethical dilemmas that have been experienced in the past
- Referring to a code of ethics[15] that typically prescribes or proscribes the treatment concerning ethical and corrupt conduct, fairness and equity to employees and stakeholders,

---

13 Values such as honesty, trust, responsibility and accountability, good faith, fidelity, fairness, care and compassion, pursuit of professional excellence, taking a principled position on issues of importance within area of expertise may lead to an ethical dilemma.

14 For example in Australia (1) Computer professionals and contractors have a code which describes six values and ideals, summarised as: priorities; competence; honesty; social implications; professional development; and information technology profession (Australian Computer Society nd); (2) various accounting bodies have non-exhaustive standards explaining how their code applies to a member's professional work (e.g. Institute of Management Accountants USA, 2005); and (3) legal practitioners have their own principles and standards (e.g. Law Society of New South Wales, 2009).

15 Codes are not a substitute for thinking about ethics but may be a point of reference in civil and criminal proceedings.

the use of information (e.g. public comment), post separation use of information (e.g. disclosure to the new employer), receipt of gifts, conflict of interest and enforcement mechanisms (e.g. sanctions for breaches)

- Using knowledge gained from training in applying ethics in case scenarios which may also involve role-playing followed by a discussion of the role-play behaviour
- Applying various tests such as the newspaper front page test[16]
- Re-framing the situation that has ethical issues into another context to assess the appropriateness of the proposed action
- Seeking advice from a mentor, coach or counsellor who specialises in ethical matters.

The managerial decisions and judgements for seeking assistance to make an ethical decision usually include:

- What is the ethical outcome we are trying to strive for?
- What is the influence of values and incentive systems (including rewards)?
- What is fair to equity holders, stakeholders and social responsibility?
- How can future reputation be safeguarded?
- How is it possible to move beyond considering self-interest alone in reaching a decision?
- Is it capable of being defended with reasons (beyond bias and preference)?
- How is it possible to encourage others to pursue ethical principles and standards?

In summary, seeking assistance may involve reviewing guidelines or contacting an appropriate advisor to discuss the circumstances. Most professional associations have guidelines which include specify the principles and standards which should be observed.

13.5 Consider making information public

In some cases one of the information possessors may decide it deserves disclosure to the public.[17] In general, it is expected that any issues regarding the information would have been previously brought to the attention of the supervisor and where an unsatisfactory response was obtained, then to a senior person within the business. Disclosure can take many forms: (1) It may be done by concealing identity (anonymously) or not;[18] (2) It may be done by the original possessor of the information; or (3) The possessor may provide it to another party for them to disclose.[19]

---

16 Perhaps in countries where there is a high use of media, the newspaper front-page test would be replaced by the prime-time television news story test.

17 There are many pitfalls if this approach is not carefully thought through beforehand (Martin 1999).

18 The security over electronic data and its transmission makes it likely that any thorough forensic examination will lead back to the whistle blower. An anonymous disclosure may therefore only be temporary.

19 The interests of any third party recipient of the disclosure (e.g. journalist, politician, politician's assistant or advisor; police) may be such that they use the information in unexpected ways with other consequences. For Microsoft, see Carter

The broad management issues and challenges in making information public include:

- The legal consequences of releasing the information[20]
- The likelihood of success in getting the details they seek to disclose published[21]
- The effect on the business which employs them
- The likely short-term and long-term effect on their personal career including the likelihood of a prosecution action and its success.[22]

The principal tools and techniques in making information public include:

- Providing the details to a member of parliament in an opposition party to the party in government
- Providing the details to a journalist or contact in the media
- The anonymous delivery to a person who as sufficient influence to carry through the disclosure
- Giving information at a public enquiry (such as a Corruption Inquiry, Royal Commission; or other inquiry with terms of reference to seek information).

The managerial decisions and judgements concerning making information public include:

- What kind of information is likely to be disclosed by employees or contractors?
- What kind of effect may such disclosures have on the business which employs them?
- What kind of protection is afforded 'whistle-blowers'?[23]

In summary, public disclosure requires careful consideration. The disclosure itself and the person making the disclosure need to have credibility. The person who is initiating the disclosure should protect themselves from punitive action.

Chapter summary

Use ethical principles and standards to make judgements and encourage others to behave ethically. This may involve recognising different ethical moralities between as well as within different stakeholders. Recognising an ethical dilemma is always the starting point. It is difficult to pre-specify the form that an ethical dilemma will take. There may be legal aspects of

---

(2002).

20 Criminal as well as civil penalties may apply. Psychiatric treatment may also be used (Arantz 1993).

21 The controversial nature of some allegations may discourage third parties from publishing the disclosure. One course of action, less frequently resorted to nowadays, is private publication (e.g. Arantz 1993; Kildall 1993).

22 The employee may choose to be named or have their details withheld. For example the Independent Commission Against Corruption investigation into the misuse of Sydney Ferries corporate cards names the whistleblower (ICAC 2009: 5) apparently because she consented.

23 Those countries who have legislated to protect whistleblowers have also limited their rights. In practice, there are many avenues for both seeking information about the action of the whistleblower and for bringing action against a whistleblower so they must realise is quite likely to occur.

an ethical dilemma which also need to be resolved. Timely resolution may be require seeking assistance to make an ethical decision. In some cases, where information is being withheld, consider 'whistle blowing' or making a disclosure to the public. The inertia for ignoring or covering up an ethical dilemma is under-appreciated. This concludes the review of adaptation to circumstances and the allocation of resources for performance is next considered.

14 Improve the conceptualisation, reasoning, business judgement and decision making of employees and managers

Many approaches for improving the business judgement and decision making of employees and managers, as individuals or in groups,[1] focus on the better use of information and avoiding errors in drawing conclusions. A wider understanding is necessary beginning with forming in the mind, of concepts and giving attention to reasoning. In this respect judgement is the end product of searching for information, formulating and evaluating alternatives and attempting persuasion. Some businesses ignore the cognitive and behavioural factors which influence most employees and managers faced with making a judgement or decision.[2]

Disciplinary perspectives on decision-making

Decision-making is studied in many different disciplines including economics, forecasting, marketing and psychology. The common conclusions are: (1) most decision-making is considered rational,[3] that is, conscious reasoning is substituted for emotion and unconscious motivation;[4] (2) models that provide an ideal standard or norm hold the decision-maker

---

1 Where a decision is to be made by a committee or a group the same process should be used and the same biases will be evident. This is partly due to their being framed by an agenda and recommendation, and partly because individuals are subject to group psychological factors where they may be unduly influenced by some members.

2 'Just exercise good judgment' was a motto at Microsoft. See the account by insiders at Microsoft when it was a small company in the Pacific Northwest that wrote software before it became an industry leader (Carter 2002).

3 Dawes and Hastie (2001) use a reverse definition of rationality claiming that the law of contradiction suggests that reasoning using the same evidence that reaches contradictory conclusions is irrational. Moreover, selection of choices involves transitivity, which is the selection of preferences where two choices are available should also apply when the preferences from several of those choices are compared. For example, a preference for A when presented with A and B and a preference for B from B and C should mean that A is preferred to C.

4 Recently the 'irrationality' movement has argued that emotion, including mood, play a large and undetected part in making decisions (e.g. Ariely 2008/2009). This may provide a partial explanation for violations of consistency in decision-making. Early proponents of decision-making accepted this was the case and sought to overcome it by preceding decision-making with sequential process and explicit criteria (e.g. Kepner-Tregoe 1965). More recent studies (e.g. Frank 1988) suggest that there may be positive outcomes from emotions in decision-making as they invoke principles.

to a much stricter criterion since they are prescriptive;[5] and (3) expertise is based on extensive knowledge.[6]

Phases or stages in decision-making

Early investigations of logical-rational and the non-logical-intuitive decision making by Barnard (1938) sought to replace narrower descriptors such as 'resource allocation' and 'policy making' with a focus on deliberation and action. Simon (1945/1997; 1987) suggested that there were four phases in decision-making (intelligence, design, implementation and review). However these are too broad. A more granular description is provided in Table 6 below.

Table 6. Nine stages in decision making.

	Decision stage	Purpose	Simon's Decision (1945/1997) Phases
1	Problem recognition	Scan the environment for conditions calling for a decision.	Intelligence: gathering information
2	Problem representation	Formulate the problem, opportunity or uncertainty in relation to the goal of the business.	
3	Make predictions about the future	Determine the cluster of outcomes from the problem, opportunity or uncertainty on the business (These can be tested and modified during the information gathering phase).	
4	Information gathering	Obtain information to gain a better understanding of the problem, opportunity or uncertainty.	
5	Devise alternatives	To ensure that alternatives are not overlooked	Design
6	Create logical evaluation criteria	To rank the alternatives using weightings and identify those which can be quickly discarded and those requiring further investigation	
7	Select the preferred alternative	To select the highest ranked alternative	Choice
8	Implement	Consult on proposal and proposed implementation arrangements	
9	Evaluate the process and outcomes	Collect information on implementation and operation and provide feedback to improve future decision making	Review

---

5 If a decision does not conform to the criteria of rational then it will violate normative standards.

6 Simon (1991) lists this as first among his generalisations.

In the above stages, considerable emphasis is placed on defining the problem, opportunity or uncertainty because until there is a clear understanding it is meaningless to proceed. Moreover, if the problem, opportunity or uncertainty is stated incorrectly or unclearly then the resulting decision will be wrong.

Topics in improving business judgement and decision making

Decision-making in business is multi-faceted.[7] There are five aspects to improving the business judgement and decision-making of employees and managers:

1. Recognise the basis for making effective business decisions and judgements
2. Consider the cluster of outcomes from making decisions and judgements
3. Search for and evaluate relevant information to the decision or judgement
4. Devise a criteria to evaluate the information and weight the options
5. Consider persuasion from behavioural bias, errors and pitfalls in forming judgements and making decisions.

14.1 Recognise the basis for making effective business decisions and judgements

General economic theory is premised on individuals maximising their benefits and minimising their costs. So most decision-making theories assume that the various factors leading to a decision can be combined into an overall value or subjective utility. In practice, employees and managers are usually unclear about the bases for their decision-making.

The broad management issues and challenges in making effective business decisions include:

- Most decisions have to be made in a specified time frame[8]
- Making use of an abundance of information[9]
- Having only limited relevant and rigorous information
- Balancing financial and non-financial criteria[10]

---

7 Decision-making uses tangible and intangible measures as well as financial and non-financial measures.

8 This is considered a characteristic of bounded rationality when considered in conjunction with the limited cognitive abilities of an individual and the limited information they have available (Simon 1945/1997). The idea that human rationality is goal-directed but humans have limited information-processing capability has been widely adopted since proposed by Simon (1945/1997).

9 The availability of considerable information (an 'information-rich' decision-making situation) also affects prediction accuracy and consistency of decision-makers with expected value theory and expected utility theory. Often an information-rich situation is termed 'computational complexity' (Payne 1988). Sometimes this is just described as 'complexity' meaning 'task complexity' (Payne 1976).

10 Businesses needs to use a range of accounting and non-accounting methods to decide how to proceed with projects. The well understood and tried and tested DCF methods consider revenue benefits and costs but should not be the sole basis for allocating capital to projects. A business that relies on innovation has to balance its short-term and long-term

- Avoiding an unproductive over-simplification of choices
- The cost of obtaining information[11]
- Information has varying degrees of reliability and there may be difficulties in corroborating information particularly where it is known only to a few people
- Information may come in a format that makes it difficult to assess[12]
- Deciding which tool or technique to use when faced with unfamiliar information or having to make a decision.[13]

The principal tools and techniques for making effective business decisions and judgements include:

- Using a theory of decision-making appropriate to the business and the individual employee or manager. Consider:
  - Bounded rationality
  - Expected value theory[14]
  - Expected utility theory[15]
  - Prospect theory which is a modification of expected utility theory[16]
  - Regret theory which is a modification of expected utility theory.[17]
- Using a suitable process for making the decision.[18] Consider:
  - Recognising the need for a decision

---

vision and may allocate 50% of its capital budget on low risk projects, 30% on medium risk and 20% on high risk projects. The value of the higher risk projects (medium and high) may increase the potential value of the business.

11 It may not be readily measurable. The cost may be direct such as purchasing a newspaper subscription, purchasing advice from consultants and indirect being the time spent searching for suitable information.

12 Aggregation, consolidation and summarisation of information are usually preferred by managers particularly if it is possible to 'drill down' (obtain detail behind the same figures). It may be too general or too detailed in the judgement of a particular employee or manager.

13 Wickelgren (1974: ix, 1, 4) recommends learning by example distinguishing between recognising a class of problem and applying specific techniques using general problem solving methods where the issue involves many component steps and differs from known problems.

14 This implies that the decision-maker is aware of all possible outcomes and the likelihood (probability) they will occur. That is, all possible outcomes are identified, their values (positive or negative) are determined, the probabilities for each course of action are calculated and the values are multiplied by probability to give an expected value.

15 The attitude toward risk introduces both risk aversion and the different utility that an outcome provides to a person with particular preferences and assets (von Neumann & Morgenstern 1944/2004),

16 Prospect theory is described in Kahneman and Tversky (1979) and revised in Tversky and Kahneman (1992). In the preface, Kahneman (2000: ix-xvii), describes their 'unusual mode of empirical research' (p x) cumulating in prospect theory (p xi).

17 Anticipated feelings including regret may occur where the difference between outcomes is large and may influence a decision-maker (Gilovich & Medvec 1995).

18 The process outlined is listed as a linear sequence. However, this does not mean that the steps have to be completed strictly in order without any repetition, branching or iterations. There are many guidelines for decision-making. Many have similarities with problem solving. From an information point of view, the decision involves available data (which may be incomplete), the goal (or expected outcome) and the operations which are deemed acceptable. The well accepted guides include Baron (1988), Bazerman (1986/2002), Dawes and Hastie (2001), Plous (1993) and Russo and Shoemaker (1989/1990).

- – Identifying what is known and what is uncertain
- – Specifying the outcomes
- – Identifying all the alternatives using a decision tree
- – Undertaking a comprehensive statement of the alternatives
- – Using heuristics[19] carefully (see Topic 14.5)
- – Determining the criteria for selecting the preferred alternative
- – Weighting the criteria[20]
- – Determining the alternatives
- – Rating the alternatives on each criterion
- – Determining the optimal decision
- – Obtaining approval for the recommended alternative
- – Implementing the preferred alternative.
- • Involving others in the process[21]
- • Opening the resulting decision up to review or rest before implementation.

The managerial decisions and judgements for making effective business decisions and judgements include:

- • Is the intention to produce a decision that is satisficing[22] rather than optimising?
- • Is the focus too strongly on the individual aspects or components of an option instead of each of the options, resulting in the elimination of some options?[23]
- • Are time constraints[24] being allowed to impact the quality of the decision?
- • To what extent are the personal values of the employees recommending the decision or the decision-maker[25] affecting the decision?

In summary, making effective decisions involves being aware of the circumstances, the limitations of tools and the motives of the parties.

---

19 This shift in decision-making is considered an adaptive response to computational complexity (Payne 1988).

20 Bazerman (1986/2002: 3-4) emphasises that it is not sufficient just to determine the elements of the selection criteria although doing so is often time consuming and very difficult in itself.

21 A group is more likely to make a better decision than even the best result achieved by its individual best member (Collins & Guetzkow 1964).

22 Satisficing decisions aim to achieve that which will satisfy or suffice (Simon 1955) rather than produce the best possible outcome (optimising) and use bounded rationality (Simon 1955).

23 They may be used several times to eliminate options. This approach known as elimination by aspects (Tversky 1972) is an alternative to being goal focused. Eventually, either only one choice remains or the number of options remaining can be examined in detail.

24 Time constraints may act as a cost associated with gathering and evaluating information in making decisions even where the amount of available information is modest. Where there are time limitations (which are high costs) decisions may use simplifying heuristics (or rules of thumb). For example, in capital budgeting using number of years payback is quicker than calculating discounted cash flow.

25 For example the Stoics considered that the duty of the virtuous person was to simply do their best in the circumstances with benevolence and calm (Aurelius 1998).

14.2 Consider the cluster of outcomes from making decisions and judgements

The effectiveness and quality of decision-making in business is shown ultimately through performance. However there are a cluster of outcomes from making decisions and judgements that should be considered.

The broad management issues and challenges concerning the cluster of outcomes from decisions and judgements include:

- Isolating the separate outcomes for strategy, governance, regulatory compliance, morality (ethics), social responsibility, performance/behaviour and human resources
- Ensuring that some decisions made by humans are at least as accurate as those made using algorithms[26]
- Making clear the basis for the judgement. Consider:
  - The extent of value or utility[27]
  - Whether it is influenced by a prior social relationship.
- Determining the place of a social relationship in making the decision
- Avoiding sub-optimal decisions owing to common errors in comprehending the world and form opinions.

The principal tools and techniques for producing a cluster of outcomes from decisions and judgements include:

- Synthesizing large amounts of data by finding relationships between ideas[28]
- Using a dual horizon (short-term and long-term)
- Determining the effect on stakeholders and other parties
- Evaluating the effect (win-win or zero sum)
- Awareness of the common types of cognitive bias which produce failures in or violations of consistency
- Using a systematic method for identifying outcomes irrespective how improbable they may appear at first glance.

---

26 For example early studies (Sarbin 1944; Meehl 1954) found clinical prediction less accurate than formulas based on observable variables. Forecasting studies have shown 'megamistakes' (Schnaars 1989).

27 Assuming relationships between a buyer, a seller and a price characterise most transactions. The view of mental accounting is discussed in Topic 13.3.

28 Affinity diagrams may be created from masses of disparate data using the KJ Method which generates ideas, displays them, sorts them into groups of like ideas and identifies relationships between them (Kawakita, 1991).

The managerial decisions and judgements for producing a cluster of outcomes from decisions and judgements include:

- Are decision-makers being biased by the 'certainty effect,[29] particularly in relation to non-fianancial (non-monetary) events?[30]

- Are there preference reversals where outcomes that are more highly valued are priced higher?

- Is selective attention being given to properties may result in some characteristics being ignored when it is difficult to evaluate them?[31]

- Does the context influence the evaluation of an option?[32]

- Does preference framing[33] direct the decision-maker to toward positive or negative properties or components of choices?[34]

- Is there a tendency toward the use of mental accounting where financial resources are believed to fall into distinct accounts (or calculative categories)?[35]

In summary, knowledge management has suggested that unfavourable outcomes (including failure) are more likely to be given attention than favourable outcomes. Cognitive psychology suggests that expected favourable outcomes may weigh unduly high with decision-makers to the extent that potential unfavourable outcomes are cognitively masked from their attention.

14.3 Search for and evaluate relevant information to the decision or judgement

The pressure for completing the decision process quickly often manifests itself as being selective with the information sought and used. With the availability of internet search engines (e.g. Google) and encyclopaedias (e.g. Wikipedia) searching information is usually reduced

---

29 Outcomes that are perceived as certain are overweighted relative to uncertain outcomes. This overweighting is not expressed within the scope of expected utility theory.

30 Tversky and Kahneman (1981) found that people preferred to avoid a certain loss. The experiment involved using a hypothetical epidemic where the ratio of survival and death remained constant.

31 For example, only one of the choices may provide details of a property which itself is difficult to judge as good or bad (Hsee et al. 1999).

32 Other options tend to affect any particular option. Rather than evaluate the intrinsic properties the presence of a dominant alternative tends to attract the decision-maker to select it.

33 Framing appears to be relevant when considering sunk costs. Decisions concerning the use of purchased resources (a sunk cost) in business are sometimes unclear. On one hand, sunk costs should not influence decisions about the future. On the other hand, persistence in a task can be adaptive, particularly where the task has a negative modest outcome followed by strongly positive outcomes (Tan & Yates 1995). A lack of information may also make the correct decision unclear (Heath 1995).

34 A framing effect (Tversky & Kahneman 1981) variant occurs when options unfold over time. Normally, decision-makers prefer (1) to receive valuable outcomes sooner rather than later and/or (2) outcomes that improve over time suggesting that decision-making over time also shows violations to expected utility theory (Lowenstein & Prelec 1993).

35 These categories may reflect the different purposes of money or its different functions.This also calls into question the standard economic theory which relies on monetary values as a common system of value.

to finding hits on the internet. Apart from their dubious accuracy, the search engines do not provide a balanced set of views nor sort them in any sequence relevant to the user's enquiry. The time spent on gathering information particularly from knowledgeable employees repays itself by not overlooking what is already known that can contribute to the decision.[36]

The broad management issues and challenges in searching for and evaluating relevant information to the decision include:

- Allocating sufficient time and a sufficiently competent person to analyse, evaluate and summarise what will be relevant

- Conducting a search for information that includes both internal and external sources. Consider:

    - In-house informants with knowledge of earlier answers to the same question but who may be in information silos

    - Suppliers and stakeholders with knowledge of previous or current arrangements who will be willing to discuss them.

- Critically evaluating the information that has been assembled. Consider:

    - Separating measures for inputs from measures for productivity and outcomes

    - Avoiding input measures that are used for efficiency and effectiveness

    - Checking whether productivity measures can be equated with achievements or results.

- Identifying whether any information is superseded

- Identifying any gap, discrepancy or bias in the information.

The principal tools and techniques in searching for and evaluating relevant information to the decision include:

- Calculating the time value of money if there is more than one period. Consider:

    - A cash flow worksheet showing whether the cash inflow occurs at the beginning or end of the period will be important

    - The number of periods over which cash inflows or outflows occur will have a substantial effect on the value of the financial transaction

    - The anticipated interest rate (or rate of return) will have a substantial effect on the value of the financial transaction

    - Whether a decision to adopt different rates of return for a multi-year project will produce a different conclusion on its viability than using a constant rate of return.

- Conducting a sensitivity analysis. Consider:

---

36 Many, many times has the author heard this plaintive refrain from an employee 'Why wasn't I told?' To which the reply also has been often heard, 'Well, why didn't you ask?'

- The assumptions[37] behind the result which if changed affect the outcomes
- The effect of adverse or favourable circumstances.

- Accepting that different costs or prices may coexist for the same activity. Consider:
  - There are many different methods for computing and comparing costs and prices for the same activity[38]
  - Different purposes that have led to different costs being derived may not be apparent.[39]

- Using the Pareto principle[40] also known as the Law of the Vital Few as a guide to analysis. Consider:
  - Causal and non-linear relationships;[41] and applications outside economics[42]
  - Major misuses involve aggregation and misclassification.[43]

The managerial decisions and judgements in searching for and evaluating relevant information to the decision include:

- Is the decision one of effectiveness, efficiency or economy? Consider:
  - Is effectiveness is the paramount consideration particularly if resources are utilised productively but fail to achieve expected results?
  - How is the current decision different to earlier decisions that appear similar?

- Is the decision well founded? Consider:
  - Is it likely to be sub-optimal owing to insufficient research?
  - Is it likely to be sub-optimal owing to lack of alternatives being considered?
  - Is it likely to be sub-optimal owing to poor comprehension of the world and re-searched opinions?

- How does the decision affect policy? Consider:

---

37 A sensitivity analysis assumes that the proposed approach is the expected or average result. Therefore worst case and best case outcomes should also be provided for the reader to judge their impact. For example, if the revenue from traffic on a toll road is studied, then high as well as low traffic flows should be calculated as well as an average. Of particular importance is showing the assumptions since the range of sensitivity is dependent upon the assumptions.

38 This can be summed up in the expression 'Different costs for different purposes'.

39 This was recognised early in the 20th century by Clark (1923).

40 Pareto's initial finding was that the distribution of wealth was not random. Further investigations found that 80% of the land in Italy was owned by 20% of the population (Pareto 1909/1971).

41 As a generalisation it suggests that for many events 80% of the effects arise from 20% of the causes. There are many varieties of it but they all have in common a non-linear relationship.

42 Some examples of the Pareto principle include: (1) 80% of invoices are of low value; (2) 80% of errors are caused by 20% of the defects; and (3) 80% of debt resides with 20% of the customers. Parmenter (2007) focuses on the effort-reward relationship: typically 80% of the reward arises from 20% of the effort. As a consequence he proposes a number of improvements which can be made in the accounting function to streamline reporting efficiencies.

43 The Pareto principle is a heuristic on the imbalance of effort which is commonly misused. The aggregation error results from accumulating several categories on a Pareto chart until approximately 80% are accounted for. The proper approach is to ascertain which 20% of the factors are contributing to about 80% of the issues. The second error is relying on data which uses classifications that are neither mutually exclusive nor collectively exhaustive. These misuses of the Pareto principle are found even in quality management, (see Bhalla 2009).

- Has the distinction between defining policy and detailing the steps in a procedure been appropriately made?

- Have the outcomes to be measured been specified if the effect of policy is being evaluated?

- Is the efficiency and effectiveness of a policy affected by detailing the procedure or process?

- Are policy statements and procedural descriptions prevented from becoming dense by lists, tabular comparisons and diagrams.

In summary, the search for and evaluation of relevant information deals with two separate aspects of decision making. During the search for information it takes into account the need to differentiate between policy and process (procedures) and conducting a sufficiently wide search. Evaluation of information considers the purpose, the measures used (including a sensitivity analysis) and the time value of money where applicable.

14.4 Devise criteria to evaluate the information and weight the options

The use of a criteria not only assists selecting the information to be sought but gives a means of balancing different demands and expectations across many different alternatives.[44] It provides a means of allowing them to be compared, and for different aspects of the criteria to be weighted according to the perceived benefit (or potential detriment). The time spent developing and refining the criteria is repaid by the potential failure avoidance as well as by better understanding the properties of the decision.

The broad management issues and challenges in using criteria to weigh the alternatives include:

- For financial outcomes, ensuring they are consistently applied across different alternatives; considering the outcomes from different alternatives in both financial and non-financial terms

- Recognising that the different alternatives will affect human behaviour in different ways because a business has social relationships where human attitudes, motivations[45] and perceptions influence behaviour

- Taking a project viewpoint for the different alternatives to consider the timetable, cash flows and deliverables

- The availability of a fall-back plan.

---

44 Sometimes your only alternatives are to do it or don't do it. Usually there are more than two alternatives and you have to devise them. It is important to be able to have a spectrum of alternatives.

45 Herzberg (1968) distinguished between hygiene or context factors which demotivate when absent and satisfiers or content factors which can motivate or demotivate. (Herzberg's studies focused on accountants and engineers).

The principal tools and techniques in using criteria to weigh the alternatives include:

- Determining whether benefits exceed costs.[46] Consider:
  - Conventions should be set out stating the basis for determining costs (relevant costs, opportunity costs, sunk costs)
  - Conventions should be set out stating the basis for determining benefits (whether only tangible benefits and costs are to be counted or whether intangibles can be counted)
  - Conventions for attributing dollar amounts to fuzzy costs and benefits
  - Conventions as to whether the determination will be a cost-benefit analysis or a wider investment appraisal
  - The time-frame for measuring benefits and costs
  - Whether benefits as savings can be actually realised
  - Using an opportunity cost perspective
  - Considering relevant costs where alternatives are being considered.
- Identifying the impact of the decision on human behaviour. Consider:
  - Agreements which require notification and consultation
  - Time allowed for consultation and feedback
  - The need to hold meetings to explain and answer questions.
- Ensuring that explicit criteria is used. Consider:
  - The criteria is equally applied for each alternative
  - The weightings are fairly applied to each alternative
  - The criteria is issued for comment to avoid disputes
  - Where utilisation of resources are involved it is made clear if economy and efficiency are the primary measures of productivity.

The managerial decisions and judgements for using criteria to weigh the alternatives include:

- Will making some policy decision may incite dysfunctional behaviour ? Consider:
  - Are there likely to be any unintended outcomes?
  - Will the use of consultants mitigate, mask or delay dysfunctional behaviour?
- Is there a sound basis for the decision? Consider:
  - Do benefits actually exceed costs?
  - Have both the financial and non-financial outcomes been considered?

---

46 The principle that benefits must exceed costs is an important guide to determining feasibility of any informal suggestion or formal proposal. There will be some effort needed to determine how the dollar amounts are attributed to agreed costs and benefits.

- – Are costings for the alternatives documented and available so that they can be validated as viable?
- – Are there qualitative factors which over-ride a favourable or unfavourable conclusion to a financial cost-benefit analysis.[47]

- What is the implementation plan? Consider:
  - – What will trigger (activate) implementation?
  - – What are the remedies and alternatives in the event that the execution of the decision encounters impediments?
  - – What are the stages for the implementation?
  - – Has the implementation plan been documented?

- What is the fall-back plan?[48] Consider:
  - – What will trigger (activate) implementation and fall-back?
  - – What are the remedies and alternatives in the event that the execution of the decision encounters impediments?
  - – What are the stages for the fall-back?
  - – Has the fall-back plan been documented?

- Is decision making fair and reasonable?[49] Consider:
  - – Has the governance or decision making protocol been made clear beforehand?
  - – Will the presumption in law that rules or principles of natural justice, also known as procedural fairness, be followed?

- Is this an attempt to fix human problems using a technical solution? Consider:
  - – Will changing the location overcome work restrictions?
  - – Will new systems or working arrangements bypass or eliminate human errors?
  - – Will short-term projects 'sideline' difficult or valued employees?
  - – Are new hierarchical structures or lines of reporting being introduced to minimise conflicts between employees, managers or departments?
  - – Are changed or special responsibilities being introduced to overcome employee or managerial weaknesses?

---

47 The failure to subject public projects to cost-benefit analysis will compromise the credibility, standing and future public investment evaluation. The fact that cost-benefit analyses of many different kinds of public infrastructure projects have been completed in many other countries is a foundation for any new study. Ultimately, the quality of any project evaluation depends upon the importance that governments place on it. The scope to transfer the costs of wasteful projects to future generations who currently have no say in the political process magnifies the risk of enduring inefficiencies. The scope to transfer the political consequences to future governments may also make for them to make bad decisions of their own from the bad decisions they inherited. These issues were also canvassed by the Vernon Inquiry on into Australian economic performance (1965).

48 All fall-back arrangements should take place in the context of wider business contingency planning.

49 Natural justice has four important elements: (1) ensuring that a person is informed of the case against them or their interests; (2) giving them a right to be heard (the 'hearing' rule); (3) not having a personal interest in the outcome (the rule against 'bias'); and (4) acting only on the basis of logically probative evidence (the 'no evidence' rule).

- Have the new or changed arrangements been constituted as a project?[50]
  - Does the project have well defined stages and outcomes?
  - Does the project have an appropriate budget?
  - Is a post project evaluation planned to identify the barriers and facilitators of success?

In summary, any criterion needs to consider both financial and non-financial outcomes. The use of weightings is always recommended as it furthers discussion on the decision. Since human problems are often symptoms of other issues identifying any potential human reactions is essential. Often political and economic influences cause delays in recognising an initiative as a project, for example, a lack of funding until the next financial year. This makes costings inaccurate and may lead to suboptimal decisions.

14.5 Consider persuasion from behavioural bias, errors and pitfalls in forming judgements and making decisions

The process of gathering information, developing alternatives and weighting them against a criterion involves a systematic and skeptical approach to human judgement and decision-making. Research has identified a common set of biases, errors and pitfalls that can apply to forming judgements (as presenter and as audience). These are particularly prevalent where complex judgements are required. Persuasion[51] and biases originate from self-interest as well as misperception.

The broad management issues and challenges which arise from behavioural bias, errors and pitfalls in forming judgements include:

- The human tendency to try to make order out of chaos even when there is no order in the first place[52]

---

50 Many initiatives are not recognised as such and as a result they do not receive appropriate resources and attention. Their conduct as a product will introduce additional costs which may not have been considered in the cost benefit analysis.

51 Persuasion may be repetitive (e.g. advertising) or split-second persuasion which involves the use of a single brilliant, pertinent handful of words to change a person's mind. According to Dutton (2009: 5) we encounter persuasion about 400 times per day. Persuasion can be reduced to a five point model: (1) simplicity that is, persuasive ideas are simple although not all simple ideas are persuasive; (2) perceived self-interest, that is, persuasive approaches involve an appeal to the benefit of the hearer; (3) incongruity, that is something unexpected changes your point of view and renders all rational debate, or irrational argument completely irrelevant; (4) confidence; and (5) empathy, that is, the ability to read someone else's emotions and to respond to them (Dutton 2009).

52 A general discussion is provided by Gilovitch (1993) with a more scholarly and detailed example in Gilovitch, Vallone and Tversky (1985). A primary conclusion from these reviews is that there is a natural tendency to impose order on random and irregular data either through clustering or looking for confirmation.

- The considerable reluctance to initially spend time establishing the details and then planning action[53]
- The opinion of the majority is able to influence a minority ('group think[54]). This can lead to agreement on facts which are incorrect or actions which are suboptimal
- The tendency to rely on prior experience, that is, to see a new situation in terms of a previous experience and act in the same ways
- The use of cognitive heuristics[55] (or 'rules of thumb') which may be either effective or misleading[56]
- To become preoccupied with a single aspect of a decision and become 'blind' to its other ramifications which have unforeseen consequences.

The principal tools and techniques associated with behavioural bias, error and pitfalls in judgements and decision-making include:

- Goal definition (clarification of outcome)
- Satisficing
- Elimination by aspects
- Recognising biases which affect the value of a heuristic because they introduce over-simplification.[57]

The managerial decisions and judgements that are likely to be affected by bias, errors and decision pitfalls can be subject to seven tests[58]:

1. Is the availability bias operative?[59]
2. Is the representativeness bias operative?[60]

---

53 A comparative study of students and managers established one of the few differences was the tendency of managers to 'gain an overall picture, by asking questions' and 'coordinate[ing] data' compared to students who were more likely to make a decision (Dörner & Schölkopf 1991: 227).

54 The effect of groupthink may be masked by the apparent harmonious and agreeable nature of members of a team (Janis 1972/1982).

55 Cognitive heuristics are more commonly referred to simply as 'heuristics'.

56 Cognitive heuristics are used by novices and experts.

57 Judgement and decision-making has been portioned into rational and emotional components. It is more likely that normal cognitive processes give rise to non-rational by-products, perhaps associated with systematic misperceptions (Kahneman, Slovic & Tversky 1982).

58 These tests identify biases which are not obvious like many others kinds such as favouritism of an individual, group or region, ideological preference, nepotism, selecting the quote stating the lowest number and fawning to vested interests.

59 The mental retrieval process may be biased through failing to distinguish special from general cases, or by attention to solo or token members or by simply bringing some details readily to mind. This is also known as 'The Von Restorff effect'. This may also result in the misperception of minorities (Hamilton 1976).

60 Representativeness has three biases where the chance similarity or typicality of the features of a category are seized upon. First, there is the conjunction fallacy where two or more factors are believed to be more typical than a single instance or event. Second, there is the bias which is the misperception of chance. Random patterns appear non-random. Moreover, the pattern may be attributed to a cause. Third, there is the bias known as the gambler's fallacy (that prior outcomes affect the outcome of probabilistic events). A decision-maker may judge extreme values (such as a run of successes or failures) as non-chance. The common feature of these biases is a failure to consider probabilistic events (that is previous success

3. Has anchoring and adjustment occurred?[61]

4. Is a causal schema being relied upon?[62]

5. Is there hindsight bias?[63]

6. Is there overconfidence?[64]

7. Is there mutability?[65]

In summary, there is a tendency to use heuristics because they are cognitively undemanding.[66] Representativeness tends to dominate thinking so that events that are presentative of the kind of event being considered are deemed to have a high probability of occurrence. It may also lead to a mistaken belief that the conjunction or combination of two events makes them more likely. Other judgement errors arise from estimating the frequency of events on the basis of how easy it is to retrieve relevant information from long-term memory although there are some confounding aspects. For example, the description of the event that is presented for consideration. Since employees have limited time and are likely to use heuristics as means of shortening the process their comments may appear better than an educated guess, making an intuitive judgment, or using common sense but their apparent persuasiveness may introduce errors and biases.

Chapter summary

Improving the business judgement and decision-making of employees and managers is a matter of awareness of models of business judgement and decision-making. The process of making a decision is described as a linear process. Most decision-making uses expected utility theory which has limitations. Often human decision-making overlooks ancillary judgements and decisions so guidelines are provided. A major area of weakness in forming

---

and failure does not affect an outcome. A string of successes or failures may still affect an individual. It may encourage an individual to try harder or result in them becoming demoralised.

61 These biases arise if (1) the initial estimate or reference is influential or (2) an insufficiently large adjustment is made to offset an initial low estimate. An influential anchor may be generated by an arbitrary or biased source.

62 A bias arises where a causal direction is inferred where there is merely a (non-directional) correlation. A causal schema may lead people to ignore other information which may be relevant. It may also result in the expectation that predictions will be more accurate because they are presented in ways consistent with expectations about underlying stability or causes.

63 It is not always clear to individuals that something they learnt after the fact would have been unknown beforehand. A hindsight bias often leads to an under-appreciation of the initial difficulty in making a decision. In practice, it is almost impossible to ignore knowledge of the outcome or a correct solution and make use of the other information available (Fischoff 1982).

64 Overconfidence is confidence greater than is objectively justifiable. This may occur from hindsight bias, lack of training in using probabilities, or lack of feedback when incorrect.

65 Bias can creep in when a comparison is made with easy to imagine alternatives associated with the events themselves. Aspects of the situation that are the focus of attention are also more easily imagined to be different or contributing to the situation.

66 The experiments conducted by Kahneman and Tversky (1982) found two major classes of heuristic: (1) representativeness which allocates an event or activity to a class; (2) availability or how easy it is to recall an instance. A third error arises from ignoring base rate (that is, given) information (Koehler 1996).

judgements and making decisions is the operation of heuristics and biases. Awareness of these heuristics and biases may help improve decision-making. Common heuristics and biases are discussed. The next chapter provides a standpoint to review an integrated approach to financial performance evaluation.

15 Evaluate productivity and profitability with financial and related non-financial information

The evaluation of performance typically makes reference to financial information accompanied by related non-financial information.[1] There a mistaken tendency to automatically prefer some forms of financial information as absolutely superior. This chapter explores a framework for evaluating financial and related non-financial information. It is acknowledged that employees may not see the financials.

Financial and related non-financial information in evaluation

Earlier chapters emphasised the importance of using financial and related non-financial information to exercise proper financial control and consider risk. Financial and non-financial information is directly used in many aspects of business. For example, in managing growth by balancing flexible external debt and equity and the acquisition and allocation of resources within the business (discussed in Chapter 3). Financial and non-financial information is used when evaluating the cost of any adjustments, which become necessary as the rationale for the existence of the business changes, to organisation structure and business function (discussed in Chapter 6). It assists sensemaking leading to revised financial projections based on current circumstances while controlling costs (Chapter 7). Financial and related non-financial information can be effectively used to evaluate past performance and create models of future cash flows. Financial information can motivate and control employees and managers responsible for costs, revenues and investments.

Financial and non-financial information also has many indirect uses. It contributes to the formulation of policies, controls and reviews bringing flexibility to operation with non-financial aspects (discussed in Chapter 8). It allows judgements to be made on the range of benefits from the intangible resources of employee ability and expertise (discussed in Chapter 10). It makes clear that information is a resource in its own right (discussed in Chapter 11).

---

1 Related non-financial information includes quantities of products or services manufactured, purchased, placed in inventory, sold, scrapped or written-down in value. It also includes transaction throughput volumes (purchases, sales, replacements, returns/refunds). This information supplements the financial data produced in both subsidiary and general ledgers.

It suggests that some of the tangible benefits from resources such as capital investments in systems and technology may be overlooked (discussed in Chapter 12). These indirect uses emphasise that they should be evaluated solely on financial criteria.

Factors in selecting financial measures

Five factors are used to select financial measures that can be used to monitor performance, that can be integrated and that reduce the opportunity for manipulation by introducing relationships and dependencies outside the control of an individual employees and managers identifies five factors: (1) the decision-making horizon (short-term or long-term); (2) the business control structure (centralised or decentralised); (3) the kind of strategic business unit (cost, profit or investment centre); (4) cultural factors; and (5) motivational forces (incentives and cultural orientation).

When this more complex set of factors is recognised, the typical reaction of automatically preferring investment return measures can be seen to create new problems which may be quite difficult to understand and which may have counterproductive effects. Any evaluation of performance with financial and related non-financial information should therefore consider all options not just investment oriented measures. These options are introduced in the following topics.

Topics in the evaluation of productivity and profitability

The approach proposed for the evaluation of performance begins by profiling the potential use of the financial and related non-financial information and the relevant strengths and weaknesses for the user of the information:

1. Maintain a watchful financial perspective

2. Evaluate cost centre productivity

3. Evaluate profit centre productivity and profitability

4. Evaluate investment centre long-term profitability

5. Select for routine reporting the critical success factors.

15.1 Maintain a watchful financial perspective

Maintaining a watchful financial perspective means takes an in-the-rounded view of the financial implications of all the business operations and strategies. While it honours the partnership with business unit managers, a financial perspective involves being a conscience in the planning and oversight of all aspects of the business, asking the difficult questions sufficiently early to pre-empt loss of competitive advantage.[2]

---

2 Industries such as the automotive and mechanical, books, cosmetics, clothing, electronics, footwear and retail are particularly in need of outspoken financial managers. For public companies, investors can express their dissatisfaction by selling their shares. Institutional investors can engineer a share price slide to signal something needs to be done to

The broad management issues and challenges in maintaining a watchful financial perspective include:

- Making a decision within a specified time frame[3]
- Concentrating on business-wide problems and opportunities
- Managing in a decentralised structure without constraining innovation or allowing waste
- Obtaining impartial knowledge of business operational performance
- Ensuring the correct definition of organisation centres (cost, profit, investment) where the business including customers are changing
- Achieving reasonable rents
- Achieving goal congruence
- Selecting methods of evaluation that do not penalise business units for their size or productive capacity
- Being seen to be fair in the allocation of fixed costs and overhead.

The principal tools and techniques for maintaining a watchful financial perspective include:

- Not relying entirely on financial reports
- Determining an acceptable rate-of-return for the business units
- Using short-term financial evaluation methods. Consider:
  - An annual master budget set
  - Cost-Volume-Profit (CVP) planning.
- Using long-term financial evaluation methods. Consider:
  - Return on Investment (ROI)
  - Residual value
  - The proprietary form of residual value, Economic Value Added (EVA).

The managerial decisions and judgements for maintaining a watchful financial perspective include:

- What are difficult operational questions that need to be addressed? Consider:
  - Will revenue and profitability targets be reached?

---

address an erosion in wealth. For example, Myer which listed at AUD4.10 reached an all time low in January 2012 of AUD1.93.

3 This is considered a characteristic of bounded rationality when considered in conjunction with the limited cognitive abilities of an individual and the limited information they have available (Simon 1945/1997). The idea that human rationality is goal-directed but humans have limited information-processing capability has been widely adopted since proposed by Simon (1945/1997).

- – Are costs being sufficiently controlled so that when the financial reports are received they will be satisfactory?
- – What should be the wholesale selling price and the recommended retail prices?
- – Should a special order be accepted at a reduced selling price?
- – Should the product mix be changed owing to restrictions on production or sales?
- – Should a product be sold as is or further processed?
- What are the difficult strategic questions that need to be addressed? Consider:
  - – Is the business model outdated?
  - – Have we become too reliant on suppliers?
  - – Should a product or activity be outsourced?
  - – Should a product or a product line, or presence in a territory be eliminated?
  - – Is there sufficient research and development and innovation?

In summary, a watchful perspective goes beyond the evaluation of measures and the use of financial and related non-financial information. The finance team is also concerned with weak and ambiguous signals. The recent history of financial management confirms that reliance on reports can overlook looming problems.

15.2 Evaluate cost centre productivity

Since the cost centre is an expenditure centre, it is primarily responsible for meeting goals and budgets in a short-term time frame. In the short-term, financial decisions do not include calculations of the time value of money of revenues and expenses.

The broad management issues and challenges in evaluating cost centre productivity include:

- The level in the organisation unit at which a cost centre is established[4]
- Ensuring that there is no overlap in responsibility and accountability between units
- Ensuring that the leadership is clearly delineated for each unit.

The principal tools and techniques associated with evaluating cost centre productivity include:

- A fully articulated annual master budget (discussed in Topic 15.2.1)
- Standard costs with variance reporting (discussed in Topics 15.2.2 and 15.2.3).

---

4 Cost centres may be established at the level of the business unit, a business subunit or an even smaller organisational subunit).

The managerial decisions and judgements associated with evaluating cost centres for productivity include:

- Is this approach appropriate for the organisation and its industry?
- Does the organisation have sufficient competency to set-up and manage these systems?
- Will the benefits exceed the costs?

15.2.1 Use a fully articulated annual master budget

An annual budget for a business unit (or subunit) must contain those costs over which it has control. However, it is not necessary for the manager to have total control over a cost to be held accountable for it. It is sufficient for the manager to be able to influence the cost.

The broad management issues and challenges with the annual budget include:

- Ensuring that budgets are realistic given the macro and the micro environment
- Determining the relationship between budget outcomes and performance evaluation
- Making clear how budget shortfalls will be treated.

The principal tools and techniques associated with the annual budget include:

- Having the manager of the subunit who is most familiar with the business operations participate in preparing the budget (participative budgeting) rather than using authoritative budgeting
- Making the nominated manager aware that they will be responsible for variances in the controllable costs
- Ensuring that the submitted budget is reviewed by other managers familiar with the operation to avoid budgetary slack.
- Enforcing disciplines around the master budget system. Consider:
  - Creating supporting schedules to detail the supporting calculations for experience-based decisions including revenues, expenses and uncollectible debts which can then be available to explain variances
  - Flexing the budget to keep it relevant by recalculating it based on actual sales or production level to ensure the calculation of variances is soundly based
  - Determining whether an incremental or zero-base budget will be justified[5]
  - Using a continuous budget allows the budget to retain its horizon (e.g. twelve months, three years, ten years) by adding on the relevant time period (month, quarter, year).

The managerial decisions and judgements associated with the annual budget include:

---

5 Periodically reviewing all costs for a budget item using zero-base budgeting can be useful for establishing the cost/benefit analysis for all expenses rather than the incremental increase over the previous year.

- Is information being concealed?[6]
- Does the budget balance planned cash outflows with funding[7] (for public sector agencies)?
- Does the budget engender the efficient planning and control of operations?

In summary, businesses of all sizes and with all kinds of accounting systems benefit from a budget particularly where the manager is involved in its preparation. The budget facilitates the use of standard costs.

15.2.2 Set standard costs

Standard costing goes beyond the actual costs incurred to use a predetermined dollar cost based on the expected or budgeted cost of materials, labour and manufacturing overhead to produce one unit or product.

The broad management issues and challenges with setting standard costs include:

- Whether to determine standard costs by ideal or attainability[8]
- The variances that will be reported using standard costs
- The changes that will be made to standard costs at the time they are reviewed (for example, in producing the next annual master budget).

The principal tools and techniques associated with setting standard costs include:

- Setting standard costs and ensuring that all costs are included in the standard. Consider:
  - Standards for direct materials based on (1) the quality of the material, allowances for wastage and the typical reject rate and (2) the price paid based on the quantities usually ordered including purchase discounts, freight costs based on the shipment arrangements and receiving, inspection and storage costs
  - Standards for direct labour[9] based on either (1) time and motion engineering studies or (2) performance level achieved by benchmarking either a single competitor or across an industry

---

6 A difficulty with annual budgets is the upward flow of financial and related non-financial information may lead to restricted disclosure where effort is directed toward concealing or filtering the information made available to be aggregated or provided to higher managers. The rationale for this may be to be eligible for incentive payments or simply to create a favourable impression.

7 The cash outflow is a spending plan limited directly by the budget of the government appropriation or indirectly by the provision of funds to supplement revenues raised. As governments attempt to eliminate deficits there is a reluctance to increase funding beyond the CPI or inflation index. This usually results in the agencies establishing priorities for expenditure and developing a program to improve the efficiencies in the delivery of services.

8 While ideal standards based on plentiful materials, reliable machines and skilled employees can be set, variances become difficult to analyse since employees and managers can attribute deviations to an unattainable standard rather than inefficiencies. Currently attainable standards recognise allowances for machine downtime and employee rest periods and are kept up-to-date. In this regard currently attainable standards may be informed by historical costs but will need to be set on the basis of the latest information including anticipated changes.

9 The standard rate will include the wages earned plus allowances for breaks, personal needs, rework, clean-up and down-time as well as labour costs such as employee benefits and taxes including taxes on benefits.

- Standards for manufacturing overhead standards based on the amount of variable manufacturing overhead incurred and fixed manufacturing overhead per volume of completed production.[10]

- Ensuring that all costs are included in the standard.

The managerial decisions and judgements associated with setting standard costs include:

- Are the standard costs calculated in ways which managers and employees understand?

- Are the standard costs stored in accounting systems so they can be automatically calculated for product or service costing and control?

- Does standard costing accompany quality management programs?

In summary, setting standard costs is an important activity because it has wide applicability in all sectors.

15.2.3 Decompose and report variances

Since a variance is the difference between an actual amount and a pre-determined standard amount a single variance will only identify the existence of a potential problem for further investigation of what can be done to improve future results. Further investigation involves both decomposition and examination of the variance.

The broad management issues and challenges with decomposing and reporting variances include:

- Using standard costs to allow comparison with actual quantity and with actual price paid so three variances (price, efficiency and volume) be calculated.[11] Consider:

  - A price[12] variance is the difference between the actual price of an input and its standard price for the quantity of input

  - An efficiency[13] variance is the difference between how much input was actually used and the standard input in monetary terms

  - A volume variance[14] is the error that occurs when the level of activity is incorrectly estimated and the costing system assumes fixes costs behave as if they are variable.

---

10 Common cost-allocation bases used for manufacturing overhead that encompass both fixed and variable costs are (in order of popularity): (1) direct labour, (2) machine-hours, (3) units of production, (4) direct material cost. However, there is also a trend toward the use of multiple allocation bases. Where businesses use activity drivers such as setup hours and inspection hours less of the overhead manufacturing cost is allocated to products using direct labour and machine hours.

11 The two variances (price and efficiency) are the peak of the hierarchy of variances. By convention variances are computed as actual costs minus budget costs and are labelled favourable if actual costs are less than the budget (a negative variance).

12 The price variance is referred to as 'price' or 'input price' for materials, 'rate' for labor and 'spending' for variable manufacturing overhead.

13 The efficiency variance is referred to as 'quantity' or 'usage' for materials, 'efficiency' for labor and 'efficiency' for variable manufacturing overhead.

14 This figure is considered in calculating overhead variances.

- Viewing the relationship between variances in three levels as a top-down hierarchy. Figure 11 below depicts the hierarchy of variances

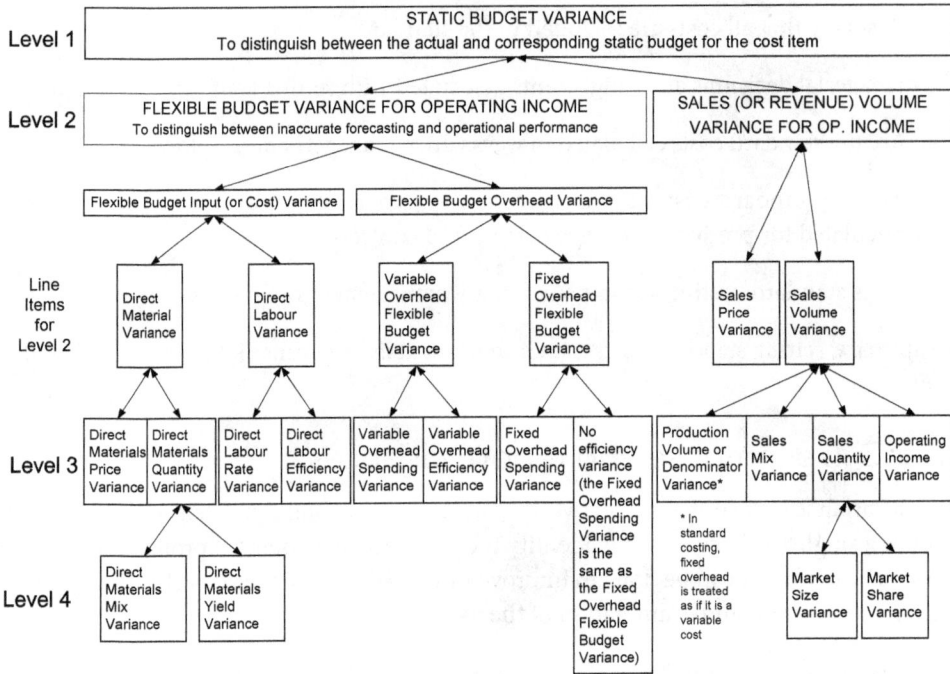

Figure 11. The three level top down hierarchy of variances with price and efficiency variances at the lowest level

The principal tools and techniques associated with decomposing and reporting variances include:

- For a price variance, the generic formula is: $(AQ * AP) - (AQ * SP)$[15] which can be simplified using the common term to: $AQ * (AP - SP)$

- For an efficiency variance, the generic formula is: $(AQ * SP) - (SQ * SP)$ which can be simplified using the common term to: $SP * (AQ - SQ)$

- For an efficiency variance, the generic formula is: $(AProd) - (BProd)$.

- Using the four-way overhead variance matrix (shown in Table 7 on next page) to analyse overhead cost variances. Consider:

  - Variable overhead does not have a production volume variance as variable costs never have any unused capacity

  - Fixed overhead does not have an efficiency variance as fixed costs are unaffected by the degree of operating efficiency in a given budget period

---

15 The generic formula can be reduced to the shortcut formula AQ (AP-SP) where AQ = Actual Quantity, AP = Actual Price and SP = Standard Price.

- The four-way variance analysis ideally allows the total overhead actually incurred to be reconciled with the overhead amounts allocated during the period

- Although, in practice, it may not be possible to separate fixed and variable manufacturing overhead in a cost-efficient manner, the resulting combined variance analysis simplifies the reporting process with a loss of detail.

Table 7. Four-way overhead variance matrix

	Variance		
	Spending	**Efficiency**	**Production volume**
Variable	Actual quantity and actual rate compared to actual quantity budgeted rate	Actual quantity budgeted rate compared to budgeted quantity and budgeted rate	No variance: The allocated amount is always the same as the amount in the flexible budget
Fixed	Actual costs compared to budgeted cost (in static budget)	No variance: Fixed costs are unaffected by any efficiencies in a period.	Budgeted cost (in static budget) compared to output quantity and flexible budget rate

The managerial decisions and judgements associated with decomposing and reporting variances include:

- Have the basic variance calculations (shown in Table 8 on next page) been performed?

- Have the basic variance calculations been performed as soon as practicable (shown in Table 6) to allow time for corrective action?

- When will variances be reported (e.g. monthly, quarterly, for seasons)?

- What resources will be allocated to investigating the different variances?

- What reporting is appropriate where majority of costs are fixed overhead costs (for example, equipment, buildings or building leases and employees) and these resources are therefore a capacity which needs to be utilised effectively?

- Is the variance material?[16]

- Does the variance recur across periods (whether small or large)?

- Does the variance make a significant immediate impact or long-term effect on the overall profitability of the business?

16 In the service sector (for example, airlines, hospitals, hotels, freight) very few of the costs can be traced to the outputs (for example passenger kilometres flown, patient days, room days, ton kilometres of freight) of the business in an effective manner.

- Does the responsibility centre manager have the ability to influence the variance?[17]
- Does a payoff probability table suggest an investigation is warranted?

Table 8. Selected variances with typical business function responsible for it and the frequency of calculation

Variance Name		Responsible Business Function	When Calculated
Direct Materials	Materials price (or rate) variance	Purchasing Department	At time of purchase
	Materials efficiency (or quantity) variance	Production Department	When material issued or used in manufacturing
	Reconciliation	Total of price and efficiency variances reconciled to total overall material variance	Completion of the job order
Direct Labour	Labour price (or rate) variance	Human Resources Department	Completion of the job order
	Labour fficiency (or quantity) variance	Production Department	Completion of the job order
	Reconciliation	Total of rate and efficiency variances reconciled to total overall labour variance	Completion of the job order
Overhead	Variable	Production Department	Completion of the job order
	Fixed	Production Department	End of period
Seling	Price and Income	Sales and Marketing Department	End of period

---

17 Some managers will claim that an unfavourable material price variance or rate variance is the responsibility of support departments (typically purchasing and human resources respectively) who are responsible for keeping production (or services) moving. In this case the root cause of the variance needs investigation to determine what instigated the need for materials or labour (e.g. were they additional to budget, the result of poor quality materials received or allowed to deteriorate). Even if it is not under the control of the manager, it is still prudent for the variance to appear on performance reports.

In summary, the standard costing system for job order or process costing creates additional financial and related non-financial information for employees and managers. It can be used for product costing and pricing. The variances act as an exception reporting system[18] for management but misunderstandings may lead to wasted investigations and demoralise employees, creating new behavioural problems.

15.3 Evaluate profit centre productivity and profitability

Since a profit centre is not only responsible for costs under its control but also generating revenues it ought not to contain large amounts of invested capital. Like cost centres it makes short-term financial decisions and does not calculate the time value of money of revenues and expenses. The ideal form of evaluation uses the standard variable cost income statement provided there is a soundly prepared budget.

The broad management issues and challenges with evaluating profit centre productivity and profitability include:

- The level in the organisation unit at which a profit centre is established (e.g. the business unit, business subunit or an even smaller organisational unit)

- Ensuring there is no overlap in responsibility and accountability between units

- Ensuring that the leadership is clearly delineated for each unit.

The principal tools and techniques associated with the evaluating profit centre productivity and profitability include:

- The design of the standard variable cost income statement. Consider:

  - It is modularised so that within the profit centre financial information is grouped around segments (for example, divisions, product lines within a division, factory producing a product, sales territory) to allow recombination

  - It is based on the revised or latest budget which takes into account all current circumstances

  - Where costs are allocated by head office to the profit centre they are not held accountable for them.

- Using the three profit categories in the standard variable cost income statement. Consider:

  - Contribution margin to focus on the attainment of business goals in the short-term

---

18 In fact, all variances only reveal a possible exception and not the cause, which requires a decision on whether to investigate and the allocation of resources to complete the investigation.

    – Controllable margin to assess management performance where programmed fixed costs (for example, advertising) are under control of the profit centre or a unit within it

    – Segment (for example, division, product or factory) margin or income to identify the amount the segment contributes toward the common fixed costs and profit.

The managerial decisions and judgements associated with evaluating profit centre productivity and profitability include:

- How to treat business-wide and head office costs?[19]

- How to balance reporting between short-term and long-term measures?[20]

In summary, the evaluation of profit centres is primarily a financial assessment. While other forms of assessment are fashionable (e.g. Balanced ScoreCard) there is no substitute for ensuring the profit centres are profitable in terms of straightforward financial measurements.

15.4 Evaluate investment centre long-term profitability

Since an in investment centre also controls significant amounts of investment capital as assets (which are a long-term investment), it is appropriate for these calculations use the time value of money. The criterion for an investment centre is the income that it generates.

The broad management issues and challenges for a DuPont single measure summary calculation include:

- The financial horizon for returns

- The expected level of return

- The risk associated with the loss of capital and the expected level of return

- The criteria for comparable returns in terms of benchmarks or targets.

The principal tools and techniques associated with the evaluating investment centre long-term profitability include:

- Return on Investment (ROI) (discussed in Topic 15.4.1 below)

- Residual income (discussed in Topic 15.4.2 below)

- Residual income's proprietary refinement, Economic Value Added (EVA) .

---

19 For example, the legal costs, interest expense and salaries of head office employees should not be charged to profit centres unless it is possible to directly trace costs and benefits to the profit centre. If allocations are arbitrary (for example based on revenue or profit) then this will make the most successful business unit shoulder most of the corporate cost burden.

20 Although these are viewed as short-term measures segment margin or income is also one measure of long-term profitability of the segment (for example, division, product or factory) margin or income segment since it must in the long run cover direct fixed expenses.

The managerial decisions and judgements associated with evaluating investment centre long-term profitability include:

- Is an annual review appropriate given the typical financial horizon is twelve months?[21]

- Is an integrated financial framework an attractive means of systematically and consistently measuring the performance of the business since it must be successful in (1) producing an operating profit from its activities, (2) effectively managing its level of assets and (3) managing the amount of it debt?

- What responsibilities are not discharged by the investment centre alone?[22]

15.4.1 Integrate ROI with the DuPont analysis framework

The DuPont analysis framework provides a means of integrating a number of separate financial ratios from the balance sheet and the income statement. Because it links critical ratios which influence company performance the DuPont Formula can diagnose the factors which influence performance of the business. If operations are successful (high Profit Margin) and management of assets is strong (high Total Asset Turnover) and management of the capital structure is tight (low Equity Margin), then for sound business reasons the ROI will be high. The business is then assessed as having a strong financial position.

The broad management issues and challenges for a DuPont single measure summary calculation include:

- Whether to use the DuPont formula at the business unit level where it is usually known as return on investment or the project level of analyses where it is usually known as accounting rate of return or accrual accounting rate of return

- Which particular formula is appropriate.[23]

The principal tools and techniques for a DuPont single measure summary calculation include:

- The formula for the DuPont single measure[24] summary is: Return on Investment = (Selected Income[25]) / (Investment Base[26])

---

21 For interim periods of less than one year it would be more appropriate to use the standard variable costing income statement previously discussed.

22 It is usual for there to be both oversight of the investment at proposal stage as well as in the viability of the continuing investment. In some cases this will result in an investment being deferred owing to an unfavourable investment climate and this needs to be considered in making any performance evaluation in terms of the viability of investments proposed.

23 Different formulas would be of interest to particular stakeholders. For example, share holders who are interested in the assets available to them would consider ROE. Long-term lenders who are interested in the viability of the business would consider ROI. Short-term lenders who are interested in the short-term liquidity provided by net profits and asset turnover would consider ROA.

24 A Du Pont analysis relies upon the accounting identity of Assets equal liabilities plus owners equity which is a formula that is by definition true.

25 'Selected Income' is used as a placeholder for 'Net profit' or 'Segment Income'. Income before interest and taxes is conveniently chosen to give an undiluted analysis of the operations of the investment centre. Gains or losses on fixed asset disposal are also outside the ambit of operations.

26 'Investment base' is used as a placeholder for (1) 'Total Gross Assets', or (2) 'Total Net Assets', or (3) 'Total Net Assets less any currently unproductive assets' or (4) 'Total Net Assets (with or without any unproductive assets minus current

- The single measure summary formula is usually decomposed into three factors namely (1) Operating efficiency; (2) Asset productivity; and (3) Financial leverage (which are separately detailed below)

- In the expanded alternative the factors are replaced by their measures and the formula becomes: Return on Investment = (Net profit margin or return on sales) * (Total asset turnover [27] or total capital turnover or investment turnover) * (Equity multiplier[28])

- The DuPont analysis framework as a hierarchy is depicted visually in Figure 12 below

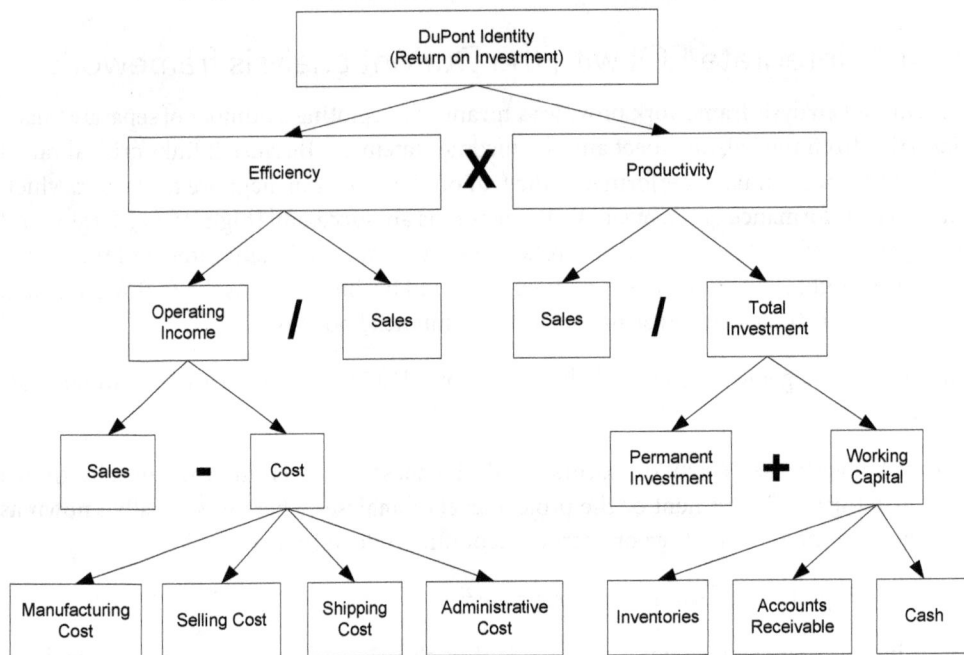

Figure 12. DuPont analysis framework

The managerial decisions and judgements for a DuPont single measure summary calculation include:

- Is the result acceptable in terms of the overall performance of the business?[29]

- Have the calculations been checked using the proof (See Figure 13 on the next page)?

---

liabilities controllable by the investment centre'.

27 If only (Net profit margin) * (Asset turnover) is considered then it is equal to (Return on Assets).

28 If (Total assets) / (Shareholder equity) then it is equal to (Return on Equity).

29 A typical maximum level is 15% with many businesses achieving well below. It can be calculated before or after extraordinary items.

Given that the Dupont identity states ROI = P / E
Then multiply by 1 (A / A)
So ROI = (P / E) * (A / A)
and then rearrange
ROI = (P / A) 8 (A / E) = ROA * EM
Multiply by 1 (R / R)
ROI = (P / A) * (A / E) * (R / R)
and then rearrange
ROI = (P / R) * (R / A) * (A / E)
ROI = PM * TAT * EM
Or ROI = Profit Margin * Total Asset Turnover * Equity Multiplier

Where:
A = Total Assets; D = Total Debt; E = Total Equity; EM = Equity Multiplier = A/E = 1
+ D / E; P = Net Profit; PM = Profit Margin; R = Revenue; ROA = Return on Assets;
ROI = Return on Investment; and TAT = Total Asset Turnover.

Figure 13. Proof for the DuPont identity

1. Operating efficiency DuPont factor

The broad management issues and challenges for assessing the operating efficiency component include:

- Whether all relevant inputs have been systematically measured.

The principal tools and techniques for assessing operating efficiency measured by the Profit Margin Ratio include:

- The key data is: Revenue (also known as sales revenue); and Net Profit (also known as net income) meaning profit after taxes

- The formula is: Profit Margin = Net Profit / Revenue, where the numerator Net Profit is after tax but it may be the operating income before tax

- The interpretation of the result is the ability to control operating expenses relative to sales within a period, so it is the amount of every revenue dollar left after tax. Improvement occurs when revenue increases and costs do not increase proportionately or when costs are reduced for a given level of sales. Net profit margins vary by industry; and a low profit margin ratio means there is little scope for management to miscalculate its strategy or its execution.

The managerial decisions and judgements for the operating efficiency component include:

- Should the selling price be increased?
- Can the costs be reduced?

2. Asset productivity DuPont factor

The broad management issues and challenges for assessing the asset productivity component include:

- Whether all relevant inputs have been systematically measured.

The principal tools and techniques for assessing asset productivity measured by asset turnover include:

- The key data is: Revenue (also known as total sales revenue); and Assets (includes fixed assets and working capital)
- The formulas is: Total asset turnover = (Revenue) / (Total assets) where the denominator Total assets is after tax but it may be those assets financed by long-term debt and shareholder equity that is, less current liabilities
- The interpretation of the result is a measure of the sales generated by each dollar invested in operating assets so it is the notional flow of money through the business or intensity of capital use. Asset turnover ratio tends to be inversely related to net profit margin (that is, low profit and high volume or high profit and low volume. A current industry average is often needed to interpret this ratio. For example, a manufacturing ratio = 1-2 times; and a retailing ratio= 4-6 times. An improvement occurs when investment decreases for a given level of revenue. A high ratio may mean that the business is not adequately replacing its assets which would be a sign of poor management. A rising ratio means that the business is able to produce increasing sales from its assets. Different businesses can be compared as it is a measure of how effectively a business converts its assets into revenue (sales).

The managerial decisions and judgements for the asset productivity component include:

- How to decrease idle cash?
- How to judiciously manage credit?
- What figure should be set for inventory levels?
- What are wise investments in long-term assets?

3. Financial leverage DuPont factor

The broad management issues and challenges for assessing the financial leverage component include:

- Whether the business is using debt to finance its asset base.

The principal tools and techniques for assessing financial leverage measured by the equity multiplier include:

- The key data is: Assets; and Shareholder equity (also known as Shareholder funds)

- The formula is: Equity multiplier = (Assets) / (Shareholder equity)

- The interpretation of the result is the proportion of return on equity that is the result of debt which reveals the extent to which sales and debt are responsible for return on equity (or, more simply, whether the business is using debt to finance its asset base).

The managerial decisions and judgements for the financial leverage component include: :

- How to choose wise investments in long-term assets?

- How to preserve capital and obtain acceptable growth?

15.4.2 Use Residual Income (RI)

The broad management issues and challenges for using residual income[30] include:

- Measuring the dollar amount of profits in excess of a required rate of return

- The minimum required rate of return expected for investments.

The principal tools and techniques for residual income include:

- The formula is: Residual income = (Operating income) – [(Required rate of return) * (Average operating assets)] where [(Required rate of return) * (Average operating assets)] is the imputed cost of the investment which can be recognised but not included in the financial statements

- The interpretation of the result is subject to overweighting information in required rate of return and under-weighting information from current earnings and book value.

The managerial decisions and judgements for residual income include:

- Which investment will benefit the business?

- Is the manager of the business unit refraining from a worthwhile investment because residual income analysis predicts the business unit ROI will decrease.

- Do industry factors such as concentration and barriers to entry affect residual income?

- Do accounting standards and industry accounting practices within the industry affect residual income?

15.4.2.1 Use the proprietary form of RI economic value added (EVA)

The broad management issues and challenges for using economic value added[31] (EVA) include:

---

30 The objective of maximising residual income is to give a business unit a threshold to guide it on whether to continue making investments where the ROI for a particular investment is less than the business hurdle ROI rate.

31 Economic value added uses residual income with adjustments. It is the after-tax operating income minus the (after-tax) weighted average cost of capital multiplied by total assets minus current liabilities.

- Maximising residual income is to give a business unit a threshold to guide it on whether to continue making investments where the ROI for a particular investment is less than the business hurdle ROI rate.

The principal tools and techniques for using the proprietary economic value added (EVA) include:

- The formula is: Economic value added = (Adjusted after tax operating income) – [(Weighted average cost of capital) * (Adjusted total assets) – (Current liabilities)] where Weighted average cost of capital = After-tax cost of all long-term financing for the business or business unit taking into account the industry risk and characteristics
- The interpretation of the result is dependent upon the specific assumptions and adjustments made for the particular business.

The managerial decisions and judgements for EVA include:

- How can more after-tax operating profit be earned than was previously obtained?
- How can less capital earn the same after-tax operating profit than previously obtained?
- What projects offer a high return on investment?

15.4.3 Use financial ratio analysis for comparisons

The financial statements of a business contain many items that, taken by themselves, have no clear meaning. Financial ratio analysis is one means of appraising their relative importance. It can be used to compare: (1) the performance of a business with that of other businesses in the same industry; (2) with the performance of industry in general; or (3) to study trends in the performance of the business over time and thus to anticipate problems before they develop. External parties can also use financial analysis provided sufficient information is available.

The broad management issues and challenges with external financial analysis include:

- The selection of tools for which sufficient financial data is available
- The need to use agreed ratios
- The difficulty in interpreting the results from calculations given there is a range of commentary on acceptable or expected figures
- The problem of comparability given the different reporting dates, segment analysis and accounting practices in organisations.

The principal tools and techniques associated with the evaluating profit centres for evaluating investment centres for long-term profitability include:

- Common size statements (vertical analysis) of the balance sheet and income statement (discussed in topic 15.4.3.1 below)

- Financial ratios[32] (discussed in Topic 15.4.3.2 below).

The managerial decisions and judgements associated with evaluating investment centres for long-term profitability include:

- Which results from external financial ratios will be accorded the most attention?
- Will the results offer any predictive advice that facilitates decision-making
- Are the results from competitors or benchmarks sufficiently up-to-date to be comparable?

15.4.3.1 Apply common size statements (vertical analysis) to the balance sheet and income statement

The broad management issues and challenges with common size statements (vertical analysis) of the balance sheet and income statement include:

- The identification of trends over time
- The comparison of different businesses.

The principal tools and techniques associated with common size statements (vertical analysis) of the balance sheet and income statement include:

- For the common size balance sheet. Consider:
  - Express each item as a percentage of the total asset total liabilities or shareholder equity as appropriate
  - Depict in a line graph the asset items (cash and cash equivalents, receivables, inventories, other current assets, non-current assets and property plant and equipment), and liability items (accounts payable, short-term debt, other current liabilities, long-term debt, non-current liabilities).
- For the common size income statement. Consider:
  - Express each cost element as a percentage of sales
  - Depict in a line graph cost of sales, gross operating profit, selling, general and administrative expenses, depreciation and amortisation and pre-tax income.

The managerial decisions and judgements associated common size statements (vertical analysis) of the balance sheet and income statement include:

- Are the overall trends and comparisons (see above) satisfactory?
- Are specific trends and comparisons (see above) satisfactory?

---

32 Although often calculated for market comparison purposes, Rappaport (1999) identifies the benefits that follow from using indexed options to reward managerial performance in preference to fixed price share options.

15.4.3.2 Calculate a range of financial ratios on recast financial statements

The broad management issues and challenges with financial ratios include:

- Selecting the financial ratios that are the best tests for the stability of the business[33]

- Calculating the ratios that market analysts would routinely calculate.

The principal tools and techniques associated with financial ratios include:

- There are six areas where ratios can be usefully calculated.[34] Consider:
  - Profitability:
    - o Return on assets
    - o Return on common equity
    - o Basic earnings per share
    - o Dividend yield ratio.
  - Efficiency:
    - o Gross profit margin
    - o Operating profit margin
    - o Net profit margin.
  - Financial leverage:
    - o Debt/equity ratio
    - o Debt ratio.
  - Liquidity:
    - o Current ratio[35]
    - o Quick ratio
    - o Times interest earned
    - o Free cash flow.
  - Asset use (productivity):
    - o Accounts receivable turnover
    - o Inventory turnover
    - o Total asset turnover.

---

33 Since these tests are well-known to investors of all types it is likely that some calculators can be found by using a search on the internet.

34 In noting apparent serious trends it is prudent to first investigate whether other factors have intervened. For example share issues will affect the price to earnings ratio.

35 Various commentators have observed that almost 'every company that has got into financial strife has had a sound current ratio right to the end.' (Jamieson 1995: 11).

- – Market value:
  - o Price earnings ratio
  - o Market to book ratio.
- Calculate a range of financial ratios either directly on the data available in accounts or by recasting the data to simplify it[36]
- Understanding their limitations.[37]

The managerial decisions and judgements associated with financial ratios include:

- Do the regrouped and renamed accounts that have been constructed contain all the relevant information?
- Does the financial ratio use the top 100/200 company ratios and industry ratios?
- Is the interpretation consistent with analysts and experts?
- Should any financial ratios be investigated?
- Have any ratios been interpreted in isolation even if the interpretation is done in an acceptable range?
- Is there an industry context to support interpretation for each ratio of interest.[38]

In summary, the advantage of attempting external control through financial ratio analysis lies in the comparison with competitors and industry performance. These are the same bases that external analysts and media commentators are either most likely to calculate or use and which will therefore be reported in the public press.

---

36 Usually when attempting to compare different businesses it is prudent to modify the accounts presented to ensure a consistent basis for calculations. This will involve regrouping and renaming account items for consistency and recasting the financial statements themselves into a simplified form. While judgement is required on what information to include in the simplified financial statement (from the source financial statement, disclosure notes and commentaries) the result should be a standardised set of financial statements. A template for recast financial statements is provided in Form 8 of the form supplement (available at the book's website – details given in Introduction) which can simplify financial ratio analysis.

37 Since all ratio calculations are based on historical results they have an inherent limitation. They ignore the results of any proposed strategic initiatives. The effects of any current initiatives may be incomplete. It would then be meaningless to project past data to predict future performance or to adjust available data to create projected future performance.

38 In noting apparent serious trends it is prudent to first investigate whether other factors have intervened. For example share issues will affect the price to earnings ratio. Industry and competitor comparisons may need to be adjusted where the competitor or the industry is different. For example, there may be differences in the product range or they may use different accounting treatments. Where the are environmental factors such as a recession the appropriate or acceptable value for a ratio may be difficult to determine. Where seasonal factors prevail any snapshot needs to ensure it covers a sufficient period to allow a representative ratio. Finally the possibility that a business will misrepresent financial information or manipulates its financial information will produce misleading ratios.

15.5 Select for routine reporting the critical success factors

Most financial measures have a specific purpose. Managers also need a routine report on what they determine to be the critical success factors of the business in the short and long-term. The high regard with financial and time value of money measures inevitably means that they will be some of the indicators in most routine reports.

The management issues and challenges with selecting critical success factors for routine reporting include:

- Selecting indicators which are relevant to the same industry and similar businesses
- Selecting a suitable set of indicators which are appropriate to the role and responsibilities
- Selecting indicators which suggest how to improve critical success factors
- An awareness of the particular advantages (shown in Table 9 below) and disadvantages (shown in Table 10 on the next page) of three financial methods for analysing business success.

Table 9. Advantages of each of the three financial methods of analysing business success

Comparison of the three financial methods		DuPont	Residual Income	EVA
Comparability and accountability	Readily compare the ROE of different business units ROE with other business units	✓		
	Readily compare the ROE of different business units with external benchmarks	✓		
	Hold managers accountable for ROE to reduce the tendency to overinvest in projects	✓		
	Changes occur in investments		✓	
	Investments in projects with lower returns than current projects are not penalised		✓	
	Allows the calculation and use of the cost of capital in decisions at the business unit which reflect the cost of capital for the business unit			✓
Influences on the calculation	Effect of the size of the investment (values the expected return)		✓	
Tax issues	Using after-tax operating income for EBIT is an incentive for managers to reduce taxes		✓	✓

Comparison of the three financial methods		DuPont	Residual Income	EVA
Behavioural influences	When decomposed into components managers are motivated to increase sales, decrease costs and minimise asset investments	✓		
	Sub-optimal decision-making should be minimised as long-term asset investment decisions should the benefit to the business			✓
Standardisation	Measures do not necessarily follow generally accepted accounting principles as they are for internal purposes (e.g. some items are therefore treated as capital while remaining as expenses in the financial statements)			✓
	Adjustments are made to customise the measure to the business and the industry and align goals of the managers and owners.			✓

Table 10. Disadvantages of the three financial methods of financial analysis

Comparison of the three financial methods		DuPont	Residual Income	EVA
Comparability and accountability	The use of financial information to measure operating income results in some assets being understated	✓	✓	
	The use of financial information to measure operating income results in some costs being over or understated in relation to their utilisation of resources	✓	✓	
Influences on the calculation	There is a bias to larger business units owing to their larger residual incomes because it uses an absolute dollar value		✓	
	The complexity of the adjustments requires the use of consulting firms on long and expensive engagements			✓
	Judgement is required to assess the level of risk and the costs of capital for the business unit and the business			✓

Comparison of the three financial methods		DuPont	Residual Income	EVA
Behavioural influences	Managers are discouraged from investing in projects that may benefit the business but decrease the business unit ROE	✓		
	If managers are rewarded solely on ROE then they may prefer to gamble with high risk projects particularly if there is a short time horizon without considering the added risk borne by the business	✓		
	Cutting costs such as employee training, maintenance or research and development is attractive as it increases residual income perhaps reducing longer term benefits	✓	✓	
	There is a temptation to set the required rate of return low to select less profitable but safe projects		✓	

The principal tools and techniques for selecting critical success factors for routine reporting include:[39]

- A combination of financial performance measures with related non-financial measures
- A combination of short and long-term indicators
- A combination of lead and lag indicators
- Indicators that cover the breadth of the business in terms of business units and products and services
- Systems that will produce information in a timely and efficient manner. Consider:
  - General purpose productivity software applications such as spreadsheets which have been created by current or former employees[40]
  - Specialised software applications which contain reporting modules (e.g. general ledger software packages)
  - Integrated software applications which handle a wide range of business transactions and provide preformatted reports (e.g. enterprise resource planning software packages)

---

39 Where the indicators are performance focused, they may be better termed key performance indicators.

40 Care needs to exercised when using general purpose tools such as spreadsheets. Since they have very few internal controls the accuracy of any worksheet created depended entirely upon the knowledge and skill of the operator. It is possible for errors to be introduced which are not detected.

- Custom software applications tailored to the in-house business activities.
- The particular indicators which should be reported. Consider:
  - Product or service costing
  - Product or service acceptance (for example by share of the market)
  - Product or service availability (for example by growth in sales of new and existing products or services)
  - Product or service quality
  - Product or service innovation
  - Satisfaction of existing customers
  - Financial well-being of the overall business.

The managerial decisions and judgements in selecting critical success factors for routine reporting include:[41]

- Are the critical success factors sufficiently well balanced? Consider:
  - Do they engender short-term performance (e.g. quarterly and half year)?
  - Is there a suitable mix of lead and lag indicators?
  - Are the lead indicators reliable?
  - Are there sufficient indicators to give a rounded understanding?[42]
  - What is the effect on the CSF's of the limitations of the indicators?[43]
- Are there likely to be detrimental outcomes from relying on ratios? Consider:
  - Is there reluctance to invest in assets with a medium to long-term horizon for returns?[44]
  - Are there creation of de facto benchmarks for financial investment and financial performance?
  - Is the difficult task of assessing the value of intangible improvements to the business avoided?

---

41 Both financial and non-financial measures may be collected.

42 The emphasis on tools and techniques to value financial assets or to demonstrate short-term performance overlooks the resources that can improve the operational position of a business.

43 Limitations include the assumptions that (1) the relationship between the denominator and numerator of the ratio are the same irrespective of the size of the entity; (2) the presence of different fixed costs, (3) timing differences in collecting the data, (4) different periods reflecting a different economic environment and (5) different policies leading to different counting and presentation.

44 The conceptual weaknesses of these analytic investment techniques include (a) the use of rates of return as though they are certain, (b) assumptions on opportunity cost returns, that is external investment opportunities and (c) arbitrary estimates of asset deterioration (Hayes & Garvin 1980: 75-77).

  - Will the effect of discounting theory be the progressive disinvestment of the existing investment infrastructure[45] and a minimalist approach to new investment in infrastructure?[46]
- What conclusions should be drawn? Consider:
  - What immediate action is essential from the apparent trends?[47]
  - What long-term planning is essential?

In summary, there is often a reluctance by senior management to recognise that relying on one of these investment measures is too narrow and suffers from the faults of using an aggregated, delayed, sole measure. Preoccupation with abstract metric return on investment on quarterly periods may result in unethical behaviour[48] or poorly undertaken innovation. A proactive senior management will complement its financial measures with non-financial measures which have a longer-term focus.

Chapter summary

Matching the kind of financial performance evaluation to the kind of responsibility centre in the business unit will produce more useful information for decision-making. In a decentralised business the use of different kinds of controls can reduce the administration in monitoring and controlling operations. The features and likely behavioural outcomes from the different financial measures should be appreciated before they are implemented.

Financial measures are lag oriented. There are some attempts to make them coincident indicators by using sales. In all cases, the goal is to identify the main economic effects closer to when plans were made and activities occurred. Businesses develop preferences for particular integrated measures and then rely on them for extended periods. This may allow them to better understand the nuances of the data. In other cases, the combination for a quick figure and loss of employee knowledge may give the figures a credibility they do not intrinsically possess.[49]

---

45 This can take the form of (a) maximising utilising of the existing infrastructure, or (b) replacing it with less expensive infrastructure at the end of its life. The less expensive infrastructure itself may be outright cheaper or have fewer capabilities.

46 This arises owing to a reluctance to seek investments or approve investments which have an expected return less than the average return (or hurdle rate). However, a profit-seeking business would be expected to make investments (in order of declining profitability) until the marginal cost of capital of the last dollar equals the marginal return generated by that dollar. This reluctance is exacerbated where return on investment is used in a performance evaluation.

47 Businesses with access to borrowings frequently leverage their assets to acquire other businesses and become conglomerates. This changes the skill set and experience required from operational matters to capital allocation (Hayes & Abernathy 1980). Moreover, the divestment of strategic business units within conglomerates also highlights valuation skills. The reluctance to invest in the development of innovative manufacturing and service processes discards long-term technological superiority as a basis for competition (Hayes & Abernathy 1980).

48 Where there are strong business incentives (e.g. financial remuneration including large bonuses) employees can be motivated into neglecting or skirting around ethical codes.

49 While the traditional expression is 'garbage in, garbage out' often abbreviated GIGO, in these circumstances it is more likely to be 'garbage in, gospel out' with people believing in whatever the output states.

16 Pursue a quest for value in business operations and strategy

The prevailing criterion for assessing value is the value chain (Porter 1985/1998). It offers a proven method for businesses to analyse their operations to provide insights into their costs and competitive advantage. Although it is frequently discussed in the strategy literature, textbooks and media there has been oversimplification and use of secondary sources which has introduced misunderstandings and misapplications of it. This chapter conducts a detailed examination of the source (Porter 1985/1998)[1] to identify how Porter intended to be applied. The examples frequently found in searching the internet are usually a superficial diagram displayed on one page or in presentation slides.[2] Some attempts to use it in conjunction with activity based costing have shown the fragility of the latter when used as an amalgam.

Value chain as an activity-based approach to value

The value chain uses the activities that take place in a business and relates them to an analysis of the competitive strength of the business. Although descriptions of the activities in the value chain are provided at a high level it is necessary to disaggregate them into discrete or distinct activities. The value chain comprises primary activities complemented by support activities as shown in Figure 14 on the next page.

---

1 The terminology used by Porter (1985/1998) is used for ease of checking so the relevant page number from Porter (1985/1998) is specified.

2 This has been encouraged by academic courses which make data collection instantaneous and allows attribution of value without any rigorous justification and prediction.

Support Activities	Margin between each adjacent and interrelated support activities					
	Organisational Infrastructure (Organizational structure, control systems, organisation culture)					Margin from each Support Activity
	Human Resources Management (Employee advertising, selection, recruitment, learning, development, and compensation)					
	Technology Development (Equipment, tools and systems that support value-creating activities)					
	Procurement of Resources (Specifying, tendering and purchasing inputs such as materials, technology, and services)					
	Margin between primary and support activities					
Primary Activities	**Inbound Logistics**	**Operations**	**Outbound Logistics**	**Marketing & Sales**	**Service**	Margin from each Primary Activity
	Receiving, and storing raw materials, and their release to operations.	Transforming inputs into finished products or services.	Warehousing and distributing finished products.	Identifying customer needs and generating sales.	Supporting customers after they acquire a product or service.	
	Margin between each adjacent and interrelated primary activities					

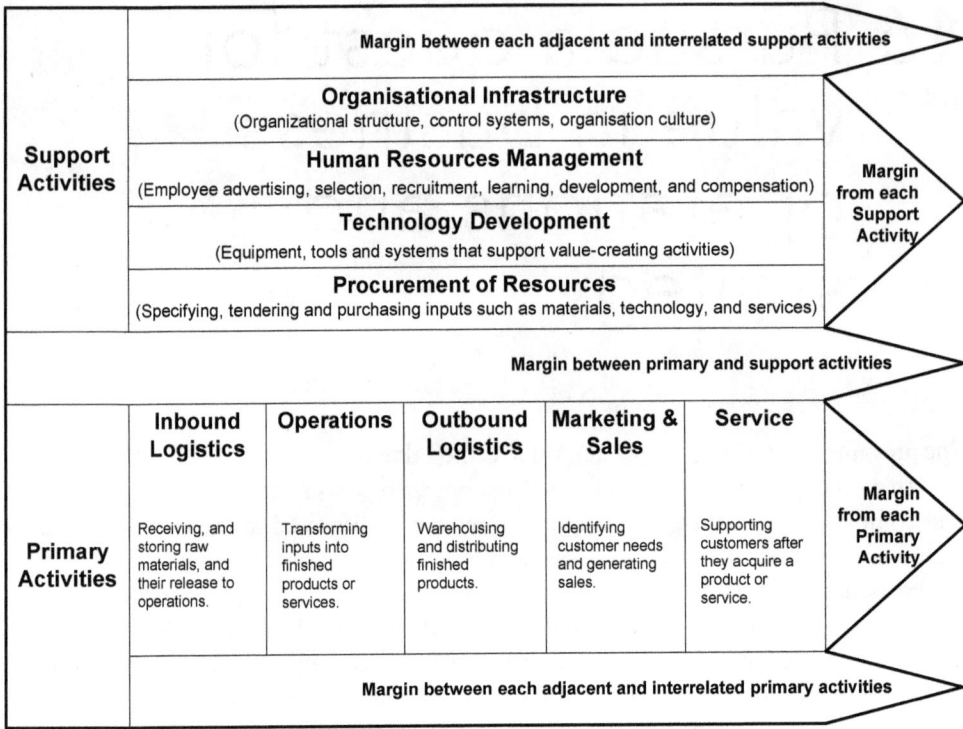

Figure 14. Traditional, generic value chain separating the value from primary activities (vertical columns), support activities (horizontal rows) showing the five value elements from activities (Revised and adapted from Porter 1985/1998)

The five generic primary activities (Porter 1985/1998: 39–40) comprise:[3]

1. Inbound logistics (the receiving and warehousing of purchased inputs and distribution to production as they are required)

2. Operations (that transform inputs into finished products or services)

3. Outbound logistics (associated with collecting, storing and physically distributing the finished product or service

4. Marketing and sales (to identify customer needs and generate sales)

5. Service (to maintain or enhance the value of the product or service.

---

3 All five primary activities are present to some extent although the industry sector determines which generic primary activities are critical (Porter 1985/1998: 39–40).

Four generic support activities are involved in 'competing in any industry' (Porter 1985/1998: 40). They comprise (pp 41–43):

1. Firm infrastructure (including general management, planning, finance, accounting, legal, government affairs, business structure, control systems, business culture and quality management)

2. Technology development (technology, know-how or procedures to support value-creating activities)

3. Human resource management (recruiting, hiring, training, development and compensation of employees and contractors)

4. Procurement (the function of purchasing inputs).

Five elements of margin can be identified from Figure 14 above:

1. Margin from each of the primary activities

2. Margin between each adjacent and interrelated primary activity

3. Margin from each of the support activities

4. Margin between each adjacent and interrelated support activity

5. Margin between the primary and support activities.

The aggregated margin or profit depends on effectively performing the both the primary and support activities efficiently and effectively. The amount that a customer is willing to pay for the product or service should exceed the sum of the cost of the activities in the value chain. A cost advantage can be pursued by reducing costs within primary and support activities as well as by reconfiguring the activities within the value chain.

Topics in the quest for value in business operations and strategy

There are five considerations when using a value criterion to assess business operations and generic strategy:

1. Establish what value means to the business in its industry

2. Identify the value within each activity in the business functions

3. Determine the competitive advantage value from the existing value chain

4. Configure each of the alternative value chains and devise the new value strategy for competitive advantage

5. Implement the new value strategy for competitive advantage.

16.1 Establish what value means to the business in its industry

The quest for value is an unending attempt to discover the best way for the business to generate value. Many descriptions of business value depend upon direct contribution to sales, improvement of processes and enabling better service and communication. While these are important, the value must also be sufficiently substantial to allow the business to remain viable. The business needs to provide dependable products or services, usually creatively collaborating with supply and delivery partners to fulfil particular needs and expectations of each customer. This occurs in an ever-changing marketplace in which it is likely that multiple sellers and multiple buyers come together to trade.[4]

The broad management challenges and issues in establishing what value means to the business in its industry include:

- Developing a shared view of value[5] throughout the business
- Distinguishing value producing from non-value producing activities
- Reducing effort on non-value producing activities
- Removing policy and routines which allow justification for continuing non-value producing activities
- Overcoming resistance to change in focusing on value adding activities[6]
- Identifying the linkages in the interfaces between value producing activities[7]
- Developing criteria for reducing non-value producing activities
- Developing criteria for improvements in value producing activities.

The principal tools and techniques establishing what values means to the business in its industry include:

- An agreed definition of value
- Using a value chain for existing arrangements
- Using value chains for each of the alternative arrangements
- Using a value chain for preferred arrangements

---

4 These comments take into account the growing place of e-business (Accenture 2000; Weill & Vitale 2001) which also depends on recognising the new place for information which is beside the products and services of the business.

5 Many businesses state their value in terms of product or service superiority, customer intimacy or operational excellence. It is difficult make a competitor product or service obsolete for any length of time so segmenting and targeting markets precisely and then tailoring offerings to match exactly that demands of those niches is a more realistic approach. Operational excellence then focuses on providing customers with reliable products or services at competitive prices and delivered promptly.

6 These may be associated with threats to employment, loss of remuneration, or loss of power and prestige.

7 That is, between the primary activities themselves, between the support activities themselves and between the primary and support activities.

- Reconciling the value reported with actual value received under the existing systems
- Ensuring consistency with (but not necessarily emulation of) value chains of other businesses in the industry.[8]

The managerial decisions and judgements that arise from establishing what values means to the business in its industry include:

- What will be the strategy[9] of the business to generate sustainable and superior value?
- Does the gross margin in the value chain reconcile with the value attributed to individual activities and linkages?
- Does the gross margin in the value chain reconcile with the value reported from an assessment of intangibles?
- Are linkages optimised or have they been outmoded by changes in the business?
- Should the current arrangements for in-house and outsourced arrangements be changed?
- What will be the effect of changes to value activities on competitors with regard to innovation, the pricing package and customer service?
- What will the effect be of changes to value activities on customers with regard to buying loyalty, volume and product preferences?

In summary, business functions do not provide a sufficiently granular base to facilitate assessment of value. Moreover, ad hoc approaches to value (e.g. asking if an activity is value adding) are approximate at best. A proven means of establishing value is provided by the value chain where value is tested against each point and interface in the value chain.

16.2 Identify the value within each activity in the business functions

Starting with the value chain is a cumbersome means of identifying the value elements. Since it is difficult to create the value chain from scratch, one approach is to map the business functions to the value chain and then conduct further analysis. Table 11 on the next page provides a mapping of the generic business functions discussed in Chapter 6. It assumes the business has chosen to retain all its business functions in-house.

---

8 These may be publicly available value chains reported in scholarly research or released to the media by the business. There may also be instances where businesses disclose their value chain privately, for example, at industry conferences, seminars and showcases.

9 This uses the Porter (1980) definition of strategy: to provide products or services at lower cost or with better differentiation than competitors.

Table 11. Generic business functions mapped to activities in the value chain

Business function	Mapping to the value chain	
	Activity	Type
Procurement (including tenders, purchase order placement, follow-up of back orders and monitoring supplier performance)	Procurement function	Support
Receiving and warehousing raw materials (including collections and returns)	Inbound logistics	Primary
Product, service or process design and re-engineering and improvement (including R&D)	Technology development	Support
Production (including assembly, testing, packaging)	Operations	Primary
Distribution (including processing customer orders, storage and handling of finished products and scheduling delivery)	Outbound Logistics	Primary
Sales and marketing (including advertising, promotion, pricing, territory and sales outlet and the sales force management)	Marketing and sales	Primary
Recruit, select, induct, train and develop employees	Human resource management	Support
General management	Firm infrastructure	Support
Finance and accounting	Firm infrastructure	Support
Quality management	Firm infrastructure	Support
Planning including strategic planning	Firm infrastructure	Support
Government relations and lobbying	Firm infrastructure	Support
Facilities (including physical location of departments, utilities such as electricity and water and security)	Service	Support
Human resources	Firm infrastructure	Support
Information systems, technology and communication	Human resource management	Support

The broad management issues and challenges in mapping the business functions to the value chain include:

- Recognising that business functions overlap elements of the value chain
- Ensuring that business functions are divided into discrete value activities which are specific to the industry
- Ensuring that the accounting distinction between direct and indirect costs is not equated to primary and support activities in the value chain[10]
- Avoiding allocating functions to particular elements of the primary and support activities of the value chain based on their perceived 'line and staff' relationship
- Ensuring that the mapping is properly and thoroughly documented and involves employees who are knowledgeable about the operations of the business
- Eschewing using parts of other value chains as a shortcut[11]
- Ensuring that the point of view adopted is that of the customer.

The principal tools and techniques for mapping the business functions to the value chain include:

- Investigating the activities roughly in the order or sequence of 'processes' (Porter, 1985/1998: 48) in the business
- Allocating all the functions of the business to the primary and support activities in the value chain based on the Porter (1985/1998) definitions and commentary
- Using the Porter (1985/1998) form of the value chain, not the simplified versions which appear in many textbooks[12]
- Creating the value chain[13] diagram in several parts so that all the functions of the business are visually captured in the sufficiently detailed value chain
- Ensuring the process of creating the value chain allows sufficient time for wide verification and discussion.

---

10 The knowledge required is not necessarily available from accounting systems (Porter 1985/1998: 39) or other internal reporting systems. These systems may however, provide some useful background data.

11 Since the value chain deals with competitive advantage for the particular business it has to be assembled from knowledge of the business: its history, strategy implementation and economics of its business activities (Porter 1985/1998: 36). Appropriation of knowledge from similar value chains is likely to produce a misleading diagnosis.

12 Textbook diagrams and discussions of value chains available from Google searches tend to incorrectly emphasise the linear sequencing of activities and overlook the important linkages between them. Linkages mean that performing a single activity affects the costs and performance in others (Porter 1985/1998: 48, 75). Their impact may not be adequately recognised.

13 A single value chain diagram unlikely to be sufficient. Typically modelling the value chain of a business requires several diagrams and is accomplished by an iterative process usually involving some workshops.

The managerial decisions and judgements that arise from for mapping the business functions to the value chain include:

- Have all the currently executed functions of the business been identified in the value chain?
- Have all the functions of the business been identified in the value chain in the way they are currently executed?
- Has the value chain been made specific to the industry (avoiding any generic value chain descriptions)?
- Does the value chain move away from specific performance measures to concentrate on the contribution of the business functions?
- Is the value chain at a sufficient level of detail to identify the discrete activities within functions?
- Has the final version of the value chain been reviewed by knowledgeable operational employees to establish its credibility?
- Should any functions or activities be further investigated or further disaggregated?

In summary, the document describing a value chain that can be found by a Google search is usually considerably oversimplified. Attention is required to properly create a value chain of the existing activities. The approach of mapping allows the project to be managed and completed in a shorter time frame than might normally be the case.

16.3 Determine the competitive advantage value from the existing value chain

Primary and support activities combine together to produce value or margin.[14] In his 1998 introduction, Michael Porter emphasises (1985/1998: *xvii*) that competitive advantage is connected to the 'many activities' (p *xvii*) which comprise an 'interdependent system' (p *xviii*) to 'design, produce, market, deliver and support [the] product[s of a business unit]' (p 36). The sum of the value comprises the value from the primary activities involved in the physical creation of the product and its sale and transfer to the buyer as well as after-sale assistance' (p 38) and the support activities that 'support the primary activities and each other' (p 38).

The broad management issues and challenges in determining competitive advantage value from the value chain include:

- Obtaining reliable information from customers that indicates which activities that are valued by them
- Ensuring that the value identified is consistent with the opportunities for the industry

---

14 This may be measured using revenue (as the amount the customer is willing to pay) or buyer payments less cost (Porter 1985/1998: 38) more accurately than value added (Porter 1985/1998: 38).

- Ensuring that all individual activities, activity combinations and activity interrelationships which customers regard as having value have been identified

- Ensuring value is properly calculated for individual activities, activity combinations and activity interrelationships which customers regards as having value

- Identifying whether there are any value overlaps between individual activities.

The principal tools and techniques for determining value from the value chain include:

- Examining each of the activities individually that produce value

- Identifying combinations of activities that produce value

- Identifying activity interrelationships that produce value

- Looking broader than the value chain to what Porter calls a 'value system'[15]

- Quantifying the value produced from individual activities, activity combinations and activity interrelationships.

The managerial decisions and judgements for determining value from the value chain include:

- Does the value chain produce value based on concentration (every activity is located in one separate location) or on dispersion (every activity is performed in every location)?

- How does the prevailing view of profitability fit with that suggested by the value chain analysis?

- Are there learning advantages in favour of concentrating the value chain?

- Are there comparative advantages in favour of concentrating the value chain?

- Are there coordination advantages in favour of concentrating the value chain?

- Do different local needs favour dispersing the value chain?

- Are there transport, communication and storage cost advantages in favour of dispersing the value chain?

- Do favourable political environments encourage dispersing the value chain?

- What should be the strategy[16] of the business to generate sustainable and superior value?

- How can the interrelationships between activities create competitive advantage be exploited?

In summary, value is produced from (1) individual activities, (2) the combination of activities and (3) their linkages or interrelationships. However, the value identified only has utility if their foundations are robust. The level of analysis needs to be set to reveal the value

---

15 The value system is a larger stream of activities in which the organisation's value chain is embedded (Porter 1985/1998: 15). It should be considered when constructing any alternative value chain.

16 This uses the Porter (1980) generic strategies to provide products or services at lower cost or with better differentiation than competitors to a broad or niche market avoiding becoming 'stuck in the middle' and becoming vulnerable should a capable competitor emerge (Porter 1985/1997: 19, 535).

of activities and to achieve this primary and support activities need to be disaggregated to establish the linkages between activities.

16.4 Configure each of the alternative value chains and devise the new value strategy for competitive advantage

Interpreting the value chain is the basis for configuring three alternative value chains: (1) the same value chain as the industry leader;[17] (2) with new activities; and (3) a new chain. The alternative value chains will assist in devising a new value strategy for competitive advantage. All alternative value chains will be prepared at a sufficient level of detail[18] to establish meaningful linkages between the disaggregated activities and reveal their value.

The broad management issues and challenges in constructing the alternative value chain and new value strategy for competitive advantage include:

- Establishing the quality of the existing analysis[19]

- Ensuring the level of analysis allows identification of distinct or discrete value activities[20]

- Examining the linkages within the value chain

- Examining the linkages associated with the value chains of suppliers, channels and buyers.[21]

---

17 The leader may choose a defensive strategy reducing the chance of a successful attack by a challenger by building structural barriers, by offering deterrents or by retaliating (Porter 1985/1997: 483–512).

18 Too high an analysis (such as the industry or sector) obscures sources of value (Porter 1985/1998: 36) that an individual firm may possess (Porter 1985/1998: 36; 36 note 2). Typically a sub-business focus is required and the strategic business unit (Porter 1985/1998: 36) is the relevant level of analysis to (a) capture 'everything' (Porter 1985/1998: 48) that the business does and (b) pinpoint the sources of competitive advantage.

19 Before adopting the set of value chain documents it is usual to complete a quality assurance review of the data. This can be done by the subject matter experts 'walking through' the document in an unscripted discussion to an audience of the management team. The first review is the basic document which identifies all the distinct or discrete value activities (Porter 1985/1998: 40, 45–46) within each of the generic primary and support activities for the business unit. This is followed by a review of the linkages within the value chain in which each is identified and described. The value chains of the supplier (Porter 1985/1998: 50–52) and the buyer (Porter 1985/1998: 52) also need to be described to establish all important external value chains. It is not sufficient to do it by naming the pairs of activities (Porter 1985/1998: 133). Usually the quality assurance review stimulates debate and further revision as omitted or insufficiently valued activities are identified. Frequently ideas emerge for refining the value chain and improving competitive advantage. These should be separately recorded so they are separate from the existing value chain. It is important that the existing chain can stand as a benchmark for considering alternatives.

20 The level of analysis (Porter 1985/1998: 40, 45–46) within each primary and support activity is based on the 'economics of the activities and the purposes for which the value chain is being organised' (p 45). The criteria are 'different economics, potential impact on differentiation and significant or growing proportion of costs' (Porter 1985/1998: 45).

21 While this contains a subjective element (since the reference point is the customer), it can be compared with the existing or apparent value from the other forms of classification such as business system functions for example, manufacturing, marketing (Porter 1985/1998: 36) and accounting classifications (Porter 1985/1998: 39). The customer expects better pricing or better performance (Porter 1985/1998: 75, 131, 133).

The principal tools and techniques for constructing the alternative value chain and new value strategy for competitive advantage include:

- Considering each activity in three ways: direct , indirect and quality[22]
- Reconfiguring the value chain for improved competitive advantage to meet the strategic objective of the business (provide lower cost or better differentiation) and generate superior value
- Considering information intensity[23] if applicable
- Identify improvements to the value chain through evaluating the value that each discrete disaggregated activity provides.[24]

The managerial decisions and judgements that arise from reviewing the value chain include:

- What is the value from each disaggregated activity?[25]
- What business functions can be restructured?[26]
- What is the estimated cost position of the business relative to competitors?[27]
- Are the direct, indirect and quality assurance activities performed by the business or to which it is subjected[28] clearly specified for each alternative?
- Are there clearly identified cost drivers which enable aggregation of costs?[29]
- Are there clearly identified cost drivers which explain the interaction of costs (Porter 1985/1998: 84–87)?
- Are there clearly identified cost drivers (Porter 1985/1998: 84–88) for the economies of scale (Porter 1985/1998: 88)?
- Are there economies of scale in favour of concentrating the value chain?
- Are there learning advantages in favour of concentrating the value chain?
- Are there comparative advantages in favour of concentrating the value chain?
- Are there coordination advantages in favour of concentrating the value chain?

---

22 The three views of activities are: direct (directly creating value); indirect (enabling the direct activities to continue functioning); and quality activities (that ensure the quality of other activities) (Porter 1985/1998: 76).

23 Porter and Millar (1985) proposed the use of an information intensity matrix to assess the impact of information. A two by two matrix evaluates the information intensity of the value chain against that of the product. They suggested that IT will play a strategic role in an industry that is characterised by high information intensity in the value chain and information content in the product.

24 It is usual to consider scope for optimisation, coordination and re-configuration of activities with respect to costs. Differentiation is also used if that strategy is chosen instead of low cost leadership.

25 Negligible and low value activities should be flagged for attention.

26 Those which have similarities or are associated with specific primary and support activities may be restructured to exploit the coordination within the hierarchical structure (Porter 1985/1998: 59).

27 Costs can be categorised as purchased operating inputs, human resource costs and assets by major category (Porter 1985/1998: 33, 67).

28 To identify the relative proportions of activity costs (Porter 1985/1998: 43–44, 67) in value creation.

29 Cost drivers (Porter 1985/1998: 84–88) are variables which causally affect costs over a medium-term time horizon which facilitate the aggregation of costs (Porter 1985/1998: 39; 84).

- Are there different local needs in favour of dispersing the value chain?
- Are there transport, communication and storage cost advantages in favour of dispersing the value chain?
- Are there favourable political environments in favour of dispersing the value chain?
- What short-term further refinements of the existing value chain are essential?
- Does the current generic strategy (cost/differentiation and niche/broad) require further attention?
- What roles and responsibilities will be recognised (as individual or committee functions) and what special project resources (people, money and technology) are required for successful project (change) outcomes?

In summary, to develop alternative value chains requires creative thinking to identify scope for optimisation, coordination and re-configuration of the costs and differentiation of activities which will create and sustain (Porter 1985/1998: 59) competitive advantage. The alternative value chains previously prepared should receive a formal quality assurance review. This will usually result in their consolidation into the preferred proposed value chain. A preferred proposed value chain can then be finalised for review.[30]

16.5 Implement the new value strategy for competitive advantage

Many methods exist for implementing new value strategy. Two popular methods include creating employee performance incentives and using Key Performance Indicators (also known as dash board measures). Porter (1985/1997: 115) counselled 'Costs do not go down automatically or by accident but rather as a result of hard work and constant attention.' In other words, there is a need to focus directly on the activities themselves. This will include 'training, motivation a culture of cost reduction, automation and improvement of the learning curve (Porter 1985/1997: 113). This topic follows Porter's recommended approach rather than the popular alternatives.

The broad management issues and challenges in implementing the new value strategy for competitive advantage include:

- Testing the adequacy of the preferred alternative value chain with a five forces analysis
- Ensuring commitment to the preferred alternative value chain
- Having a comprehensive implementation plan which takes into account competitor reactions.

---

30 Discussion should also generate much of the supporting materials for the implementation of the preferred proposed value chain including estimated (budgeted) costs and benefits, change schedule (timetable) and the allocation of roles/responsibilities for key change milestones.

The principal tools and techniques for implementing the new value strategy for competitive advantage include:

- Constructing and analysing industry scenarios
- Providing improved reporting of value
- Meshing scenarios, five forces, competitor behaviour and competitive advantage into an implementation plan.

The managerial decisions and judgements that arise from implementing the new value strategy for competitive advantage include:

- What will be the staged approach to implementation?
- What is the combination of attack and defence which reinforce on a scenario while preserving flexibility for others built into the new value strategy?

In summary, the realisation of value requires careful planning and progressive implementation. Not only must there be flexibility in the strategy to deal with unexpected external events but changes in the industry must be factored into the implementation so that the promise of additional value is realised.

Chapter summary

The value chain constitutes intellectual capital for the business. The information contained in the proposed value chain document makes it a commercial-in-confidence document. However, aspects of it will find their way into strategy statements and operational instructions.

17 Automate transactions and improve decision support using business system, business process, workflow and data analyses

A system may operate at four different levels of automation: (1) entirely manual; (2) semi-automated; (3) fully automated; or (4) all systems are fully integrated. The level of automation[1] affects the boundaries and interfaces between the systems. Different systems may be at different levels of automation. For example, sales may be fully automated but back orders may be semi-automated. Business functions may be automated in three different forms: (1) a single business function may be automated which is either a core[2] or a subsidiary[3] business function; (2) several business functions in the one department may be automated as a whole[4]; and (3) a business function that overlaps several departments can be automated into a single system.[5] The level of automation may also be affected by its source of hosting. In-house systems may satisfactorily have a level of automation that is manual or semi-automated. Where hosting is provided by a third party the level of automation is more likely to be semi or fully automated.

Approaches to automation and analysis

The integrating MIT90s model introduced in Dimension Two proposes that the use of an information technology, like e-mail, is a function of the task to be accomplished, the role of the individual, the structure and the strategy of the organisation. A detailed view of systems, processes, data and workflow should always be informed by an analytical framework such as MIT90s which guides analysis. Analysis is a prerequisite for: (1) removing anomalies that

---

1 Since systems interface one another a workflow may be routed through many different levels of automation. This provides both opportunities for efficiency improvement as well as project pitfalls since improved automation for its own sake may not provide the customer with any additional value.

2 One of the earliest business functions to be automated was accounting.

3 One of the earliest subsidiary functions to be automated was payroll.

4 Warehousing and distribution of finished products is often automated as logistics where there is an in-house transport fleet.

5 Inventory control spans production, warehousing and distribution.

develop in a system over time; (2) making changes including complying with mandatory requirements; (3) designing a new system from a blank sheet of paper; (4) integrating different processes or systems; and (5) imposing workable controls. Neither business functions (discussed in Topic 6.2) nor the value chain (introduced in Topic 11.3 and discussed in Chapter 16) are suitable methods for analysing systems, processes or data. Business functions do not comprise homogeneous business processes[6] because they encourage giving priority to the needs of the employee's own department.[7] They provide insufficient detail to permit confident assessment of the value of activities.

Systems theory provides a unified view of the business systems and processes. Given the confusion that usually arises when considering systems within systems, an overarching view is provided by the business transaction cycle. There is no 'universally accepted' definition of business cycles. This view is synthesised from many accounting textbooks which is where the primary discussion of business cycles is provided.[8] Traditionally, business transaction cycles are used to categorise business activities and systems. The business transaction cycles exist in all types of businesses (profit seeking and non-profit) and all sectors (manufacturing, merchandising and service). The transactions cycles differ depending upon the size and complexity of the business.[9] The business cycle approach provides a template to analyse unfamiliar systems using a set of factors which are expected to be found in each cycle. A systems perspective brings a different approach to looking at the world.[10] It considers at least three characteristics: (1) seeing interrelationships among systems rather than linear cause-effect chains; (2) seeing processes of change among systems rather than discrete snapshots of change; and (3) seeing systems, subsystems and components of systems. However, there is a third way. It is possible to map the business functions to the business transaction cycle and system as shown in Table 12 on the next page. It can be seen that a function has more than one system assuming that the business has chosen to retain all its business functions in-house.

Unsatisfactory attempts to use business functions

Frequently an attempt is made to use business functions either as a starting point or for the whole analysis. There are two problems with this approach as shown in Table 12 on the next page. First, a business function contains more than one system. Second, a system is too high a level for analysis although it does show interrelationships between different systems in the business.

---

6 This is to be expected since their purpose is to allow economies of specialisation.

7 This is sometimes referred to as a 'silo mentality'. It may also lead to information silos where very few people know what information might be useful and available.

8 There are differences in the nomenclature of the transaction cycles and there are also some differences in the detail with which they are treated. A sample of three contemporary accounting textbooks were consulted (Brockholdt 1999; Hollander, Denna & Cherrington 2000; Romney & Steinbart 2009). The summary provided is broadly consistent with them but is in greater detail with additional commentary.

9 As the transactions cycles increase in size and complexity it is usually the case that there is greater automation of the processes. Since the advent of virtual proprietary networks in the 1990's followed by e-business using the internet, part of the business transaction cycles are conducted via websites.

10 The systems approach is more generally known as general systems theory (Bertalanffy 1969/1976; Weinberg 1975/2005). It emphasises wholes without considering operations mechanically or technically.

Table 12. Business function mapped to business cycle and system

Business function	Mapping to	
	Business cycle	System
Procurement	Expenditure	Supplier selection
		Purchasing
		Receiving
Sales and marketing	Revenue	Marketing
		Sales order entry
Production and engineering	Expenditure	Production planning
		Production operations
		Production control
Distribution	Revenue	Distribution
Research and development	Expenditure	Product design
Accounting and finance	Revenue	Cash receipts
		Billing
		Revenue collection
	Expenditure	Cash disbursements
		Accounts payable
		Fixed assets
Information systems, technology and communications	Expenditure	-
Human resources	Expenditure	Payroll
		Leave
Facilities	Expenditure	Facilities management

Topics in automating transactions and decision support

Automating transactions and support decisions using system, process, data and workflow analyses comprises five general-purpose approaches to manage the detail of business operations and administration:

1. Standardise and integrate business operations to achieve goals

2. Determine the formality and effort of the analysis

3. Take a unified view of the business using systems, business processes and workflows

4. Make wise capital investments in systems and technology

5. Constitute a project to plan and implement change.

17.1 Standardise and integrate business operations to achieve goals

A standardising and integrating business operations approach provides a new view of business cycles and systems. Instead of treating them simply as solutions to business opportunities and problems they become a means to develop flexible procedures for business operations. Once these are known it is possible to integrate them to serve the larger goals and strategies of the business.

The broad management issues and challenges in standardising and integrating business operations include:

- Setting standards meaningful to the industry, customers and suppliers
- Identifying risks including early obsolescence of the investment
- Ensuring availability of the system to customers[11]
- Differentiating the systems of the business from those of its competitors
- Making strategic investments in a timely manner
- Completing any change project quickly
- Ensuring the availability of historical data created in/by earlier systems where is affects competitive position or the accuracy of records
- Determining the competitive advantage of in-house or outsourced systems
- Reducing dependence upon suppliers where it may lead to inflation of costs.

The principal tools and techniques for standardising and integrating business operations include:

- For conducting a background analysis. Consider:
  - Business functions
  - Role and responsibilities of employees and managers.
- For conducting a detailed analysis. Consider:
  - Business transaction cycle
  - Systems
  - Business processes (generic and unique)
  - Business rules and workflow.
- For conducting a specialised analysis. Consider:

---

11 This is an added challenge where third parties are involved. For example, service providers may have an outage discovered only by their customers; service hosting may experience congestion and reduced throughput and/or telecommunications networks can be affected by weather conditions.

- – Value chain
- – Capital budgeting
- – Project management.
- For modelling the systems analysis. Consider:
  - – Entity Relationship (E-R)
  - – Data flow (DF)
  - – Unified Modelling Language (UML) for an object oriented approach.

The managerial decisions and judgements that arise from standardising and integrating business operations include:

- Will selection of a few suppliers results in over dependency and negotiation weaknesses?
- What is an acceptable balance between new projects and existing operations?
- Is there capability to execute all vital projects simultaneously?
- Does the reporting format provide Board members with sufficient relevant information?
- For any particular project and operations, is in-house preferable to outsourcing?
- For any particular project and operations, is an off-the-shelf software package preferable to custom development?
- Should the hurdle rate be the same for all projects?[12]
- Where should the information systems and technology function report in the business?[13]

In summary, standardising and integrating business systems, processes and data offer considerable payback to the business if accomplished on time and within budget. However, the history of success with such projects is rare. Any attempt should only be commenced when there is a preparedness to spend time in planning.

17.2 Determine the formality and effort of the analysis

Before commencing any analysis it is prudent to determine how formal or extensive the analysis should be and how much effort or resources should be expended. For example, changes to strategic business operations should be thoroughly investigated. Two separate

---

12 This will exclude projects which are solely for compliance with government legislation and which have no business by-product benefits.

13 There appears to a pendulum-like change with information systems and technology reporting to the CEO then being downgraded and situated with the finance/accounting function or as one of the shared services functions. It is lamentable that this decision is often made to reduce the number of direct reports to the CEO rather than fitting business strategy. The issue of governance in information systems and technology is discussed in detail by Weill and Ross (2004).

kinds of investigations are proposed: (1) profiling the business and (2) determining the context of the business. The templates provided below allow understanding to be reached quickly and easily. The resulting documents should be referenced by during the analysis and amended where new understandings are reached.

The broad management issues and challenges in determining the formality and effort of the analysis include:

- Matching importance with the formality of the project management and the effort in design
- Ensuring preparatory understanding is gained by the team members working on analysing the systems.[14]

The principal tools and techniques in determining the formality and effort of the analysis include:

- Constructing a business profile[15] (see Form 1 in the Forms and Templates Supplement) comprising simple, obvious, important but underestimated characteristics
- Business context (see Form 2 in the Forms and Templates Supplement) of the external environment and business culture with particular attention to threats and opportunities.

The managerial decisions and judgements associated with determining the formality and effort of the analysis include:

- Is the resulting document of sufficient quality?
- Will the release of the resulting document be accompanied by briefings?
- Do the employees (and outsiders) involved in the analysis comprehend the business culture and strategy for which capital expenditure is approved?

In summary, the profile and context of the system ensures the analysts of the existing and proposed system, as well as the designers, developers and implementers of the new or proposed system have sufficient regard for the business context to minimise the chance of either failure or reluctant use.

---

14 Frequently where consultants or contractors are employed, this step is skipped with the result that the ensuing systm contains deficiencies though lack of appreciating its place in the business.

15 The Business Profile template is the first step in prearing the Business Context template below. They provide a background the analysis with threats and opportunities that can become part of the specification for any new or improved system.

17.3 Take a unified view of the business systems, business processes, workflows and data

A unified view considers business systems, processes, workflows and data. The advantage of a unified view is that it is easy to detect duplication, partial overlap, shadow systems and shortcomings. Practitioners disagree on which of business systems,[16] processes and data give the best view. Business processes[17] have the advantage of a compact focus. Their disadvantage is their detail is always cumbersome. However, the advent of data flow modelling has made clear that business processes could be decomposed to different levels until a primitive business process was reached.

The broad management issues and challenges in taking unified view of the business systems and processes include:

- Appreciating the scope of the task. Consider:
  - Allowing sufficient time for the analysis ensuring that there are interim deliverables of value produced
  - The time taken will depend upon whether inexperienced employees are allocated to the work (e.g. for job rotation, career enhancement or because they are surplus to requirements)
  - Recognising the knowledge gained from developing an accurate account of systems, processes, workflow and data
- Adopting an independent management review and evaluation stance. Consider:
  - Recognising that there is some arbitrariness to what is defined as a system since by convention, several systems are identified for each business transaction cycle and in practice a business may shift elements in the generic system to another system
  - Whether the current actual physical implementation (comprising the processes, source documents, technology, internal control goals and plans, reports (financial and non-financial) and technologies) has any value worth salvaging
  - Clarifying the purpose of each systems so effectiveness can be judged

---

16 Often a system is an information system. This emphasises that there are multiple related inputs which interact and are processed into outputs which then become inputs to another step. These may include storage and distribution for planning, decision making and control. It is often convenient to group several related processes as subsystems and treat them as a whole (which can be combined with other subsystems into greater wholes). The distinction between a system and a subsystem therefore depends upon the point of view of the observer or analyst.

17 Business processes are defined either broadly (as identifiable aggregates) or narrowly (as units). By convention in data flow modelling they can be further decomposed until they are no longer subdividable. Such processes are atomic or a 'primitive process' (DeMarco 1978/1979).

    – Ensuring that all the physical interfaces between different systems, and what data actually moves between them and in what direction, is examined.[18]

The principal tools and techniques in unified view of the business systems, and processes include:

- Selecting a specific or proprietary methodology which contains a framework for the business cycles, systems, business processes, workflow and data

- Taking a top-down approach by focusing on the business transaction cycles which are partitioned as shown in Figure 15 on the next page. Consider:

    – Four separate operating cycles:[19]

      o Revenue (or collection) cycle

      o Expenditure (or acquisition and payment) cycle

      o Conversion (or production)[20] cycle

      o Investment (or finance) cycle.

    – One non-operating cycle[21] which is not decomposed any further.

- Appreciating the relationships between all the business transaction cycles (four operating and one non-operating).

---

18 Although management itself will not clarify the physical interfaces and subsystems their disciplined request for this and review of this information will establish an understanding for any improvement to business systems and processes

19 There is an argument, on logical grounds, for labelling the Operating and Non-operating cycles as subcycles. However, by convention it is not done. A similar case would apply to the Revenue, Expenditure, Conversion and Investment cycles.

20 The conversion cycle is exclusive to businesses which undertake manufacturing businesses. The manufacturing may be assembly of components (e.g. motor vehicles), the processing of raw materials (e.g. flour and other ingredients produce bread, pastries and cakes).

21 The expression 'non-operating' emphasises it is a by-product of the operating cycles. Although the trial balance and general ledger are tangible processes producing financials and related reports, this only is possible through the underlying transactions.

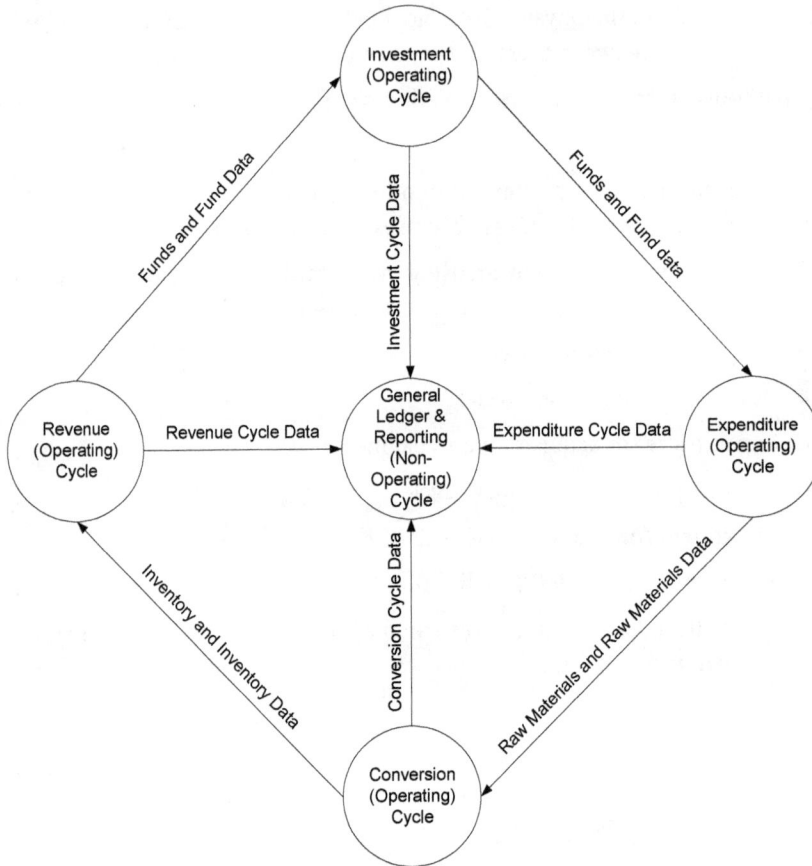

Figure 15. Business transaction cycle diamond showing the circularity of the operating cycles, their common interrelationship with reporting and the flows of physical and logical items

- Working at the business system level within the operating cycle, as shown in Figure 16 on the next page. Consider:

  - Grouping systems in the business cycles according to the class of economic event

  - Moving between the physical view (how it might be implemented) and the logical view (what needs to be accomplished) of systems, processes and data[22]

  - Identifying the role of three systems (inventory system, the general ledger system and the budget system) that are central to all other systems.[23]

---

22 The logical system is described after the physical view as it requires the implementation features to be abstracted. The advantage of taking a logical view is that the artefacts of the system that distract attention from its essence are eliminated. A logical view enables a more succinct view of the systems and their interfaces.

23 The business cycles group systems according to the common economic events. The four operating cycles (revenue, expenditure, conversion and investment) are depicted in Figure 16 to show their interrelationships between data flows at the logical level. It shows the common role of the inventory system to all business cycles. It also shows that the general

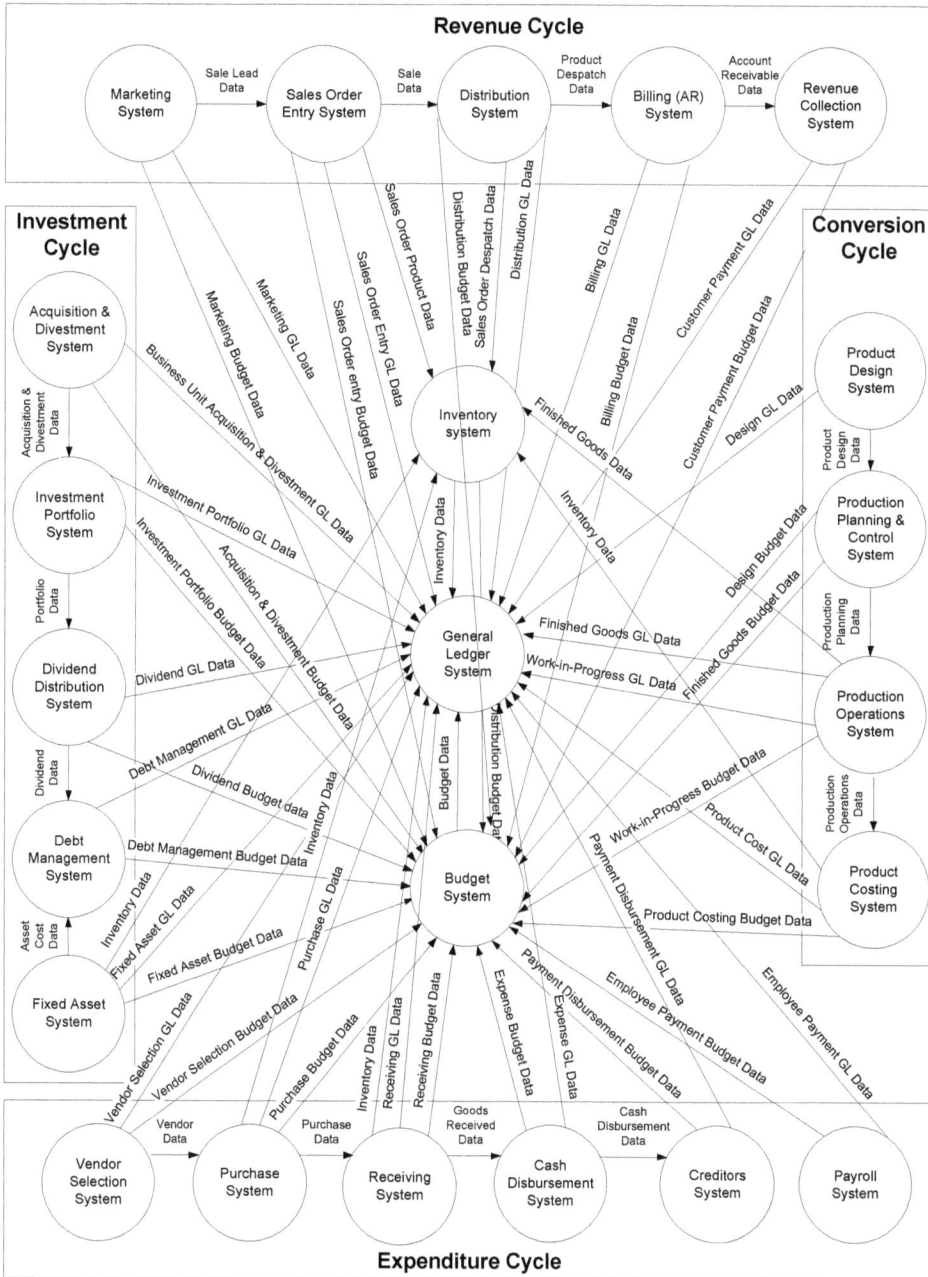

Figure 16. Systems within the operating cycle showing
the inventory system, the general ledger system and the budget system
are each common to all business cycles

ledger system and the budget system are central to all other systems. Only the net data flows between systems are shown. Separate data flows are aggregated. All trivial data flows are essential if the system is a high reliability system (e.g. avionics, nuclear power generation) but are usually omitted in other cases. On a data flow model the external entities and data stores would be shown. This would introduce additional data flows which cannot be accommodated in the space.

- Working at the process level. Consider:
  - The data flow context model is a superb tool to elicit and reinforce this understanding
  - Recognising that there are generic business processes and unique business processes
  - Using the basic input-process-output sequence[24] shown in Figure 17 below to identify processes:
    - o Inputs (information or materials is recorded)
    - o Process (Methods to transform the inputs into value added output)
    - o Output (products from processing desired by the customer or another process).

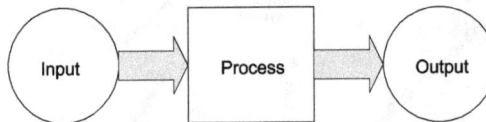

Figure 17. The basic input-process-output linear model

  - Adding controls and feedback to the basic input-process-output model shown in Figure 17 above to create the extended input-process-output model shown in Figure 18 below:
    - o Controls (Monitoring and evaluating feedback to determine whether a system is moving toward achievement of its goal)
    - o Feedback (Output that is used to make changes to input and/or processing). It may be reactive or pro-active (forecasting).

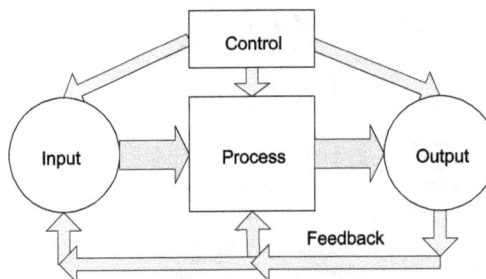

Figure 18. The extended input-process-output linear model

The managerial decisions and judgements that arise from unified view of the business systems and processes include:

- Does the system have a clear purpose which creates value for the business?

---

24 Both the basic input-process-output model and the extended input-process-output model are frequently useful for quickly deducing one or two missing elements.

- What are the apparent discrepancies between how things are really done and what is believed to occur?

- How will overlaps between functions under the control of different managers be resolved?

- How interdependent is the system under consideration with other systems?

- How effective and efficient is the current physical system in terms of source documents, technology, internal control goals and plans, reports (financial and non-financial) and technologies?

- How important is the system under consideration in terms of what data it creates, stores and transfers?

- When the business systems of outsourced functions are included, are there any gaps?

- What are the major limitations in the existing business systems?

The principal features of the business transaction cycle depicted in Table 13 commencing on the next page show the four operating cycles and the non-operating cycle. For each of the cycles, the following are considered: (1) objective of the business transaction cycle; (2) key question; (3) industry sector; (4) profit sector; (5) selected examples from the sector (6) operational model for the business transaction cycle; (7) key operational decisions; (8) key accounting events; (9) major systems (transactional or operational, tactical, and strategic) in the business transaction cycle (these are separately detailed in Tables 14 to 18); (10) auxiliary systems; (11) reports (financial and non-financial); and (12) technologies (infrastructure and architecture). The description is of the physical system as it deals with the actual manifestations of the systems.

The heading of the columns in Table 13 on the next page show each of the business cycles while the rows detail important aspects of the business cycles.

Table 13. Principal features of the operating and non-operating business transaction cycles

Business Cycle: Major cycle:	Operating				Non-operating
	Revenue	Expenditure	Conversion	Investment	Business reporting
Also Known As:	Collection; Order-to-cash;	Acquisition & Payment; Purchase-to-pay	Production or manufacturing	Finance	Financial reporting
Objective	Provide products and services to customers.	Acquires products and services.	Transforms acquired resources into products and service.	Obtain funds and provide equity to establish, operate and expand the business.	Produce reports containing financial and non-financial data to be distributed to stakeholders.
Key question (Note 1)	How does the business create wealth from its products/services?	How does the business use its expenses to create wealth?	How does the business use its funds to create wealth?	How does the business use its funds to create wealth?	How much wealth has the business created this period?
Industry Sector	Manufacturing Merchandising Resource Service	Manufacturing Merchandising Resource Service	Manufacturing Resource	Manufacturing Merchandising Resource Service	Manufacturing Merchandising Resource Service
Profit sector	Not-for-Profit Private Public	Not-for-Profit Private Public	Not-for-Profit Private Public	Not-for-Profit Private Public	Not-for-Profit Private Public
Sector Example — Manufacturing	Ford Australia	Ford Australia	Ford Australia	Ford Australia	Ford Australia
Merchandising	Woolworths	Woolworths	Not applicable	Woolworths	Woolworths
Resource	BHP Billiton	BHP Billiton	BHP Billiton	BHP Billiton	BHP Billiton
Service	Macquarie Bank	Macquarie Bank	Not applicable	Macquarie Bank	Macquarie Bank
Not-for-Profit	Salvation Army	Salvation Army	Salvation Army	Salvation Army	Salvation Army
Private	Consolidated Press Holdings (The private company of Mr James Packer)	Consolidated Press Holdings	Not applicable	Consolidated Press Holdings	Consolidated Press Holdings
Public	Dept. of Immigration	Dept. of Immigration	Not applicable	Dept. of Immigration	Dept. of Immigration

Continued over page

Business Cycle:	Operating				Non-operating
Major cycle:	Revenue	Expenditure	Conversion	Investment	Business reporting
Also Known As:	Collection; Order-to-cash;	Acquisition & Payment; Purchase-to-pay	Production or manufacturing	Finance	Financial reporting
Operational model for the cycle	Revenue model (cash, pre-billing or post-billing including invoice with goods) Accounts receivable options (balance only, balance forward, open-item)	Expenditure models: - Delegated functions - Project	Conversion models: - Continuous processing - Batch processing - Make-to-order processing	Finance models: - Long-term debt funding - Equity funding	Reporting models: - Statutory or Financial - Management accounting - Performance reporting
Key operational decisions	Authorise credit terms for customer Allow discount on price Allow sale on credit Authorise special order Authorise backorder	Authorise supplier Authorise purchase product and quantity Authorise acceptance of received products	Authorise production Authorise release of finished products	Authorise business investment placements Authorise balance of investments Authorise continuation of an investment strategy Authorise discretionary repayments	Review performance Authorise financial statements
Key accounting events	Accept an order Despatch the products or services Request payment Receive payment	Order the items Receive the items Record the obligation to pay Make payment	Consume materials Employ labour Incur overhead	Raise capital Use capital to acquire property, plant and equipment	Periodic reporting to the sources of capital and the end users of financial and non-financial information

Continued over page

239

Business Cycle:	Operating				Non-operating
Major cycle:	Revenue	Expenditure	Conversion	Investment	Business reporting
Also Known As:	Collection; Order-to-cash;	Acquisition & Payment; Purchase-to-pay	Production or manufacturing	Finance	Financial reporting
Transactional or Operational	Marketing Customer/Sales Order entry Distribution Cash receipts Billing Revenue collection (accounts receivable) Sales returns	Supplier selection and requisitioning Purchasing Receiving Cash disbursement Accounts Payable Payroll Inventory control	Production planning and control Production operations Product costing	Investment portfolio Dividend payment Debt management Fixed assets	Compliance reporting including consolidations General purpose financial statements and footnote disclosures
Tactical and Strategic	Sales reporting	Expenditure reporting and management	Product design	Acquisition & divestment	Budget Profit forecast Key Performance Indicators Critical Success Factors Service Delivery Outcomes
Auxiliary Systems	Human resources benefit plan administration Human resources Superannuation Human resources leave	Human resources benefit plan administration Human resources Superannuation Human resources leave	Property accounting Human resources benefit plan administration Human resources Superannuation Human resources leave	Non-current (Fixed) assets Human resources benefit plan administration Human resources Superannuation Human resources leave	All auxiliary systems

Major Systems

Continued over page

Business Cycle:			Operating			Non-operating
Major cycle:		Revenue	Expenditure	Conversion	Investment	Business reporting
Also Known As:		Collection; Order-to-cash;	Acquisition & Payment; Purchase-to-pay	Production or manufacturing	Finance	Financial reporting
Reports	Financial	Revenue	Expenditure	Variances	Cash flow	Cash flow / Income and Expenditure / Balance sheet
	Non-Financial	Productivity measures	Resource measures	Quality measures / Cycle measures	-	-
Technologies	Infrastructure (Note 2)	Hardware (e.g. Servers & Clients) / Communications and networks (e.g. firewalls; switches; routers) / Databases (e.g. non-relational databases and relational databases) / Software (e.g. application software; decision support systems; collaboration tools; electronic payment systems); / Programming and web page languages / Security / Electronic commerce payment systems				
	Architecture	Client: Personal Digital Assistant (PDA); Cell phone, Browser / System: Legacy, web server, mail server; directory server; wireless server; application server				
Notes	1.	For public sector activities, 'wealth' can be replaced by outcomes expected by the activity'.				
	2.	Suitable business processes are necessary to accompany the infrastructure. For example, self-service requires simple and informative product selection and confirmation steps, security of the transaction including privacy and supply chain management and coordination to deliver the product.				

241

Analysing systems

A systems perspective brings a different approach to looking at the world.[25] It has three advantages: (1) seeing interrelationships among systems rather than linear cause-effect chains; (2) seeing processes of change among systems rather than discrete snapshots of change; and (3) seeing systems, subsystems and components of systems. The data flow context model[26] is a superb tool to elicit and reinforce this understanding. Its disadvantage is that it is difficult to document and to agree boundaries (sometimes known as interfaces).

A system offers a means of grouping independent yet related functions together. By convention, several systems are identified for each business transaction cycle. Similarly, within a system it is convenient to group related functions together and refer to them as a subsystem.[27] It can be seen that there some arbitrariness operating. The acceptability of the use of system or subsystem is dependent upon whether the bundles of functions are processes that are coherently interrelated. In practice a business may shift elements in the generic system to another system.[28]

To analyse a system it is necessary to find a sequence of activities or logically related tasks. An analysis can take a physical or the logical view of a system. The physical view of a system describes how it might be implemented. The logical view of a system describes what needs to be accomplished.

17.3.1 Physical view of systems, processes, workflow and data

Generally, a physical view is created by examining how the existing system actually operates. This requires time to be spent in closely examining how work is performed by employees, taking into consideration their knowledge, familiarity and degree of reticence. A physical view should reveal where the existing (perhaps taken for granted) arrangements work satisfactorily as well as any shortcomings.

The broad management issues and challenges in taking physical viewpoint of the business systems, processes and data include:

- Clarify the systems analysis. Consider:
  - The likelihood that this will not have been previously documented or analysed

---

25 The systems approach is more generally known as general systems theory (Bertalanffy 1969/1976; Weinberg 1975/2005). It emphasises wholes without considering operations mechanically or technically.

26 The context model formally declares the boundary of analysis. It represents the highest level of generalisation of the processes that comprise the system. The model defines the environment within which the system functions. It shows the set of data flows that cross into and out of the domain and the sources/sinks which will be treated as entities external to the system (DeMarco 1978/1979).

27 A subsystem must have its own goal just as does a system.

28 The argument in favour of doing this is that it makes if difficult for outsiders to understand and thus acts as a barrier. The argument in favour of retaining the generic view of systems is that it encourages the business to focus on features and business rules that will create competitive advantage for it.

- – The difficulty in undertaking the analysis and documentation.
- Clarify the relationship of business rules to systems. Consider:
  - – Identifying the statutory obligations, standards, benchmarking best practice and incidents with customers and suppliers to see business rules in action
  - – Reviewing the business rules to check the suitability of their constraints on the business
  - – Assessing the extent to which the business rules can facilitate the automation of the processes.
- Clarify the relationship of automation to systems. Consider:
  - – The feasibility of a single automated system.[29]

The principal tools and techniques in taking physical viewpoint of the business systems, processes and data include:

- For systems. Consider:
  - – Information elicitation skills to obtain information about current work practices
  - – Developing conventions and protocols to ensure the documentation methods are used consistently by different employees.
- Clarify the relationship of business rules to systems. Consider:
  - – Devising the business rules expressed in succinct syntax.
- Clarify the relationship of workflow to systems. Consider:
  - – Basing sequencing on the order of input-output and business rules
  - – Using the traditional approach recommended by organisation and methods studies.

The managerial decisions and judgements that arise from taking physical viewpoint of the business systems, processes and data include:

- What are the satisfactory aspects of the current physical system, processes and data?
- Should the unsatisfactory aspects of the current physical system, processes and data be improved or replaced?

Taking a physical view of the existing systems often saves a project by revealing what is actually being done as opposed to what employees and managers think is being done. Any changes are therefore solidly grounded in an understanding of the effect on existing arrangements.

Tables 14–17 present a physical view of each of the four operating cycles (revenue, expenditure, conversion and investment) using the same row format for the four systems. Although the tables identify the key, major or important aspects of the physical view of the system, other physical variations will be found. The listings are not exhaustive. No exceptions identified.

---

29 It is not expected that the workflow will be accomplished by a single system (Kobielus, 1997: 4). Workflow attempts to provide a complete description of activities as they are physically completed (Sharp & McDermott 2001: 148–59).

A physical view of each of the systems for each of the four operating cycles (revenue, Expenditure, Conversion and Investment) is depicted in Tables 14 to 17 commencing on the next page. In each Table the following are considered: (1) key source documents;[30] (2) key internal controls (as control goals of the business process[31] and control plans); (3) example of specific internal control checks; (4) budget; (5) key reports (financial and non-financial); and (6) key technologies associated with the system. However, the Tables are an 'ideal' characterisation and others may be found. The listings are not exhaustive and exceptions are not identified.

---

30 In a traditional (non-computer) system these documents are usually completed by employees. In a computer-based system which has web enablement (internet access) the customer or end user may complete the initiating, confirmation and payment documents.

31 Controls goals over operations and information. Operation processes includes compliance with regulations, conformance with specifications and agreements, utilisation of resources and security of resources. Information processes concern input and update accuracy, validity and completeness. To avoid repetition, the listed control goals exclude the goals common to all activities such as separation of duties, supervision and independent verification.

Table 14. Physical view of the systems in the revenue cycle

	System:	**Marketing**	**Sales order entry**	**Distribution**	**Billing**	**Cash receipts**	**Revenue collection**
	Also Known As:		**Order entry**	**Logistics**	**Debtors** **Accounts receivable**		**Collections**
	Source documents	Advertisement Sales catalogue Product brochure	Sales quotation Sales order Sales order acknowledgement Return of product	Packing slip (Despatch advice) Return of damaged product	Sales invoice Statement	Cash receipt Bank deposit form	Payment receipt Bank deposit slip
Internal controls	**Goals (Note 1)**	Profit budgeting Issue refund or replacement	Timely response to inquiry Acknowledge order Sale authorisation Ensure adequate inventory	Despatch authorisation Timely shipment Collect product authorisation Delivery acceptance authorisation	Charge freight Allow discounts Billing authorisation	Payment in full Timely banking	Endorse cheques Bank reconciliation (monthly) Identify unpaid (unmatched to invoice) accounts
Internal controls	**Plans**	Ensure appropriate product pricing	Grant credit to credit worthy customers Accept and finalise orders for stocked products	Correctly fill customer orders Ensure safe undamaged delivery Ensure timely delivery	Correctly bill the customer	Avoid mishandling of cash receipts	Ensure receipts correctly allocated to customer accounts and invoices

Continued over page

System:	Marketing	Sales order entry	Distribution	Billing	Cash receipts	Revenue collection
Also Known As:		Order entry	Logistics	Debtors Accounts receivable		Collections
Examples of specific internal control checks	Conduct spot checks of prices in the inventory master file	Identify missing numbered forms Reliable customer data entry Entitlement to supply (customer credit) determined independent of the sales function Allow backorders Accept returns	Despatch of appropriate products and quantities Independent order checking Adequate packing Insure products in transit	Bill exactly what has been shipped Frequent reconciliations of debtor accounts	Use numbered receipts	Doubtful debt collection Bad debt write off Bank deposit reconciliations
Reports — **Budget**	Advertising and promotion budget	Sales volume budget	Cost of Goods Sold budget	Budgeted receivables	Cash receipts forecast	Articulated master budget
Reports — **Financial**	Advertising costs Advertising expenditure	Sales analysis report	Inventory valuation	Revenue invoiced	Monies banked	Revenue banked Bad debt report
Reports — **Non-financial**	Advertiser listing Advertising schedule	Customer listing Product listing	Inventory movements	Billing run completion details	Receipts issued	Ageing of debtors
Technologies associated with system	Database of products/services Web based product specifications, catalogues and pictures	Online real-time order entry (24/7) Automation of order status	Bar-code materials Computer Aided Design (CAD) Computer controlled machining Computer reported production	Online real-time billing (24/7)	Multiple copy receipting form sets Cash register	Electronic funds transfer
Notes 1.	The goals have the following generic objectives: (1) To execute transactions in accordance with management authorisations; (2) To promptly and correctly record the transaction; and (3) To ensure security of assets.					

Table 15. Physical view of the systems in the expenditure cycle

System: Also Known As:	Supplier selection Vendor selection	Purchasing Procurement	Receiving Goods received	Cash disbursements Expense	Accounts payable Creditors	Payroll
Source documents	Approved supplier list	Purchase requisition Purchase order Purchase acknowledgement	Supplier packing slip Goods received slip Claim for damaged or surplus product	Petty cash voucher Expenditure requisition authorisation	Payment voucher Journal forms Adjustment authorisation Supplier invoice Supplier remittance advice Petty cash form	Offer of employment Attendance sheet
Goals *(Internal controls)*	Supplier selection criteria	Purchase order authorised Purchase from approved supplier	Receipt authorisation Ensure correct supply	Expense declaration Eligibility for reimbursement	Payment voucher authorisation	Employment offer in writing Pay authorisation
Plans *(Internal controls)*	Use appropriate authorised supplier	Avoid ordering unwanted products	Detect and reject unordered or defective products Detect theft of products	Detect theft of cash	Detect errors on invoices for payment Detect payment of duplicate invoices Obtain payment discounts where advantageous	Detect errors in payment rates or entitlements

Continued over page

System:	Supplier selection	Purchasing		Receiving	Cash disbursements	Accounts payable	Payroll
Also Known As:	Vendor selection	Procurement		Goods received	Expense	Creditors	
Examples of specific internal control checks	Ensure appropriate authorised supplier is used	Confirm order details Check for missing transaction documents Set minimum and maximum order levels Determine stocking options (in-stock versus special order)		Inspect inwards goods against order Checks for quantity, damage and order Optimise cash discounts	Ensure sufficient cash held Comply with reimbursement terms	Frequent reconciliation of creditor accounts Comply with payment terms Variance reporting	Employment offer made by other than the employing department
Budgets	Supplier purchase budget	Materials or inventory budget		Budgeted supplier payments	Cash receipts forecast	Cash disbursement forecasts	Payroll budget
Financial	Purchases with suppliers	Raw materials valuation Supplier order accruals valuation		Production planning schedule Finished goods Scrap and waste Labour efficiency Machine utilisation	Petty cash claims	Supplier payment (remittance) Supplier refund claim	Employee wages Deductions Bank deposits (by institution)
Non-financial	Approved supplier listing	Inventory on hand Inventory on order		Production output (units)	Type of expenditure	Number of transactions processed Number of transactions by supplier	Payroll count
Technologies associated with system	Database of supplier products/services Web based product details	Electronic Data Interchange (EDI) Automatic stock replenishment		Bar code identification Radio frequency ID	Electronic claim lodgement	Electronic Funds Transfer (EFT):	Electronic attendance recording Electronic Funds Transfer (EFT):

Reports

Table 16. Physical view of the systems in the conversion cycle

System: / Also Known As:	Product design	Production planning / Material requirements planning	Production operations / Factory operations	Production control / Shop floor control
Source documents	Design specification	Production job ticket / Bill-Of-Materials (BOM)	Finished goods test result / Quality inspection certificate	Finalised job ticket
Goals	Design authorisation	Production authorisation / Raw materials planning	Job authorisation / Quality levels / Completion by deadline	Efficiency in processes / Effectiveness of operations / Acceptable quality / Completion authorisation / Resource security / Inventory level
Plans *(Internal controls)*	Ensure customer is credit worthy / Reliable design	Purchase from approved supplier / Confirmation of order details / Check raw materials are available / Inventory status	Prior authorisation of overtime / Investigation of standard costs and variances / Machine utilisation / Labour utilisation	Quality of raw materials / Quality of work-in-process / Quality of finished product
Examples of specific internal control checks *(Internal controls)*	Ensure there is a valid customer request or order / Ensure the proposed design is authorised	Ensure raw materials ordered at acceptable prices	Quality of work-in-process / Authorisation for each processing stage	Variance reports on pricing and efficiency
Budgets	Budgeted design cost	Budgeted raw material costs / Budgeted direct labour costs / Budgeted manufacturing overhead costs	Budgeted production costs / Flexible budget	Standard costs
Technologies associated with system	Computer Aided Design (CAD)	Computer manufacture or assembly (e.g. robotics)	Bar-code materials / Computer controlled machining / Computer reported production	Automated warehousing of finished product

Continued over page

System: Also Known As:	Product design	Production planning Material requirements planning	Production operations Factory operations	Production control Shop floor control
Reports — Financial	Design cost	Raw material costs	Finished goods Scrap and waste Labour efficiency	Factory efficiency
Reports — Non-financial	Customer listing	Non-approved supplier purchases	Production planning schedule Production output (units) Machine utilisation	Factory utilisation
Technologies associated with system	Computer Aided Design (CAD)	Computer manufacture or assembly (e.g. robotics)	Bar-code materials Computer controlled machining Computer reported production	Automated warehousing of finished product

Table 17. Physical view of the systems in the investment cycle

	System:	Acquisition & divestment (Mergers & acquisitions)	Investment portfolio	Dividend distribution	Debt management	Fixed asset
Internal controls	Source documents	Contractual agreement and schedules	Approved investment list; Investment prospectus	Dividend letter/certificate; Change of shareholder details	Money market confirmation; Loan contract	Asset tagging (ID's); Radio-Frequency tagging
	Goals	Proposal supported by evidence; Compliance with acquisition and divestment regulation; Compliance with investment criteria	Acceptable rate of return; Investment authorisation	Compliance with legislative framework controlling dividend payment; Dividend authorisation	Acceptable rate of borrowing; Debt authorisation	Ensure utilisation; Maximise sale value
	Plans	Acquisition or divestment authorisation	Ensure authorised purchase of bonds etc. Obtain appropriate interest and repayments	Identification of recipient; Payment of dividend according to schedule	Issue and repay equity and debt	Asset acquisition and disposal authorisation
	Examples of specific internal control checks	Physical stock-takes of inventory and non-current assets; Bank deposit reconciliations; Debtor reconciliations	Identification of supplier; Reconciliation of investment portfolio; Valuation of investment portfolio	Dividend payment reconciliations	Identification of lenders; Use of accounting records for authorised borrowings and dividend payments	Threshold amount for fixed assets; Depreciation rate; Asset expected life; Salvage value
	Budgets	Acquisition & divestment budget; Goodwill	Investment income budget	Dividend payment budget	Cash flow and debt budget	Fixed asset budget and depreciation
Reports	Financial	Acquisition profit (loss); Divestment profit (loss)	Investment income	Dividend payment schedule	Capital schedule	Schedule of assets; Asset depreciation schedule
	Non-financial	-	-	-	-	Remaining operating life
	Technologies associated with system	Spreadsheets and specialist applications to model the business	Electronic Funds Transfer (EFT)	Electronic Funds Transfer (EFT)	Electronic Funds Transfer (EFT)	Bar code tags and readers

17.3.2 Logical view of business systems, processes and data

The logical system is described after the physical view as it requires the implementation features to be abstracted. However, the table is an 'ideal' characterisation and others may be found. The listings are not exhaustive. The tables identify the key, major or important aspects of the logical view of the system and other logical variations will be found. The listings are not exhaustive. No exceptions identified.

The broad management issues and challenges in taking a logical viewpoint of the business systems, processes and data include:

- The novelty in a non-physical representation takes some learning time and effort
- The accuracy of the non-physical representation is difficult to check.

The principal tools and techniques in taking a logical viewpoint of the business systems, processes and data include:

- Developing a disciplined mindset that can abstract from the physical and eliminate all physical aspects
- Ensuring rigorous quality assurance of any drafts.

The managerial decisions and judgements that arise from taking a logical viewpoint of the business systems, processes and data include:

- Is the current system as documented similar to the management understanding and intention of how the system should operate?
- Is the current system comparable to desirable benchmark systems?

Taking a logical view of the existing systems often saves a project by allowing employees and managers to consider what they want to accomplish.

The tables for the logical view of each of the four operating cycles (revenue, expenditure, conversion and investment) provide a side-by-side format for the systems in each cycle. A logical view of each of the systems for the four operating cycles (revenue, expenditure, conversion and investment) is depicted in Tables 18 to 21. In each table, the following are considered: (1) processes for products; (2) products for services;[32] (3) key data;[33] and (4) external entities.[34] The convention with entity-relationship modelling is to show entities in CAPITALS and this has been done. The logical features of systems in the business transaction cycle are summarised with reference to the four operating cycles and the one non-operating cycle (the same cycles shown in the physical view).

---

32 There are several differences where services are provided rather than products. This is due to the intangible nature of most services unlike the sale or use of products.

33 When the data is normalised for use in a relational database, redundancy is eliminated (Date 1975/1999). This is not shown in the descriptions provided in Tables 13 to 18.

34 An external entity identifies a source or destination for data that is outside the boundary defined for the system. It will therefore include customers, suppliers and other systems.

Table 18. Logical view of the systems in the revenue cycle

System: Also Known As:	Marketing	Sales order entry Order entry	Distribution Logistics	Billing Debtors Accounts receivable	Cash Receipts	Revenue collection Collections
Processes for Product	Plan campaign Assess effectiveness	Respond to customer inquiry Provide quote Accept customer order Agree credit sale Check inventory available Provide confirmation acknowledgement Handle returns	Pick product Pack product Issue product Obtain despatch receipt Obtain delivery receipt	Issue payment request: invoice Issue accounts receivable statement	Check cash amount Issue receipt Post to account Bank monies	Collect deposit Collect payment Deduct sales returns Deduct oversupply Deduct discount errors
Processes for Service	Plan campaign Assess effectiveness	Respond to customer inquiry Provide quote Accept customer order Agree credit sale Check appointment available Provide confirmation acknowledgement	Arrange onsite service (if applicable) Obtain receipt for provision of service	Issue invoice Issue statement Obtain payment	Check cash amount Issue receipt Post to account Bank monies	Collect deposit Collect payment Deduct discount errors Deduct discount allowances
Key Data	Credit worthiness Order fulfilment Collections	Customer inquiry Product details	Product details Shipment details	Customer details Discount entitlements	Payment details	Customer details Payment details
External Entities	SUPPLIER	CUSTOMER	SUPPLIER	CUSTOMER	BANK	BANK

Table 19. Logical view of the systems in the expenditure cycle

System: Also Known As:	Supplier selection Vendor selection	Purchasing Procurement	Receiving Goods received	Cash disbursements Expense	Accounts payable Creditors	Payroll
Processes for Product	Make versus buy decision Select supplier	Raise internal purchase requisition for input resources Authorise purchase Issue purchase order	Receive input resources Check input resources Store input resources	Replenish petty cash float Lodge expense form Receive reimbursement	Receive supplier invoice Authorise supplier invoice payment Deduct discounts Adjust payment for returns, damage and shortages Pay supplier invoice	Authorise employee hire Authorise compensation package Prior authorisation of overtime
Processes for Services	Make versus buy decision Select supplier	Raise internal purchase requisition Authorise purchase Issue purchase order	Obtain service	Replenish petty cash float Lodge expense form Receive reimbursement	Receive supplier invoice Authorise payment of supplier invoice Adjust payment for allowable discounts Adjust payment for errors in supply of product or service (e.g. damaged goods, incorrect supply) Pay supplier invoice	Authorise contractor hire Authorise compensation package Prior authorisation of overtime
Key Data	Supplier details	Product purchase Product replenishment Service provision Supplier details	Product details Service details Supplier details	Purchase details	Supplier details	Employee details Contractor details Payment rate details Job details Leave details Superannuation details
External Entities	SUPPLIER	SUPPLIER	SUPPLIER	BANK	SUPPLIER	BANK

Table 20. Logical view of the systems in the conversion cycle

System:	Product design	Production planning	Production operations	Production control
Also Known As:	Research and Development	Material requirements planning	Factory operations	Shop floor control
Processes for Product	Finalise design of product Acceptance of the terms of the order	Request input resources Specify manufacturing processes Schedule production Detail costs for production Obtain input resources Specify production arrangements	Allocate resources Complete operations Verifying quality Store finished product	Accumulate costs Identify variances
Processes for Services	The conversion cycle is only applicable for products.			
Key Data	Product design details	Product design details Product manufacture details	Product manufacture details Inventory holdings	Cost of operations Worker productivity Equipment performance & repairs
External Entities	CUSTOMER	SUPPLIER	-	-

255

Table 21. Logical view of the systems in the investment cycle

System:	Acquisition & divestment	Investment portfolio	Equity	Dividend distribution	Debt management	Fixed asset
Also Known As:	Mergers & acquisitions					
Processes for Product	Investigate mergers Investigate acquisitions Preparing proposal Negotiate the terms Finalise acceptance Implementation	Forecast cash needs Assess performance Determine balance Rebalance portfolio	Determine suitability of equity Sell stock or securities to investors Retire stock	Determine available funds for dividend distribution Declare dividend Lodge compliance documents Make dividend payment	Determine preferred funding source Determine required funds Determine period for funding Negotiate loan Pay interest Retire debt	Submit proposal Order asset Install asset Commission asset
Processes for Services	Prepare valuation	Prepare valuation	-	-	-	-
Key Data	Cash flow	Investment return	Profitability		Borrowings Investor details Lender details	Asset details
External Entities	-	SHAREHOLDER LENDER	SHAREHOLDER		LENDER INVESTOR	LENDER

17.3.3 Analysing with generic and unique business processes

Business processes[35] have the advantage of a compact focus. Their disadvantage is that their detail is often cumbersome.

There are generic and unique business processes. Generic business processes are common to most businesses. For example, most businesses choose very similar coordination, activities and workflows for sales to customers. Unique business processes represent the interpretation of reports and the decisions that are converted into actions. Some controls are imposed on business processes, for example, customer policies on refunds, warranties and after-sales support. Some outputs from business processes are also unique. For example, the ease of use or reliability of products, the quality of product documentation, the friendliness, helpfulness and knowledge of sales and customer service employees.

17.3.4 Relationship between the physical and logical views

The physical view is concerned with inputs including source documents, the business processes, the workflow of business processes, business rules that govern business processes, the output including reports, and their organisational allocation into business functions. The logical view concerns systems but also concerns data, decisions and judgements. Figure 19 on the next page shows how these are interconnected.

17.4 Make wise capital investments in infrastructure, systems and technology

Many benefits can flow from investing in systems and technology. Wise investments are based on a project approach and a clear plan to realise the benefits.

The broad management issues and challenges in considering investments in infrastructure, systems and technology include:

- The fact that there is a low success rate with technology investments[36]
- Maintaining the relevance of accounting technologies in a rapidly changing, complex business environment

In summary, a unified view of business systems, processes, workflow and data requires both physical and logical views.

---

35 Business processes are defined either broadly (as identifiable aggregates) or narrowly (as units). By convention in data flow modelling they can be further decomposed until they are no longer subdividable. Such processes are atomic or a 'primitive process' (DeMarco 1978/1979).

36 There are many reasons why technology investments are unsuccessful. The common causes include the acceptance of an overly ambitious goal, the changing nature of the target product or service and the partial obsolescence of technology where a long development and implementation timeframe is involved.

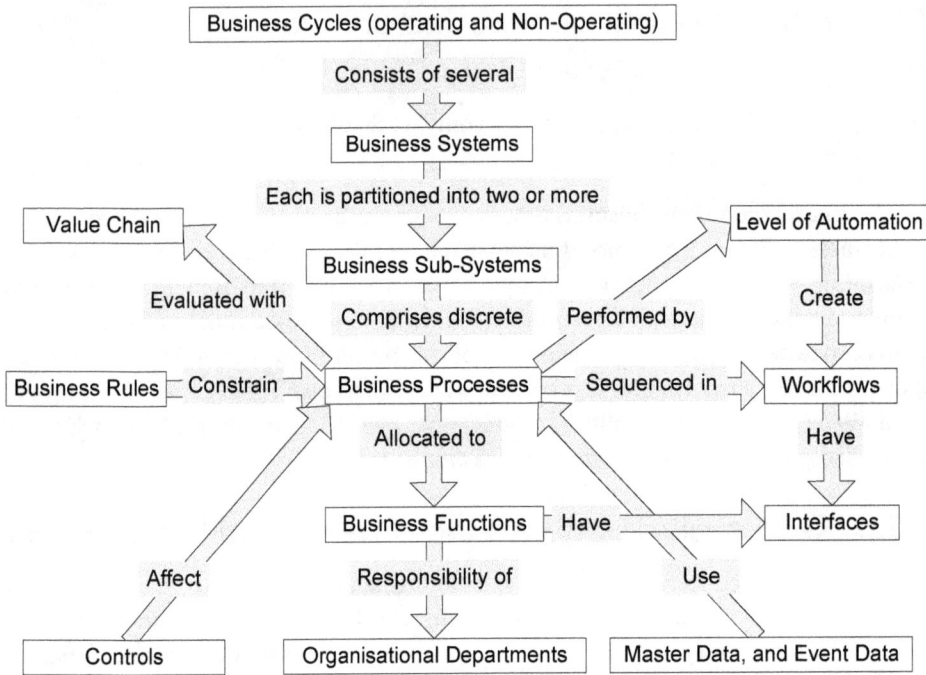

Figure 19. Interconnection between physical and logical views of the system

- If competitors have access to the same technology then the opportunity for gaining competitive edge is minimised[37]

- Any implementation of new technology should occur within a project management framework

- The life cycle of a technology means that it is necessary to realise benefits over a short time[38]

- Making cost systems accommodate needs for more diverse business analysis and more complex business processes.

The principal tools and techniques for considering investments in infrastructure, systems and technology include:[39]

---

37 There is a view that use of the same technology by different businesses can be differentiated by different implementations, meaning different surrounding systems or customer service policies.

38 Technologies have a time frame in which they remain current. The finite period before obsolescence may be as little as six months. For example, the new product cycle for mobile phones is six months. In the semi-conductor industry Moore's Law (Moore 1965) describes the doubling of transistors on an integrated circuit which can be extrapolated to digital devices in terms of processing power and random access memory capacity.

39 The extent to which technology can improve operations is unclear. Some implementations of technology have higher costs than benefits. A project that involves technology will always be inherently attractive because a spreadsheet can easily be created which promises high return and substantial benefits.

- Establishing a clear business case
- Requirements elicitation
- Feasibility study[40]
- Project management[41]
- Capacity and load planning
- Prototyping
- Software engineering
- Network analysis (including critical path analysis and project evaluation and review technique)[42]
- Disaster recovery and business contingency planning.

The managerial decisions and judgements associated with investments in infrastructure, systems and technology include

- Is the existing infrastructure adequate? Consider:
  - What is the obsolescence timeframe?
  - When are replacements budgeted?
  - Should the initiative be constituted as a project?
  - What is the method for benchmarking and negotiating the price for infrastructure and services?
- Are there suitable projects to develop new products or services? Consider:
  - Should the initiative be constituted as a project?
  - What resources should be made available to the project?
  - Has the project clear and measurable milestones?
  - Will the historical data be converted or available in the new system?
  - When should the migration/cut-over event occur?
  - Have the planned benefits been realised?
- Are there suitable projects to acquire new products or services? Consider:
  - How will the project be managed?
  - How will relationships change with the supplier when the project moves from pre-sales to post sales?
  - What are the contractual terms for licensing or acquisition?

---

40 Three tests for feasibility should be used: (1) technical, (2) operational: and (3) economic (McKinsey 1968/1971: 104–05).

41 A project management structure and responsibilities must be accompanied by a rigorous reporting regime. Details are provided in Oliver and Walker (2006).

42 Network analysis may also be used when comparing incremental costs and benefits (Moore & Hodges 1970).

- What are the vendor policies on audits or validation of licenses?
- What is the guaranteed life of the product or service?
- What are the annual licence fees, maintenance and other fees?
- How are fees set and what is the policy for setting prices for the expected life of the product or service?
- What is the extent of 'lock-in' once the product or service is adopted?

In summary, the value promised by infrastructure, systems and technology is frequently not delivered owing to inadequate specification and testing, poor project management or unsatisfactory operationalisation.

17.5 Constitute a project to plan and implement change

A heuristic provided by Davenport and Prusak[43] (1998/2000) is that a project becomes a information technology project when over a third of its budgeted time and expenditure is related to information and communication technologies. The typical information and communication technology project comprises phases and stages such as those listed in Table 22. The list is a 'waterfall' implying that the activities occur in a sequential manner but in practice some activities begin earlier and culminate where shown, some activities proceed in parallel and some are iterative.[44] Their heuristic also suggests that a project to improve business systems, process or data with a high technology expenditure is likely to overlook changes to the human side of the enterprise. In business, this suggestion that humans resist change is based on imposing systems which the employees find either don't save them the work promised or impose additional work to produce customer satisfaction.

---

43 While Davenport and Prusak (1998/2000: 78) use this heuristic to distinguish a knowledge project from a technology project it seems reasonable to expand the ambit of their observation to distinguish a management project from a technology project. It also serves to remind that it is more difficult to build ownership and acceptance when a project is handed over to the information and communication technology department.

44 Some insight into the difficulties of making software development visible is provided by Marciniak (1990).

Table 22. Overview of phases and stages in a software project.

Phase	Objective	Stage	Activities based on type of software selected		Deliverable	Project or business event
			Acquisition of a software package	**Custom software development**		
Initiative	Recognise the need for a solution	Inception	Prepare proposal		Proposal	Recognition as a project Assess fit with strategy
		Adoption	Inclusion in capital budget Formalise project team			
Analysis (Investigation)	Analyse the and specify the requirements for the software and the hardware on which it will run	Feasibility		List of options for implementing the application and a recommendation as to the preferred option	Feasibility study	Determination of feasibility Budget approval (if to proceed)
				Feasibility tests (Technical, economic and operational)		
				Schedule of costs and benefits (tangible only or tangible and intangible)		
				Identify and validate high level requirements which are the scope of the application and the project		
				Risk management plan (e.g. Loss of key project staff; Delay in going live'; Problems in processing transaction types; Problems handling the volume of transactions; disaster)		
				Schedule of work with tasks and milestones to indicate when the application can reasonable be made available		

Continue next page

Phase	Objective	Stage	Activities based on type of software selected		Deliverable	Project or business event
			Acquisition of a software package	Custom software development		
Design	Either code the application or evaluate packages against the requirements specification	Requirements definition	Preliminary investigation for shortlisting (Vendor assessment and Product assessment)	Preliminary (high level requirements)	Requirements in progressive detail;	Select development/developer option (in-house or external)
			Initial intensive review of product to determine preferred package	Detailed requirements	Detailed matching of preferred package to requirements or develop database, screens and reports	
			Inspect user sites and obtain referee opinions	Procedural requirements		
		Programming	-	Programming (usually prototyping)		
		Hardware	Hardware specification (make and model)		Hardware installation	Operating hardware
		Network	Network activation		Network installation	Active network
		Licensing	Licensing of application modules and any third party packages	-	Software package as modified	Sign licence contract
		Configuration	Configuration of the package	-	Configured	
		Testing	Create the test environment		Test plan, test scenarios, test results	Decision on test results
			Validate routine and exception controls			
			Testing	Unit, function, system testing		
			Volume, error handling and system restart and recovery testing			
			Local and online or remote testing			
			Integration with related systems			
			End-user acceptance testing			
		Documentation	Finalise policies including changes of policy		Policies	Approved documentation
			Finalise user documentation		User manual	
		Training	User training (may involve certification)		Completed training	Operators trained

Continue next page

Phase	Objective	Stage	Acquisition of a software package	Custom software development	Deliverable	Project or business event
			Activities based on type of software selected			
Implementation	Application commences day to day use	Cutover	Cutover (Method: pilot, direct, phase-in, parallel)		Cutover plan	Commissioning and operation 'Day 1'
		Restructuring	Appointment of end-user Administrator			
			Change operational roles and responsibilities documented and authorised		Restructure finalised	
			Change technology access and protocols authorised and documented			
		Migration	Migration of prior data and balances with selective and random comparison checks		Migrated data	
			Retention of old system to access non-migrated data (if applicable)			
		Go Live	Notify users, clients of new arrangements and procedures		Client awareness	
			Service level agreement for vendor support	Retention of programming resolution support and prioritisation of urgent fixes	Support agreements	Project implementation finalised; Decommission old systems
			Hours of operation (initial and routine)		Operation agreements	
			Random internal audit checks of transactions and controls		Audit assurance	
Evaluation	Implemented system is assessed and the adequacy of the project management is examined	Review	Post implementation review to compare what has been delivered with what was approved and reported as being delivered		Review with recommendations	Assessment of products and services
		Evaluation	Post project evaluation (or lessons learnt; also known as after action review		Evaluation with recommendations	Assessment of project
		Realisation	Realisation of benefits according to the realisation of benefits plan and organisation change plan		Realisation of revenue gains and savings as budgeted	Reorganisation

Continue next page

Phase	Objective	Stage	Activities based on type of software selected		Deliverable	Project or business event
			Acquisition of a software package	Custom software development		
Maintenance	Provide support to make continued use possible	Development	Program fixes prioritised according to an authorised schedule based on impact on customers, back office processing overhead, cost/benefit and strategic and competitive position.	Modifications to comply with amendments to existing or new legislation (enacted or forthcoming)	Improved functionality	Prioritise system stability
				Modifications to enable execution of new or revised business strategy		
				Enhancements for new functionality		
		Support	Training of new users		Trained and competent users	
			Training in new functionality			
			Technical support and help desk facility for resolving enquiries (e.g. volume, response time, errors)			
		Renewal	Renewal of maintenance agreement(s) for software and hardware with appropriate response level	Retention of analysts and programmers) and renewal of hardware maintenance with appropriate response level	License	Budget
		Retirement	Retirement (with or without replacement) at end of product life, at change in business strategy or to satisfy compliance obligations		Plan for replacement	Life cycle

The broad management issues and challenges in planning and implementing change include:

- Ensuring that the task is a project and not research
- Making clear the triad of management expectations (cost, time and quality).
- Ensuring the scope[45] of the project is well defined at the outset

The principal tools and techniques in planing and implementing change include:

- Preparing a Work Breakdown Structure (WBS) and having it reviewed for comprehensiveness and tasks which require spare time owing to the risk of running late or requiring rework[46]
- Techniques for appreciating constraints (e.g. Theory of Constraints)
- Using a change framework[47]
- Communicating in a manner appropriate to the recipients and culture.

The managerial decisions and judgements that arise from planing and implementing change include:

- Is it possible to verify appropriate plans have sufficient detail? Consider:
  - Is there an overall, detailed project timetable?
  - Is there a risk plan[48] covering the project and operations?
  - Is there a comprehensive software testing plan (including user acceptance testing)?
  - Is there a plan to realise benefits?
  - Is there a disaster recovery plan?
- Are there adequate governance and reporting arrangements? Consider:
  - Are there appropriate reporting arrangements within the project team?
  - Will the calculation of resources at feasibility be confirmed at commencement to avoid cost over-runs through under-costing?[49]

---

45 Scope depends upon: (1) number of sub-systems forming part of the application; (2) the complexity of those sub-systems; (3) extent to which an application handles industry and organisation-specific needs; (4) extent of automation of sub-systems; (5) perceived adequacy of standard controls forming part of the application; and (6) Availability of suitable related systems.

46 The work breakdown structure needs an overall framework comprising both activities and events.

47 Theories of change include: (1) Lewin's force field analysis which considers driving and restraining forces; (2) Senge's fifth discipline which uses systems thinking, personal mastery, mental models, shared vision and team learning; (3) Schein's model of cognitive re-definition (with unfreezing); and (4) various complexity theories derived from scientific disciplines such as meteorology, biology, physics, chemistry and mathematics which take into account the possibility of temporary chaos.

48 Project risk will encompass: (1) loss of key project staff; (2) delay in 'going live'; (3) problems in processing transaction types; (4) problems handling the volume of transactions. Operations risk will encompass: (1) cost of readiness to recover from a disaster; (2) hardware failure, incompatability or inadequacy; (3) Network failure, incompatability or inadequacy; (4) viability of an alternate site.

49 Resource costs include staffing and overheads (including facilities taking into account major resource consuming tasks including testing).

- – Have expenditure approvals been authorised?
- – Has reporting (format, frequency and recipients) been determined?[50]
- – Has an oversight committee (membership, meeting frequency and rights) been appointed and empowered?
- – What is the potential for escalation of commitment?[51]

- Does the project have a clear objective and achievable scope? Consider:
  - – Are the symptoms and problems comprehensively identified?
  - – Has the existing system been adequately examined?
  - – Is the level of automation proposed realistic?
  - – Have the requirements been adequately specified?
  - – Has any 'gold plating'[52] been eliminated?
  - – Has the feasibility of the project been thoroughly explored?
  - – Have the whole-of-life costs been considered?

- Is there appropriate compliance? Consider:
  - – Are all software applications properly licensed for the number of users at their locations?[53]
  - – Are there enterprise bargaining agreements which have to be followed?

In summary, a project should be managed in a framework. Feasibility of the specified requirements should be established and the project managed appropriat to the level of formality and effort agreed at the outset. Care should be taken to ensure oversight by management and avoid escalation of commitment. Important aspects of any project are the clear definition of requirements, testing including user acceptance and post implementation realisation of benefits. Once it is complete, there should also be an evaluation of the conduct of the project.

---

50 Oliver and Walker (2006) have suggested some templates as well as committee responsibilities.

51 Staw (1976) identified the phenomenon where people increase their investment in a decision despite new evidence suggesting that the decision was probably wrong. In software projects past evidence of accomplishment may not indicate future accomplishments. However, a failing project may be rescued by careful management or scaling back its scope.

52 There are at least three kinds of gold plating: (1) it can be the inclusion of desirable rather than only the essential requirements; (2) it can be the selection of higher quality items when average quality would be sufficient; and (3) it can be the inclusion of exceptional transactions rather thn just the routine transactions. There is no end to a list of desirable requirements and thus the scope of a project will continue to expand. Attempting to automate exceptional transactions will often prove insurmountable; typically exceptions should be separately handled with manual intervention as they require both judgement and discretion.

53 Licensing should encompass (1) the number of end users included; (2) the locations of the end users; (3) the location of the software application in terms of hosting; (4) the frequency of maintainenance updates and upgrades (5) the availability of technical advisory support from the vendor (6) the horizon for support to be discontinued; and (7) the date when a replacement software application is to be available that will supersede the current generation.

Chapter summary

Examination of the business cycle, systems, process, business rules, workflow and data offers a detailed analysis of business operations. This is essential for standardising and integrating business operations. While time and effort to create a detailed analysis often does not exist, the simple input-process-output models provide an entry point into back-of-the-envelope analyses which can reveal areas for attention. Although value chain analysis provides a view of where value is being created and captured it lacks sufficient detail to pinpoint the primitive processes which are involved. The hierarchy of business transaction cycle, systems, subsystems and the business processes allow a structured immersion in detail. The level of automation establishes the options for the system and then allows consideration as to whether it is in-house or outsourced. This avoids premature commitment. Accompanying the processes are the business rules and the workflow which allow policies and practices to be codified and thus be made transparent for review. The standardisation and integration of systems and processes is only accomplished by experienced analysts in conjunction with employees well versed in the particular operations of the business possessing the assumed business body of knowledge. Wise investments will avoid sunk costs in obsolete infrastructure, systems and technology.

DIMENSION FIVE
VOCABULARY OF
THE *BOSBOK*

Context of the vocabulary of the *BOSBOK*

The vocabulary of the *BOS*BOK is sourced from the four dimensions. Some similarities and overlap will be found between concepts from different disciplines. Within the same discipline, some concepts from different times in its history may not necessarily be interchangeable.

Perspective on the vocabulary of the *BOSBOK*

The nature of assumed business knowledge is interdisciplinary. No discipline dominates the vocabulary of assumed business knowledge. However, disciplines[1] do contribute 'families' of terms and expressions which can be compared and cross-referenced.

Impact of the vocabulary of the *BOSBOK*

For convenience, the vocabulary is listed alphabetically. This requires the reader to select the usage and meaning. Some of the vocabulary is misleading or unhelpful to a novice. For example, the subtleties of system and subsystem depends upon the reference system rather than any absolute definition. In any business conversation the prudent reader will probe and pursue meaning with their discussants as a part of normal communication.

Chapters in Dimension Five (Vocabulary or glossary)

Some instances of the vocabulary of each of the four dimensions is reviewed in chapter 18 which follows. They are:

1. Vocabulary of the business life cycle (discussed in Topic 18.1)

2. Vocabulary of adaptive behaviour to continuous and discontinuous changing circumstances (discussed in Topic 18.2)

3. Vocabulary of leverage resources to improve performance (discussed in Topic 18.3)

4. Vocabulary of recurring themes in employee and manager behaviour (discussed in Topic 18.4).

---

1 While there are various disciplinary dictionaries (e.g. Dictionary of Accounting, Dictionary of Mathematics; Dictionary of Psychology) their orientation is technical rather than business.

18 Vocabulary across all dimensions

The vocabulary of the *BOSBOK* can replace the rigid mental model of terms and expressions that employees bring to with them the business, allowing them to absorb new meanings and new terms and expressions. The advantage of considering the vocabulary is that it offers a top down approach to the dimensions as shown in Figure 20 below.

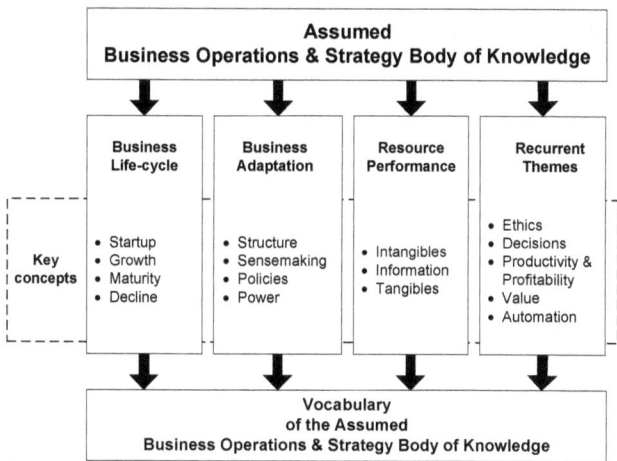

Figure 20. Top down view of the sources of the vocabulary in the *BOSBOK*

Since the vocabulary of the assumed business body of knowledge is quite substantial and broad it needs a systematic means to approach it. As shown in the diagram above, the four dimensions (business cycle, adaptive behaviour, leveraging resources and recurrent themes) provide such an approach.

18.1 Vocabulary of the business life cycle

The vocabulary of the business cycle (with its four stages startup, growth, maturity and decline) provides many terms and expressions to discuss routine, unexpected or uncertain business events.

During the startup stage the success of the business depends largely upon the vision of the owner. Central to the vocabulary is strategy, the industry, competition and the basics of management including marketing, external relationships, budgeting and taxation. The business decides if it operates on a cash or accrual basis. It also decides how to handle one-time special orders and whether to use penetration pricing. Related terms and expressions were introduced in Chapter 2.

To grow the business requires a different strategy to start-up, financing and prudent allocation of resources to enable growth through expansion. Central to the vocabulary are mergers, acquisitions, joint ventures, financing with debt or equity, diversification and coordination of the business units (strategic business units) with key performance indicators. The major issues of resources, the principal and agent problem and management controls are introduced. Related terms and expressions were introduced in Chapter 3.

During maturity revenues and market share are stable necessitating a review of strategy and operations. Central to the vocabulary is profitability in terms of cash flow, products and markets. Controls and costs of procurement and investment as well as considerations of goodwill are paramount. Issues of quality management arise with just-in-time purchasing and production and outsourcing. Threats to employment and employee security depend upon contractual obligations and workload. Related terms and expressions were introduced in Chapter 4.

Decline may be prevented by turnaround or may lead to exploring and finalising the sale of the business. Central to the vocabulary are the legal options of cessation. There are human consequences including redundancy and retrenchment as well as the disposal of assets and intellectual property. Related terms and expressions were introduced in Chapter 5.

Much of the vocabulary associated with the business cycle is associated with performance measures, estimates and indicators, including key performance indicators, variances and operating income. There are dangers in using indicators which are inappropriate to the cycle or lead indicators which no longer forewarn what the lag measures will state. This is exacerbated where lead indicators are input measures. Another problem can exist where several lead indicators are used. A contradiction between them introduces a difficult decision choice. An additional difficulty is the use of criteria which can be manipulated. Recent attempts to overcome these by indicators of the balanced scorecard type, which depend upon a definitive and linear causal chain between them, are problematic as it is difficult to select reliable lead indicators. The number of businesses affected by the global financial crisis of 2008 supports this suggestion.

18.2 Vocabulary of adaptive behaviour to continuous and discontinuous changing circumstances

The vocabulary of adaptive behaviour assumes that the business is in a continuous state of flux and the basis for change is itself varying.

Changes are manifested in the hierarchy (organisational roles and responsibilities), business functions and the legal structure of the business. Central to the vocabulary are organisational structure and business functions. These can be changed relatively easily and these are made frequently. A change to the legal structure incurs considerable expenses and these changes are considered for both their impact on financial statements and the tax advantages. Related terms and expressions were introduced in Chapter 6.

Scanning the external and internal events for their impact on the business brings about changes in priorities. Central to the vocabulary is sensemaking as it gives the widest view of its customers and suppliers, to bring concerns to the fore in sufficient time for the business to adapt. As many changes occur imperceptibly, the formal strategy can be outmoded even with financial projections, pricing, controls and supplier arrangements including just-in-time with lean manufacturing. Related terms and expressions were introduced in Chapter 7.

The reliance on policies controls and reviews is designed to bring flexibility to operations while ensuring there is intrinsic motivation. Central to the vocabulary is risk, policies, standard operating procedures and controls over administration and overhead. The efficiency, economy and effectiveness of systems and processes will not necessarily prevent defection of major or regular customers, or major suppliers changing their product or arrangements at short notice. Retention clauses may affect the legal position in the event of non-payment.[1] Well written service-level agreements and sensitivity analyses may overlook intangible benefits. Related terms and expressions were introduced in Chapter 8.

There are many difficulties in interpersonal relationships in organisations. Central to the vocabulary is power, authority, corruption and conflict deal with authority, concealment and trust. Internal relationships established through informal lines of reporting can exert more influence on the business than the Board and top management. Power relations affect the future behaviour of existing and new employees. Where employees feel that Boards, senior managers or managers are working mainly for their personal benefit or do not recognise their effort they can feel justified in pursuing their own interests. Related terms and expressions were introduced in Chapter 9.

Much of the vocabulary associated with adaptive behaviour centres on the information available to managers and employees. The modern business uses computers and software for routine reporting.[2] Reports may assist determine where attention should be directed for action (e.g. concerning cash position, trading arrangements, inventory management, expenditure and debt) in different functional areas.[3] It is notable that most businesses fail to foresee and mitigate the most serious hazards. Their adaptation is mostly either ad hoc or

---

1 This becomes complicated if the product sold was a component that is used in the fabrication of another product or is embodied in a construction (e.g. the steel rods in concrete for a road).

2 The use of packaged software with predefined reports may delay consideration of the information needed by the business for its operations. For example, customer dissatisfaction with products and services may be masked by efficient refund and return transactions.

3 Chapter 7 on priorities and sensemaking emphasises responses that can prevent premature action that may create a tipping point (Gladwell 2000/2001; Granovetter 1978; Schelling 1971), especially if a system has been propped up by dedicated employees.

a copy of other businesses (sometimes prompted by consultants). Policy-making may become a substitute for action and cost reduction may become a substitute for pride and innovation. A business regulated by controls for monitoring performance becomes dominated by its administration and overhead. A powerful source of adaptation is customer feedback but it is frequently misused or affected by performance measures and so becomes a lag instead of a leading indicator of failure.

18.3 Vocabulary of leveraging resources to improve performance

The vocabulary of leveraging allocated resources to improve performance covers both tangible and intangible resources.

Most businesses are aware of the potential contribution that their employees can make but are unable to unlock it. Central to the vocabulary are the intangible resource of employee abilities and judgement. Some resources are durable, appropriable, reproducible and transferable. Frequently management places such an emphasis on the performance of its employees that it overlooks the notion that their knowledge is contributed voluntarily[4] and depends on peers as much as policies.[5] Related terms and expressions were introduced in Chapter 10.

Information and knowledge are themselves resources. Central to the vocabulary are resources, capabilities and core competencies. An operating/non-operating cycle and systems view provides a means for grouping primitive processes to better understand them. Information may arise from the 'knowing' of individual employees, their innovation or through feedback from experts or novices. The format and content of some publicly available information is prescribed but should not override the needs of employees and managers. Assurance is used to determine the quality of the processes and information. Information is essential to suggest how best to improve the value of resources using both the physical and logical views of a system. Information is important in production planning (e.g. MRP/ERP). Related terms and expressions were introduced in Chapter 11.

Making improvements to tangible resources calls for judgement. Central to the vocabulary are the criteria for the use of scarce resources. Quality products and services will facilitate cash flow and the profitability of the business. A value focus will result in careful control, prioritising expenditure, minimising interest expense and can avoid intervention by the

---

4 Many businesses have found that their smarter employees quietly make their own career decisions to leave and it is then bereft of valuable knowledge and skill. A business lacking employee knowledge, skill and loyalty will find it makes poor decisions.

5 The use of morale as an indicator is often manipulated by 'morale booster' events. In these circumstances morale will continue to plummet. Morale is also affected by decisions which are perceived as 'out of touch'. Examples of this include a promotion or a recruitment which does not have credibility, avoiding difficult situations, agreeing with decisions made higher in the business that are considered counterproductive and not sponsoring new initiatives which require real effort from them to succeed.

lender. The improvement of business activities is always time consuming and requires detailed attention. Related terms and expressions were introduced in Chapter 12.

Considered use of resources is critical for competitive advantage. Profitability reports and variance reports on efficiency and prices can reveal the use of resources in terms of targets but may overlook organisational learning through training and mentoring. Communicating to employees that discounts, operations and expansion all have to be funded can make them aware of the value of resources to the organisation. A value focus will result in economising on the use of resources as well as using resources more intensively.

Of course, the three dimensions (stages of the business life cycle, continuous and discontinuous change and leveraging resources for performance) use a vocabulary which itself is specific to the business and its industry. All adaptation requires consideration of the resources that can improve the business. There is a fourth dimension which overlaps the previous three dimensions.

18.4 Vocabulary of recurring themes in employee and manager behaviour

The vocabulary of the fourth dimension of recurring themes concerns behaviours which affect all employees and managers.

Ethical principles and standards alter behaviour and encourage others to behave ethically. Central to the vocabulary are the concepts of ethics, morality, ethical dilemma and whistle blowing. There is ethical drift and the influence of peers is considerable so an ethical code is a major touchstone when supported by opportunities for mentoring. The limited time for reflection increases the importance of ethics. Related terms and expressions were introduced in Chapter 13.

Improving business judgement and decision-making in financial evaluation, the search for value and the improvement of systems has considerable payback. Central to the vocabulary are the heuristics, uncertainty, satisficing and value or utility. Often the outcomes from making decisions are delayed so a poor choice (perhaps from a poor analysis) results in the adoption of unworkable arrangements which have to be amended consuming additional resources. Related terms and expressions were introduced in Chapter 14.

Evaluating performance with financial and non-financial information involves the accounting standards followed in the financial statements (balance sheet, profit and loss, cash flows) usually assisted by budgets, standard costs and total cost of ownership. Public companies will have their accounts audited. Central to the vocabulary are ratios, cost-volume-profit analyses, budgets, variances and return on investment. There are competing methods including economic value added (EVA). A complete evaluation of productivity and profitability requires two forms of knowledge (external and internal) to be absorbed and meshed. Related terms and expressions were introduced in Chapter 15.

Creating and capturing value in the business is an area where there is divergent opinion both on the avenues for achievement and determining success. Central to the vocabulary are the value chain with its primary and support activities. Related terms and expressions were introduced in Chapter 16.

Standardising and integrating business operations using multiple simultaneous task and process analyses provides many benefits. Central to the vocabulary are the speed of change of technology compared with the speed of change of the business processes. Consideration of systems includes scope or boundaries and sub-systems. A transaction cycle view of the business helps categorise systems and decompose them into processes. This can be done by focusing on their physical or their logical attributes. Related terms and expressions were introduced in Chapter 17.

The common element in the four recurring themes is the desirability of involving the actual operational employees, although this often requires trade-offs between day-to-day workload of the current system and work on improving the system (or envisioning a new system) which should be grounded in an understanding of the current system. It takes committed and pains-taking managers for this effort to succeed. Standardising and integrating systems is always difficult. Thirty years' experience suggests the movement of prices, changes in supplier relationships and shorter product fashions requires faster analyses and better decision-making with closer attention to problem solving and negotiation. It should always be remembered that advances in technology in the last decade have done little to improve the chances of success while employee initiatives have provided considerable achievements .

Chapter summary

The final dimension is that of the assumed business body of knowledge vocabulary found in the glossary. In many respects it is the most difficult of all the dimensions. There is loose usage, overlapping meaning and sometimes unknowing ignorance by the speaker which can mislead even an attentive listener. Not only is the vocabulary taken for granted but the particular sense of meaning that is appropriate is often assumed. The glossary therefore identifies the preferred sense of meaning. Where there is more than one meaning in use, the alternative sense is described. There are also many instances of equivalent usage and these are also recognised in the glossary.

Nevertheless, specifying much of the vocabulary used in the book makes the assumed business body of knowledge clearer and sensitises the reader early to expect they will have to probe and pursue some meanings with their discussants as a normal part of prudent communication

CONCLUSION
USING THE *BOSBOK*

Leading Board members and senior executives are emphatic that a comprehensive understanding of business characteristics, drivers and their relationships – why and how it works – is more important than learning facts and principles.[1] This perspective reinforces the assumed Business Operations and Strategy Body of Knowledge.

The business life cycle, continuous adaptation to circumstances, leveraging resources to improve performance, the recurring themes and vocabulary are the five dimensions of the *BOSBOK*. These provide the foundation insights into assumed business knowledge.

Two commentaries conclude this *BOSBOK*:

1. Issues with sharing the assumed business knowledge. Sharing is not necessarily guaranteed because it is discretionary and not necessarily amenable to rewards or policy exhortations. Even the diffusion of assumed business knowledge does not guarantee it will be comprehended.

2. The future of the *BOSBOK* depends upon several factors. It depends partly upon fads and fashions in writing on business and management which distract attention from the solid foundations of traditional business knowledge. It also depends upon the expansion of assumed business knowledge framed in terms of the dimensions that comprise the *BOSBOK* or the are expanded.

Chapters in the Conclusion

Using the assumed business body of knowledge has two aspects. They are:

1. Factors in sharing assumed business knowledge (discussed in Chapter 19)
2. Future of the *BOSBOK*: Reflection and execution (discussed in Chapter 20).

---

1 This is the message from 60 alumni from UNSW over 60 years (UNSW World 2009).

19 Factors in sharing assumed business knowledge

With shared knowledge there are two perspectives, the provider and the recipient. Since the business life cycle, adaptation and resources reciprocally affect one another it is desirable to consider as much knowledge as possible within the constraints of availability, time or pricing. A common phrase wherever business is undertaken is 'Why wasn't I told?' Sharing assumed business knowledge is influenced by the factors in Figure 21 below which distinguish between the provider and a recipient.

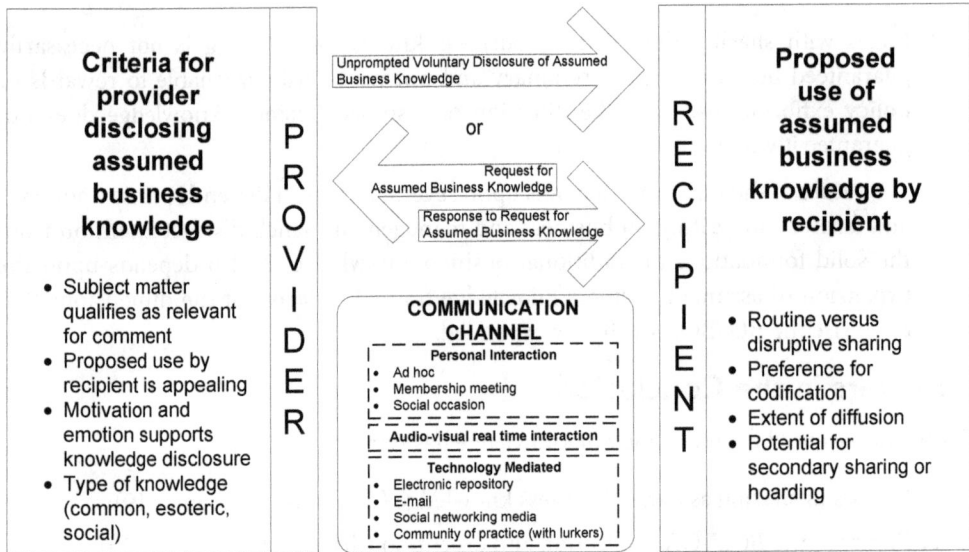

Figure 21. Factors influencing the sharing of assumed knowledge between provider and recipient.

19.1 Provider sharing assumed business knowledge

The provider tends to be influenced by three factors although the weight on any particular factor will vary and thus will influence the extent of sharing. The first factor is the subject matter of the knowledge itself. The provider must possess subject matter knowledge or be willing to express an opinion on the subject.[1] Assumed business knowledge involves a wide ranging subject matter so it is unlikely that one provider can be relied upon for all matters and therefore there may be multiple providers acting as knowledge brokers.

A second factor is its apparent purpose that is, its intended use. As shown earlier in the *BOSBOK*, sensemaking involves reaching a personal opinion on 'what is going on' and 'how it affects me' so any ostensible statement may be interpreted for its motives and possible repercussions. Threats and opportunities are considered by the provider. Typically there is the related consideration of trust. Business norms may assist determining whether the use is acceptable although organisation-wide norms may be modified by peer influences. Many aspects of assumed knowledge rely on being trusted with descriptions and rationales for behaviour or for understanding why certain kinds of behaviour are prevalent.

The final factor concerns motives and emotions of the provider. Motives may be extrinsic. Incentives or benefits offered and granted by the business both gain attention and usually ensure fulfilment, at least in the early stages of their availability. After the passage of time , employees may find other ways of obtaining the incentive through less effort. Motives may also be intrinsic. Personal belief and value systems may engender feelings of self-worth and meaning. This factor therefore covers both sharing for rewards as well as sharing for altruistic reasons. Emotions are closely linked to motivation as they influence empathic and altruistic behaviour. For example, mood and facial expression affect perception and interaction. Assumed business knowledge may be disclosed as part of trading and valuation of the knowledge market-place. In such circumstances, sharing assumed knowledge becomes a selective and showcase phenomenon. The assumed knowledge of business that has been discussed depends upon the willing contribution of knowledge.[2]

For these reasons, Figure 21 does not specify separately the factors shown for the provider. Sharing is contingent upon the the provider's motivation and emotional state when there are both opportunities and suitable recipients; their propensity to share differs with the type of knowledge and its particular subject matter. An employee may share common or social knowledge but hoard esoteric knowledge until it is strategic to provide it.

19.2 Recipient of shared assumed business knowledge

In looking at the recipient side of sharing assumed knowledge different problems become apparent. As noted in Chapter 11, there are several difficulties in recognising information as a resource and one of the major issues is the interpretation made by the recipient of the

---

1 Considering the information to be shared may involve reformulation or redrafting to ensure the best effect on the recipient (Adamson, 1983).

2 Using the question format advocated in the *BOSBOK*, these three factors could be reworded as 'What kind of information do you want me to reveal?', 'How do you intend to use it?' and 'Why should I share it?'

information. The recent example of Markopolos with regard to Madoff Investment Securities suggests that recipients of information may interpret publicly shared knowledge differently. It is another example of assumed business knowledge at work. In this case, Markopolos was unable to persuade government regulators that their assumed business knowledge was incorrect. His testimony makes clear that routinely shared knowledge can have greater credibility than information which is disruptive or disagreeable.

A major issue for the recipient of assumed business body of knowledge is its form. Nowadays there is a preference for making tacit knowledge explicit, usually by capturing it as text. It appears that codification gives the recipient greater control of the assumed business knowledge. Not only does codification potentially reduce delay in making knowledge available but it can have the weight of evidence should it be required.

Each recipient has different intentions for diffusion. Apart from the free movement of employees between businesses with different owners, there is the function of advice seeking and gossip. A recipient is usually not bound by constraints on secondary sharing of their assumed business knowledge. Alternately they may hoard the knowledge so they themselves can be a strategic provider of assumed business knowledge at a later time to selected recipients. In such circumstances it is unlikely to be to benefit the business.

19.3 Knowledge sharing instigation

Assumed business knowledge may be shared through the provider determining that knowledge should be disclosed to a recipient. This form of voluntary disclosure occurs where the provider is aware of that a target recipient exists and considers that they would benefit from being given the knowledge. The recipient's role may be used to make this judgement or they may simply be known to the provider as someone from a business unit. The alternative is the recipient seeking a potential provider. Again the same reasons for selecting the individual employee may apply. In the latter case, the assumed business knowledge may be incomplete or out of context if provided summarily.

19.4 Communication channel between provider and recipient

Sharing between provider and recipient may be personal, mediated by technology or a hybrid with audiovisual technology. While employees have their own preferences for the communication channel there is no longer a trade-off between richness and reach. Contact can be made using asynchronous communication. The distribution of employee functions in different locations (e.g. branches) as well as the outsourcing of routine business functions (e.g. distribution) and cost reduction measures reduce the frequency of personal interaction making it more difficult for employees to meet and know many of the other employees with whom they have dealings. Assumed business knowledge is becoming more technology mediated communication.

In some technology mediated communications the provider is anonymous. A seeker of information may turn to content aggregator websites such as Wikipedia and various publications. Often this is because the information is required to complete a task and the seeker either does not have it or wants to verify knowledge that they have. The ethos of verifying knowledge with sources is largely unknown outside journalism so there is a loss of the authentication that occurs when the provider is known to the recipient. Sharing assumed business knowledge within the business somewhat overcomes this problem even if technology mediated communication is used.

19.5 Assumed common, esoteric and social business knowledge

A major argument threaded throughout the book has been that common knowledge, which is readily available, is often overlooked. It is acquired from a variety of sources (discussion, textbooks, journal articles, conferences) but what is salient depends upon the employee's or manager's role and their personal preferences. Employees have common knowledge about the business even if they are not recipients of official reports. For example, a sales employee knows whether products are selling or services are being supplied even if they do not receive a daily sales report, a cash balance, or a stock summary. Similarly, while the business periods (e.g. weekly, monthly half year and annual events) are also well-known, their seasonal and budgetary significance may not be appreciated. Procedures and policies may be both codified[3] and available online to employees but there may be so many documents that comprehending them becomes next to impossible. Common knowledge is greatest for the activities in close proximity to the employee provided they notice it. It is also where there can be pitfalls through familiarity. For example, many frauds use well-known techniques. The common knowledge elements of assumed business knowledge are substantial.

The other disclosure is esoteric knowledge which has value if shared but is usually retained for strategic disclosure because it but is otherwise difficult to obtain, to summarise and to understand. It may be rules, capabilities or judgements including what is the essential information necessary for a decision. For example, capital budgeting, which is common knowledge, also has esoteric knowledge concerning the degree of confidence that can be placed in it for particular circumstances, the value judgements in interpreting and then optimising calculations and predicting the likely outcome if implemented. Esoteric knowledge may need to be acquired through learning which takes time. Assumed business esoteric knowledge can be embodied in employees in the business if the business is prepared to

---

3 The champions of codification were Nonaka and Takeuchi (1995) achieving it in four steps with their SECI model (socialisation, externalisation, combination and internalisation). Regrettably the process is neither as straightforward as described them nor guaranteed to produce the expected outcome. Instead, any approach should begin by determining which of two strategies should be preferred that is, either personalisation or codification (Hansen *et al.* 1999).

allow time for the learning to occur. However the business benefits from the knowledge being customised for it.

The final kind of assumed business knowledge is social knowledge. This knowledge is relative to the moment or to the circumstances of the employee. It includes gossip, rumour, immediate interpretations of current events and delayed interpretations as historical accounts and myths. It can background exceptional successes and notable failures in the business, competitors or the industry as well as interpretations of the selected actions of employees and managers and events in the business. This form of assumed business knowledge is frequently shared as stories and anecdotes although the social contribution of activities may be overlooked. Social knowledge can appear irrelevant or an interruption yet it may contain knowledge that confirms or supplements common and esoteric business knowledge.

The three kinds of assumed business knowledge do not easily fit the available views of knowledge or knowing. While some writers on general management recognised the knowledge of white collar workers was different to operational knowledge, (Drucker 1985/1994) he did not further explore the kinds of knowledge available to them and how there are different providers and recipients for sharing. A parallel view of knowledge developed by Grant (1996), in the field of leadership, considered it only in relation to recipients in senior management in terms of strategy. This may be one of the rare occasions when the forecasters were correct. Machlup (1962) identified the knowledge economy and sociologists of the future (particularly Bell 1967, 1973), predicted knowledge leading a service-oriented economy.

Chapter summary

Assumed business knowledge is not exclusively possessed by an individual and thus its diffusion in the business is essential for it to be available for use by its employees. While this is a welcome change to the perennial attempts at codification and the extensive preoccupation of administrators for rules, it creates its own difficulties. The outsourcing of many business functions makes it difficult to recognise assumed business knowledge for what it is. Providers are the key to promoting understanding of activities and breaking down the knowledge silos within the business. The reliance of software packages has also fragmented the intimate knowledge of processes which manual procedures inevitably engendered. It is now likely that more assumed business knowledge is being retained by individuals to justify their continued employment. Even when assumed business knowledge is shared it can be brief, keeping some detail in reserve to be strategically disclosed depending upon the feedback from the other party and the disclosures that they make even when business norms dictate otherwise.

20 Future of *BOSBOK*: Reflection on execution

The argument of the earlier chapters suggests that assumed business knowledge is more than the technical capacity to execute a variety of sophisticated techniques which have been practised by consultants and highly ranked businesses. It is a combination of analytical frameworks, ad hoc learning and reflection of experience and observation.

The assumed business knowledge becomes visible in the depth and range of knowledge associated with any given managerial conceptualisation, reasoning, judgement and decision making. Decision heuristics and biases are a reminder that usually favourable results are contemplated and risk is also considered mechanistically so there is often a sense that the tools and techniques constitute an infallible method. In many cases the employee or manager simply does not call upon their assumed business knowledge but makes quick decisions. It is common for a manager to reach their decision based on limited knowledge, a simple criterion and no reflection (or delay) between decision and execution.

Using the *BOSBOK* promises a different future for judgement and decision making. It shows many strategic and operational benefits of allowing time for broader considerations. In other words, making an inquiring rather than a procedural due diligence with nuanced criteria, gathering knowledge rather than relying on codified information and being aware of biasing heuristics. For improved decision making there also needs to be time for the potential business direction to be considered and adequate time for the formulation of substantive alternatives. Senior management often regard time spent on these activities as unnecessary delay. The *BOSBOK* makes clear that this is a sign of competent judgement and decision making.

Using the *BOSBOK* also links the future to the past. Its emphasis on asking many questions about issues and challenges, tools and techniques and managerial judgement and decision making takes a social complexity approach, probing the multiple aspects of phenomena to make sense of it. Sensemaking is more likely to accept diversity in perspectives on the current state of the business and reject any single solution to prepare for the future. It removes reliance on what was previously done in similar situations. Since the BOSBOK also presents a range of tools and techniques greater effort can be placed on understanding how employees see the current position and the future. Quicker challenges can be perceived at all levels in the business and the more comprehensive the proposed response the better the adaptation.

The existence of the *BOSBOK* will assist recall of relevant assumed business knowledge reducing the tendency to take a financial approach. While budgets, threshold earning levels, rates of return and expense reduction targets continue to play a large part in performance evaluation, they are models which exclude the unpredictable people factor. Although evaluation of performance will continue to be firmly rooted in such measures the *BOSBOK* emphasises their uncertainty. While targets may be met in the short-term this may have a detrimental effect which becomes apparent in the medium term. Qualitative factors appear to be playing a larger part in business success, witness the resurgence from Apple Inc. (formerly Apple Computer Inc.). In future, having the *BOSBOK* is a reminder to balance assumed quantitative and qualitative business knowledge when making judgements and decisions.

The *BOSBOK* is an artefact of the knowledge-based view of the firm suggesting that resources are inert unless converted to capabilities through routines and instructions. For the *BOSBOK*, they are the triumvirate of questions, the topics and the dimensions. They can be used alone with careful observation, or in discussion with peers, managers and mentors as well as in reflecting the rationale behind decisions and behaviour. While the future of the *BOSBOK* is in its contribution to individual understanding or knowing, that is, personal knowledge, it is not confined to it. More generally the *BOSBOK* reminds senior managers that sharing the assumed knowledge found in their business will not be accomplished by a policy exhorting employees to do so.

Business is a social activity and what constitutes assumed business knowledge is changing and the means for leveraging it also vary. The future will be one of scarce resources and plenitude of knowledge. Since the exploitation of resources is becoming more difficult and costly, businesses must look to the value or profit from sharing knowledge. Sharing knowledge should not be redefined as improving the intellectual capital position of the business but in enriching business practices with knowledge. Customers, innovation and reputation are long-term business basics. Businesses depend upon assumed business knowledge in routine as well as novel situations to reveal new insights and additional opportunities. The *BOSBOK* brings much of this together. It is the beginning of a process which can be ably concluded by managers and employees with reference to the knowledge surfaced in the *BOSBOK*.

Glossary of the *BOSBOK*

The glossary is a vocabulary of the business. It provides succinct definitions for the terms and expressions, and identifies common abbreviations used in earlier chapters. Many terms have synonyms or are known by alternative names. These are identified using the expression 'also known as'. When there is a preferred term cross references point to the preferred term. Some terms form a family. These are identified by the expression 'see also' at the end of the entry so they also can be checked. Some terms have more than one definition. The preferred definition will depend upon the circumstances and whether a narrow (or strict) or broad definition is appropriate. For ease of reading, terms and their definition are stated in the singular not plural.

Some confusion with terms and expressions also arises from terms becoming truncated in usage (e.g., 'floor plan financing' becomes 'floor plan'). Both the truncated and full term and expression are identified.

An up-to-date version of the glossary is available as an iPhone app from the iTunes store. Search under BOSBOK or Business Assumed Knowledge.

A	
ABC Analysis	The classification of line items of inventory into three categories (A, B, and C) based on their value or overall inventory cost. Category A contains about 20% of the line items that account for 80% of the value. Category B contains about 30% of the line items that account for 15% of the value. Category C contains about 50% of the line items that account for 5% of the value. There is a similar heuristic to the 80/20 rule known as the Pareto Principle. Also see *Pareto Principle*.
ABC Costing	See *Activity Based Costing*.
Ability	The ability to think ('intelligence') motor ability and artistic abilities as well as skill. Also known as Competence. Also see *Human Capital*, and *Skill*.
Abnormal Spoilage	The spoilage that would not arise under efficient operating conditions; it is not inherent in a particular production process.
Absorption Costing	A method of inventory costing. All variable manufacturing costs as well as all fixed manufacturing overhead costs are applied to or assigned to manufactured products when costs are incurred as Work-in-Process inventory on the Balance Sheet and when as Finished Goods inventory on the Balance Sheet and are then recorded as expenses on the Profit and Loss Statement when goods are sold. Thus inventory 'absorbs' all manufacturing costs. The difference between absorption and variable costing is the timing with which fixed manufacturing overhead becomes an expense. Under Absorption Costing, fixed overhead is inventoried until the accounting period during which the manufactured goods are sold. Also known as Full Costing. Contrast with *Variable Costing*.

Access Key	See *Entity Identifier*.
Account Analysis	The use of judgement by managers to allocate costs as fixed, variable or mixed (semi-variable).
Account Form	A layout which uses two columns (assets, and liabilities and owner's equity). It may be used for the Balance Sheet and is used for the Profit and Loss. Also see *T Account* and *Narrative Form*.
Accounting (Business Function)	The provision and analysis of financial and non-financial information for a variety of decision-making, managerial, accountability, regulatory, governance and resource allocation purposes. Also see *Distribution (Business Function), Finance (Business Function), Manufacturing (Business Function), Marketing (Business Function), Procurement (Business Function), Research and Development (Business Function),* and *Sales (Business Function)*.
Accounting Cycle	See *Business Transaction Cycle*.
Accounting Entity	A real or artificial unit of the business defined for the purpose of recording and reporting economic events. Also see *Legal Entity*.
Accounting Event	1. An external transaction. For example, sale to a customer 2. An internal transaction that is recorded in the accounting system. For example, an adjusting entry 3. Also see *Business Event,* and *Economic Event*.
Accounting Rate of Return	See *Accrual Accounting Rate-of-Return*.
Accrual Accounting Rate of Return (AARR)	An accrual accounting measure of average annual income of a project divided by an accrual accounting measure of its investment. Also known as Accounting Rate of Return. Also see *Return on Investment* (ROI).
Accrual Basis	Accounting that recognises economic events when they occur regardless of when the cash transaction occurs. The matching principle requires that future cash inflows/outflows are matched with any corresponding current cash inflows/outflows. Income is recorded when a sale occurs or when services are provided, regardless when the payment occurs and expenses are recorded when goods are received or services are provided, regardless when the payment occurs. Also known as Accrual Method. Also see *Cash Basis*.
Acquisition and Payment Cycle	See *Expenditure Cycle*.
Activity	An event, task, or unit of work with a specified purpose.
Activity Analysis	See *Value Analysis*.
Activity Based Budgeting (ABB)	A budgeting approach that focuses on the budgeted cost of those activities necessary to produce and sell products and services.
Activity Based Costing (ABC)	An approach to costing that focuses on individual activities as the fundamental cost objects. The costs of these activities are used as the basis for assigning costs to other cost objects such as products or services.
Activity Centre	A work area in which all the activities have a common purpose.

Activity Driver	A cost driver used to estimate the cost of an activity consumed by the cost object.
Actual Cost	A cost incurred (a historical or past cost), as distinguished from a budgeted or forecasted cost.
Actual Costing	A costing system that (a) traces direct costs to a cost object by using the actual direct-cost rates times the actual quantities of the direct-cost inputs, and (b) allocates indirect costs based on the actual indirect-cost rates times the actual quantities of the cost allocation bases at the end of each accounting period. Contrast with *Normal Costing*.
Actual Manufacturing Overhead	The actual amount of manufacturing overhead costs incurred in production.
Actual Overhead Rate	The actual amount of overhead divided by the actual volume of production.
Adhocracy	An organisational form in which interactions and activities are largely informal and work teams which represent different parts of the business. This may allow innovation to build on standard skills.
Adjusting Entry	A change to accounts on the last day of the reporting period to reflect accrual or deferral of non-cash transactions. The five main adjusting entries are: (a) prepaid expenses, (b) revenue received in advance, (c) accrued expenses, (d) accrued revenue, and (e) depreciation of non-current assets.
Administrative Expenses	See *Selling, General and Administration Costs*.
After-Tax Cash Flow	The cash flow expected after all tax implications have been considered.
Affinity Diagram	A method (a) to organise facts or thoughts that are uncertain, (b) to overcome pre-existing ideas or paradigms, (c) to clarify ideas, or (d) to create unity within a team. The process comprises: (a) a focus question is agreed, (b) a pool of items is assembled, (c) individuals work in silence to place them in groups based on similarity or difference, (d) when all items are allocated to give each group a name, (e) vote for the most important groups, and (e) rank the most important groups. A name is a noun cluster. Items may be duplicated if necessary so they can be in more than one group. Groups may be combined during voting if all participants are agreed. Also known as KJ Diagram. Also see *Innovation*, and *Market*.
Agency Costs	The costs of managing employees and coordinating their work (otherwise they pursue their own interests rather than those of the owners).
Allowable Cost	A cost that may be reimbursed. This is often made explicit in a contract but it may also be allowable under a policy.
Analysis	1. The abstract separation of a whole (e.g. a project or a proposal) into its constituent parts in order to study its elements and their relations. 2. The process of examining, identifying, or separating a complex to isolate and define the relationship of its components (people, machines, rules and procedures), including the definition of problems, objectives, requirements, priorities, and constraints of systems (and the extent to which they have been satisfied) plus identification of cost, benefit, and schedule estimates for potential solutions.
Anecdote	A simple and short description of an event. Also see *Micro Narrative*.
Annual Budget	See *Master Budget*. Also see *Articulated Budget*.
Annual Report	See *Financial Statement*.

Application Software	Processes data to structure or automate a business process or help users solve particular computing problems. Platform may be from mainframe to personal digital assistant. Examples are music players and payroll.
Appraisal Costs	The costs incurred to detect which individual units of product do not conform to specifications, that is, possess defects.
Appropriability of Resources	A resource position barrier. The extent to which a business can control the profit-generating potential of a resource or capability. Examples of resources with different appropriabilities include freehold land, and employee ingenuity. Also known as Transferability. Also see *Durability*, *Replicability*, and *Substitutability*.
Aretaic Turn Ethical Theories	An ethical theory concerning the moral development and moral education that depends on uniform community standards for morality. Also see *Consequential Ethical Theories*, *Obligation-Based Ethical Theories*, and *Social Contract Based Ethical Theories*.
Articulated Budget	1. A budget which states its expectations concerning all aspects of the business (e.g. personnel, technology and other physical operations) in financial terms. 2. A hierarchical budget in which all the subordinate and supporting schedules have been integrated so the relevant output data from a lower schedule is the input data for a related higher schedule. 3. Also see *Master Budget*.
ASCII	An abbreviation for the American Standard Code for Information Interchange (ASCII). A method for representing characters (alphabetical upper and lower case letters, numerals, symbols and control characters) in computers communications equipment, and other devices that use text. Developed by a committee of the American Standards Association from telegraphic codes.
Asset	A measure of costs where the benefits extend into the future.
Assign	See *Assignment*.
Assignment	The transfer of a property right or title to some particular person or entity under an agreement, usually in writing. Also known as Assign; Bargain; Grant; Sell; Set Over; or Transfer. Also see *Lease*; *Lessee*; and *Lessor*.
Assurance	An independent professional service with the goal of improving the confidence in a decision with reference to the past data available. Examples of assurance services include an accounts receivable review, an assessment of business risk, issuing a letter of comfort, completing a customer satisfaction survey, conducting a review of information systems security and evaluating a business contingency and disaster recovery plan. Also see *Audit*.
Audit	The systematic examination of accounts for the purposes of determining their validity and accuracy. It covers the nature and purpose of auditing, the accountability of external auditors under statutory and professional requirements, the conduct and reporting of an audit. Also see *Assurance*.
Audit Committee	The committee responsible for financial management, financial performance and financial reporting of the business.
Authoritative Budgeting	A superior informs subordinates what their budget will be without requesting input. Also see *Participative Budgeting*.
Autonomy	The degree of freedom to make decisions. Most are 'semi-autonomous'.
Available Market	See *Market Narrowing*.

Average Cost	See *Unit Cost*.
Average Cycle Time	The ratio of total processing time to total product units produced.
Avoidable Costs	The costs that will not be incurred in the future if a particular option is not selected. Also see *Unavoidable Costs*.
B	
B2B	Business to Business. The e-commerce activities that occur between a business and customers who are businesses in their own right.
B2C	Business to Consumer. The e-commerce activities that occur between a business and customers who are not businesses in their own right.
Back Office	Those activities that occur without the customer being present.
Backflush Costing System	A system of product costing that simplifies recording. It occurs after the product is complete and omits the recording of some journal entries that would usually arise from purchase of direct material up to the sale of finished products.
Balance Sheet	A financial statement of an accounting entity that summaries at a given date the financial position of an accounting entity with the goal of presenting a true and fair view of the information. It may use a narrative form or an account form. It answers the questions 'Where have we obtained funding?' and 'What assets have been acquired with those funds?' Also known as Statement of financial position as at the end of the period. Also see *Account Form, Financial Statements,* and *Narrative Form.*
Balanced ScoreCard	A framework for implementing strategy that translates an organisation's mission and strategy into a set of performance measures for lower level goals that use four perspectives (Financial, Customer, Process, and Learning) to assess the implementation of strategy. Also see *Critical Success Factors, Key Performance Indicators,* and *Service Delivery Outcomes.*
Bank Overdraft	A means of allowing the borrower to write cheques up to an agreed limit without having the funds in the account when the cheque is presented.
Bargain	See *Assignment*.
Batch-Level Costs	The costs of activities related to a group, set or block of units of products/services rather than to each individual unit of product or service.
Batch Manufacturing	A process in which individual products are produced in quantity using a specific sequence of production processes.
Belief Systems	One of the four levers of control (Simons, 1995) that articulate the mission, purpose, norms of behaviours, and core values of a business intended to inspire managers and other employees to do their best. Also see *Boundary Systems, Diagnostic Control Systems, Interactive Control Systems,* and *Levers of Control.*
Benchmarking	The continuous process of comparing the levels of performance in producing products and services and executing activities against the best levels of performance in competing companies or in companies having similar processes. The objective is to identify areas for improvement.
Benefit	The tangible and intangible improvements. Also see *Cost, Cost Benefit, Intangible Benefit, Intangible Cost, Intangible Resource, Tangible Benefit, Tangible Cost,* and *Tangible Resource.*
Bill	See *Invoice*.

Billable Hours	The number of hours per year that an employee has available to service customers.
Billing System	A system that estimates the fees to be charged to a client for a service based on the charge-out rate for different types of services per billable hour.
Black Box	A system program, module, or component with known inputs, known outputs, and a generally understood function, but with unknown or irrelevant detailed contents.
Body of Knowledge	A collection of essential concepts, terms and activities within a profession or subject area.
BOK	See *Body of Knowledge*.
Book Value	The original cost minus accumulated depreciation of an asset.
Bookbuild	A three step process where (a) the investor market bids the value of share price rather than setting a fixed price, (b) the company or its advisor examining the bids against a criteria and (c) the final issue price is then set.
BOSBOK	The Business Operations and Strategy assumed Body of Knowledge which is represented in five dimensions (1) position in the business life cycle, (2) continuous and discontinuous adaptive behaviour to changing circumstances, (3) leveraging available resources to improve performance, (4) recurring themes in employee and manager behaviour and (5) the vocabulary of assumed business knowledge.
Bottleneck	An operation where the work to be performed approaches or exceeds the capacity available to do it.
Bottom-Up Budgeting	A participative process in which people in operational levels and lower managerial levels play an active role in setting their budget.
Boundary Systems	One of the four levers of control (Simons, 1995) that describes standards of behaviour and codes of conduct expected of all employees, especially actions that are off-limits. Also see *Belief Systems, Diagnostic Control Systems, Interactive Control Systems*, and *Levers of Control*.
Bounded Rationality	The limitations to making an optimal decision owing to the constraints of information available, time and cognitive processes. It rejects Expected Utility Theory. Also see *Expected Utility Theory, Expected Value Theory*, and *Prospect Theory*.
Breakeven Point	The quantity of output sold at which total revenues equal total costs, that is, where the operating income is zero.
Bricks and Mortar	A retail or wholesale business usually with a storefront. Also see *Clicks and Mortar*, and *Pure Play*.
BSC	See *Balanced SoreCard*.
Budget	A quantitative expression of a proposed plan of action for a specified period summarising the financial consequences of operations. It is used to coordinate what needs to be done to implement that plan. It is prepared by management and approved by senior management. Also see *Articulated Budget*.
Budgetary Slack	The practice of deliberately underestimating budgeted revenues or overestimating budget costs to make it easier to achieve the target budget. This may be prevalent where (1) the actual-budget variance is used for performance evaluation, or (2) where an across-the-board cost reduction is implemented in the face of a projected revenue reduction.
Budgeting	See *Incremental Budgeting* and *Zero-Base Budgeting*.
Budget Manual	A set of instructions that communicate the procedure for preparing the budget and the deadlines for submission and authorisation.

Budgeted Overhead Rate	See *Indirect Manufacturing Costs.*
Budgeted Performance	The expected performance or a point of reference to compare actual results.
Bullwhip Effect	See *Forrester Effect.*
Bundled Product	A package of two or more products (or services) that is sold for a single price, but whose individual components may be sold as separate items at their own 'stand-alone' prices.
Business	Any trade, profession or occupation; or organisation to conduct a commercial or industrial operation. Also known as Company (to emphasise the legal entity), Corporation (also to emphasise the legal entity), Firm (to emphasise competitive activity) and Organisation (to emphasise the structure of management). Also see *Company, Cooperative, Enterprise, Incorporation, Partnership, Sole Proprietorship,* and *Trust.*
Business Case	A detailed argument usually in financial terms with sufficient supporting evidence in favour of a preferred course of action. Also known as a Business Plan or a Proposal.
Business Cycle	A convenient sequence of stages that over the passage of time a business may experience. The four stages of the business cycle are *Startup, Growth, Maturity,* and *Decline.* Also see *Economic Cycle.*
Business Event	Any internal or external change that affects the business. Also see *Economic Event, Decision Event, Information Event,* and *Operations Event.*
Business Function	An organising principle to cluster activities that accomplish the result that is the name of the business function. Also see *Accounting (Business Function), Distribution (Business Function), Manufacturing (Business Function), Marketing (Business Function), Procurement (Business Function), Research and Development (Business Function),* and *Sales (Business Function).*
Business Plan	See *Business Case.*
Business Process	1. Strict: The transformation of input data flow(s) into output data flow(s). For example, a customer payment is converted into a receipt for the product. 2. Broad: A series of work tasks which organise resources to satisfy a goal or outcome. 3. Also see *Generic Process,* and *Unique Process.*
Business Process Reengineering	The fundamental rethinking and redesign of business processes to achieve considerable improvements in critical measures of performance, such as cost, quality, service, speed, quality, and customer satisfaction.
Business Rule	A statement that defines or constrains some aspect of the business that facilitates the automation of the business. It is intended to assert business structure or to control or influence the behaviour of the business. Also see *Internal Control.*
Business Strategy	See *Competitive Strategy.*
Business Transaction Cycle	The sequence of major activities comprising manufacture of products, expenditure of products, revenue from the sale of the products, financing the business and recording in the general ledger and reporting. Also known as the Accounting Cycle and the Transaction Cycle.

Buy-Sell Agreement	Specifies ownership arrangements in the event that one or more of the owners die or wish to sell their shareholding. It may be tied to an insurance policy that provides the surviving business partner with the money to buyout the deceased partner's holding from the beneficiaries of the deceased person's estate. Also see *Shareholder Agreement*.
By-Product	One or more products from a joint production process that have low total sales values compared with the total sales value of the main product or of joint products. Also see *Joint Product*, and *Main Product*.
Buyer	See *Customer*.
C	
CAGR	See *Compound Annual Growth Rate*.
Capabilities	See *Capability of Resources*.
Capability of resources	Routines (that is, patterns of activities and decision rules) to productively deploy resources usually in combination. Also see *Resources*, and *Core Competencies*.
Capacity	A constraint or upper limit to production based on full efficiency all the time. It may be measured in terms of supply or demand of capacity. For capacity supplied see *Practical (Available) Capacity* and *Theoretical (Available) Capacity*. For capacity demanded see *Normal (Demand) Capacity Utilisation* and *Master-Budget (Demand) Capacity Utilisation*.
Capex	See *Capital Expenditure* and *Capital Expenditure Budget*.
Capital Budgeting	The planning and evaluation of a long-run investment in a project or investments across many projects. Also see *Discounted Cash Flow*.
Capital Expenditure	The expenditure carried forward as an asset in the balance sheet which will be progressively allocated as expenses in determining profit and loss.
Capital Expenditure Budget	A plan for the acquisition of long-term assets. Usually prepared for plant, building, equipment and technology.
Carrying Amount	1. The cost of asset acquisition minus accumulated depreciation. 2. The amount at which an asset is recognised in the balance sheet after deducting accumulated depreciation and accumulated impairment losses. 3. Also see *Impairment of Assets* and *Mark to Market (MTM)*.
Carrying Costs	The costs that arise while holding inventory of products for sale.
Cash Basis	The recognition of income when cash, cheque or deposit is actually received and expenses are counted when they are actually paid. Also known as Cash Method. Also see *Accrual Basis*.
Cash Budget	A schedule of expected cash receipts and disbursements for the budget period. Also see *Cash Flow Statement*.
Cash Flows	The amount and timing of all revenue, all expenses, wages, capital expenditure, debt repayments, dividends and taxes.
Cash Flow Statement	A financial statement of an accounting entity that summarises the actual flows of cash for a period. It answers the questions 'How much money was made?' and 'Where have the profits/losses gone?' Also known as a statement of cash flows for the period. If projected for future periods it will be a Cash Budget. Also see *Financial Statements*, and *Funds Statement*. If projected for future periods it will be a *Cash Budget*. Also see *Financial Statements*, and *Funds Statement*.
Cash Inflows	Cost savings, revenues and proceeds from sale of assets in a project.

Cash Method	See *Cash Basis*.
Cash Outflows	The initial cost of a project and any increases in costs that will be incurred over the life of a project.
Causality	The explanation of a phenomenon using theory and constructs and interconnected relations between them. Manipulations may be used to see whether the claims of a theory actually occur including predictions, which can be tested over time as the phenomenon unfolds or evolves. Measurement assumptions, evidence and validity need deep thinking, careful theory, and creativity.
Cause-and-Effect Diagram	A diagram that identifies potential causes of defects. Four categories of potential causes of failure are human factors, methods and design factors, machine-related factors, and materials and components factors. Also known as a Fishbone Diagram.
Chasm Theory	Early adopters of a technology are different to the mainstream market. Also see *Technology Adoption Life Cycle*.
Chargeout Rate	The hourly charges for different levels of service or types of employee.
Chief Accounting Officer (CAO)	See *Financial Controller*.
Chief Executive Officer (CEO)	The senior executive responsible for overseeing all the operations of a business. The leader of the executives responsible to the Board for business strategy and its execution. Also known as Managing Director.
Chief Financial Officer (CFO)	The senior executive responsible for overseeing the financial operations of a business. Also known as Finance Director or Executive Director Finance.
Choice Criterion	An objective that can be quantified in a decision model.
Classics	Considering truth, beauty, goodness, liberty, equality, and justice for an evolving perspective and understanding.
Clicks and Mortar	A business model with a combination of e-business and a traditional bricks and mortar business. Also see *Bricks and Mortar*, and *Pure Play*.
Client	See *Customer*.
Closing Entry	The clearing of all revenue and expense accounts on the last day of the financial year so on the first day of the new financial year they commence with a zero balance.
Code	Any set of computer instructions. Also see *Program, Routine,* and *Software*.
Code of Ethics	See *Ethical Principles*, and *Ethical Standards*.
Coefficient of Determination	A measure of the percentage of variation in a dependent variable explained by one or more independent variables.
COGS	See *Cost of Goods Sold*.
Coincident Indicator	1. An indicator that normally moves in line with the target object. 2. In economics the indicator moves in line with the overall economy. 3. Also see *Lag Indicator*, and *Lead Indicator*.
Collection Cycle	See *Revenue Cycle*.
Collusion	An arrangement between two or more companies in an industry on how they will achieve a price above the competitive price and so restrain trade. This may involve conspiring to set prices, make contract bids, limit production, or any combination of them.

Collusive Pricing	See *Collusion*.
Command and Control Management	The top down exercise of authority and direction by a person in charge to accomplish an objective.
Commercial Judgement	Taking a pragmatic approach to business recognising that (a) there is incomplete information available, (b) there is limited time available for action to be taken, (c) there may not already exist detailed procedures which can be followed, and (d) it is desirable that action is taken promptly.
Committed (Fixed) Cost	A fixed cost which is difficult to change in the short term as it arises from investments in productive capacity (e.g. plant and employees). Also see *Fixed Cost*.
Common Cost	The cost of operating a facility, activity, or like cost object that is shared by two or more business units or departments.
Common Off The Shelf Software (COTS)	A software package developed by a third party and generally available that can be used without considerable changes. Also known as Off-The Shelf package (OTS).
Community Service Obligations (CSO)	A function, service or concession performed by a commercial business to deliver non-commercial products and services to entitled members of the general public.
Company	A form of incorporation or legal structure which creates an artificial legal person with recognition under law and limitation of liability. The forms of company are proprietary (private) or public. Also see *Business, Cooperative, Enterprise, Incorporation, Partnership, Sole Proprietorship*, and *Trust*.
Comparable Uncontrolled Price	A comparison of price paid by the target business with the price paid by comparable independent businesses. Also see *Transactional Net Margin Method*, and *Transfer Price*.
Competence	See *Ability*.
Competitive Advantage	The significant and ideally, long-term, benefit that a business enjoys compared to its competitors.
Competitive Bid	Two or more companies submit sealed offers in response to a specification to a potential buyer for a product, service or project.
Competitive Strategy	The chosen means for competing in a market. The broad choices are low cost or differentiation. The market focus may be narrow (niche) or broad. Also see *Low Cost Leadership*, and *Product Differentiation*.
Compound Annual Growth Rate (CAGR)	A business and investing term for the smoothed annualised gain of an investment over a given time period. It is also described as the year-over-year growth rate of an investment over a specified period of time. It has the advantage of comparing the growth rates of two investments because it dampens the effect of volatility of periodic returns that can render arithmetic means irrelevant.
Conformance Quality	The performance of a product or service relative to its design and product specifications.
Consequentialist Ethical Theories	An ethical theory concerned with the potential results of a behaviour. Also see *Aretaic Turn Ethical Theories, Obligation-Based Ethical Theories*, and *Social Contract Based Ethical Theories*.

Consideration	The amount of cash or shares (scrip) offered per share in respect of (on-market or off-market) takeover offers.
Constant	A quantity which does not change despite changes in situation or circumstances and the passage of time.
Constraint	A limitation that a business cannot escape (Goldratt, 1999). It may be access to resources. Also see *Theory of Constraints*.
Consumption Tax	A tax levied on purchases. The consumption tax may be titled a Goods and Services Tax or Value Added Tax.
Continuous Budget	See *Rolling Budget*.
Continuous Variable	A variable (such as time or weight) that is infinitely divisible into whatever units a researcher may choose.
Continuous Improvement	The ongoing incremental attempt to reduce or eliminate waste and improve costs, quality and customer service. Also known as Process Improvement.
Contract Rent	The actual payments made by tenants for the use of the property owned by others. Also see *Economic Rent*, and *Ricardian Rent*.
Contribution Income Statement	An income statement that groups costs into variable costs and fixed costs to highlight the contribution margin.
Contribution Margin	The revenues minus total variable costs. Also see *Fixed Cost*, and *Gross Margin*.
Contribution Margin Format	Operating income is driven by the unit level of sales. Also see *Income Statement Format*.
Contribution Margin Per Unit	The selling price minus the variable cost per unit.
Contribution Margin Percentage	The contribution margin per unit divided by unit selling price multiplied by 100.
Contribution Margin Ratio	The contribution margin per unit divided by unit selling price.
Contribution Margin Statement	An income statement that separates fixed and variable costs and calculates a contribution margin.
Control	1. The actions that implement the planning decisions, deciding how to evaluate productivity and profitability, and providing feedback and learning to help future decision-making. 2. The capacity of a business to dominate decision-making directly or indirectly in relation to the financial and operating policies of another entity to achieve the objectives of the controlling entity. 3. Monitoring and evaluating feedback to determine whether a system is moving toward achievement of its goal. 4. Also see *Internal Control*.
Control Account	An account in the general ledger which shows the aggregate balance of a number of separate but related ledger accounts. For example, the creditors control account shows the balance for all individual creditor accounts. Also see *General Ledger, Ledger, Ledger Account, Posting,* and *Trial Balance*.

Control Chart	A graph of a series of successive observations of a particular step, procedure, or operation taken at regular intervals of time. Each observation is plotted relative to specified ranges that represent the limits within which observations are expected to fall.
Control Concepts	These concepts relate to the comparison of actual results to the plan. Also see *Controllable Costs, Direct Costs, Indirect Costs, Non-Controllable Costs,* and *Plan Concepts.*
Controllability	The degree of influence that a specific manager has over costs, revenues, or related items for which he or she is responsible.
Controllable Cost	Any cost that is primarily subject to the influence of a given responsibility centre manager for a given period. Usually direct and variable costs are controllable by a particular manager. Also see *Control Concepts, Direct Costs, Indirect Costs,* and *Non-Controllable Costs.*
Controlled Entity	An entity controlled by a parent entity.
Controller	See *Financial Controller.*
Conversion Costs	The sum of all direct manufacturing labour costs and indirect manufacturing costs (excluding direct material costs) to convert raw material into a finished product.
Conversion Cycle	The business activities and information processing operations associated with the production of finished products from raw materials using batch processing, continuous processing or make-to-order processing. Also known as the Production Cycle. Also see *Expenditure Cycle, Investment Cycle, Non-Operating Cycle,* and *Revenue Cycle.*
Cooperative	A form of incorporation or legal structure with limited liability legal entity whose members share the authority for making decisions. Cooperatives are usually organised by employees or by consumers. Also see *Business, Company, Enterprise, Incorporation, Partnership, Sole Proprietorship,* and *Trust.*
Core Business Functions	See *Distribution (Business Function), Procurement (Business Function),* and *Sales (Business Function).*
Core Business Markets and Products	The strategy of a business to concentrate on the products or services which is both experienced in and which it has reputational advantage in the marketplace.
Corporate Strategy	1. Making decisions about the types of businesses to acquire, operate or divest and how to best structure those operations. 2. The plan concerning the types of businesses to acquire, operate or divest and how to best structure those operations.
Cost	Any resource that is either sacrificed or forgone to achieve a specific objective. Costs may be tangible or intangible. Also see *Benefit, Cost Benefit, Intangible Benefit, Intangible Cost, Intangible Resource, Tangible Benefit, Tangible Cost,* and *Tangible Resource.*
Cost Accounting	The measurement, analysis, and reporting of financial and non-financial information relating to the costs of acquiring or using resources in a business. It provides information for both accounts and non-accountants.
Cost Accumulation	The collection of cost data in some organised way by means of an accounting system.
Cost Allocation	The assignment of indirect costs to a particular cost object.

Cost-Allocation Base	A factor that links in a systematic way an indirect cost or cost pool of indirect costs to a cost object. A cost allocation base can be financial (e.g. direct labour costs) or non-financial (e.g. machine hours, direct labour hours; direct material usage, units of production of output).
Cost Application Base	A *cost allocation base* where the *cost object* is a job, product or customer.
Cost Assignment	A general term that refers to (a) *Cost Tracing* of accumulated costs that have a direct relationship to the *Cost Object*, and (b) *Cost Allocation* of accumulated costs which have an indirect relationship to the *Cost Object*. Also see *Cost Object*.
Cost Behaviour	The relationship between a cost and the level of activity or cost driver. Also see *Fixed Costs, Mixed Costs, Step Costs*, and *Variable Costs*.
Cost Benefit Analysis (CBA)	An analysis of the costs (initial investment, subsequent investment, operational and maintenance costs) and benefits (outputs, and outcomes) of a decision, program, project or different alternatives over a defined period to produce a comparison for unbiased evaluation. It is usually restricted to those economic, social and environmental costs and benefits that can be reasonably quantified. Most analysts will also factor opportunity cost into the analysis. Also see *Benefit, Cost, Intangible Benefit, Intangible Cost, Intangible Resource, Tangible Benefit, Tangible Cost*, and *Tangible Resource*.
Cost Budget	A series of budgets that detail the cost of operations required to support a forecast sales volume.
Cost Centre	A *Responsibility Centre* where the manager is accountable for costs only. Also see *Investment Centre, Profit Centre*, and *Revenue Centre*.
Cost Driver	A factor or activity that causes a cost to be incurred. Also see *Resource Driver*.
Cost Management	The approaches and activities of managers to use resources to increase value to customers and to achieve organisational goals.
Cost Object	An accounting item for which a separate measurement of costs is desired. Examples include a contract, customer, product, project, service, or a process. Also see *Revenue Object*.
Cost of Capital	See *Required Rate of Return*.
Cost of Goods Manufactured	The cost of products brought to completion, whether they were started before or during the current accounting period.
Cost of Goods Sold	1. The cost of producing, converting or acquiring the inventory during a period. It may be recorded using the perpetual or periodic method. 2. The account 'Cost of Goods Sold'.
Cost of Quality (COQ)	The costs incurred to prevent, or the costs arising as a result of, the production of a low-quality product.
Cost-Plus Pricing	The calculation of the selling price by adding a mark-up to the cost price.
Cost Pool	A grouping of individual cost items. The basis for grouping may be the different types of cost drivers, cost allocation bases, the different degrees of difficulty in determining cause and effect relationships, or different degrees of difficulty in determining benefits received.
Cost Prediction	A forecast about future costs.

Cost Structure	A combination of *Cost Assignment*, *Cost Behaviour*, *Cost Hierarchy*, *Cost Pool* and their associations and causal relationships.
Cost Tracing	The assignment of direct costs to a particular cost object. See also *Cost Object*.
Cost-Volume-Profit (CVP) Analysis	The behaviour of total revenues, total costs, and operating income as changes occur in the units sold, the selling price, the variable cost per unit, or the fixed costs of a product.
Creative Destruction	New and better technologies displace old but sound technologies.
Critical Success Factors (CSF)	A measure of the factors considered to influence the success of a project, initiative, project or programme. Also see *Balanced ScoreCard*, *Key Performance Indicators (KPI's)*, and *Service Delivery Outcomes*.
Crowd-Out	To overwhelm so as to force out either partly or completely.
Current Cost	An asset measure based on the cost of purchasing an asset today identical to the one currently held, or the cost of purchasing an asset that provides services like the one currently held if an identical asset cannot be purchased.
Customer	Sometimes it is useful to differentiate among the different kinds of customers: (a) people who make buying decisions (often termed Buyers or Consumers); (b) People who make use of products and services (often termed End Users); and (c) People who provide the money or authorise the expenditure (often termed Clients). See also *Client*.
Customer Life Cycle Costs	The total costs incurred by a customer to acquire, use, maintain, and dispose of a product or service.
Customer-Profitability Analysis	The reporting and analysis of revenues earned from customers and the costs incurred to earn those revenues. See also *Revenue*.
Customer Service	The pre-sale after-sale support provided to customers. In the Porter (1985/1998) value chain it is providing after-sale support to customers.
D	
Data	1. Facts. 2. Values. 3. Enquiries, statements or commands. 4. Symbols. 5. An input or output.
Data Flow Diagram (DFD)	See *Data Flow Model*.
Data Flow Model	1. A graphic tool to depict what data is stored and transformed within a business showing all interfaces between processes and systems by partitioning a system into its components parts. 2. A graphic tool to represent a network of related functions.
Data Model	A data model depicts the internal, logical relationships between data.
Data Store	A repository for data at rest.
Data Structure Model	A graphic tool used to represent entities, attributes, and data inter-relationships in a data store.
Database	A data store of interrelated data that are stored together to serve one or more applications and that can be modified in format without affecting the program that accesses it.

Decentralisation	The structuring the business into units and assigning decision-making responsibilities to each unit.
Decision Event	A decision (or management) event (De) will plan and control use of resources associated with operations events using information events. It will also evaluate use of resources and implementation of decisions associated with Operations events using Information events. Also see *Information Event*, and *Operation Event*.
Decision-Making	The process of generating, evaluating and selecting among a set of relevant choices which involve some form of risk.
Decision Table	A summary of the alternative actions, events, outcomes, and probabilities of events in a decision model.
Decision Tree	A graphic tool used to describe the conditions and actions in a problem using a chart in a branching format.
Decline (Business Cycle)	In decline the business faces closure or takeover. The four stages of the business cycle are *Startup*, *Growth*, *Maturity*, and *Decline*. Also see *Business Cycle*, and *Economic Cycle*.
Decremental Costs	A reduced total cost incurred as a result of a lower differential cost. Also see *Differential Costs, Differential Revenues, Discretionary Costs, Incremental Costs, Imputed Costs, Incremental Revenues, Opportunity Costs, Out-of-Pocket Costs, Plan Concepts, Relevant Costs, Sunk Costs*, and *Unavoidable Costs*.
Degree of Operating Leverage	The contribution margin divided by operating income at any given level of sale.
Delivery Lead Time	1. The time elapsed from order until the finished product or service is delivered to the customer. 2. The time elapsed from despatch until the finished product or service is delivered to the customer. 3. Also see *Manufacturing Lead Time, Purchase Order Lead Time, Service Response Time*, and *Waiting Time*.
Delta	Difference.
Deterministic View of the Marketplace	Success of a product or service, or an employee is governed mainly by the intrinsic qualities of the person or the product or service. Also see *Non-Deterministic View of the Marketplace*, and *Random*.
Denominator Level	The quantity of cost driver used to determine the budgeted fixed overhead rate computation. The denominator may be based on *Theoretical (Available) Capacity, Practical (Available) Capacity, Normal (Demand) Capacity*, or *Master-Budget (Demand) Capacity*.
Denominator-Level Variance	See *Production-Volume Variance*.
Deontology (Ethical Theories)	See *Obligation-Based Ethical Theories*.
Dependent Variable	The dependent variable is the result measured from the treatment. Also see *Independent Variable*.

Design of Products, Services, or Processes	The detailed planning and engineering of products, services, or processes.
Design Quality	The extent to which the characteristics of a product of service meet the needs and wants of customers.
Designed-In Costs	See *Locked-In Costs*.
DFD	See *Data Flow Model*.
Diagnostic Control Systems	One of the four levers of control (Simons, 1995) that measures critical performance variables such as Return on Investment, Residual Income, Economic Value Added, customer satisfaction, and employee satisfaction, that monitor critical performance variables that help managers track progress toward achieving strategic business goals. Also see *Belief Systems, Boundary Systems, Interactive Control Systems*, and *Levers of Control*.
Differential Cost	The difference in total cost between two alternatives. Usually variable costs however, if the decision is outside the relevant range then fixed costs are included. Also see *Decremental Costs, Differential Revenues, Discretionary Costs, Incremental Costs, Imputed Costs, Incremental Revenues, Opportunity Costs, Out-of-Pocket Costs, Plan Concepts, Relevant Costs, Sunk Costs*, and *Unavoidable Costs*.
Differential Rents	See *Ricardian Rents*.
Differential Revenue	The difference in total revenue between two alternatives.
Diminishing Returns	A situation where production is continuing to rise but productivity is declining as input yields progressively smaller increases in output. Also known as Diminishing Marginal Returns and the Law of Diminishing Returns. Also see *Marginal Cost*.
Direct Costing	A misnomer for Variable Costing because the indirect cost of variable manufacturing overhead is included while some direct costs (e.g. direct marketing costs) are excluded. Also see *Variable Costing*.
Direct Costs of a Cost Object	The costs related to the particular cost object that can be traced to that object in an economically feasible (cost-effective) way.
Direct Labour Efficiency Variance	See *Efficiency Variance*.
Direct Manufacturing Labour Costs	The compensation of all manufacturing labour that can be traced to the cost object (work in process and then finished products) in an economically feasible way.
Direct Material Costs	The acquisition costs of all materials that eventually become part of the cost object (work in process and then finished products), and that can be traced to the cost object in an economically feasible way.
Direct Materials Efficiency Variance	See *Efficiency Variance*.
Direct Materials Inventory	The direct materials in stock and awaiting use in the manufacturing process.

Direct Materials Mix Variance	When substitute inputs can be used, a materials efficiency improvement relative to budgeted costs may arise from using a cheaper input or using less input. There is no mix variance if there are no substitutes. The variance is the difference between (a) budgeted cost of budgeted mix of the actual total quantity of direct materials used, and (b) budgeted cost of direct materials based on actual total quantity of direct materials used. The actual quantity of direct materials is held constant. The variance has a favourable effect on operating income if the actual material used is cheaper than the budgeted material. Also see *Direct Material Yield Variance*.
Direct Materials Yield Variance	When substitute inputs can be used, a materials efficiency improvement relative to budgeted costs may arise from using a cheaper input or using less input. There is no yield variance if there are no substitutes. The variance is the difference between (1) budgeted cost of direct materials based on the actual total quantity of direct materials used and (2) flexible-budget cost of direct materials based on the budgeted total quantity of direct materials allowed for the actual output produced. The budgeted input mix of direct materials is held constant. The variance has a favourable effect on operating income if less actual material is used than was budgeted. Also see *Direct Material Mix Variance*.
Direct (Cost Allocation) Method	A cost allocation method that allocates each support department's costs to operating departments only.
Disclosure Notes	A summary of significant accounting policies and other explanatory information. Also known as Notes. Also see *Financial Statements*.
Discount Rate	See *Required Rate of Return*.
Discounted Cash Flow (DCF)	A capital budgeting method that use the time value of money to measure all expected future cash inflows and outflows of a project as if they occurred at the present point in time.
Discretionary (Fixed) Cost	The costs that arise from periodic (usually annual) decisions regarding the maximum amount to be incurred and have no measurable cause-and-effect relationship between output and resources used. Also see *Decremental Cost, Differential Costs, Differential Revenues, Discretionary Costs, Incremental Costs, Imputed Costs, Incremental Revenues, Opportunity Costs, Out-of-Pocket Costs, Plan Concepts, Relevant Costs, Sunk Costs,* and *Unavoidable Costs*.
Distribution (Business Function)	The delivery of products or services to wholesalers, retailers or end use customers. Also see *Accounting (Business Function), Finance (Business Function), Manufacturing (Business Function), Marketing (Business Function), Procurement (Business Function), Research and Development (Business Function),* and *Sales (Business Function)*.
Disruptive Innovation	Provides characteristics that are of no interest to traditional customer segments while being cheaper, simpler and perhaps of inferior quality if compared to existing products, forcing the business to search for either a marginal or new customer segment who will value it (Christensen, 1997). For example the smaller disk drive (5.25 inch and 3.5 inch) was of no interest to mainframe and mini computer manufacturers. Also known as Disruptive Technology. Also see *Innovation, Invention,* and *Sustaining Innovation*.
Double-Loop Learning	Double-loop learning is the learning about single-loop learning. That is, after individuals, groups or organisations question the assumptions, values, and policies that led to the actions in the first place; and then are able to view and modify their assumptions, values, and policies. Also known as Second-Order Learning. Also see *Single-Loop Learning*.

Downsizing	An integrated approach of configuring processes, products, and people to match costs to the activities that need to be performed to operate effectively and efficiently in the present and future.
Downward Demand Spiral	The reduction in demand that can occur if prices are raised to recover the fixed costs over a smaller number of output units. Also see *Capacity*.
Dual Pricing	An approach to transfer pricing using two separate transfer-pricing methods to price each transfer from one subunit to another.
Dual-Rate Method	An allocation method that classifies costs in each cost pool into two pools (a variable-cost pool and a fixed-cost pool) with each pool using a different cost-allocation base.
Dumping	The selling of a product in an overseas market below the market value in the country where it is produced. If this lower price materially injures or threatens to materially injure an industry in the overseas country government action may result. Differential costing may make sense for a business seeking to be competitive overseas or expanding into new markets. It is not harmful if it promotes competition and benefits consumers. World Trade Organisation (WTO) specifies tests for imposing anti-dumping by considering the public interest.
DuPont Profitability Analysis	A framework which identifies linkages between key performance drivers, key performance indicators and financial performance measures.
DuPont Identity	See *DuPont Profitability Analysis*.
Durability of Resources	A resource position barrier. The rate at which the benefits of a resource or capability depreciate or become obsolete. Examples of resources with different durabilities include land, patents, product designs, and customer relationships. Also see *Appropriability*, *Replicability*, and *Transferability*.
Dysfunctional Decision-making	The decisions which are not congruent with the goals of the business (Rydgway, 1956). It results in behaviour designed to avoid following the policy, undermine the policy, or achieve personal advantage from the policy. For example, a policy to work harder may encourage employees to try and loaf without their supervisor realising that loafing is occurring. Also known as Incongruent Decision-Making.
E	
Earnings Before Interest and Tax	The net profit for a period without deducting payments for interest on non-current liabilities and tax.
EBIT	See *Earnings Before Interest and Tax*.
E-business	Electronic business is the use of information and communication technologies to support the entire business value chain servicing customers and collaborating with suppliers: It is broader than e-commerce. Also see *E-commerce*.
E-commerce	The process of buying, transferring, or exchanging products, services, and/or information via computer networks, including the internet. It may also involve automated business processes, customer service, online learning, virtual collaboration, and community. Also known as Electronic Commerce. Also see *E-business*, and *Forms of E-commerce*.
Economic Cycle	The economic cycle is the periodic but irregular rise and fall of economic activity, measured by fluctuations in real GDP and other macroeconomic variables. Also see *Business Cycle*.
Economic Event	An action by a business that affects its assets, liabilities or owner's equity. Also see *Business Event*, *Decision Event*, *Information Event*, and *Operations Event*.

Economic Exchange	Value chain activities that directly affect the quantity of resources.
Economic Feasibility	Resolved by asking the question: 'Do its tangible benefits exceed its costs?' Also see *Feasibility, Operational Feasibility* and *Technical Feasibility.*
Economic Order Quantity (EOQ)	A decision model for determining the optimal order size for individual inventory items to minimise total order costs and carrying costs, under a set of assumptions.
Economic Rent	A payment in excess of the amount required to draw the factor of production into the process or to sustain its current use. Also see *Contractual Rent, Factor of Production* and *Ricardian Rent.*
Economic Resource	The tangible benefits of profitability, net assets, cash generation and the capacity to borrow or attract cash. Also known as Financial Resource. Also see *Human Resources, Physical Resources, Reputational Resources,* and *Technological Resources.*
Economic Substance	A qualitative characteristic of accounting information. A financial report should reflect the underlying substance of the transaction not its legal form. Also see *Materiality of Information, Relevance of Information,* and *Reliability of Information.*
Economic Value Added (EVA)	After-tax operating income minus the (after-tax) weighted average cost of capital multiplied by total assets minus current liabilities.
Economics	The combined areas of microeconomics and macroeconomics. Also see *Macroeconomics,* and *Microeconomics.*
Economy	The frugal and judicious expenditure of material resources. Economy is a measure of the costs. Also see *Efficiency, Effectiveness, Input,* and *Risk.*
Effectiveness	The degree to which a predetermined objective, goal or target is met. Also see *Economy, Efficiency, Input,* and *Risk.*
Efficiency	A measure of the usage of inputs in relation to outputs. The relative amount of inputs used to achieve a given output level. It may also be considered as performance within a process measured using capacity, cycle time, consistency, flexibility, productivity, or security. Also see *Economy, Effectiveness, Input,* and *Risk.*
Efficiency Variance	See *Efficiency Variance for Direct Cost Inputs.*
Efficiency Variance for Direct Cost Inputs	The difference between (1) the actual input quantity used and (2) the budgeted input quantity allowed for actual output, multiplied by budgeted price. Also known as Quantity or Usage Variance for direct materials, Efficiency Variance for direct labour, and Efficiency Variance for variable manufacturing overhead. A variance has a favourable effect on operating income if smaller quantities of inputs are used than budgeted for the actual output produced. There are two manufacturing efficiency variances: Direct Materials Efficiency Variance and Direct Labour Efficiency Variance which are calculated with the same formula. An Efficiency Variance is also known as a Usage Variance.
Efficient Market Hypothesis (EMH)	Existing share prices always incorporate and reflect all relevant information so shares always trade at their fair value on stock exchanges. Investors should not be outperforming the overall market through expert stock selection (purchasing undervalued stocks) or market timing (selling stocks for inflated prices). The only way an investor can possibly obtain higher returns is by purchasing higher risk investments. Also see *Fundamental Analysis, Random Walk* and *Technical Analysis.*

Effort	The physical or mental labour exerted toward achieving a predetermined objective, goal or budget target.
Electronic Commerce	See *E-commerce*.
Electronic Data Interchange (EDI)	The electronic connections that link the information systems of different businesses. Also see *E-commerce*.
Elimination by Aspects	Each alternative is viewed as a set of aspects. The aspects are sequentially based on order of importance and starting with the most important. At each stage an aspect is selected. All alternatives that do not include that aspect are eliminated. The process stops when all but one alternative are eliminated.
Empower	The process of providing an employee with knowledge and enabling or authorising them to make decisions and quickly take action within their sphere of responsibility and accountability.
End User	See *Customer*.
Engineered Costs	The costs that result from a cause-and-effect relationship between the cost driver, output, and the (direct or indirect) resources used to produce that output.
Enterprise	An entity organised for commercial purposes. A public enterprise is a government owned commercial activity. For the concept, also see *Business, Company, Cooperative*, and *Incorporation*. For legal entity also see *Cooperative, Partnership, Sole Proprietorship*, and *Trust*. For employer sectors, also see *Large Business, Medium Business, Micro Business*, and *Small Business*.
Enterprise Resource Planning System	An integrated software package which supports the different business functions.
Entity	1. A person, place, object, event or concept in the user environment about which the business wishes to maintain data. Also see *External Entity*. 2. Also see *Accounting Entity*, and *Legal Entity*.
Entity-Relationship Model	An Entity-Relationship model is a documentation technique which identifies entities and the relationships between them.
Equivalent Units	The derived amount of output units that (a) takes the quantity of each input (factor of production) in units completed and in incomplete units of work in process and (b) converts the quantity of input into the amount of completed output units that could be produced.
Error Data	1. Data presented to the system when the user makes a mistake. 2. An analytical event because the process is unable to deal with the input.
Ethical Absolutism	A position where ethics are unchanging and apply to everyone. Also see *Ethical Nihilism*, and *Ethical Relativism*.
Ethical Dilemma	A position where each of two alternative courses (or of all the feasible courses) is equally desirable (or undesirable). Also known as a Moral Dilemma.
Ethical Nihilism	A position where there is the absence of any ethical approach. Also see *Ethical Absolutism*, and *Ethical Relativism*.

Ethical Principles	The broad considerations which should guide behaviour. Examples include honesty, fairness, objectivity and responsibility. Encouraging others to adhere to them is also expected.
Ethical Relativism	A position where any determination of moral right and wrong is subject to change and no single position applies to everybody. Also see *Ethical Absolutism*, and *Ethical Nihilism*.
Ethical Standards	The criteria for evaluating an action. Examples include competence, confidentiality, integrity and credibility.
Ethical Theories	See *Aretaic Turn Ethical Theories, Consequential Ethical Theories, Obligation-Based Ethical Theories*, and *Social Contract Based Ethical Theories*.
Ethics	The science of morals or rules of behaviour. A branch of philosophy which is concerned with human character and conduct.
Evaluation	See *Program Evaluation*.
Event	1. A business event effects a change in resources. A business event may be either an economic or non-economic event. An economic event is an action by a business which affects its assets, liabilities, and owner's equity. 2. A business event is a single activity that occurs during execution of a business process. Several events may comprise an activity. 3. A possible relevant occurrence in a decision model.
Exception	An atypical event or condition, based on a criterion of volume, financial cost or implication, urgency of processing activity.
Excess Capacity	See *Idle Capacity*.
Excess Present Value Index	See *Profitability Index*.
Executive Director, Finance	See *Chief Financial Officer*.
Expected Monetary Value	The weighted average of the outcomes of a decision with the probability of each outcome serving as the weight.
Expected Utility Theory	A theory of decision-making based on maximising benefits and minimising costs which assumes that the personal value to the decision-maker of an outcome differs from its monetary value. It takes into account the goals of the decision-maker. Also known as Rational Choice Theory, or Rational Action Theory. Also see *Bounded Rationality, Expected Value Theory, Prospect Theory*, and *Regret Theory*.
Expected Value Theory	A theory of decision-making based on maximising benefits and minimising costs based on the outcomes expressed as monetary values and the option selected is the one with the highest value. Where attitudes toward risk prevail then Expected Utility Theory will weight the uncertain choices. Also see *Bounded Rationality, Expected Utility Theory, Prospect Theory*, and *Regret Theory*.
Expenditure Cycle	The business activities and information processing operations associated with the purchase of and payment for products and services. Also known as the Acquisition and Payment Cycle. Also see *Conversion Cycle, Investment Cycle, Non-Operating Cycle*, and *Revenue Cycle*.
Expense	A cost incurred in the generation of revenue.

Experience Curve	A graph (function) that measures the decline in cost per unit in various business functions of the value chain (e.g. logistics, marketing), as the output of these activities increases.
External Entity	A source or destination of data on a data flow model.
External Failure Costs	Costs incurred on defective products because they have been shipped to customers.
Externality	A class of economic relationships not efficiently controlled by prices. It is a cost imposed (negative externality) or benefit conferred (positive externality) on people affected by the externality that are not accounted for by the person who causes or creates these costs or benefits.
Extrinsic Motivation	The motivation that derives from sources external to the individual.
F	
Facility-Sustaining Costs	The costs of activities that cannot be traced to individual products or services but support the business as a whole.
Factor of Production	The resources employed to produce products and services which facilitate production (but do not become part of the product) or are significantly transformed by the production process. The traditional factors of production are land, labour and capital goods (tools, equipment and technology). Also known as Productive Inputs.
Factoring	The sale of accounts receivable from trade debtors to a financier who accepts responsibility for their collection.
Factory Burden Costs	See *Indirect Manufacturing Costs*.
Factory Overhead Costs	See *Indirect Manufacturing Costs*.
Fair Value	The amount of cash obtainable from the sale of an asset in an arm's length transaction between knowledgeable, willing parties. Also see *Carrying Cost*, *Impairment of Asset*, and *Recoverable Amount*.
Favourable Variance	A variance that has the effect of increasing operating income relative to the budgeted amount. It is identified by adding the letter F as a suffix. Also see *Unfavourable Variance*.
Feasibility	1. A study to specify all possible options and justifies the selection of the preferred option. 2. The tests for determining feasibility. It may be solely an economic case or may consider economic and non-economic factors. Also see *Economic Feasibility*, *Operational Feasibility*, and *Technical Feasibility*. 3. A feasibility report provides: (a) a list of options for implementing the application and a justification for the recommended preferred option; (b) a schedule of costs and benefits with savings by period and how they may be realised as well as the method by which they were reached and any sensitivities; (c) a list of validated requirements which constitute the scope of the application (compared with the features offered by various packages if selected from COTS); and (d) a schedule of work with tasks and milestones to indicate when the application can reasonable be made available evidenced by resource calculations. Also see *Common Off The Shelf Software (COTS)*.

Feedback	Output that is used to make changes to input and/or processing). It may be reactive or pro-active (forecasting).
FIFO	See *First-In, First-Out*.
File	An arrangement in an orderly way of data in any format (manual or electronic).
Filtering	A special type of data transformation (in a data flow model) in which the data are not physically changed but out knowledge about that data is changed.
Finance (Business Function)	The management of funding encompassing investment and risk. Also see *Accounting (Business Function), Distribution (Business Function), Manufacturing (Business Function), Marketing (Business Function), Procurement (Business Function), Research and Development (Business Function)*, and *Sales (Business Function)*.
Finance Cycle	See *Investment Cycle*.
Finance Director	See *Chief Financial Officer*.
Finance Lease	An arrangement where the lessee owns the asset. It is similar to a loan. Also see *Loan* and *Operating Lease*.
Financial Accounting	The measurement and recording of business transactions and providing financial statements that are based on the Generally Accepted Accounting Principles (GAAP). It focuses on reporting to external parties such as investors and banks.
Financial Budget	The part of the master budget that focuses on how planned capital outlays affect cash. It comprises: the capital expenditure budget, the cash budget, the budgeted balance sheet, and the budgeted statement of cash flows. Also see *Articulated Budget, Master Budget*, and *Operating Budget*.
Financial Controller	The financial executive primarily responsible for day to day oversight of management accounting and financial accounting. Also known as Chief Accounting Officer.
Financial Crises	The substantial downturn in the market that occurs without easily being controlled. In Australia, financial crises have occurred recently in 2008, 2001, 1994, 1987, 1981, 1974 and 1952.
Financial Engineering	Devising legal structures, arrangements and using measures that ensure that the investments maintain their impact and contribute a return for the business.
Financial Information	The information that is expressed in units of currency.
Financial Markets	Any marketplace where eligible buyers and sellers trade capital or credit (e.g. equities, bonds, currencies, derivatives, bills of exchange, commodities, futures and options, foreign currency) or fungible items. Financial markets ought to have transparent pricing, basic regulations on trading, costs and fees, and market forces determining the prices of securities that are traded. Prices should reflect supply and demand. Prices may rise owing to heavy demand or fall where there are low levels of demand or macroeconomic forces (e.g.taxes, heightened gross production or low employment levels). The rise and fall may be beyond the past levels of the intrinsic value of the product. There are two ways to look at financial markets: (a) *Fundamental Analysis* and (b) *Technical Analysis*.
Financial Planning Models	A mathematical representation of the relationships among operating activities, financial activities, and other factors that affect the master budget. Also see *Articulated Budget, Master Budget*, and *Operations Budget*.

Financial Position	See *Balance Sheet*.
Financial Resource	See *Economic Resource*.
Financial Statements	The general purpose financial statements of an accounting entity is a document reporting the business financial performance and business resources. Its purpose is to show how a firm has used the funds entrusted to it by its stockholders (shareholders) and lenders, and what is its current financial position. They usually comprise: (a) A Profit and Loss Statement which shows how the net income of the business is arrived at over a stated period of time. (b) A Statement of Changes in Equity to show the link between the Profit and Loss statement and the Balance Sheet. (c) A Balance Sheet which shows firm's assets, liabilities, and net worth on a stated date. (d) A Cash Flow Statement which shows the inflows and outflows of cash caused by the firm's activities during a stated period of time. (e) Notes to the individual summary reports.
Finished Goods	See *Finished Goods Inventory*.
Finished Goods Inventory	The products which have completed all the manufacturing processes and ready for sale but are not yet sold.
First-In, First-Out (FIFO)	A method of process costing used for assigning costs to inventory. It assumes products are used in the order purchased. The raw materials unused and inventory on hand at period end are valued as though they were most recently purchased or produced. Usually abbreviated FIFO. Also see *Last In First Out (LIFO)*.
First Principles	The fundamental or foundational propositions, assumptions or elements that cannot be deduced from any other proposition or assumption on which a particular theory or procedure is based.
Fishbone Diagram	See *Cause and Effect Diagram*.
Five Whys	A technique from Toyota (Ohno, 1988) in which the question 'why' is repeated a minimum of five times so that the past and the present, long-term factors, and any layers of symptoms are all considered. Further iterations are acceptable.
Fixed Cost	A cost that remains unchanged in total for a given time period, despite wide changes in the related level of total activity or volume. Strictly the term should be 'Fixed Cost for the relevant Range' to remind the reader to enquire 'What is the relevant range?' Also see *Contribution Margin*, *Gross Margin*, *Mixed Cost*, *Relevant Advantage*, *Step Cost*, and *Variable Cost*.
Fixed Overhead Flexible-Budget Variance	There is no efficiency variance for fixed costs because these costs are unaffected by any production efficiency. Also see *Fixed Overhead Spending Variance*.
Fixed Overhead Spending Variance	The difference between (a) the actual fixed overhead costs, and (b) the fixed overhead costs in the flexible budget. Also known as Fixed Overhead Flexible-Budget Variance.
Flash Cash	See *Flash Report*.
Flash Report	A report containing critical information usually produced each day. Also known as Flash Cash.

Flat Organisation Structure	A structure that has very few layers of management.
Flexible Budget	A budget developed using budgeted revenues and budgeted costs based on the actual output in the budget period.
Flexible-Budget Variance	The difference between (a) an actual result, and (b) the corresponding flexible-budget amount based on the actual output level in the budget period.
Flexing the Budget	See *Flexible Budget*.
Floor Plan Financing	A system of financing where the inventory is the security for the loan which is retired when the merchandise is sold and repayment is made. Often used by motor vehicle dealerships.
Flow	A business distinguishes between the units of measurement used for quantities that are stocks and those that are flows. A flow is measured over an interval of time and represents an amount per unit of time (say a year). Usually inflows (adding to the stock) are distinguished from outflows (subtracting from the stock). Examples are the total value of transactions (sales or purchases, incomes or expenditures) during an accounting period. Some accounting entries are normally always represented as a flow (e.g. profit or income). Some accounting entries may be represented both as a stock and as a flow (e.g. capital). Also see *Stock*.
Flowchart	A graphic tool to show the sequence and control of program or module logic.
Form	A part of a procedure. Also see *Template*.
For-Profit Business	See *Private Sector*. Also see *Profit*.
Forms of E-commerce	(a) Business to Business, abbreviated B2B, which is inter-organisational and may operate as an electronic marketplace for recognised business partners and their representatives or as a direct link between businesses; (b) Business to Consumer, abbreviated B2C, which entices customers to the business; (c) Consumer to Consumer, abbreviated C2C, which is trading between consumers themselves often using an intermediary to provide the infrastructure to enable consumers to make known their needs and fulfil those needs; and (d) Intra-organisational which allows e-mail, video and workflow processing among individuals and workgroups in the organisation. Also see *E-business* and *E-commerce*.
Forrester Effect	In the supply chain orders progress from the end-use customer ultimately to the raw material supplier. The further away they are from the end-use customer the greater the amplification of variations as each intermediary makes their own adjustment based on their expectation of rising or falling demand and the inventory they wish to carry. A simulation known as the beer (distribution) game allows all players to know each other's inventory shows the Forrester Effect. Also known as Bullwhip Effect or Whiplash Effect.
Franchise	A marketing technique to distribute products and services through the owner of the business (franchisor) allowing others (franchisees) to run a semi-independent branch of the business in return for initial and ongoing fees.
Fraud	The intentional misrepresentation, misstatement or omission of information which affects an action or outcome. Also see *Theft*.

Friendly Takeover	A takeover which is supported by the Board of the target company.
Front Office	Those activities in which employees interact with customers.
Full Costing	See *Absorption Costing*.
Full Costs of the Product	The sum of all variable and fixed costs in all business functions of the value chain: inward logistics, operations, outward logistics, sales and marketing, and customer service.
Fundamental Analysis	A method of evaluating a security that entails attempting to measure its intrinsic value by examining the qualitative and quantitative factors in terms of macroeconomic factors (e.g. overall economy and industry conditions) and company-specific factors (e.g. financial condition and management). This can determine the position to take with that security (if under-priced then buy, if overpriced then sell or short). Also see *Efficient Market Hypothesis*, *Random Walk*, and *Technical Analysis*.
Funds Statement	A financial statement of an accounting entity that summarises the resources made available to finance the activities for the period and the uses to which the resources have been put. It shows the link between the Profit and Loss statement and the Balance Sheet. A report which answers the question 'Why has net worth increased/diminished over the period?' Also known as statement of changes in equity for the period. Also known as Funds Movement Statement or a Statement of Sources and Application of Funds. Also see *Financial Statements*.

G

GAAP	See *Generally Accepted Accounting Principles*.
Game Outcome	Determining the effect of the decision on the other party. Also see *Win-Win*, and *Zero Sum*.
Garbage In, Garbage Out	A reminder that the quality of output is determined by the quality of the input. Where there is an emphasis on process, it emphasises that regardless of the correctness of the logic built into the program, no answer can be valid if the input is incomplete, erroneous or uncertain. A variation on the term, 'garbage in, gospel out' refers to a tendency to put unwarranted faith in the accuracy of data produced using technology and this includes models.
Generalisation (Function)	The same person performs more than one business function. For example in a small corner store, the owner will be the both the procurement clerk and the sales clerk. Also see *Specialisation*.
Generally Accepted Accounting Principles (GAAP)	The standard framework of guidelines for financial accounting used in any given jurisdiction. GAAP includes the standards, conventions, and rules accountants follow in recording and summarising transactions, and in the preparation of financial statements. The concepts and assumptions are: (a) Accounting entity assumption (business is separate to its owner); (b) Historical cost assumption (initially recorded at cost); (c) Going concern assumption (continue to operate); (d) Accrual accounting principle (match to period incurred); (e) Accounting period assumption (equal periods); (f) Qualitative characteristics of information (relevance, reliability, materiality, and economic substance); and (g) Accounting equation (assets = liabilities + owner's equity).

Generic Process	Generic business processes are those common to most businesses and which are conducted in a similar manner in most businesses. For example, most businesses choose very similar coordination, activities and workflows when a customer queues at a counter to make a purchase. Also see *Business Process*, and *Unique Process*.
Generic Skills	Skills not specific to work in a particular occupation or industry but are important for work, study and life in general. Also known as Employability Skills or Capabilities, or Transferable Skills.
GIGO	See *Garbage In, Garbage Out*.
Glossary	1. An explanation of terms and expressions. 2. An indexed store of terms and expressions peculiar to the business function(s) used in process analysis (e.g. Data Flow Model).
Goals of the Business	The basic goals are improving customer value and creating shareholder value. Also see *Objective*.
Goal Congruence	The state where individuals and groups work toward achieving the goals of the business while still satisfying their personal goals. Managers working in their own best interest take actions that align with the overall goals of top management.
Gold plating	The addition of unnecessary features or the provision of a feature at a higher standard than is necessary. Since resources are finite this consumes scarce resources which could be better utilised. Since the cost of the feature has to be funded there is additional interest is incurred.
Good; Goods	See *Product*.
Grant	See *Assignment*.
Green Whiskers Project	William Vickrey used the term to describe a recurring feature of public decision-making: the tendency to spend substantial resources on a project or policy, only to then to do things inconsistent with that policy's or project's stated goals. The example Vickrey gave was that of costly airport expansion projects: runways were upgraded so as to allow large airplanes to land, but then charges were levied on runway use which discouraged them from actually using the airport. The term is found in Lewis Carroll's poem, The White Knight's Song where the subject planned to dye their whiskers green, only to then 'use so large a fan/that they could not be seen.'
Gross Margin	The revenue minus cost of goods sold. Also see *Contribution Margin*, and *Fixed Cost*.
Gross-Margin Format	Operating income is driven by the unit level of production, the unit level of sales, and the denominator level for assigning fixed costs. Also see *Contribution-Margin Format*.
Gross Margin Percentage	The gross margin divided by revenues.
Growth (Business Cycle)	Initial growth is focused on the defined customer base and establishing a market presence. Secondary expansion is establishing new markets and distribution channels. The four stages of the business cycle are *Startup*, *Growth*, *Maturity*, and *Decline*. Also see *Business Cycle*, and *Economic Cycle*.
Growth Component	A change in operating income attributable solely to the change in the quantity of output sold between one period and the next.
H	
Hardcopy	Output from an information system using the traditional paper format. Also see *Softcopy*.

Hawthorne Effect	The finding that when employees receive attention they perform better. It has also become known as the observer bias.
Heuristic	1. A general method for problem solving, learning, and discovery that is expected to produce an acceptable solution to a problem. 2. A trial and error method for reaching an acceptable solution. 3. Also known as a Rule of Thumb.
High-Low Method	A method used to estimate a cost function that uses only the highest and lowest observed values of the cost driver within the relevant range and their respective costs.
HIPO	An acronym for Hierarchy-Input-Process-Output. An IBM documentation technique for representing the modules of a system as a hierarchy and for documenting the contents of the module.
Historical Cost Accounting	The original monetary value of an economic item is used to determine its value. It assumes that there has been no change in value since the date of acquisition. For example, assets, property, plant and equipment not generally restated when values change. Also see *Mark to Market*.
Holding Cost	See *Opportunity Cost*.
Homogeneous Cost Pool	A cost pool in which all the costs have the same or a similar cause-and-effect or benefits-received relationship with the cost-allocation base.
Horizontal Integration	The degree to which the same stage of production in the same industry is owned by the same business. This may be accomplished by acquisition, merger, or failure of the other businesses. For example, Standard Oil (USA) acquired over 25 other oil refineries.
Hostile Takeover	A takeover which is rejected by the Board of the target company.
Human Capital	The competencies, intelligence, motor abilities, artistic abilities, skills, and personality attributes embodied in the ability to perform labour. Competencies can be expanded, shared and mobilised. Also see *Human Resources*.
Human / Machine Boundary	The interface(s) between procedures which are manual and those which are automated.
Human Resources	1. The intangible resources of the competence profile of employees (full and part-time) casual and contractors as well as their creativity, commitment and intellectual capital. Also see *Economic Resources*, *Physical Resources*, *Reputational Resources*, and *Technological Resources*. 2. A general term for full-time employees, part-time employees, casual employees, contractors, casuals who have various responsibilities which may also include supervision or management. Also known as Human Capital.
Hurdle Rate	See *Required Rate of Return*.
Hybrid-Costing System	A costing system that blends characteristics from both job-costing systems and process-costing systems. Also see *Job Costing*, *Operation Costing*, and *Process Costing*.
Hygiene Factors	The factors that provide a basis for motivation but which do not motivate.
I	
Idle Capacity	The situation in which equipment, labour or other inputs to production are not being utilised and are available for other purposes. Also known as Excess Capacity, or Spare Capacity.

Idle Time	The wages paid to employees for unproductive time. It may occur as a result of lack of orders, machine breakdowns, material shortages, poor scheduling, incomplete specification, or machine set-up.
Imitability	See *Replicability of Resource*.
Impairment of Assets	1. An asset is impaired when its carrying amount exceeds its recoverable amount. 2. Impairment extends to determining how the recoverable amount is calculated. 3. Also see *Carrying Amount, Fair Value,* and *Recoverable Amount*.
Imputed Costs	1. The costs recognised in particular situations but not incorporated in financial accounting records. Also known as Managed Fixed Costs 2. The interest earnings foregone as a result of monies expended on assets. For example, average balance of accounts receivable multiplied by the interest rate. 3. Also see *Decremental Costs, Differential Costs, Differential Revenues, Discretionary Costs, Incremental Costs, Incremental Revenues, Opportunity Costs, Out-of-Pocket Costs, Plan Concepts, Relevant Costs, Sunk Costs,* and *Unavoidable Costs*.
Incentive Compensation Systems	See *Performance-Related Pay Systems*.
Income Statement	See *Profit and Loss Statement*. Also see *Contribution Margin Statement,* and *Financial Statements*.
Income Statement Format.	The format is either *Contribution Margin format,* or *Gross-Margin format*.
Incongruent Decision-making	See *Dysfunctional Decision-Making*.
Incorporation	One of the legal structures of a business. Also see the common legal structures are: *Business, Company, Cooperative, Enterprise, Partnership, Sole Proprietor,* and *Trust*.
Incremental Budgeting	The budget for an item in the previous year is taken as accepted and any increase has to be justified. Also known as Traditional Budgeting. Also see *Zero-Base Budgeting*.
Incremental Costs	An additional total cost incurred as a result of a higher differential cost. Also see *Decremental Cost, Differential Costs, Differential Revenues, Imputed Costs, Incremental Revenues, Opportunity Costs, Out-of-Pocket Costs, Plan Concepts, Relevant Costs, Sunk Costs,* and *Unavoidable Costs*.
Incremental Cost-Allocation Method	A method that ranks the individual users of a cost object in the order of users most responsible for the common cost and then uses this ranking to allocate cost among those users.
Incremental Revenue	Any additional total revenue that will be gained as a result of selecting one activity over an alternative.
Incremental Revenue-Allocation Method	A method that ranks individual products in a bundle according to criteria determined by management (for example, sales), and then uses this ranking to allocate bundled revenues to the individual products.
Incremental Unit-Time Learning Model	A learning curve model in which the incremental time needed to produce the last unit declines by a constant percentage each time the cumulative quantity of units produced doubles.

Independent Variable	A variable manipulated to create a treatment condition.
Indicator	A set of values used to measure against. Their purpose is to help us understand where we are, where we are going and how far we are from the goal, that is, an indicator provides evidence that a certain condition exists or certain results have or have not been achieved. There are many different kinds of indicator including Coincident Indicator, Lag Indicator, and Lead Indicator. Indicators can measure inputs, process, outputs, and outcomes. Input indicators measure resources, both human and financial, devoted to a particular program or intervention. Process indicators measure ways in which program services and goods are provided (e.g. error rates). Output indicators measure the quantity of goods and services produced and the efficiency of production (e.g. number of people served, speed of response from a defined contact event). Outcome indicators measure the broader results achieved through the provision of goods and services. Population-level indicators measure a condition or changes a condition (e.g. work OH&S accident rate). Indicators can exist at various levels: population/group, program/project and organisational unit. Also see *Coincident Indicator, Lag Indicator*, and *Lead Indicator*.
Indirect Costs of a Cost Object	A cost related to the particular cost object that cannot be traced to that object in an economically feasible (cost-effective) manner.
Indirect Labour	The labour used in production that cannot be directly traced to a product or service in an economically feasible (cost-effective) manner.
Indirect Manufacturing Costs	All the manufacturing costs that are related to the cost object (work-in-process and then finished products) that cannot be traced to that cost object in an economically feasible way. Also known as Manufacturing Overhead Costs, Factory Overhead Costs, or Factory Burden Costs.
Indirect Materials	The materials used in production that cannot be directly traced to a product or service in an economically feasible (cost-effective) manner.
Industrial Engineering Method	See *Time and Motion Studies*.
Inflation	The decline in the general purchasing power. Usually measured in the monetary units.
Information Event	An information event involves the recording (input), maintenance and reporting of data about operations events. Also see *Decision Event*, and *Operations Event*.
Information Silo	A situation where very few employees know what data is available in other departments that would be useful for their decision-making. Also see *Silo Mentality*.
Infrastructure	1. Business infrastructure refers to buildings, equipment and technology. 2. IT infrastructure refers to hardware, software, storage, communications and networks.
In-house	The process of producing products or providing services within the business rather than purchasing those same products or services from outside suppliers.
Innovation	The commercialisation of an idea. It may refer to either the process itself or any output from the process. Schumpeter (1934) defined an economic innovation as a new product, method of production, market, source of supply or form of organisation. Also see *Disruptive Innovation, Invention*, and *Sustaining Innovation*..
Input	Those resources allocated to an activity or project. Also see *Economy, Efficiency, Effectiveness*, and *Risk*.

Input-Price Variance	See *Price Variance*.
In-Source	See *In-house*.
Inspection Point	The stage of the production process at which products are examined to determine whether they are acceptable or unacceptable units.
Instruction	1. A direction from a manager or supervisor to a lower level manager, supervisor or employee. 2. A direction from a business or person being represented to their legal counsel. 3. A portion of a computer program more properly termed a *Routine*.
Institutional Theory	A theory that highlights the need for legitimacy and the tendency for businesses to imitate the practices of other businesses. The three processes of institutions are (a) regulative (b) normative and (c) cognitive.
Intangible Benefit	A benefit capable of expression only in words (qualitative). Intangible benefits include: (a) customer goodwill; (b) employee morale; (c) job satisfaction; (d) improved decisions; and (e) community service. Also see *Cost, Tangible Benefit, Tangible Cost, Tangible Resource, Intangible Cost,* and *Intangible Resource.*
Intangible Cost	A cost capable of expression only in words (qualitative). Intangible costs include: (a) employee development costs; and (b) loss of morale costs. Also see *Cost, Tangible Benefit, Tangible Cost, Tangible Resource, Intangible Benefit,* and *Intangible Resource.*
Intangible Resource	The non-physical assets of a business. Also see the three forms of intangible resources namely *Human Resources, Reputational Resources,* and *Technological Resources.*
Interactive Control Systems	One of the four levers of control that managers use to focus organisational attention and learning on key strategic issues (Simons, 1995). Also see *Belief Systems , Boundary Systems, Diagnostic Control Systems,* and *Levers of Control.*
Interface	A common boundary between two devices, subsystems, programs or modules.
Intermediate Product	A product transferred from one subunit to another subunit of a business. The product is then further processed by the receiving subunit. In some cases there may be a market for intermediate products.
Internal Control	The systems, plans, methods and procedures adopted by management to assist achieving the objective of ensuring efficient conduct of the business including adherence to policies, safeguarding assets, prevention of fraud, detection of fraud and error, the accuracy of records and the timely preparation of reliable accounting information.
Internal Customer	The next individual or group in a sequence of processes.
Internal Failure Costs	The costs incurred on defective products before they are shipped to customers.
Internal Rate-of-Return Method	A capital budgeting Discounted Cash Flow (DCF) method. It calculates the actual economic return earned by the project over its life as a discount rate at which the present value of expected cash inflows from a project equals the present value of its expected cash outflows.
Intrinsic Motivation	The motivation that derives from interest in and enjoyment of the work itself.
Invention	A discovery, that is making manifest a new form, composition or process. Also see *Disruptive Innovation, Innovation,* and *Sustaining Innovation.*

Inventoriable Cost	All costs of a product that are considered as assets in the balance sheet when they are incurred and that become cost of goods sold only when the product is sold.
Inventoried Cost	See *Inventoriable Cost.*
Inventory Accounting	Making decisions concerning the inventory system (perpetual or periodic), the inventory valuation (cost, market or replacement value), and the cost flow assumption (e.g. First In, First Out, Last In First Out).
Inventory Management	The planning, coordinating, and controlling activities related to the flow of inventory into, through, and out of a business.
Inventory Reorder Point	See *Reorder Point.*
Inventory Write-Down	An accounting entry made to reduce the inventory value shown in the balance sheet to the lower of cost or net realisable value.
Investment	The resources or assets used to generate revenue. The cash outflows of an investment are compared with the net cash inflows discounted by the cost of capital, interest and risk.
Investment Allowance	A one-off taxation deduction that businesses receive in the year the asset is purchased.
Investment Centre	A *Responsibility Centre* where the manager is accountable for investments, revenues, profits and costs. Also see *Cost Centre, Profit Centre,* and *Revenue Centre.*
Investment Cycle	The business activities and information processing operations associated with obtaining the necessary funds to continue operations. Also known as the Finance Cycle or the Financial Cycle. Also see *Conversion Cycle, Expenditure Cycle, Non-Operating Cycle,* and *Revenue Cycle.*
Invoice	A report source document identifying the product or service, the unit cost for the product or service, the quantity and therefore the cost.
ISO 9000	The international quality management standard. Also see *Standard.*
J	
Job	A distinct unit or batch of a distinct product or service
Job-Cost Record	A source document that records and accumulates all the costs assigned to a specific job, starting when work begins. Also known as Job-Cost Sheet.
Job-Cost Sheet	See *Job Cost Record.*
Job-Costing System	A costing system in which the cost object is a unit or multiple units of a distinct product or service called a job. Also see *Hybrid Costing, Operation Costing,* and *Process Costing.*
Job Order	See *Job.*
Joint Cost	All the manufacturing costs incurred in a production process that yields multiple products simultaneously.
Joint Products	The two or more products that have high total sales values compared with the total sales values of other products yielded by a joint production process. For example, crude oil produces petrol, kerosene and benzene. Also see *Main Product,* and *By-Product.*

Joint Venture	A relationship which exists between parties carrying on a particular commercial undertaking in common for their individual gain as a result of contributing assets. Unlike a partnership it does not seek mutual benefits. Also see *Partnership*, and *Strategic Alliance*.
Journal	A chronological record of accounting transactions (usually made at the time the transaction occurs). In practice, the transactions are usually recorded in dedicated separate journals although a general journal may still be necessary. Also known as a Daybook. Also see *General Ledger, Ledger, Ledger Account, Posting*, and *Trial Balance*.
Just-In-Time (JIT) Production	A demand-pull manufacturing system in which each component in a production line is produced as soon as, and only when, needed by the next step in the production line. Also known as Lean Production.
Just-In-Time (JIT) Purchasing	The purchase of materials (or products) so that they are delivered just as needed for production (or sales).
K	
Kaizen Budgeting	A budgetary approach that explicitly incorporates continuous improvement anticipated during the budget period into the budget numbers.
Kanban	A Japanese term for card or visible record (Ohno, 1988). A visible record is used to signal a request for new production or inventory.
Key Performance Indicators (KPI)	The financial and non-financial measures agreed beforehand that are used to evaluate achievement of goals related to strategy. Also see *Balanced ScoreCard, Critical Success Factors*, and *Service Delivery Outcomes*.
Keywords	A word that summarises the topic or main idea selected from a hierarchical classification of terms (thesaurus). It is sometimes erroneously used as a synonym for *Tag* Also see *Tag*.
KJ Diagram	See *Affinity Diagram*.
KJ Method	See *Affinity Diagram*.
Kludge	A clumsy or inelegant yet effective solution to a problem.
L	
Labour On-Costs	The additional costs that are incurred when employing employees. They include payroll tax, worker's compensation levy and the employer's contribution to superannuation.
Labour-Time Record	See *Timesheet*.
Lag Indicator	1. A measure of the outcomes of progress toward objectives. 2. In economics the indicator changes direction after the overall economy does. 3. Also see *Coincident Indicator*, and *Lead Indicator*.
Lamarckian Evolution of Markets	Learning or acquiring characteristics through observation or copying.
Large Business	The definition is country dependent. As a guide it is a business which employs 250 or more. (Europe also considers turnover and balance sheet details). Also known as Large Enterprise. Also see *Medium Business, Micro Business*, and *Small Business*.

Last In First Out	A method of process costing used in historical cost accounting for assigning costs to inventory. It assumes the last purchased products are first to be used. The raw materials unused and inventory on hand at period end are valued as though they were the earliest purchases or earliest production. Usually abbreviated LIFO. Also see *First In First Out (FIFO)*.
Law of Economy	See *Ockham's Razor*.
Law of Diminishing Returns	See *Diminishing Returns*.
Law of Large Numbers	In statistics, the theorem that, as the number of identically distributed, randomly generated variables increases, the mean (average) of the sample approaches the theoretical mean.
Law of Parsimony	See *Ockham's Razor*.
Law of Plenitude	Some digital objects provide increasing returns when their distribution is increased. Kelly (1998) gives the example of facsimile (fax) machines where the more machines that are interconnected, the greater the advantage of owning one.
Lead Indicator	1. A measure that drives outcomes and provides information that is actionable and manageable. 2. In economics a lead indicator reliably changes before the overall economy does. 3. Also see *Coincident Indicator*, and *Lag Indicator*.
Lead Time	The duration between any two events. Also see *Delivery Lead Time, Manufacturing Lead Time,* and *Purchase-Order Lead Time*.
Lean	Creating more value for customers with fewer resources. Also see *Just-In-Time Production*.
Lean Accounting	A costing method that supports creating value for the customer by costing the entire value stream, not individual products or departments, thereby eliminating waste in the accounting process.
Lean Production	See *Just-In-Time Production*.
Learning	The examination of past performance and the systematic exploration of alternative ways to make better-informed decisions and plans in the future.
Learning Curve	A mathematical function that measures the reduction in labour-hours per unit as units of production increase owing to efficiency increasing with employee experience.
Learning Outcomes	The set of knowledge, skills and/or competencies a person has acquired and is able to demonstrate after completion of specified learning activities.
Leasing	A legal arrangement that allows the owner of an asset (lessor) to allow another party (lessee) to use the asset. Also see *Finance Lease,* and *Operating Lease*.
Ledger	1. The collection of accounts used by an accounting entity for recording its financial transactions. The accounts are usually listed by their order in the balance sheet. 2. The manual book or electronic record which contains the transactions for a nominated account. 3. Also see *Subsidiary Ledger*.
Ledger Account	A particular account in the ledger which records transactions of a particular type. It contains the debit and credit ledger entries and the balance after each entry.

Legal Entity	A form of legal incorporation to give legal status to the business or organisation. Also see *Accounting Entity*.
Lessee	A person or entity who receives the use and possession of leased property (e.g. real estate or equipment) from a lessor in exchange for a payment of funds. The person or entity to whom a lease is made. The duties of the lessee are twofold: (a) to fulfil all express covenants of the lease, and (b) to fulfil all the implied covenants of the lease. A lessee of land is a tenant.
Lessor	An owner of property who rents it to another party (the lessee) under an agreement allowing use the equipment or property for the lease term, and who is entitled to receive rental fees. A lessor of land is a landlord. A lessee of land is a tenant.
Letter of Comfort	A document prepared by an accounting firm assuring the financial soundness or backing of a company. The letter may be used to 'comfort' another party as to the ability or willingness to company to fulfil its obligations.
Level of Activity	The volume or intensity of work performed in the business.
Levers of Control	The critical performance variables used by managers to monitor progress in achieving business goals. There are four levers: Belief Systems, Boundary Systems, Diagnostic Control Systems, and Interactive Control Systems. Belief Systems and Interactive Control Systems resemble positive and inspirational forces (yang) of sun, warmth and light. Boundary Systems and Diagnostic Control Systems create constraints and ensure compliance with orders and represent the yin forces of darkness and cold. Also see *Belief Systems*, *Boundary Systems*, *Diagnostic Control Systems*, and *Interactive Control Systems*.
Life Cycle	See *Business Life Cycle*, *Customer Life Cycle Costs*, *Life Cycle Budgeting*, *Life Cycle Costing*, *Product Life Cycle*, *Project Life Cycle*, *Sales Life Cycle*, and *Technology Adoption Life Cycle*.
Life Cycle Budgeting	A budget that estimates the revenues and business function costs over the entire life of the product. The value chain is used to estimate the planned costs and predicted revenues attributable to each product from initial Research and Development to final customer service and support. Also see *Research and Development (Business Function)*.
Life Cycle Costing	A cost management approach that tracks and accumulates business function costs of the value chain attributable to each product from initial Research and Development to final customer service and support.
LIFO	See *Last In First Out*.
Line Employee	An employee (including a manager) who is directly responsible for achieving the goals of the business. They will include sales, production and distribution employees. Also see *Staff*.
Linear Cost Function	A cost function in which the graph of total costs versus the level of a single activity related to that cost is a straight line within the relevant range.
Linear Programming	An optimisation technique used to identify linear relationships between variables or functions (for example, contribution margin of a mix of products), to determine an optimal solution when there are multiple constraints.
Line Item	The detail entries or accounts in a chart of accounts. For example, salaries, office supplies or telephone expenses.
Line Item Budgeting	A form of budgeting where resources are allocated to detailed entries or accounts in a chart of accounts.

Line Management	See *Line Employee*.
Loan	An agreement by which an asset is transferred from its owner (the lender) to a user (the borrower) for a specified period of time in return for a fee (usually interest payments).
Locked-In Costs	The costs that have not yet been incurred but, based on decisions that have already been made, will be incurred in the future. Also known as Designed-In Costs.
Logical View of a System	The logical system describes what needs to be accomplished. It is implementation-independent; pertaining to the underlying policy rather than to any way of that policy might be physically manifested. Format, size and medium are irrelevant.
Long Term	Decisions involving periods longer than one year. Also see *Short Term*.
Long-Term Decisions	The decisions that have strategic considerations and which focus on major changes in resources for the business.
Loss on Disposal	The loss made when an asset is sold for less than its carrying amount.
Low Cost Leadership	A generic strategy based on the capability of the business to produce and deliver products of competitive quality at lower costs. Also see *Competitive Advantage*, and *Product Differentiation*.
M	
Macroeconomics	The study of the performance and structure of an economy at the aggregate level (national economy). It considers income, output, and the interrelationship among diverse economic sectors. It uses indicators such as business cycles, inflation, unemployment, balance of trade, and the government fiscal policy of taxation and spending.
Main Product	The product from a joint production process yields one product that has a high total sales value compared with the total sales values of all other products. Also see *By-Product*, and *Joint Product*.
Make-or-Buy Decision	The decision by a producer of products or services whether to in-source (produce products or services within the business) or outsource (purchase them from outside suppliers).
Managed (Fixed) Costs	See *Discretionary Costs*.
Management Accounting	The use of numerical and analytical skills, the demonstration of current theoretical knowledge and the understanding of the nature, functions, structure and operations of management to measure, evaluate, and report financial and non-financial information that helps managers make decisions to use resources to fulfil the goals of a business. It focuses on internal reporting.
Management Accounting System	An information system that produces financial and non-financial information to assist managers to manage resources and create value.
Management By Walking About (MBWA)	The making of first-hand observations by visiting the employees (including managers) while they actually perform their daily tasks.
Management by Exception	The practice of focusing management attention on areas not operating as expected and giving less attention to areas operating as expected. A threshold may be used so only significant variances are investigated.

Management by Objectives (MBO)	The assignment of targets, usually for the next twelve months, to employees.
Management Control System	A means of gathering and using information to aid and coordinate the planning and control decisions throughout a business and to guide the behaviour of its managers and employees.
Management Event	See *Decision Event*.
Management Performance Indicator	See *Performance Measurement System*.
Managing Director	See *Chief Executive Officer*.
Manufacturing (Business Function)	The production of finished products from raw materials using batch processing, continuous processing or make-to-order processing. Also see *Accounting (Business Function), Distribution (Business Function), Finance (Business Function), Marketing (Business Function), Procurement (Business Function), Research and Development (Business Function)*, and *Sales (Business Function)*.
Manufacturing Cell	The grouping together of all the different types of equipment for different processes used to complete the manufacture of a given product.
Manufacturing Cost	The sum of direct materials, direct labour and manufacturing overhead.
Manufacturing Cycle Efficiency (MCE)	The value-added manufacturing time divided by manufacturing cycle time.
Manufacturing Cycle Time	See *Manufacturing Lead Time*.
Manufacturing Department	See *Production Department*.
Manufacturing Lead Time	The elapsed time between when an order is received by manufacturing and when a finished product is completed. Also known as Manufacturing Cycle Time. Also see *Delivery Lead Time, Purchase-Order Lead Time, Service Response Time*, and *Waiting Time*.
Manufacturing Overhead Allocated	The amount of manufacturing overhead costs allocated to individual jobs, products, or services based on the budgeted rate multiplied by the actual quantity used of the cost-allocation base. Also known as Manufacturing Overhead Applied.
Manufacturing Overhead Applied	See *Manufacturing Overhead Allocated*.
Manufacturing Overhead Cost	See *Indirect Manufacturing Costs*.
Manufacturing Sector	The businesses that purchase materials and components and convert them by assembly or conversion of raw material inputs into various finished products. It may produce products in a batch process such as a motor vehicle or use a continuous process such as producing petrol. Also see *Merchandising Sector, Resource Sector*, and *Service Sector*.

Margin of Safety	An amount by which budgeted (or actual) revenues exceed breakeven revenues.
Marginal Cost	The cost of producing one additional unit of production.
Marginal Cost Curve	A graph of the change in total cost that accompanies a change in the quality of product produced and sold.
Marginal Revenue Curve	A graph of the change in total revenue that accompanies a change in the quality of product sold.
Mark to Market (MTM)	The value of an asset or liability is based on (a) the current market price of the asset or liability, or (b) the current market price of similar assets and liabilities, or (c) another objectively assessed 'fair' value. Values on the balance sheet may change frequently, as market conditions change. Also known as Fair Value Accounting. Also see *Carrying Cost, Fair Value, Historical Cost Accounting*, and *Recoverable Amount*.
Market	1. Any place where the sellers of a particular product or service can meet with the buyers of that product or service with potential for a transaction to occur. 2. The consumers or organisations that (a) are interested in the product or service, (b) have the resources to make the purchase, and (c) are permitted by laws and regulations to acquire the product. 3. Also see *Market Cap, Market Failure, Market Narrowing*, and *Marketing (Business Function)*.
Market Cap	The market value of the equity capital of a company. Usually calculated by multiplying the number of ordinary shares by the current price.
Market Failure	An economic term that encompasses a situation where, in any given market, the quantity of a product demanded by consumers does not equate to the quantity supplied by suppliers. This is a direct result of a lack of certain economically ideal factors, which prevents equilibrium.
Market Narrowing	The market is narrowed from the population by considering: the potential market (those interested), the available market (those with resources to purchase), the qualified available market (those legally entitled to make the purchase), the target or served market (those targeted by the business), and the penetrated market (those who have made the purchase). Also see *Market*, and *Marketing (Business Function)*.
Marketing (Business Function)	The promotion and selling of products or services to customers or prospective customers. Also see *Accounting (Business Function), Distribution (Business Function), Finance (Business Function), Manufacturing (Business Function), Procurement (Business Function), Research and Development (Business Function)*, and *Sales (Business Function)*.
Marketing Cost	The costs of selling products and services.
Market-Share Variance	The difference in budgeted contribution margin for actual market size in units caused solely by actual market share being different from budgeted market share. Also see *Market-Size Variance*.
Market-Size Variance	The difference in budgeted contribution margin at the budgeted market share caused solely by actual market size in units being different from budgeted market size in units. Also see *Market-Share Variance*.
Master Budget	An expression of management's operating and financial plans for a specified period (usually a fiscal year) including a set of budgeted financial statements. Also known as Pro Forma Statements. Also see *Articulated Budget, Operating Budget*, and *Financial Budget*.

Master-Budget Capacity (Demand) Utilisation	The expected level of demand capacity utilisation for the current budget period (typically one year). Also see *Normal Capacity (Demand) Utilisation*.
Mastery	Demonstrating a comprehensive knowledge and understanding of a field of work or learning.
Materiality of Information	A qualitative characteristic of accounting information. The extent to which information can be omitted, misstated, or grouped with other information without misleading a user of the information when making a decision. Also see *Economic Substance, Relevance of Information,* and *Reliability of Information*.
Materials Requirements Planning (MRP)	A push-through system that manufactures finished products for inventory on the basis of demand forecasts.
Materials-Requisition Record	A source document that contains information about the cost of direct materials used on a specific job and in a specific department. It may also authorise the movement of raw materials from the warehouse to the production department.
Maturity (Business Cycle)	The end of growth and some reductions in sales; reduced revenue, profitability or erosion of market share. The four stages of the business cycle are *Startup, Growth, Maturity,* and *Decline*. Also see *Business Cycle,* and *Economic Cycle*.
MBO	See *Management by Objectives*.
MCS	See *Management Control System*.
Medium Business	The definition is country dependent. Also known as Medium Enterprise. As a guide it is a business which employs less than 250. (Europe also considers turnover and balance sheet details). Also see *Large Business, Micro Business,* and *Small Business*.
Mental Model	The deep understanding of an individual's motivations and thought-processes. The theories used by an individual that drives their motivation and behaviour.
Merchandising Sector	A business that purchases tangible products and then sells them from inventory or special order without using any conversion process to change their basic form. For example, a fruit and vegetable retailer. Also see *Manufacturing Sector, Resource Sector,* and *Service Sector*.
Metadata	The data that describes data and processes.
Methodology	A formal specification of a system for building systems which defines the activities and the interfaces of the project.
Microeconomics	The study of the market behaviour or other mechanisms that establish relative prices among products and services and uses of societal resources at the level of small economic units. Examples of the units are individual consumers, households or businesses. It uses the concepts of money, time, resources, supply and demand, markets, income distribution, scarcity and market failure. Also see *Macroeconomics*.
Micro Business	The definition is country dependent. Also known as Micro Enterprise. As a guide it is a business which employs less than 10 employees. (Europe also considers turnover and balance sheet details). Also see *Large Business, Medium Business,* and *Small Business*.
Micro Narrative	One or several real or fictional occurrences containing a reason for its telling featuring time, place, characters and an environment in lesser or greater detail giving some account of not only what happened but how the story teller makes sense of it.

Mission Statement	A statement that defines the purpose and boundaries of the business. It states what the business will have to do to accomplisht its vision. Also see *Vision Statement*.
Mixed Cost	A cost that has both fixed and variable elements. Also known as Semi-variable Cost. Also see *Fixed Cost, Step Cost,* and *Variable Cost.*
Model / Modelling	The representation of a system using prose, graphic symbols, algebra or other notation or a combination of them.
Module	An identifiable piece, component, or continuous sequence of instructions, a component of a program.
Monopolistic Market	A market where there is a single seller. Also see *Natural Monopoly,* and *Oligopolistic Market.*
Moral Dilemma	See *Ethical Dilemma.*
Moral Hazard	1. A situation in which a person does not bear the full consequences and responsibilities of their actions, and therefore has a tendency to act less carefully than he or she otherwise would, leaving another party to hold some responsibility for the consequences of those actions. 2. A situation in which an employee prefers to report distorted information desired by the owner because the validity of the reported information cannot be accurately monitored and enforced.
Motivation	The desire to attain a selected goal (the goal-congruence dimension) combined with the resulting pursuit of that goal (the effort dimension).
Multicollinearity	Exists when two or more independent variables in a multiple regression model are highly correlated with each other.
Multiple Regression	A technique that estimates a linear relationship between a dependent variable and two or more independent variables.
N	
Narrative	An account of an event to make a point, often in first person or with personal involvement, containing some reflection about the event, experiences and social relationships. Also known as Story. Also see *Micro Narrative.*
Narrative Form	A layout which records both debit and credit items vertically using appropriate subtotals. Also known as *Report Form, Statement Form,* and *Vertical Form.* Also see *Account Form,* and *T Account.*
Nash Equilibrium	Each individual has optimised their own position relative to everyone else. That is, no individual can benefit from a change in their own strategy if the other players retain their strategy. Agreement on new strategies may result in improved payoffs. Also see *Pareto Optimum.*
Natural Monopoly	The presence of a single business on the grounds it is the most efficient approach based on obtaining the lowest long-run average cost for production. Concentration in a single form may arise from being first or from cose of the capital expenditure (e.g. water and sewerage), or from government mandate (e.g. East India Company). Also see *Monopolistic Market.*
Natural Science	The scientific study of the objects, phenomena, their interrelations and transformations, and processes of the physical world to produce a body of reliable knowledge including rules that can be logically and rationally explained. Examples of disciplines are physics, chemistry, geology, and biology. It excludes the abstract or theoretical sciences, such as mathematics, and logic. Also see *Social Science,* and *Science.*

Net Income	The operating income plus non-operating revenues (such as interest revenue) minus non-operating costs (such as interest cost) minus income taxes.
Net Present Value (NPV)	1. A capital budgeting Discounted Cash Flow (DCF) method that calculates the expected monetary gain or loss from a project by discounting all expected future cash inflows and outflows to the present point in time, using the required rate of return. 2. The sum of all the present values of the cash flows in each period.
Net Realisable Value (NRV)	The estimated sales value of the merchandise less any anticipated costs of completing and selling the products.
Net Realisable Value (NRV) Method	A method of allocating joint costs to joint products according to the relative size of the final products' net realisable value.
Nominal Rate of Return	1. The unadjusted amount of money generated by an investment without factoring in any compounding or discounting, expenses (such as taxes, investment fees) and inflation. 2. The nominal rate of return sought by a business covers three elements: (a) a risk-free element (excluding inflation), (b) a business-risk element, (c) an allowance for the expected inflation. 3. Also see *Internal Rate of Return*, *Rate of Return*, and *Real Rate of Return*.
Non-Controllable Costs	A cost that is either indirect to the particular business unit being analysed or cannot be changed or influenced by management in the short-term. Also see *Control Concepts*, *Controllable Cost*, *Direct Cost*, and *Indirect Costs*.
Non-Deterministic View of the Marketplace	Success of a product or service, or an employee is governed mainly by a conspiracy of random and minor factors, that is, luck. Also see *Deterministic View of the Marketplace*, and *Random*.
Non-Excludable Benefit	The benefit cannot be retained by the originator of the activity, innovation or discovery.
Non-Financial Information	The information which is expressed in non-financial units (e.g. inventory levels or labour hours), or which is expressed in qualitative descriptive terms (e.g.employee morale is low). The measure may be units or a ratio. For example, comparing capital expenditure projects using payback (that is, using number of years). Non-financial outcomes also include qualitative considerations. For example, a narrative of the risks of undertaking a project. Also see *Qualitative Factors*.
Non-Linear Cost Function	A cost function in which the graph of total costs based on the level of a single activity is not a straight line within the relevant range.
Non-Manufacturing Costs	All costs incurred outside manufacturing. These are the upstream and downstream activity costs.
Non-Operating Cycle	The production of financial and non-financial information (reporting) using transactions from the operating cycle. This may also involve use of the business strategy information. Also see *Operating Cycle*, *Conversion Cycle*, *Expenditure Cycle*, *Investment Cycle*, and *Revenue Cycle*.
Non-Physical	See *Logical view of a System*.

Non-Profit	A non-profit business is one where the amount which can be spent is limited by the amount of funding or amount of revenue collected. It relies on estimation of budgeted funds. Funding may be allocated to particular activities, projects or programs (that is, planned activities). The only budget/funding revision allowed may be CPI/inflation, salary increases. Funding depends upon legislative timing. Important budgetary and financial management/compliance include (a) measures may be primarily non-financial and associated to goals/outcomes; (b) direct comparison between budget and actual funding and expenditure; (c) review of expenditure and liabilities; (d) the need to demonstrate that expenditure is in accordance with reason for funding; and (e) there are projections for future activity. The typical examples are State Governments and Local Councils. Also see *Non-Profit Sector*.
Non-Profit Sector	The part of the economy that undertakes voluntary activities and does not operate for profit and is not controlled by the government. A business that does not distribute its surplus funds to owners or shareholders, but instead uses them to help pursue its goals. Examples include charities and voluntary organisations (e.g. an amateur cricket club). Also known as Not-for-Profit. Also see *Private Sector* and *Public Sector*.
Non-Value-Added Activity	An activity that if eliminated would not affect the functioning of the business. Also see *Value Added Activity*.
Non-Value-Added Cost	A cost that, if eliminated, would not reduce the actual or perceived value or utility (usefulness) that a customer obtains from using the product or service. Also see *Value-Added Cost*.
Normal Capacity (Demand) Utilisation	The level of demand capacity utilisation that satisfies average customer demand over a period (say, two to three years) that includes seasonal, cyclical, and trend factors. Also see *Master-Budget Capacity Utilisation*.
Normal Costing	A product costing system that traces direct costs to a cost object by using the actual direct-cost rates times the actual quantities of the direct-cost inputs and that allocates indirect costs based on the budgeted indirect-cost (predetermined overhead) rates times the actual quantities of the cost-allocation bases. That is the overhead rate is normalised over a fairly long period. Contrast with *Actual Costing*.
Normal Spoilage	The spoilage inherent in a particular production process that arises even under efficient operating conditions.
Normal Volume	See *Normal Capacity Utilisation*.
Normalisation	1. The removal of the effects of factors outside the business so that improvements in performance are achievable. 2. The decomposition of a data structure to remove redundant information and ensure there is a unique identifier for individual records to produce a well-structured relation.
Not-for-Profit	See *Non-Profit*.
NRV	See *Net Realisable Value (NRV)*, and *Net Realisable Value (NRV) Method*.
Null	A null represents missing or unknown information of an attribute value. It is inappropriate to refer to a 'null value' because using the term 'null' implies the lack of a value.
O	
Objective	A specific statement of what the business intends to achieve. It must be quantified and expressed for a time period or a deadline.

Obligation-Based Ethical Theories	An ethical theory concerning the role of duty and respect for persons. It may underestimate the importance of happiness and social utility. Also see *Aretaic Turn Ethical Theories, Consequential Ethical Theories,* and *Social Contract Based Ethical Theories.*
Observer Bias	See *Hawthorne Effect.*
Ockham's Razor	A principle that gives precedence to simplicity. It has two aspects (1) anti-quantity that is, use as few parameters and (2) anti-superfluity, or avoidance of parameters that are not needed to explain the data. In an explanation, between two competing theories, the simplest explanation of an entity is to be preferred. The principle is also expressed as 'Plurality should not be posited without necessity' and 'Entities are not to be multiplied beyond necessity.' Also known as Occam's Razor, and Occham's Razor, Law of Economy, or Law of Parsimony.
Off-Market	A direct offer to the shareholders of the target business.
Oligopolistic Market	A market where a small number of sellers compete among themselves. Also see *Monopolistic Market.*
On-Cost	See *Labour On-Costs.*
On-Market	Purchase of the shares of the target business by way of a stock exchange transaction.
On-Time Performance	The delivery of a product or service by the time it is scheduled to be delivered.
One-Time-Only Special Order	An order that has no long-run implications.
Operating Department	Any department that directly adds value to a product or service. Also known in manufacturing companies as a production department.
Open Book	The full display of (a) accurate input data, (b) processing methods, (c) calculations, and (d) all results as well as showing all (e) assumptions, and (f) business rules.
Operating Budget	The part of the master budget that focuses on sales, production and cash. The schedules to the operating budget include: the sales revenue budget, the production budget, the sales expense budget, the cost of goods budget, the distribution costs budget, the marketing costs budget, the ending budgeted inventory leading to the budgeted income statement. The production budget is further divisible into budgeted direct materials, budgeted direct labour and budgeted overhead. The cash budget is further divisible into budgeted cash receipts, budgeted cash disbursements and budgeted cash. Also see *Financial Budget,* and *Master Budget.*
Operating Cycles	The activities performed within businesses which provide products and services to customers. There are four operating cycles: *Conversion Cycle, Expenditure Cycle, Investment Cycle, Revenue Cycle,* and one *Non-Operating Cycle.*
Operating Income	The total of revenues from operations minus cost of products sold and operating costs (excluding interest expense and income taxes).
Operating Lease	A short-term agreement to rent an asset. Also see *Finance Lease.*
Operating Leverage	The effects that fixed costs have on changes in operating income as changes occur in units sold and hence in contribution margin.
Operating Leverage Factor	The percentage impact on net profit of a percentage change in sales revenue.
Operation	A standardised method or technique that is performed repetitively, often on different materials, resulting in different finished products. Also see *Business Process,* and *Operations Event.*

Operation-Costing System	A hybrid-costing system applied to batches of similar, but not identical, products. Each batch of products is often a variation of a single design, and it proceeds through a sequence of operations, but each batch does not necessarily move through the same operations as other batches. Within each operation, all product units use identical amounts of the operation's resources. Also see *Hybrid Costing*, *Job Costing*, and *Process Costing*.
Operational Feasibility	Resolved by asking the questions: 'Can it be put into operation?' and 'Will it be used if successfully developed?' Also see *Economic Feasibility*, *Feasibility*, and *Technical Feasibility*.
Operational Performance Indicators	See *Performance Measurement System*.
Operations Event	The production of products and or services for customers. Also see *Decision Event*, and *Information Event*.
Opportunity Cost	The contribution to operating income that is forgone or rejected by not using a limited resource in its next-best (productive) alternative use. An opportunity cost is usually expressed in monetary units but it may represent only time. The holding cost of inventory is a special type of opportunity cost since funds tied up in inventory are not available for investment elsewhere. Also see *Decremental Costs*, *Differential Costs*, *Differential Revenues*, *Discretionary Costs*, *Incremental Costs*, *Incremental Revenues*, *Out-of-Pocket Costs*, *Plan Concepts*, *Relevant Costs*, *Sunk Costs*, and *Unavoidable Costs*.
Opportunity Cost of Capital	See *Required Rate of Return*.
Optimum Order Size	An order size that minimises the total ordering and carrying costs.
Option	A contract between two parties giving the taker (buyer) the right but not the obligation to buy or sell a pre-existing underlying asset at a particular price on or before a particular date.
Order Receipt Time	The elapsed time between when the sales department receives a customer order and when the order is placed with the manufacturing (production) department.
Ordering Costs	All the costs of preparing, issuing, and paying purchase orders, plus receiving and inspecting the items included in the purchase order.
Ordinary Share	The class of shares which have no preferential rights as to dividends out of profits or capital on winding up.
Organisation	See *Business*.
Organisation Structure	The arrangement of lines of responsibility between positions in the business.
Out-of-Pocket Costs	The incremental costs that will be incurred if a particular course of action is selected. Also see *Decremental Costs*, *Differential Costs*, *Differential Revenues*, *Discretionary Costs*, *Incremental Costs*, *Incremental Revenues*, *Opportunity Costs*, *Plan Concepts*, *Relevant Costs*, *Sunk Costs*, and *Unavoidable Costs*.
Outcome	1. The predicted economic results of the various possible combinations of actions and events in a decision model. 2. An end result or consequence from an action, negotiation or situation.
Output Unit-Level Costs	The costs of activities performed on each individual unit of a product or service.

Outsourcing	The process of contracting and purchasing products and services from another, different organisation which specialises in that function rather than producing the same products or providing the same services within the business.
Over Absorbed Indirect Costs	See *Over Allocated Indirect Costs*.
Over Allocated Indirect Costs	The allocated amount of indirect costs in an accounting period is greater than the actual (incurred) amount in that period. Also known as Over Applied Indirect Costs, or Over Absorbed Indirect Costs. Also see *Under Allocated Indirect Costs*.
Over Applied Indirect Costs	See *Over Allocated Indirect Costs*.
Over Applied Overhead	See *Over Allocated Indirect Costs*.
Overdraft	See *Bank Overdraft*.
Overhead	The general expenses of a business, such as heating and lighting of premises as distinct from the direct costs of producing an article.
Overhead Costs	See *Indirect Manufacturing Costs*.
Overtime	The wage rate paid to workers (for both direct labour and indirect labour) in excess of their straight-time wage rates. Also known as Overtime Premium.
Overtime Premium	See *Overtime*.
Overtrading	The aggressive expansion of trading operations resulting in borrowings which incur interest that reduce the available working capital. Also see *Working Capital*.
P	
Padding the Budget	The practice of underestimating revenues or overestimating costs so that budget targets are easier to achieve.
Pareto Diagram	A graph that indicates how frequently each type of defect occurs, ordered from the most frequent to the least frequent.
Pareto Optimum	A condition where no individual or institution can be made better off by making another individual or institution worse off. Also see *Nash Equilibrium*.
Pareto Principle	A heuristic that highlights typically 80% of the reward arises from 20% of the effort.
Partial Productivity	A measure of the quantity of output produced divided by the quantity of an individual input used.
Participative Budgeting	An approach to budgeting that uses a joint decision-making process in which the parties set and agree the budget targets. Also see *Authoritative Budgeting*.
Partnership	A form of incorporation or legal structure which is an arrangement between persons to conduct a business and share its profits. Also see *Business, Company, Cooperative, Enterprise, Incorporation, Sole Proprietor*, and *Trust*.
Payback	See *Payback Period Method*.
Payback Period Method	A capital budgeting method that measures the time it will take to recoup, in the form of expected future cash flows, the net initial investment in a project.
PDA	See *Plan-Do-Act*.
P E Ratio	See *Valuation of Shares*.

Peak-Load Pricing	Practice of charging a higher price for the same product or service when the demand for it approaches the physical limit of the capacity to produce that product or service.
Penetrated Market	See *Market Narrowing*.
Penetration Pricing	A strategy for setting the initial price of a new product relatively low to attract market share.
Perfect Knowledge	No-one knows more than anyone else.
Perfectly Competitive Market	A market where there is a homogeneous product with buying prices equal to selling prices and no individual buyers or sellers can affect those prices by their own actions. Also known as a Perfect Market. The outcome of a perfect market is to remove profit since there are no entrepreneurs, oligopolies or monopolies.
Performance Gap	The extent to which a business needs to improve to reach agreed best practice.
Performance Indicator	See *Performance Measurement System*.
Performance Measurement System	1. A system that measures performance by comparing actual results against a pre-determined target. 2. Indicators that provide information about waste relative to volume of production, sales or some other activity.
Performance-Related Pay Systems	1. A payment system that relates pay to some measure of work performance. Also known as Incentive Compensation Systems, Merit Pay, Piecework, or Profit Sharing. 2. An individualised payment system where changes in salary depend upon individual performance appraisal. Also known as Individual Performance-Related Payment System. 3. Also see *Profit Sharing Plan*.
Period Costs	All costs in the income statement other than cost of goods sold. Costs which are expensed in the period they are incurred. Period costs include selling, administrative, and finance costs. Also see *Product Costs*.
Personnel	See *Human Resources*.
Physical Design	A physical design is one phase in a phased approach to systems development; the process of transforming a functional specification or logical design into plans for programs, modules and sub-routines, including detailed program, module, and sub-routine specifications.
Physical Record	A storage record with a specified format and a predefined size.
Physical Resource	The tangible assets of property, plant and equipment. Also see *Economic Resources*, *Human Resources*, *Reputational Resources*, and *Technological Resources*.
Physical Specification	A description of a process that can be implemented in only one physical way.
Physical Units	The units that are currently in production whether fully or partially completed.
Physical View of a System	A description of the actual or proposed implementation. It is implementation-dependent.

Physical-Measure Method	A method that allocates joint costs to joint products on the basis of the relative weight, volume, or other physical measure at the split-off point of total production of these products during the accounting period.
Plagiarism	The absence or incomplete acknowledgement by an author that the information, ideas and facts were obtained from another source. The basic principle is that it should be possible for a reader to check the information and ideas used by going to the original source material. The acknowledgment should be sufficiently accurate to enable the source to be located speedily.
Plan Concepts	This concept relates to the process of making short-term and long-term decisions. For concepts, also see *Control Concepts*. For business functions, also see *Human Resources, Marketing*, and *Production*. For costs, also see *Decremental Costs, Differential Costs, Differential Revenues, Incremental Costs, Imputed Costs, Incremental Revenues, Opportunity Costs, Out-of-Pocket Costs, Pricing, Relevant Costs, Sunk Costs*, and *Unavoidable Costs*.
Plan-Do-Act	The three steps in problem solving and process improvement. 'Plan' is establishing the objectives and creating the processes to deliver the expected output. 'Do' is implementing the new or revised processes. 'Act' is analysing the output or results. A third step is often inserted called 'check' to emphasise comparison of the output with the original specification. PDA is repeated to increase understanding and improve output.
Planning	A broad concept concerned with selecting business goals, predicting results under various alternative ways of achieving those goals, deciding how to attain the desired goals, and communicating the goals and how to attain them to throughout the business.
Poison Pill	A takeover defence strategy aimed at making the target unattractive to the bidder and creating animosity toward the bidder from existing shareholders. This may be accomplished by giving shareholders the right to purchase new shares at a discount, issue preferred shares, or stagger the election of directors. Also see *Shareholder Rights Plan*.
Posting	1. The transfer of an entry or an item from a journal to a ledger in an accounting system. 2. The actual entry or item in a ledger.
Potential Market	See *Market Narrowing*.
Power	The authority or influence that individuals exert over other individuals in a business.
Power Law	In the study of statistical distributions it is a special kind of mathematical relationship between two quantities where the frequency of an event varies as a power of some attribute of that event at least in their upper tail (large events). It underlies the frequency of extremely rare events like stock market crashes, large natural disasters and the distribution of wealth. Also known as the Polynomial Form or Polynomial Function. Also see *Pareto Principle*.
Practical (Available) Capacity	The level of capacity that reduces Theoretical Capacity as a result of unavoidable operating interruptions under normal efficient operating conditions. Examples include scheduled maintenance downtime, and shutdowns for holidays. Also see *Theoretical (Available) Capacity*.
Predatory Pricing	The action of a business to deliberately price below its costs with the intention of driving out competitors and then raising prices.
Predetermined Overhead	See *Indirect Manufacturing Costs*.

Prevention Costs	The costs incurred to preclude the production of products that do not conform to specifications.
Previous Department Costs	See *Transferred-In Costs*.
Price Discount	A reduction in selling price below list selling price to encourage additional customers to make a purchase or existing customers to make increased purchases.
Price Discrimination	The setting of different prices, discounts, services or payment terms for different customers for the same product or service.
Price Elasticity	The impact of price changes on sales volume.
Price Fixing	An arrangement that result in the fixing, control or maintenance of prices for the supply of products and services.
Price-Recovery Component	The change in operating income attributable solely to changes in prices of inputs and outputs between one period and the next.
Price Variance	The difference between (a) the actual price, and (b) the budgeted price, then multiplied by actual quantity of input. Also known as Input Price Variance for direct materials, Labour Rate Variance for direct labour, and 'Variable Overhead Spending Variance for variable manufacturing overhead.
Primary Sector	A classification based on economic development where the economic activity involves the extraction and production of raw materials. Examples include growing wheat and cutting timber. Also see *Secondary Sector*, and *Tertiary Sector*.
Prime Cost	All direct manufacturing costs (that is, direct material and direct labour).
Primitive	See *Primitive Business Process*.
Primitive Business Process	A business process that cannot be subdivided into any further detail. Also see *Business Process*.
Principal and Agent	See *Agency Costs*.
Private Sector	The part of the economy that operates for profit and is not controlled by the government. A for-profit business aims for revenue to exceed expenses by sufficient amount to allow the payment of an appropriate level of dividends to compensate the owner for the risks to which their capital is exposed. Also see *Non-Profit Sector*, and *Public Sector*.
Probability	The likelihood or chance that an event will occur.
Process	See *Business Process*.
Process Costing	A costing system that assigns all production costs to processes or departments and averages them across all units produced. Also see *Hybrid Costing*, *Job Costing*, and *Operation Costing*.
Process-Costing System	A costing system in which the cost object is masses of identical or similar units of a product or service.
Process Improvement	See *Continuous Improvement*.

Procurement (Business Function)	The combined activities of acquiring products or services, including ordering, arranging payment, obtaining transportation, inspection, storage, and disposal. For example, in a manufacturing business procurement deals with obtaining all the raw materials while in a merchandising business procurement is obtaining inventory for resale. Also see *Accounting (Business Function), Distribution (Business Function), Finance (Business Function), Manufacturing (Business Function), Marketing (Business Function), Research and Development (Business Function),* and *Sales (Business Function).*
Product	1. The end result of a natural or mechanical process offered to the marketplace to satisfy a need or want. It may be in the form of raw materials, merchandise, items for internal consumption, fixed assets, ideas, methods or information. 2. An output that has a positive total sales value (or an output that enables a business to avoid incurring costs).
Product Cost	The sum of the costs assigned to a product manufactured or purchased for resale relevant to a specific purpose. In manufacturing direct materials, direct labour and manufacturing overhead as well as costs that are a function of time (e.g. depreciation) can be charged to inventory. Also see *Period Costs.*
Product-Cost Cross-Subsidisation	A costing outcome where one under-costed (over-costed) product results in at least one other product being over-costed (under-costed).
Product Differentiation	A business strategy to offer products or services perceived by its customers to be superior and unique relative to the products or services of its competitors. Also see *Competitive Strategy,* and *Low Cost Leadership.*
Product Diversity	The number of individual product lines produced or merchandised.
Product Group	The categorisation of similar individual products together. Also see *Product Subgroup.*
Product Level Costs	See *Product-Sustaining Costs.*
Product Life Cycle	The elapsed time from conception of a product, initial Research and Development on a product to its abandonment and when customer service and support is no longer offered for that product. The product life cycle comprises (a) market introduction, (b) market growth, (c) market maturity, and (d) market decline (Levitt, 1965). The fourth stage may also be termed market saturation.
Product Mix Decision	A decision about the most appropriate range of products to offer to customers and in what quantities.
Product Over-Costing	A product consumes a low level of resources but is reported to have a high cost per unit.
Product Subgroup	The splitting of a product group into convenient and meaningful separate subordinate subcategories. Also see *Product Group.*
Product-Sustaining Costs	The costs of activities undertaken to support individual products regardless of the number of units or batches in which the units are produced.
Product Under-Costing	A product consumes a high level of resources but is reported to have a low cost per unit.
Production	The acquisition, coordination, and assembly of resources to produce a product or deliver a service.

Production and Delivery Activities	The activities undertaken to produce and deliver the products.
Production Budget	A budget that outlines the number of production units to be manufactured during the budget period to satisfy sales needs and meet inventory requirements.
Production (Business Function)	The acquisition, coordination, and assembly of resources to produce a product or deliver a service. For the Manufacturing (Business Function), also see *Manufacturing (Business Function)*.
Production Chain	See *Economic Development Sector*.
Production Cycle	See *Conversion Cycle*.
Production-Denominator Level	The estimated units of activity in standard cost systems. If the actual production level is greater than the denominator level, the volume variance will be favourable. If actual production is less than the denominator level, then the volume variance will be unfavourable (because of assumed lost sales, loss contribution margin, and lost income).
Production Department	The department that works directly on the products being produced. Also known as the Manufacturing Department.
Production-Volume Variance	The difference between (a) the budgeted fixed overhead, and (b) fixed overhead allocated on the basis of actual output produced. Also known as Denominator-Level Variance, or Output-Level Overhead Variance.
Productive Inputs	See *Factors of Production*.
Productivity	A ratio of outputs produced per unit of input. Both quantities and costs can be used. Higher productivity results from reducing the inputs for a given quantity of outputs or the increasing the outputs for a given quantity of inputs.
Productivity Component	A change in costs attributable to a change in the quantity of inputs used in the current period relative to the quantity of inputs that would have been used in the prior period to produce the quantity of current period output.
Profit	1. An accounting profit is the difference between revenue and the costs of those products or services together with any operating or other expenses. Also see *For-Profit Business*, and *Profit Motivation*. 2. An economic profit is the difference between the total revenue and the opportunity cost for a business.
Profit and Loss Account	A summary of all revenues and expenses including cost of goods sold for the relevant accounting period.
Profit and Loss Statement	A financial statement of an accounting entity that discloses the revenues, expenses, gains and losses arising in a specific period which is expressed as an operating profit or loss with the goal of presenting the information fairly. It answers the questions 'How much money did we make?' and 'What was the quality of our earnings?' Also shown will be income tax, abnormal and extraordinary items. Also known as internationally as an Income Statement. Also known as an Income and Expenditure Statement if the accounting entity is not a business. Also see *Financial Statements*, and *Quality of Earnings*.
Profit Centre	A *Responsibility Centre* where the manager is accountable for revenues and costs. Also see *Cost Centre*, *Investment Centre*, and *Revenue Centre*.

Profit Motivation	See *Profit*, and *Private Sector*.
Profit on Disposal	The profit made when an asset is sold for more than its carrying amount.
Profit Sharing Plan	A plan where a bonus is paid to an employee based on a percentage of the profit of the business.
Profit Volume Graph	A graph that shows the total amount of profit or loss at different sales volumes.
Profitability Index	The present value of cash flows excluding the initial investment divided by the initial investment.
Pro Forma Statements	See *Master Budget*.
Program	1. A set of related instructions or processing elements that meet the requirements stated in a program specification. 2. A complete set of instructions to execute a related set of tasks. 3. To code and debug the instructions or processing elements of the program specifications. 4. Also see *Code, Routine,* and *Software*.
Program Budgeting	A form of budgeting where the various programs undertaken by the business are identified, program objectives are developed and budgets are prepared for each program. Also see *Master Budget*.
Program Evaluation	An examination of the outcomes from an implementation. The evaluation relies on specified and justified criteria. The criteria may be embodied in the existing programme of activities or may need to be defined. Also known as Evaluation.
Programme	1. An outline of proceedings with relevant details. 2. A specially arranged selection of tasks to be accomplished.
Proposal	See *Business Case*.
Proration	The allocation of under allocated manufacturing overhead or over allocated manufacturing overhead proportion to the sizes of the ending account balances in Work-in-Process Inventory account, Finished Goods Inventory account, and Cost of Goods Sold account.
Prospect Theory	A psychologically motivated theory of decision-making which attempts to account for the psychological processes which affect the creation of values or utilities and modifies Expected Utility Theory to account for violations of Expected Utility Theory by assuming that utilities are evaluated relative to a reference (frame) and that a subjective form of probability is used by the decision-maker which will overweight very low and very high probabilities relative to intermediate probabilities. Also see *Bounded Rationality, Expected Utility Theory, Expected Value Theory,* and *Regret Theory*.
Protectionism	The protection of existing industries from competition. It can be achieved by tariffs (on imported products), subsidies, import quotas, and selective industry assistance. In many cases the tariff can be used for government subsidies. The alternative is either trade liberalisation or free trade.

Psychopath	The character traits of this type of person are: (a) glib and superficial; (b) ggocentric and grandiose; (c) lack of remorse or guilt; (d) lack of empathy; (e) deceitful and manipulative; (f) shallow emotions; (g) impulsive; (h) poor behaviour controls; (i) need for excitement; (j) lack of responsibility; (k) early behaviour problems; and (l) adult antisocial behaviour (Hare, 1999).
Public Sector	The delivery of products and services by the government through government departments and authorities, government instrumentalities, and government corporations. Public sector organisations may be (a) direct administration (e.g. departments) funded through taxation based on decisions are determined by government or (b) publicly owned corporations which operate according to commercial criteria using goals set for them by government. Also see *Private Sector,* and *Non-Profit Sector.*
Pull System	A system where production and inventory purchases occur as a result of demands placed by customers. Also see *Push System.*
Punctuated Equilibrium	There are long periods of small, incremental change interrupted by brief periods of discontinuous radical change that alter the industry.
Purchase Order Lead Time	The elapse time between placing an order and its delivery. Also see *Delivery Lead Time, Manufacturing Lead Time, Service Response Time*, and *Waiting Time.*
Purchases Budget	A budget that is used to determine the quantity and cost of products that needs to be purchased during the budget year.
Purchasing Activities	See *Procurement.*
Purchasing Costs	The cost of raw materials and products acquired from suppliers including incoming freight or transportation costs.
Pure Rate Variance	The difference between (a) the actual hourly wage rate, and (b) the standard hourly wage rate, then multiplied by the number of standard hours allowed.
Push System	The products that are purchased or the merchandising inventory that is acquired to meet inventory levels rather than to satisfy actual customer demand. Also see *Pull System.*
PV Graph	A graph that shows how changes in the quantity of units sold affect operating income.
Q	
Qualified Available Market	See *Market Narrowing.*
Qualitative	A complete or partial description of characteristics or properties.
Qualitative Characteristics of Accounting Information	The concepts that accounting information must satisfy. Also see *Economic Substance, Materiality of Information, Relevance of Information*, and *Reliability of Information.*
Qualitative Factors	The outcomes that are relevant to a decision that cannot be expressed effectively in numerical terms. Also see *Non-Financial Factors.*
Quality	The total features and characteristics of a product made or a service performed according to specifications to satisfy customers at the time of purchase and during use

Quality Accreditation	A formal recognition that a series of quality standards set out in the international ISO 9000 series have been satisfied.
Quality of Conformance	The degree to which a product meets its formal design specifications. Also see *Quality of Design*.
Quality of Design	The degree to which the design specification of a product meets customer expectations. Also see *Quality of Conformance*.
Quality of Earnings	1. The amount of earnings attributable to higher sales or lower costs rather than artificial profits created by outside sources including accounting anomalies. For example, inflating the value of the inventory. 2. The calculation of earnings conservatively rather than using aggressive accounting policies. Also known as Earnings Quality, and Quality in Reported Earnings. Also see *Profit and Loss*.
Quantitative	The numerical measurement of anything by counting or estimation.
Quantitative Factors	The outcomes that are relevant to a decision that can be expressed effectively in numerical terms using measurements.
Quantity Discounts	The price reductions provided by suppliers when businesses order large quantities.
R	
R&D	See *Research and Development (Business Function)*.
Random	Events that occur by chance. They are caused by randomness-prone factors (namely people). Humans are adept at finding purpose and patterns where none exist (e.g. winning and losing streaks). Also see *Random Walk*.
Random Walk	The occurrence of an event determined by a series of random movements or events. For example, share prices change randomly, making it impossible to predict stock prices and the availability of new information is seemingly random as well. Also see *Efficient Market Hypothesis*, and *Technical Analysis*.
Rate of Return	See *Real Rate of Return*.
Rate Variance	See *Price Variance*.
Raw and In Process Inventory Account	A ledger account where movements in both raw material and work in process are recorded under a backflush costing system.
Raw Material Inventory	The items, components or articles that are used in production.
Reach of Information	The number of people who participate in the sharing of that information. The richness vs. reach concept means that the richer the information is the less reach it has and vice versa. However, e-business tends to eliminate the richness versus reach trade off. Also see *Richness of Information*.
Real Rate of Return	The rate of return demanded to cover investment risk (with no inflation). It has a risk-free element and a business-risk element.
Real Time Reporting	A system that allows employees to access up-to-date information when they require it.
Realisation Rate	The final fee charged to the client as a percentage of the billing system fee based on the chargeout rates of the business.

Reciprocal Services	The services that are provided between support departments.
Reciprocal Services Method	A cost allocation method that fully recognises the mutual services provided among all support departments.
Reconciliation	A comparison of the cash record of the business with the record kept by the banks.
Reconstruction	The form of reconstruction includes share splits, consolidations, capital reduction (partial repayments) schemes of arrangement, and name changes.
Recovery	See *Turnaround.*
Recoverable Amount	The higher of an asset's fair value, less costs to sell (sometimes called net selling price) and its value in use. Also see *Impairment of Assets,* and *Mark to Market (MTM).*
Redundancy	The creation of acceptable, practical alternatives if routine arrangements are disrupted. For example, the bus has two ticket machines for passengers to use. Also see *Data Redundancy.*
Re-Engineering	See *Business Process Reengineering.*
Refined Costing System	A costing system that reduces the use of broad averages for assigning the cost of resources to cost objects (jobs, products, services) and provides better measurement of the costs of indirect resources used by different cost objects—no matter how differently various cost objects use indirect resources.
Reflection	To consider the assumptions or premises behind particular beliefs, attitudes and behaviour. These may involve the structure of the world, expectations on what ought to be done, and the causes or motives for events. Personal transformation may result from reflection.
Regression Analysis	A statistical method to estimate the average amount of change in the dependent variable associated with a unit change in one or more independent variables.
Regret Theory	A psychologically motivated theory of decision-making which attempt to account for the psychological processes which affect the creation of values or utilities and modifies Expected Utility Theory to account for violations of expected utility theory by considering the anticipated reactions of the decision-maker to various outcomes, predicting that when the difference between outcomes is large the feeling of regret is overweighted. Also see *Bounded Rationality, Expected Utility Theory, Expected Value Theory*, and *Prospect Theory.*
Reject	See *Error.*
Relative Sales Value Method	A method of allocating joint cost to joint products in proportion to their sales value at the split-off point.
Relevance of Information	A qualitative characteristic of accounting information. Information must be useful to users for making a decision.
Relevant Costs	The expected future costs that differ among alternative courses of action being considered.
Relevant Range	The band of normal volume or activity level in which there is a specific relationship between the level of activity or volume and the cost in question and the particular cost behaviour pattern is assumed valid.
Relevant Revenues	The expected future revenues that differ among alternative courses of action being considered. Also see *Economic Substance, Materiality of Information,* and *Reliability of Information.*

Reliability of Information	A qualitative characteristic of accounting information. Information is presented faithfully without bias or undue error and represents the underlying transactions and events. Also see *Economic Substance, Materiality of Information,* and *Relevant Information.*
Rent	A system of payment for the (temporary) use of something owned by someone else. For example rent to use premises. Also see *Economic Rent,* and *Ricardian Rent.*
Reorder Point	The quantity or level of inventory on hand that triggers a new purchase order.
Replicability	A resource position barrier. If acquisition of resources is not possible, rivals may want to grow the resources inside their organisation. The more complex the organisational routines are, the more difficult it will be to replicate them. Also see *Appropriability, Durability,* and *Substitutability.*
Report Form	See *Narrative Form.*
Reputational Resource	The intangible assets of brand name, relationships with key stakeholders and goodwill. Also see *Economic Resources, Human Resources, Physical Resources,* and *Technological Resources.*
Required Rate of Return (RRR)	The minimum acceptable annual rate of return on an investment. Also known as Discount Rate, Hurdle Rate, Cost of Capital, or Opportunity Cost of Capital.
Resale Price Maintenance	A supplier dictates the minimum price which a product or service is to be resold by a buyer in the wholesale or retail market.
Research	Scholarly or scientific investigation or inquiry where the outcome is uncertain.
Research and Development (Business Function)	The generation of ideas and invention of techniques related to new products, services, or processes. Also see *Accounting (Business Function), Distribution (Business Function), Finance (Business Function), Manufacturing (Business Function), Marketing (Business Function), Procurement (Business Function),* and *Sales (Business Function).*
Research and Development Costs	All the costs incurred in the development of new products and processes.
Residual Income (RI)	The profit after subtracting an imputed interest charge using the required rate of return on an accounting measure of investment.
Residual Value	The value of the business at the end of the forecast period.
Resource	A person, asset, material, or capital which can be used to accomplish a goal which is under the control of the business and has value to the business. For the categories of resources, also see *Physical Resources, Economic Resources, Reputational Resources, Technological Resources,* and *Human Resources.* For the two broad types, also see *Intangible Resources,* and *Tangible Resources.* For the hierarchy of resources, also see *Capabilities,* and *Core Competencies.*
Resource Dependency Theory	A study of how the external resources of organisations affect the behaviour of the organisation. External resources may be available through procurement, contractual arrangements or alliances.
Resource Driver	A cost driver used to estimate the cost of resources consumed by an activity. Also see *Cost Driver.*
Resource Position Barrier	A factor which makes it difficult to imitate a resource or to substitute an acceptable equivalent. In general, there are four resource position barriers. Also see *Appropriability, Durability, Replicability,* and *Substitutability.*

Resource Sector	The mining or extraction of raw materials often, but not always with some simple ancillary processes, such as crushing or refining. For example, exploration and mining for gold and refining it into ingots. Also see *Manufacturing Sector, Merchandising Sector,* and *Service Sector.*
Responsibility Accounting	A system that measures the plans, budgets, actions, and actual results of each responsibility centre to hold managers responsible for the activities and performance of their area of the business.
Responsibility Centre	A part, segment, or subunit of a business whose manager is accountable for a specified set of activities and performance. There are four kinds of Responsibility Centre. Also see *Cost Centre, Investment Centre, Profit Centre,* and *Revenue Centre.*
Retail	A business that resells products directly to the public.
Return on Investment (ROI)	An accounting measure of profit divided by an accounting measure of investment. Also see *Accrual Accounting Rate of Return.*
Return on Investment Pricing	The selling price determined by using the required rate of return to calculate the mark-up on cost.
Return on Sales	The percentage of each sales dollar that remains as profit after all expenses are covered, calculated as profit divided by sales revenue.
Revenue	The inflows of assets (usually cash or accounts receivable) received for products or services provided to customers.
Revenue Allocation	The allocation of revenues that are related to a particular revenue object but cannot be traced to it in an economically feasible (cost-effective) way.
Revenue Centre	A *Responsibility Centre* where the manager is accountable for only revenues generated by that unit. Also see *Cost Centre, Investment Centre,* and *Profit Centre.*
Revenue Cycle	The business activities and information processing operations associated with providing products and services to customers and collecting payment for them. Also known as the Collection Cycle. Also see *Conversion Cycle, Expenditure Cycle, Investment Cycle, Non-Operating Cycle,* and *Operating Cycle.*
Revenue Driver	A variable that causally affects revenues. For example, volume of product sold.
Revenue Object	Anything for which a separate measurement of revenue is desired.
Reward System	All the processes, systems and practices that are used to provide levels of pay and benefits to employees.
Rework	A finished product that does not meet the specifications required by customers for finished units that is subsequently repaired and then sold as a finished product.
Ricardian Rent	A type of economic rent created by variation in resource quality. It is the return on a productive resource (e.g. land or a product) that is greater than the amount necessary to keep it producing or in excess of what would have been the return except for some unique factor. It is equal to the economic advantage obtained by using the site in its most productive use, relative to the advantage obtained by using marginal (i.e., the best rent-free) land for the same purpose, given the same inputs of labor and capital. Also see *Contract Rent, Economic Rent, Factors of Production,* and *Rent.*

Richness of Information	There are six main aspects that define the richness of information and these are: (a) bandwidth or amount of information; (b) customisation of information to an individual buyer; (c) interactivity between buyer and seller; (d) reliability; (e) security; and (f) currency (or how current or up to-date the information is). The richness versus reach concept means that the richer the information is the less reach it has and vice versa. However, e-business tends to eliminate the richness versus reach trade off. Also see *Reach of Information*.
Risk	A set of uncertain outcomes that involve loss, catastrophe, or other undesirable outcomes. Risk can also be viewed as: 1. Volatility compared to either an average such as an average or historical rate of return or to expectations. 2. Tolerance for risk where a either lower risk or a longer horizon should be considered.
Rolling Budget	A budget or plan that is always available for a specified future period by adding a period (e.g. month, quarter or year) to the period that just ended and dropping the period just completed. Also known as Continuous Budget.
Root Cause	An initiating cause of a causal chain which leads to the outcome or effect of interest such as activities being performed and costs being incurred. There may be one or several initiating causes.
Routine	1. The regular and predictable patterns of activity which are made up of a sequence of coordinated actions by individuals. They may result from repeated interaction (learning) between people and other resources or be documented procedure descriptions provided by the business. 2. A set of instructions for a specific task. Also see *Code*, *Program*, and *Software*.
Rule of Thumb	See *Heuristic*.
S	
Safety Margin	The difference between the budgeted sales revenue and the break-even sales revenue.
Safety Stock	The inventory held at all times to cover any above average usage or demand.
Sales (Business Function)	The exploration of customer needs to encourage them to make an offer for products or services which is accepted by the business. Also see *Accounting (Business Function)*, *Distribution (Business Function)*, *Finance (Business Function)*, *Manufacturing (Business Function)*, *Marketing (Business Function)*, *Research and Development (Business Function)*, and *Procurement (Business Function)*.
Sales Budget	A detailed summary of the estimated sales units and revenues from the business' products or services for the budgeted period.
Sales Forecasting	The process of estimating the quantity and price of each product that will be sold in the budget period.
Sales Mix	The relative proportion of each type of product or service that constitute total unit sales.
Sales-Mix Variance	The difference between (a) budgeted contribution margin for the actual sales mix, and (b) budgeted contribution margin for the budgeted sales mix.
Sales Price Variance	The difference between (a) the actual sales price and (b) the budgeted sales price, then multiplied by actual sales volume.

Sales-Quantity Variance	The difference between (a) the budgeted contribution margin based on actual units sold of all products at the budgeted-mix and (b) the contribution margin in the static budget (which is based on the budgeted units of all products to be sold at the budgeted mix).
Sales Value at Split-Off Method	A method that allocates joint costs to joint products on the basis of the relative total sales value at the split-off point of the total production of these products during the accounting period. Also see *Split-Off Point*.
Sales Variance	See *Sales-Mix Variance, Sales Price Variance, Sales-Quantity Variance*, and *Sales Volume Variance*.
Sales-Volume Variance	The difference between (a) the flexible-budget amount and (b) the corresponding static-budget amount.
Schedule	An organised list. The items in the list and their arrangement depend upon the purpose of the list. For example a lease schedule will list the principal and repayments reducing for the life of the list. A depreciation schedule will list the asset details and their depreciation details for a twelve month period.
Schedule of Goods Sold	A report detailing the Cost of Goods Sold which is equal to the cost of products manufactured adjusted for changes in Finished Goods Inventory and under/over applied overhead.
Schedule of Products Manufactured	A report detailing the cost of direct materials, direct labour and manufacturing overhead applied to work in process during the period, and showing the changes to the Work in Process Inventory.
Schematic (Schematic Representation)	A diagram that specifies each of the components and depicts how each component is connected to the other components. It allows the individual components to be depicted in the abstract without specifying how they are instantiated and may give some indication of the sequencing of events.
Schumpeterian Competition	The attempt to gain a decisive competitive advantage by pursuing technological innovation.
Science	A method of inquiry requiring a theory, the use of available knowledge, the gathering evidence and relating the findings to available knowledge with the use of specific principles of reasoning. Invention, sagacity, genius are required at every step; it is not enough to rely on experience alone. In most cases it features systematic observation, measurement and recording which allows it to be repeated. The hypothetico-deductive method uses hypotheses, and the formulation, testing, and if necessary modification of the hypothesis. Also see *Natural Science*, and *Social Science*.
Scrap	The residual material remaining after making a product that cannot be used in making the next product.
Second-Order Learning	See *Double-Loop Learning*.
Secondary Sector	A classification based on economic development where the economic activity involves the transformation of raw or intermediate materials into finished products. Examples include steel manufacturing and home building. Also see *Primary Sector*, and *Tertiary Sector*.

Sector	1. An economic development sector. Also see *Primary Sector, Secondary Sector,* and *Tertiary Sector.* 2. An employer sector. Also see *Micro Business, Small Business, Medium Business,* and *Large Business.* 3. An industry sector. Also see *Manufacturing Sector, Merchandising Sector, Resources Sector,* and *Services Sector.* 4. An ownership sector. Also see *Non-profit sector, Private Sector,* and *Public Sector.*
Segment	A part of the business about which management seeks data. Examples of segments are divisions, product lines within a division, factory producing a product, sales (geographical) territory. Also see *Segment Margin.*
Segment Margin	The segment contribution margin remaining after covering the direct fixed costs of the segment. It is the amount the segment contributes toward the common fixed costs and profit. Also known as Segment Income.
Segment Performance	A breakdown of operations showing revenue, operating profitability, (before tax and interest), return on allocated assets, contribution to overall revenue and profit.
Seigniorage	1. The profit that results from the difference between the face value of that money and the cost of printing money. 2. The total amount of a currency in circulation which can be used to borrow against.
Self-Managed Team	A work team that has wide responsibilities to manage all aspects of a particular process.
Sell	See *Assignment.*
Selling Expenses	See *Selling, General and Administration Expenses.*
Selling, General and Administration Expenses (SG&A)	The cost of marketing and distributing the products or services of the business.
Selling-Price Variance	See *Sales Price Variance.*
Semi-Variable Cost	See *Mixed Cost.*
Sensitivity Analysis	A what-if technique that managers use to examine how an outcome will change if the original predicted data are not achieved or if an underlying assumption changes.
Sensemaking	A cognitive activity that interactively considers one or more mental models and phenomena. It occurs when an individual finds shortcomings in either the mental model they want to use or in the data they possess (e.g. an observation, a situation or an understanding of events).
Separable Processing Costs	All the costs (manufacturing, marketing, distribution, and so on) incurred beyond the split-off point that are assignable to each of the specific products identified at the split-off point. Also see *Split-Off Point.*
Sequential Allocation Method	See *Step-Down Method.*
Sequential Tracking	The recording of the journal entries occurs in the same order as actual purchases and progress in production.
Served Market	See *Market Narrowing.*

Service Delivery Outcomes	Measurements of the effect of program on the recipients (end users). Also see *Balanced ScoreCard, Critical Success Factors,* and *Key Performance Indicators.*
Service Department	See *Support Department.*
Service Level Agreement	A contract between two units of a business or between a business and the vendor providing the service to establish the nature of the service that will be provided and the responsibilities of both.
Service Response Time	The elapsed time between an order being placed by the customer and it being delivered to the customer. Also see *Delivery Lead Time, Manufacturing Lead Time,* and *Purchase Order Lead Time.*
Service Sector	The provision of advice or assistance such as help, utility or care to customers instead of a product. An example of advice is designing an advertisement. The advice or assistance may involve determining eligibility and delivering assistance against program or in accordance with contractual arrangements. An example is determining eligibility for disability income assistance. Also see *Manufacturing Sector, Merchandising Sector,* and *Service Sector.*
Service-Sustaining Costs	The costs of activities undertaken to support individual services.
Set Over	See *Assignment.*
Setup Time	The time taken to prepare the machine and make materials available before processing can commence.
SG&A	See *Selling, General and Administration Expenses.*
Share Registry	An organisation that handles the administration of an issuer's securities. This includes maintaining the register of security holders, recording transfers of interest in securities, posting documents to security holders.
Share Valuation	See *Valuation of Shares.*
Shared Services	The concentration into a separate unit of support services that are typically replicated in the individual units of a decentralised business so they serve multiple internal customers.
Shareholder Agreement	Specifies the voting rights for shares, how they may or may not be sold, and how they may be valued. This agreement should reflect the expectations of shareholders on how the business should be owned and managed. Also see *Buy-Sell Agreement.*
Shareholder Rights Plan	A target company in a takeover may issue rights to shareholders to purchase common or preferred shares if a threshold percentage of shares is held by same beneficial owner. A hostile takeover then becomes considerably more expensive. Also see *Poison Pill.*
Shareholder Value	1. The value that the shareholders or owners place on the business. 2. The market capitalisation of the business. 3. The expectation that the business return should outperform certain benchmarks such as the cost of capital for similar risk.
Shareholder Value Added	The basic calculation is net operating profit after tax minus the cost of capital from the issuance of debt and equity, based on the weighted average cost of capital of the business.
Short Term	Decisions involving periods of one year or less. Also see *Long Term.*
Shortage Costs	See *Stock-out Costs.*

Shrinkage Costs	The costs that result from theft by outsiders, embezzlement by employees, misclassifications, and clerical errors.
Silo Mentality	An employee gives priority to the needs of the employee's own department. Also see *Information Silo*.
Single-Loop Learning,	Individuals, groups, or organizations modify their actions according to the difference between expected and obtained outcomes. Also see *Double-Loop Learning*.
Single-Rate Method	An allocation method that allocates costs in each cost pool to cost objects using the same rate per unit of a single allocation base.
Six Sigma	A business improvement methodology which uses a structured approach involving rigorous data analysis and a unique leadership model.
Six Thinking Hats	Dividing the thinking process into six parts symbolised by six hats (De Bono, 1986/1999). Everyone wears the same coloured hat at the same time to focus on the same dimension: White (neutral or objective); Red (emotion); Black (cautious or careful); Yellow (optimistic); Green (creativity and new ideas); Blue (organising and controlling the other hats).
Skill	A narrow, domain-specific ability. Also see *Ability, Competency,* and *Human Capital*.
Skimming Pricing	A strategy of setting the initial product price high and reaping high short-term profits on a new product.
Small Business	The definition is country dependent. As a guide it is a business which employs less than 50 employees. (Europe also considers turnover and balance sheet details.) Also known as Small Enterprise. Also see *Large Business, Medium Business,* and *Micro Business*.
SME	See *Small Business* and *Medium Business*.
Social Contract-Based Ethical Theories	An ethical theory of morality based on ceding some individual rights and agreeing to some common rules to have their lives protected by law. The rules may offer only a minimal morality. Also see *Aretaic Turn Ethical Theories, Consequential Ethical Theories,* and *Obligation-Based Ethical Theories*.
Social Science	The scientific study of human interaction in society, their social relationships and their changes over time in which individuals and groups make rational and subjective valuations about meaning, self-interest and choices. Also see *Natural Science,* and *Science*.
Socio-Technical View of the Business	A socio-technical view of the business focuses on the way interactions between humans restrict or shape interactions between humans and technology. It consists of three views of the business: (a) a technical/rational emphasizes the precise organization of tasks into jobs and their execution; (b) a behavioural view that emphasizes how the organisation can adapt to its external and internal environment; and (c) a cognitive view which emphasises how the organisation learns and applies knowledge and how well managers manage new situations.
Softcopy	Data in an electronic or digital format. Usually the format depends upon the software application that created the file. Also see *Hardcopy*.
Software	A general term used to describe the coded instructions (programs) that control hardware. Also see *Code, Program,* and *Routine*.
Software Testing	Software testing comprises a sequence of tests: (a) unit; (b) function; (c) system; (d) integration with related systems; and (e) user acceptance. It also consists of different types of tests (a) volume or load testing; (b) error handling; and (c) system failure and recovery.

Sole Proprietor	A form of incorporation or legal structure which has an individual trading with full liability for the debts of the business. Also see *Business, Company, Cooperative, Enterprise, Incorporation, Partnership,* and *Trust.*
SOP	See *Standard Operating Procedures.*
Source and Application of Funds	See *Statement of Changes in Equity.*
Source Document	An original record that initiates and supports journal entries in an accounting system.
Spare Capacity	See *Idle Capacity.*
Specialisation (Business Function)	The allocation of different business functions to separate, individual employees. Also see *Generalisation.*
Spin	The art of manipulating facts to gain attention, make the client and the client's project appear in the best light and enhance the client's interests. Spin may include immediate and decisive action detailing the available information to avoid speculative fear and loathing filling the vacuum from media or individuals.
Split-Off Point	The stage in a joint-production process when two or more products become separately identifiable. Also see *Joint Products.*
Spoilage	A unit of production that does not meet the specifications required by customers for an acceptable product and is discarded or sold at a reduced price. Also see *Abnormal Spoilage.*
Staff	An employee who provide advice and assistance to line management. Examples include an accountant, a payroll clerk, and an information technology help desk employee.
Staff Manager	A manager who provides advice and assistance to line managers. They are indirectly involved in the operations of the business. Examples include a management accountant, an information systems manager, and a human resources manager.
Stakeholder	An individual or group of people who can influence the business. Traditionally, the stakeholders identified are: (a) customers; (b) shareholders; (c) suppliers; (d) employee unions; (e) financial institutions; (f) government agencies; and (g) the community. Competitors are not stakeholders. Also see *Customer.*
Stand-Alone Cost-Allocation Method	A method that uses product-specific information on the products in the bundle as weights for allocating the bundled revenues to the individual products.
Standard	1. A carefully determined price, cost, or quantity that is used as a benchmark for judging performance. It is usually expressed on a per unit basis. 2. Benchmarks or expectations of learning that have been established with stakeholders and include all the factors that influence the consistency and relevance of qualifications. 3. Also see *Standards.*
Standard Cost	A carefully determined cost of a unit of output based on estimates of the cost of material, labour and overhead resources that should be used to make one unit of product.

Standard Costing System	A costing system that traces direct costs to output produced by multiplying the standard prices or standard rates by the standard quantities of inputs allowed for actual outputs produced and allocates indirect costs on the basis of the standard overhead-cost rates multiplied by the standard quantities of the allocation bases allowed for the actual outputs produced. Standard costs of direct material and direct labour are recorded in the Work-in-Process Inventory. Cost variances are computed and production costs are entered into Work-in-Process Inventory at their standard amounts.
Standard Cost Variance	The difference between (a) the actual cost, and (b) the budgeted cost or standard cost.
Standard Direct Labour Quantity	The number of labour hours needed to manufacture one unit of a product.
Standard Input	A carefully determined quantity of input required for one unit of output.
Standard Labour Rate	The total hourly cost of wages including on-costs.
Standard Material Price	The total delivered cost of direct materials required to produce one unit of a product after deducting any quantity discounts.
Standard Material Quantity	The total amount of direct material required to produce one unit of a product.
Standard Operating Procedures	A set of mandatory instructions explicitly stating the sequence of activities to be performed and describing the means for performing the tasks. Different Standing Operating Procedures may be defined by different business units for the same task.
Standard Price	A carefully determined price that a business expects to pay for a unit of input.
Standards	1. An approved set of desirable practices for ensuring consistency in performance, methods and human practices. 2. A published description of conformance requirements having mandatory compliance authority. 3. Also see *International Organisation for Standardisation*. 4. Also see *Standard*.
Startup (Business Cycle)	The inception or acquisition of the business until the general purpose financial statements is produced for the first year. The four stages of the business cycle are *Startup, Growth, Maturity,* and *Decline*. Also see *Business Cycle,* and *Economic Cycle*.
Statement of Changes in Equity	A financial statement of an accounting entity that summarises the resources made available to finance the activities for the period and the uses to which the resources have been put. Also known as a Funds Statement or a Statement of Sources and Application of Funds. Also see *Financial Statements*.
Statement of Comprehensive Income for the Period	See *Profit and Loss Statement*.
Statement of Financial Position as at the end of the Period	See *Balance Sheet*.

Statement Form	See *Narrative Form*.
Static Budget	A detailed budget based on the level of output planned at the start of the budget period.
Static-Budget Variance	The difference between (a) an actual result and (b) the corresponding budgeted amount in the static budget.
Statistical Control Chart	A plot of the variable of interest across time compared with statistically determined upper and lower critical values. For example, it can be used to highlight variances that should be investigated.
Step Cost Function	A cost function in which the cost remains the same over various ranges of the level of activity, but the cost increases by discrete amounts (that is, increases in steps) as the level of activity changes from one range to the next.
Step-Down Method	A method of allocating support department costs that partially recognises the services provided by one support department to another support department. Also known as Sequential Allocation Method.
Step (Fixed) Cost	A cost that remains fixed over a wide range of activity levels but jumps to a different amount for levels outside that range. Also see *Fixed Cost, Mixed Cost,* and *Variable Cost.*
Stock	Business distinguishes between the units of measurement used for quantities that are stocks and those that are flows. A stock is measured at a particular point in time, and represents a quantity existing at that point in time (usually at a particular date) which is accumulated over time by inflows and/or depleted by outflows (e.g. inventory on hand at a physical stocktake and in the balance sheet). Some accounting entries may be represented both as a stock or as a flow (e.g. capital). Also see *Flow*.
Stock-out Costs	The costs that result when a business is unable to supply a particular item for which there is customer demand. The business must act to meet that demand or suffer the costs of not meeting it.
Stock Turnover	If the flow value of an economic activity is divided by the average stock value during an accounting period, we obtain a measure of the number of turnovers (or rotations) of a stock in that accounting period. Also see *Flow,* and *Stock.*
Story	A fiction with a beginning, middle and end featuring characters (protagonists, antagonists, heroes, victims etc) with dramatic tension, a temporal ordering of events and a point to give meaning to the story. Also known as Narrative. Also see *Micro Narrative.*
Strategic Alliance	A formalised cooperative arrangement between two or more parties involving the sharing of resources and activities to enhance the strategies of all participants. Also see *Joint Venture,* and *Partnership.*
Strategic Business Unit	A profit centre or investment centre that has its own clearly defined strategies and markets.
Strategic Cost Management	Cost management that specifically focuses on strategic issues.
Strategic Performance Measurement System	A system that translates strategy into an integrated set of financial and non-financial measure across a range of perspectives.
Strategic Planning	The long-term planning to achieve the objectives of the business.

Strategy	The specification of how a business matches its capabilities with the opportunities in the marketplace to accomplish its objectives.
Strategy Implementation	The execution of plans to support the strategy and act upon feedback.
Strategy Map	The establishment of cause and effect relationships between intangible assets and tangible value associated with accomplishing strategic objectives. (Kaplan & Norton, 2004).
Structured Systems Analysis (SSA)	The top-down approach to all phases of the systems development life cycle, featuring graphic tools, an awareness of classical problems, and a structured methodology.
Suboptimal Decision-making	A decision in which the benefit to one subunit is more than offset by the costs or loss of benefits to the business as a whole. Also see *Dysfunctional Decision-Making*.
Subsidiary (Company)	A business that is controlled by another separate business. The controlled business may be a private or public company, or a state-owned enterprise.
Subsidiary Ledger	A ledger containing only the accounts for a particular class of assets or liabilities which has a corresponding control account in the general ledger. Ledger entries are then posted to the subsidiary ledger and the total is then posted to the general ledger reducing the volume of entries in the general ledger. For example, there is a subsidiary ledger for accounts receivable. Also see *General Ledger*, *Ledger*, and *Ledger Account*.
Substitutability of Resources	A resource position barrier. The extent to which a resource has an acceptable equivalent. Rareness and difference will determine the degree of substitution. For example, fashion designers have differences in approach and style but only a limited number of fashion designers would be considered by an international fashion label. Also see *Appropriability*, *Durability*, and *Replicability*.
Subsystem	A grouping of several related processes in a system which comprises a major stage or results in a significant output and has its own goal as does a subsystem. A system usually contains two or more subsystems. Also see *System*.
Summation Notation	1. SUM X Squared: First square each score, then add the squared values. 2. (SUM X) Squared: First sum the scores, then square the total. 3. SUM(X - C) Squared: First subtract the constant C from each score then square each of values. Finally add the squared numbers.
Sunk Costs	The recognition that past costs that are unavoidable because they cannot be changed no matter what action is taken. Also known as Unavoidable Costs. Also see *Decremental Cost*, *Differential Costs*, *Differential Revenues*, *Imputed Costs*, *Incremental Revenues*, *Opportunity Costs*, *Out-of-Pocket Costs*, *Plan Concepts*, *Relevant Costs*, *Sunk Costs*, and *Unavoidable Costs*.
Super-Variable Costing	See *Throughput Costing*.
Supplier Performance Index (SPI)	The ratio of supplier activity costs to the total purchase price.
Supply Chain	The interlinked customers and suppliers that work together to convert, distribute and sell products and services among themselves, leading to specific end products. Also see *Bullwhip Effect*.

Supply Chain Management	The management of key business processes associated with the flow of products, services, and information from the initial sources of materials and services to the delivery of products to customers, regardless of whether those activities occur in the same business or in other businesses.
Supply Costs	The costs of sourcing and managing incoming parts, assemblies, articles and supplies.
Support Department	An internal department that provides services that assist other (operating or support) internal departments in the business. It does not directly work on producing products but is necessary for the manufacturing processes to occur. Also known as Service Department.
Support Department Cost Allocation	The process of reassigning all support department costs to the production departments.
Survivor Syndrome	The remaining employees who survived a downsizing or a takeover are overburdened and exhausted and avoid taking risks.
Sustainability	1. The ability to continue operations under the current internal arrangements and external conditions. 2. An approach that considers the interrelated impacts of their activities on the broader economy, the environment and society.
Sustainable Development	Development that meets the needs of the present without compromising the ability of future generations to meet their own needs. This requires consideration of the needs of the poor and the limitations of the state of technology and social organisation on the ability of the environment to meet future needs.
Sustaining Innovation	An innovation that brings to the market a better product or service than is available in that market which the business could sell for higher margins to its best customers. A sustaining innovation may be either a simple, incremental, year-to-year improvement or a dramatic, breakthrough technology. Also see *Disruptive Innovation*, *Innovation*, *Invention*, and *Sustaining Innovation*.
SWOT Analysis	The identification of the perceived strengths, weaknesses, opportunities and threats facing the business in the short and medium term.
System	1. Strict view: The processing of data to produce outputs that satisfy a major organisational goal. 2. Broad view: A means of grouping independent yet related functions together which are organised to form an integral whole to achieve a common objective. The functions can be a set of interdependent devices, rules, and/or procedures (automated, manual or both). 3. A system produces outputs which are significant and useful in their own right. Also see *Subsystem*.

T

T Account	An account set out with debit entries usually recorded on the left and credit entries usually recorded on the right. There is a horizontal line at the top where the account name is written. The debit and credit columns are separated by a vertical line. Also see *Account Form*, and *Narrative Form*.
Tactical Decisions	A decision that does not require significant or permanent resource commitments and that can be changed or reversed quickly.
Tag	A user selected categorisation term. Also see *Keyword*.

Takeover	The acquisition of the target company by another company (the bidder) by purchasing the target company's shares either on-market or off-market. Also see *Friendly Takeover*, *On-Market*, *Off-Market*, and *Hostile Takeover*.
Tangible Benefit	A benefit capable of being measured and expressed as a monetary amount. Also see *Benefit*, *Cost*, *Cost Benefit*, *Intangible Benefit*, *Intangible Cost*, *Intangible Resource*, *Tangible Cost*, and *Tangible Resource*.
Tangible Cost	A cost capable of being measured and expressed as a monetary amount. Tangible costs include: (a) raw material costs; (b) finished goods costs; (c) inventory holding costs; (d) selling costs; (e) administrative costs; (f) infrastructure costs; and (g) environmental costs. Also see *Benefit*, *Cost*, *Cost Benefit*, *Intangible Benefit*, *Intangible Cost*, *Intangible Resource*, *Tangible Cost*, and *Tangible Resource*.
Tangible Resource	The visible and quantifiable assets of a business. Also see the two forms tangible resources namely *Economic Resources*, and *Physical Resources*.
Target Cost Per Unit	The estimated long-run cost per unit of a product or service that enables the business to achieve its target operating income per unit when selling at the target price. Target cost per unit is the target unit price minus target operating income per unit.
Target Costing	A system of profit planning and cost management which determines the life cycle cost at which a proposed product must be produced to generate the desired level of profit based on the anticipated selling price. Also see *Life Cycle Costing*.
Target Market	See *Market Narrowing*.
Target Operating Income Per Unit	The operating income that a business aims to earn per unit of a product or service sold.
Target Rate Of Return On Investment	The target annual operating income that a business aims to achieve divided by invested capital.
Target Pricing	See *Target Costing*.
Target Selling Price	The anticipated selling price for a product or service based on market considerations and the strategic objectives for the product that potential customers will pay.
Task Analysis	See *Time and Motion Studies*.
Taxation	The legislation and compliance with business income tax, capital gains, fringe benefits, goods and services tax, payroll tax, personal income tax, resource rent tax and other taxes.
Team-Based Incentive Schemes	The rewarding of individuals when their work team exceeds certain performance targets.
Technology Adoption Life Cycle	The population is divided into the (a) innovators, (b) early adopters, (c) early majority, (d) late majority and (e) laggards. Also see *Chasm Theory*.
Technical Analysis	The method of evaluating securities by analysing statistics generated by market activity, such as past prices and volume suggesting that the future price of a share can be forecasted using historical information. Also see *Efficient Market Hypothesis*, *Fundamental Analysis*, and *Random Walk*.

Technical Feasibility	Resolved by asking the question: Can reliable hardware, software (operating system and application) and resources be obtained to solve the problem? Also see *Economic Feasibility, Feasibility Study,* and *Operational Feasibility.*
Technical Skill	An operational skill necessary to perform certain work or certain tasks and may include learning activities.
Technological Resource	The intangible assets of systems and procedures, knowledge of processes, patents, research and development. Also see *Economic Resources, Human Resources, Physical Resources,* and *Reputational Resources.*
Template	A starting point for a new document. Also see *Form.*
Tertiary Sector	A classification based on economic development where the economic activity involves the provision of services to consumers and businesses. Examples include banking and providing technology infrastructure to businesses. Also see *Primary Sector,* and *Secondary Sector.*
Theft	The unauthorised taking or retention of the property of another person combined with the intention ('mens rea' of dishonesty) to do so. Also see *Fraud.*
Theoretical (Available) Capacity	The ideal goal of capacity utilisation calculated as the maximum level of production that can be achieved in a specified period based on producing at full efficiency all the time. Also see *Practical (Available) Capacity.*
Theory of Constraints	An approach to managing costs and improving the quality and delivery performance by focusing on identifying and removing bottlenecks in operations.
Threshold	A minimum standard of achievement or attainment.
Throughput Accounting	A method of measuring the effects of bottlenecks, and operational decisions using financial measures of throughput, inventory and operating expense.
Throughput Contribution	The revenues minus the direct material costs of the finished products sold.
Throughput Costing	An extreme form of Variable Costing in which only variable direct material costs are included as inventoriable costs. Also known as Super-Variable Costing. All other costs are treated as costs of the period in which they are incurred and are deducted as expenses of the period. Also see *Absorption Costing,* and *Variable Costing.*
Time and Material Pricing	An approach to cost-plus pricing where one charge is determined for the labour used on a job and another charge is determined for the materials.
Time and Motion Studies	An approach to cost function estimation that analyses the relationship between inputs and outputs in physical terms. It can involve observation of the steps required and time taken by employees to perform particular activities or the use of activity sampling. Also known as Task Analysis or Work Measurement.
Time Driver	Any factor in which a change in the factor causes a change in the duration of an activity.
Time Value of Money	The adjustment of a monetary amount to take into account that any currency unit received today is worth more than the same currency unit received at a future time.
Timely Information	The availability of information so it can be used in the decision-making process.
Timesheet	A source document that contains information about the amount of labour time used for a specific job in a specific department.

Tipping Point	A trend or transformation where (a) there are relatively few transmitters (people or factors) (b) there is sudden or simultaneous change (c) it produces a magnified effect, and (d) behaviour is contagious. It uses the concept of social epidemics and the geometric progression of epidemics or virology.
Top Down	An approach to analysis design and implementation which requires attention to be directed to the objective of the system and the typical functions of the system.
Top Down Budgeting	A system where senior managers impose budget targets on more junior managers with little or no consultation.
Total Contribution Margin	The difference between (a) total sales revenue, and (b) total variable costs.
Total Cost Curve	A graph of the relationship between total cost and the quantity produced and sold.
Total Cost of Ownership	The sum of all the costs associated with dealing with a particular supplier. It includes the purchase price of materials, as well as all the costs that are triggered by the purchase activity or the supplier.
Total Factor Productivity (TFP)	The ratio of the quantity of output produced to the costs of all inputs used, based on current period prices.
Total Manufacturing Overhead Variance	The single variance calculated as the sum of the flexible-budget variance and the production-volume variance.
Total Quality Management	A management approach that centres on meeting the requirements of customers by achieving continuous improvements in products.
Total Revenue Curve	A graph of the relationship between total sales revenue and quantity sold.
Traditional Budgeting	See *Incremental Budgeting*.
Transaction	A signal, event, or unit of data that triggers or initiates some action or sequence of actions.
Transaction Cycle	See *Business Transaction Cycle*.
Transactional Net Margin Method	A comparison of profits earned by the target business with those earned by comparable independent businesses. Also see *Comparable Uncontrolled Price*, and *Transfer Price*.
Transfer	See *Assignment*.
Transfer Price	The internal selling price used when products or services are transferred between profit centres or investment centres. It is the price one subunit (department or division) charges for a product or service supplied to another subunit of the same business. Also see *Comparable Uncontrolled Price*, and *Transactional Net Margin Method*.
Transferability	See *Appropriability*.

Transferred-In Costs	The costs incurred in previous departments that are carried forward as costs of the product when it moves to a subsequent process in the production cycle. Also known as Previous Department Costs.
Trial Balance	A statement listing in two columns the debit and credit balances of all the ledger accounts. Since debits should equal credits it acts as a check for the correct recording of transactions. It is made before, and after closing entries.
Trigger Point	One of the four stages in the cycle from purchase of direct materials to sale of finished products at which journal entries are made in the accounting system. The four stages are purchase of direct materials, production work-in-progress, completing of finished product, and sale of inventory.
True and Fair View	The presentation of a company's financial position as shown in its accounts and confirmed by its auditors. It does not mean absolute truth since financial statements are a product of management judgments and estimates.
Trust	A form of incorporation or legal structure in which the trustee is the holder of an interest in property subject to equitable obligation to use or keep the property for the beneficiary or for a specific purpose. Also see *Business*, *Company*, *Enterprise*, *Incorporation*, *Partnership*, and *Sole Proprietor*.
Turnaround	Accomplishing satisfactory profitability that enables the business to continue trading and develop and release new products that will assure its future viability. Also known as Recovery or Revival.
Two-Dimensional Activity Based Costing	A costing system that provides information about activities, cost drivers and performance, as well as the costs of cost objects.
U	
Unavoidable Costs	The costs that will continue to be incurred no matter which course of action is decided. Also see *Decremental Cost*, *Differential Costs*, *Differential Revenues*, *Imputed Costs*, *Incremental Revenues*, *Opportunity Costs*, *Out-of-Pocket Costs*, *Plan Concepts*, *Relevant Costs*, and *Sunk Costs*.
Uncertainty	The outcome, result, value or state is either unknown or capable of more than one possibility. The possibility that an actual amount will deviate from an expected amount.
Uncontrollable Cost	A cost that a manager cannot significantly influence.
Under-Absorbed Indirect Costs	See *Under-Allocated Indirect Costs*.
Under-Allocated Indirect Costs	The allocated amount of indirect costs in an accounting period is less than the actual (incurred) amount in that period
Under-Applied Indirect Costs	See *Under-Allocated Indirect Costs*.
Unfavourable Variance	A variance that has the effect of decreasing operating income relative to the amount budgeted. Identified by adding the letter U as a suffix. Also see *Favourable Variance*.

Unique Process	Unique business processes represent the interpretation of reports and the decisions that are converted into actions. Some controls are imposed on business processes. For example, customer policies on refunds, warranties and after-sales support. Some outputs from business processes are also unique. For example, the ease of use or reliability of products, the quality of product documentation, the friendliness, helpfulness and knowledge of sales and customer service employees. Also see *Business Process*, and *Generic Process*.
Unit Contribution Margin	The difference between (a) the sale price per unit, and (b) the variable cost per unit.
Unit Cost	The cost computed by dividing total cost by the number of units. Also known as Average Cost. Also see *Contribution Margin*, *Fixed Cost*, and *Gross Margin*.
Unit Level Activities	The activities performed for each unit of product.
Unit Level Cost	The costs relating to the activities that are performed for each unit produced.
Unused Capacity	The amount of productive capacity available over and above the productive capacity employed to meet consumer demand in the current period.
Usage Variance	See *Efficiency Variance for Direct Materials*.
V	
Valuation of Shares	1. Ratio of present share price to company expected earnings (the price earnings ratio). 2. Compare the earnings yield on shares (the after tax profits earned by companies as a percentage of the current share price) with the yield on a long dated government bond. In normal times both yields are similar. 3. Compare the average dividend yield on shares with the yield on a government bond.
Value-Added Activity	An activity that provides essential value to the customer or is essential to the functioning of the business. Also see *Non-Value Added Activity*.
Value-Added Cost	A cost that, if eliminated, would reduce the actual or perceived value or utility (usefulness) a customer obtains from using the product or service. Also see *Non-Value Added Cost*.
Value Analysis	A method that classifies activities as either (a) value-added or (b) non-value added. Also see *Value Added Activity*, and *Non-Value Added Activity*.
Value-Based Pricing	A pricing strategy where customers' perceptions of value guide the price.
Value Chain	A set of interlinked processes that begin with acquisition of resources and conclude with providing and supporting products and services that customers value (Porter, 1985/1998).
Value Drivers	The activities or actions that create value for a business.
Value Engineering	The systematic evaluation of all aspects of the product to eliminate any non-value added elements to achieve a target cost while maintaining or increasing the value to the customer.
Value Proposition	The benefits, costs, and value that a product or service provides to a customer, supplier or alliance partner which engenders loyalty.

Value In Use	The discounted present value of the future cash flows expected to arise from (a) its the continuing use of an asset, and (b) from its disposal at the end of its useful life. Also see *Carrying Amount, Impairment of Asset*, and *Recoverable Amount*.
Value Stream	All the valued-added activities needed to design, manufacture, and deliver a given product or product line to customers.
Variable	A variable is a characteristic or condition that can change or take on different values.
Variable Cost	A cost that changes in total in proportion to a change in the related level of total activity or volume.
Variable Cost of Products Sold	The total amount of direct material, direct labour and variable manufacturing overhead assigned to the units sold.
Variable Costing	A method of inventory costing. Only variable costs (that is, direct material, direct labour and variable manufacturing overhead) are applied to Work-in-Process Inventory on the Balance Sheet and then as finished goods on the balance sheet. When the finished goods are sold they are then expensed on the Profit and Loss Statement. The difference between absorption and variable costing is the timing with which fixed manufacturing overhead becomes an expense. Under variable costing all fixed manufacturing overhead costs are expensed immediately as incurred and are recorded on the Profit and Loss Statement. Since non-manufacturing costs are treated as period costs they are expensed. Also known as Direct Costing. Also see *Absorption Costing, Actual Costing, Normal Costing, Standard Costing*, and *Throughput Costing*.
Variable Manufacturing Overhead Costs	The indirect manufacturing costs that vary in proportion to the level of production (or the volume of overhead cost driver).
Variable Overhead Efficiency Variance	The difference between (a) the actual quantity of variable overhead cost-allocation base used and (b) budgeted quantity of variable overhead cost-allocation base that should have been used to produce actual output, then multiplied by budgeted variable overhead cost per unit of cost-allocation base.
Variable Overhead Flexible-Budget Variance	The difference between (a) the actual variable overhead costs incurred and (b) the flexible-budget variable overhead amounts.
Variable Overhead Spending Variance	The difference between (a) the actual variable overhead cost per unit and (b) the budgeted variable overhead cost per unit of the cost-allocation base, then multiplied by (c) the actual quantity of variable overhead cost-allocation base used for actual output.
Variance	The difference between (a) expected performance, and (b) the actual result.
Vertical Form	See *Narrative Form*.
Vertical Integration	The degree to which one business owns its upstream suppliers (e.g. raw materials, manufacturing, marketing) and downstream buyers (also manufacturing, distribution, also marketing and retailing). For example, a newspaper owning the timber plantations and a mill to make its own paper.
Virtual Close	The ability to be able to close the accounting books and run reports at any point in time.

Virtuous Character (Ethical Theories)	See *Aretaic Turn*.
Vision Statement	The desired future state or aspiration of a business. Also see *Mission Statement*.
Volume-Based Driver	A cost driver that assumes that costs are driven or caused by the volume of production or sales.
Voluntary Sector	See *Non-Profit Sector*.
Von Restorff Effect	An effect of isolating a difference for example, remembering the word that is different from other words in a list.
W	
Waiting Time	The elapsed time between an order being received by manufacturing and production commencing. Also see *Delivery Lead Time*, *Manufacturing Lead Time*, and *Purchase Order Lead Time*.
Weighted-Average Contribution Margin	The average of the products' unit contribution margins, weighted by the sales mix.
Weighted Average Cost of Capital (WACC)	The weighted average of the cost of funds from all sources of borrowings and equity.
Weighted-Average Process-Costing Method	A method of process costing that assigns the equivalent-unit cost of the work done to date (regardless of the accounting period in which it was done) to equivalent units completed and transferred out of the process and to equivalent units in ending Work-in-Process Inventory.
What-If Analysis	See *Sensitivity Analysis*.
Whiplash Effect	See *Forrester Effect*.
Wholesaler	A business that resells products to other businesses for use in their production processes or for resale to the public.
Win-Win	Both the players, or both the sides, achieve acceptable outcomes. Also see *Game Outcome*, and *Zero Sum*.
WIP	See *Work-In-Process Inventory*.
Work-In-Process	See *Work-In-Process Inventory*.
Work-In-Process Inventory	A product on which manufacture has begun but is only partially completed. Often shortened to Work-in-Process or the acronym WIP. Also known as Work-In-Progress.
Work In Progress	See *Work-In-Process Inventory*.
Work-Measurement	See *Time and Motion Studies*.

Work Sheet	1. A sheet which sets out financial information, non-financial information, or both. 2. A sheet prepared by an accountant which is retained by the accountant and is used for period end adjustments and closing entries.
Working Capital	The funding of debtors, Work-in-Process Inventory and Finished Goods Inventory as a relationship between activity, and financing. The excess of current assets over current liabilities.
Working Papers	1. The documentation to support proposals or recommendations usually containing detailed calculations and supporting source data. 2. In auditing, the documentation prepared by the auditor as an aid to the audit procedures. 3. Also see *Work Sheet*.
Write Down	1. To make provision for the depreciation of an asset. 2. To record the decline in net realisable value of non-depreciable assets below the value recorded in the books of the accounting entity. For example, land or inventory is written down when its market value is reduced. Also see *Inventory Write Down*.
Write Off	1. To cancel by creating an offsetting entry. 2. To recognise a loss in the value of an asset by crediting an asset and debiting a liabilities account or an expense account. 3. To treat as an irreparable or non-recoverable loss.
Z	
Zero-Base Budgeting	The process where all activities in the organisation are initially set to zero. To receive an allocation of resources during the budgeting process, managers must demonstrate that the activity provides continued benefit to the business.
Zero Sum	One player or one of the sides benefits to the extent that the other player or side incurs losses. Also see *Game Outcome*.
Zipf's Law	The 'size' (denoted y) of an occurrence of an event relative to its rank (denoted r). Based on work by Harvard linguistics professor George Kingsley Zipf, a to determine the 'size' of the 3rd or 8th or 100th most common word based on frequency of use of the word in English text. Zipf's law also states that the size of the r'th largest occurrence of the event is inversely proportional to its rank. Also see *Pareto Distribution*, and *Power Law*.

Brief on methodology

The controversial (Fischer 1978) Delphi systematic method (Bedford 1972; Sackman 1974) for eliciting expert opinion on a variety of topics, including technological forecasting developed by the RAND Corporation (www.rand.org) and q sort methodology (Stevenson, 1953)" was used as the basis for information sharing.

Overview of Delphi method

The characteristic features of the Delphi method are (a) a central topic to elicit an answer containing the reasons, factors and conclusions, (b) a panel of experts who do not interact (c) repeated individual questioning, (d) use of controlled feedback concerning factors raised by others or answer to questions raised by the expert, and (e) applying justifiable corrections to the expert answer/consensus (Dalkey & Helmer 1963: 458–59). A variant enables policy rather than numeric information to be assessed (Strauss & Zeigler 1975).

Allowing for some fluidity in collecting data (Salancik, Wenger & Helfer 1971), the central topic was essential business knowledge and used three guiding questions[1]: (1) What kinds of knowledge did you draw on that proved valuable to you? (2) How did you use that knowledge? (3) What formed the judgements, viewpoints, decisions or opinions that you reached? and (4) What limitations or concerns did you have or did you come to perceive later?

Process

To produce the original data set between 1982 and 2000, general Managers and functional managers (or their equivalents) were interviewed from representative sectors and industries. Outcomes were the triumvirate of issues/challenges, tools/techniques and judgements/decisions, a set of topics which and a superset of organising dimensions (life cycle, adaptation resources and recurrent themes and vocabulary). The dimensions were necessary as competing frameworks could not be reconciled into a single homogeneous criterion. This resulted in several perspectives on a topic.

Validity

Selection of informants was targeted. Since responses were self-reported they lack the standards of audit or legal evidence or testimony. However, to encourage candour, all participants were guaranteed complete confidentiality of themselves and their responses. Selected commentaries were sought on the draft which informed the final result.

---

1 Some details of the motivation for the research and its outcomes are provided in Oliver (2010). Participants were prompted with: (1) Top ten ideas, principles, guidelines, topics or areas, and the top ten authors/people who changed your understanding or perception; (2) Top ten issues, top ten challenges, top ten decisions, top ten unanticipated actions of competitors, top ten causes of change in your industry, and top ten impacts; and (3) Top ten decisions in the area, topic, issue or challenge, and what influenced your understanding or perception.

References

The references[1] provided attempt to balance generally accessible monographs with articles in specialised publications and scholarly publications.[2] Employees and managers usually do not have access to library holdings with their subscriptions to hardcopy journals or electronic journal articles. A number of classic books and articles are available from the Library of Economics and Liberty (www.econlib.org). The contemporary and historical references range across the disciplines of economics, education, finance, health sciences, international politics, law, marketing, philosophy, and psychology.

Matters of public record are not referenced as they are readily available. Search engines of the internet (e.g. www.google.com) are a convenient alternative to obtaining assistance from a librarian at a public library.

The far right hand column of the lists the topic where the publication is cited. The introduction at the commencement of each number is labelled '.0' to avoid confusion with the Introduction.

Abernathy, W. J., & Utterback, J. M.	(1978)	Patterns of industrial innovation. *Technology Review, 80(7)*: 40-47.	10.4
Abrahams, J.	(2007)	*101 mission statements from top companies plus guidelines for writing your own mission statements.* New York. Ten Speed Press.	2.1
Abrahams, R., & Barrow, P.	(2005/ 2008)	*The successful business plan: secrets and strategies.* (4th ed.). New York. Capstone Publishing/Wiley. (Original work published 1991).	Intro.
Abrahamson, E.	(1991)	Managerial fads and fashions: The diffusion and rejection of innovations. *The Academy of Management Review, 16(3)*: 586–612.	9.5
Abrahamson, E. & Freeman, D. H.	(2006)	*A perfect mess: The hidden benefits of disorder.* London. Weidenfeld & Nicholson.	4.0

---

1 It should be remembered that no-one, no matter how intelligent or diligent, can be original most of the time. The most accomplished scientists, scholars, teachers and authors only make a small contribution to the sum of human knowledge. Mostly they reuse the discoveries and ideas of others, with varying due acknowledgement. This does not devalue their thinking or their teaching. The tendency of individuals who are recognised authorities or commentators to move outside their area of speciality does however, make it essential to be skeptical of public announcements or claims because they occur outside the forums of refereed debate and dialogue.

2 Scholarly publications should be identifiable by being double blind refereed, refer to previous scholarly publications and indicate directions for future research. A scholarly publication also contains a substantial literature survey in which both supporting and disagreeing approaches are discussed. If the author changes their view it is expected they will follow up with a publication which corrects or expands their earlier work.

Accenture	(2000)	*Mastering value creation in the eworld: A CEO toolkit for unlocking the total value potential of information technologies.* Melbourne, Victoria. Accenture.	15.1
Adamson, J.	(1983)	*Groucho, Harpo, Chico and sometimes Zeppo: A history of the Marx Brothers and a satire on the rest of the world.* New York: Simon and Schuster.	19.1
Akerlof, G. A.	(1970)	The market for lemons: Qualitative uncertainty and the market mechanism. *Quarterly Journal of Economics,* 84(3): 488–500. Reprinted in G. Akerlof (1984) *An economic theorist's book of tales.* Cambridge. Cambridge University Press.	12.2
Albanese, J. S.	(2008)	Risk assessment in organised crime: Developing a market and product-based model to determine threat levels. *Journal of Contemporary Criminal Justice,* 24(3): 263–73.	9.2
Alchian, A. A.	(1950)	Uncertainty, evolution, and economic theory. *Journal of Political Economy,* 58(3): 211–21.	1.2, Dim. Two, Dim. Three
Allen, L. A.	(1982)	*Making managerial planning more effective: designing, integrating, implementing managerial and strategic plans for productivity and profit.* New York. McGraw-Hill.	12.2
Altman, E. I.	(1968)	Financial ratios, discriminant analysis and the prediction of corporate bankruptcy. *The Journal of Finance,* 23(4): 589–609).	4.3
Altman, E. I.	(2000)	*Predicting the financial distress of companies: Revisiting the Z-Score and Zeta models.* <Downloaded from http://pages.stern.nyu.edu/~ealtman/Zscores.pdf on 9 November 2009>	4.3
Alvesson, M.	(2004)	*Knowledge work and knowledge-intensive firms.* Oxford, England. Oxford University Press.	13.2
Alvesson, M. & Deetz, S.	(2000)	*Doing critical management research.* London. Sage Publications.	10.1
American Psychological Association	(2009)	*Publication manual of the American Psychological Association.* (6th ed.). Washington, D. C. American Psychological Association.	Intro.
Ansoff, H. I.	(1965)	*Corporate strategy.* New York. McGraw-Hill.	7.3
ANZSIC	(2006/ 2008)	*Australian and New Zealand standard industrial classification (ANZSIC), 2006* (Revision 1.0). <Downloaded 17 November 2008 from http://www.abs.gov.au/AUSSTATS/abs@.nsf/Latestproducts/1292.0Contents12006%20%28Revision%201.0%29?opendocument&tabname=Summary&prodno=1292.0&issue=2006%20%28Revision%201.0%29&num=&view=>	2.1
Arantz, P.	(1993)	*A collusion of powers.* Dunedoo, NSW. The Author.	10.5
Argyris, C.	(1993)	*Knowledge for action: A guide to overcoming barriers to organisational change.* San Francisco. Jossey-Bass.	13.2
Argyris, C. & Schon, D.	(1978)	*Organisational Learning: A theory of action perspective.* Reading, Massachusetts. Addison-Wesley.	13.2
Ariely, D.	(2008/ 2009)	*Predictably irrational: The hidden forces that shape our decisions.* (Rev. ed.). London. HarperCollins. (Original work published 2005).	2.0, 14.0
Aristotle	(ND/ 2002)	*Nicomachean ethics.* (J Sachs, Trans.). Newburyport, Massachusetts. Focus Publishing/R. Pullins Company.	10.1

Ashby, W. R.	(1956)	*An introduction to cybernetics*. London. Chapman and Hall. <Available on the internet, 1999 and downloaded from http://pcp.vub.ac.be/books/IntroCyb.pdf 26 January, 2004>	8.3
Aurelius, M.	(1998)	*Meditations*. (A. S. L. Farquarson, Trans). Oxford. Oxford World Classics. (Originally published 1944).	14.1
Austin, R. D.	(1996)	*Measuring and managing performance in organisations*. New York. Dorset House.	12.2
Australian Computer Society	(ND)	*Code of ethics*. < Retrieved from http://www.acs.org.au/index.cfm?action=show&conID=2005090223222219027 on 4 November 2009>	10.4
Baggini, J. & Fosl, P. F.	(2003/2010)	*The philosopher's toolkit: A compendium of philosophical concepts and methods*. London. Wiley-Blackwell.	Intro.
Barnard, C.	(1938)	*The functions of the executive*. Cambridge, Massachusetts. Harvard University Press.	6.4
Barney, J. B.	(1991)	Firm resources and sustained competitive advantage. *Journal of Management*, 17(1): 99–120.	1.2
Baron, D.	(2009)	*A better pencil: Readers, writers, and the digital revolution*. New York. Oxford University Press.	11.5
Baron, J.	(1988)	*Thinking and deciding*. Cambridge, England. Cambridge University Press.	14.1
Bateson, G.	(1972)	*Steps to an ecology of mind: Collected essays in anthropology, psychiatry, evolution, and epistemology*. Chicago. University of Chicago Press.	13.2
Baumol, W. J.	(2002)	*The free-market innovation machine: Analysing the growth miracle of capitalism*. Princeton, New Jersey. Princeton University Press.	11.4
Bazerman, M. H.	(1986/2002)	*Judgment in managerial decision-making*. (5th ed.). New York. John Wiley. (Original work published 1986).	14.1
Bedford, M. T.	(1972)	The values of competing panels of experts and the impact of 'drop-outs' on Delphi results. In Delphi: The Bell Canada Experience. Bell. Canada.	Method
Becker, G. S.	(1964/1994)	*Human capital: A theoretical and empirical analysis, with special reference to education*. Chicago. University of Chicago Press.	Dim. Three
Beer, S.	(1959)	*Cybernetics and management*. London: English Universities Press.	8.3
Belfort, J.	(2007)	*The wolf of wall street*. New York. Bantam.	2.1
Bell, D.	(1973)	*The coming of post-industrial society: A venture in social forecasting*. New York: Basic Books.	19.5
Bell, D.	(1967)	Notes on the post-industrial society I and 2. *The Public Interest*, 6 (Winter 1967): 24–35 and 7(Spring 1967): 102–18.	19.5
Bentham, J.	(1983)	*Deontology together with a table of the springs of action and articles on utilitarianism. (Collected Works of Jeremy Bentham)*. Oxford, England. Oxford University Press.	10.1
Bentham, J.	(1789/1996)	*An introduction to the principles of morals and legislation*. (Eds.) H. L. A. Hart & J. H. Burns. New York. Oxford University Press.	10.1
Berle, A. A. & Means, G. C.	(1932)	*The modern corporation and private property*. New York. Macmillan.	Intro., 3.4

Berliner, J. S.	(1957)	*Factory and manager in the USSR.* Cambridge, Massachusetts. Harvard University Press.	8.3
Bertalanffy, L. von	(1969/ 1976)	*General systems theory: Foundations, development, applications.* (Rev. ed.). New York. George Braziller. (Original work published 1969).	17.3
Bhalla, A.	(2009)	Don't misuse the Pareto principle. *Six Sigma Forum magazine, 8 (3)*:15-18.	14.3
Black, F. & Scholes, M.	(1973)	The pricing of options and corporate liabilities. *Journal of Political Economy*, 81(3): 637-654.	3.2
Blau, P. M.	(1955)	*The dynamics of bureaucracy.* Chicago. University of Chicago.	8.3
Blau, P. M. & Schoenherr, R. A.	(1971)	*The structure of organisations.* New York. Basic Books.	12.5
Blaug, M.	(1958)	*Ricardian economics: A historical study.* New Haven, Connecticut. Yale University Press.	7.7, 15.1
Bloomfield, B., & Best, A.	(1992)	Management consultants: Systems development, power and the translation of problems. *The Sociological Review*, 40(3): 533–59	8.5
Boisot, M.	(1995)	*Information space: A framework for learning in organisations, institutions and culture.* London. Routledge.	8.5
Boisot, M.	(1987)	*Information and organisations: The manager as anthropologist.* London. Fontana Collins.	8.5
Boulding, K. E.	(1956)	General systems theory: The skeleton of science. *Management Science*, 2(3): 197–205.	8.3
Brackett, M.	(2000)	*Data resource quality: Turning bad habits into good practices.* Reading, Massachusetts. Addison-Wesley.	11.2
Breadmore, R. G.	(1971)	*O & M.* London. Teach Yourself Books.	11.1, 17.4.1
Brockholdt, J. L.	(1999)	*Accounting information systems: Transactions processing and controls.* (5th ed.). New York. Irwin/McGraw-Hill.	17.0
Brodie, M. B.	(1967)	*Fayol on administration.* London. Lyon and Grant.	6.4
Bromwich, M.	(1980)	*Standard costing for planning and control.* Hemel Hempstead, England. Philip Allan.	7.5
Brooker, C.	(2004)	*The seven basic plots: Why we tell stories.* London. Continuum.	11.5
Brookfield, S.	(1995)	*Becoming a critically reflective teacher.* San Francisco. Jossey-Bass.	10.1
Brown, D. S.	(1978)	Petronius or Ogburn? *Public Administration Review*, 38(3): 296.	Dim. Two
Brown, S. & Eisenhardt, K. M.	(1997)	The art of continuous change: Linking complexity theory and time-paced evolution in relentlessly shifting organisations. *Administrative Sciences Quarterly*, 42(1): 1–34.	10.4
Brown, T.	(2009)	*Change by design: How design thinking transforms organisations and inspires innovation.* New York. Harper Business.	10.4
Brundtland, G. H.	(1987)	*Our common future* (Brundtland report). Report of the United Nations World Commission on Environment and Development. Oxford. Oxford University Press.	7.1
Buckland, M.	(1991)	Information as thing. *Journal of the American Society for Information Science*, 42(5): 351–60. Reprinted in: M. Buckland (1994): *Information and information systems* (pp 43–57). Westport, Connecticut. Praeger.	12.2

Buckingham, M., & Coffman, C.	(1999)	*First, break all the rules: What the world's greatest managers do differently*. New York. Simon & Schuster.	6.5
Buffet, W. E. & Cunningham, L. A.	(2001)	*The essays of Warren Buffett: Lessons for corporate America*. (Rev ed.). New York. Cunningham Group. (Original work published 1997).	Dim. Three
Burgelman, R. A.	(1983)	A process model of internal corporate venturing in the diversified major firm. *Administrative Science Quarterly*, 28(2): 223–47.	10.4
Burgelman, R. A.	(1991)	Interorganisational ecology of strategy making and organisational adaptation: Theory and field research. *Organisation Science*, 2(3): 239–62.	10.4
Burns, A. F., & Mitchell, W. C.	(1946)	*Measuring business cycles*. New York. National Bureau of Economic Research.	1.1, Dim. Three
Buzzell, R. D.	(2004)	The PIMS program of strategy research: A retrospective appraisal. *Journal of Business Research*, 57(5): 478–83.	3.1, 6.4
Buzzell, R. D., & Gale, B. T.	(1987)	*The PIMS principle: Linking strategy to performance*. New York. Free Press.	6.4
Carnes, W. S., & Slifer, S. D.	(1991)	*The atlas of economic indicators: A visual guide to market forces and the federal reserve*. New York. Harper Business.	7.1
Carr, L. P., & Itner, C. D.	(1992)	Measuring the cost of ownership. *Journal of Cost Management*, 6(3): 42–51.	12.4
Carter, K. L.	(2002)	*Microsoft in the mirror*. Redmond, Washington. Pennington Books.	13.5, 14.0
Case, J.	(1995)	*Open book management: The coming business revolution*. New York. Harper Collins.	10.2
CCH	(2009)	*Australian master accountants guide*. Sydney, NSW. CCH Australia.	Intro.
Chambers, R. J.	(1947/ 1986)	*Financial management*. (4th ed.). Sydney, NSW. Law Book Company. (Original work published 1944).	1,1, 1.2, 3.0, 4.3, 4.4, 12.0
Chandler, A. D. Jr	(1990)	*Scale and scope: The dynamics of industrial capitalism*. Cambridge, Massachusetts. Belknap Press.	10.4
Chandler, A. D. Jr	(1977)	*The visible hand: The managerial revolution in American business*. Cambridge, Massachusetts. Belknap Press.	6.3
Chandler, A. D. Jr.	(1962)	*Strategy and structure: Chapters in the history of the American industrial enterprise*. Cambridge, Massachusetts. MIT Press.	6.3
Chatov, R.	(1975)	*Corporate financial reporting Public or private control*. New York. Free Press.	4.0
Cherry, C.	(1957/ 1966)	*On human communication: A review, a survey and a criticism*. (2nd ed.). (Original work published 1957). Cambridge Massachusetts. MIT.	11.5
Choi, S. Y., Whinston, A., & Stahl, D.	(1997)	*The economics of electronic commerce*. Indiana, Indianapolis. Macmillan Computer Publishing.	Dim. Two

Christensen, C. M.	(1997/ 2003)	*The innovator's dilemma.* (Original work published 1997). New York. Harper Business.	10.4
Cialdini, R. B.	(2001)	The science of persuasion. *Scientific American,* 284(2): 76–81.	9.3
Cialdini, R. B.	(1984/ 2008)	*Influence: Science and practice.* (5th ed.). Needham Heights, Massachusetts. Allyn & Bacon. (Original work published 1987).	6.3
Clark, C.	(1940/ 1951)	*The conditions of economic progress.* London. Macmillan.	2.1
Clarke, F., & Dean, G.	(2007)	*Indecent disclosure: Gilding the corporate lily.* Port Melbourne, Victoria. Cambridge University Press.	5.3, 12.0
Clarke, F., Dean, G., & Oliver, K.	(1997/ 2003)	*Corporate collapse: Accounting, regulatory and ethical failure.* (2nd ed.). Melbourne, Victoria. Cambridge. Cambridge University Press. (Original work published 1994).	5.3, 11.0
Clark, J. M.	(1923)	*Studies in the economics of overhead costs.* Chicago. University of Chicago Press.	14.3
Clausewitz, C. von	(1832/ 1968)	*On war.* (J. J. Graham, Trans.). (Ed. A. Rapoport). London. Penguin Books. (Original work published 1832).	3.1
Coase, R.	(1960)	The problem of social cost. *Journal of Law and Economics, 3 (1):* 1-44.	3.4, 8.4
Coase, R.	(1937)	The nature of the firm. *Economica,* 4(16): *386–405.*	8.4
Cohen, S. G., & Bailey, D. E.	(1997)	What makes teams work: Group effectiveness research from the shop floor to the executive suite? *Journal of Management,* 23(3): 239–90.	6.5
Collins, B. E., & Guetzkow, H.	(1964)	*A social psychology of group processes for decision-making.* New York. John Wiley.	3.1, 14.1
Collins, J.	(2001)	*Good to great: Why some companies make the leap … and others don't.* New York. Harper Business.	Intro., 3.1
Collins, J.	(2006)	*Why business thinking is not the answer. Good to great and the social sectors: A monograph to accompany good to great.* New York. Random House Business Books.	Intro., 2.1, 3.1
Collins, R.	(1990)	Cumulation and anti-cumulation in sociology: Reply to Gottdiener. *American Sociological Review,* 55(3): 462–43.	6.3
Commons, J.R.	(1931)	Institutional economics. *American Economic Review,* 21: 648-657.	3.4
Con Walker, B.	(2009)	*Casino clubs NSW: Profits, tax, sport and politics.* Sydney, NSW. Sydney University Press.	9.2
Cooper, R., & Slagmulder, R.	(1997)	*Target costing and value engineering.* Portland Oregon. Productivity Press.	7.3
Cootner, P.	(1964)	*The random character of stock market prices.* New York. MIT.	Dim. Three
Dalkey, N., & Helmer, O.	(1963)	An experimental application of the Delphi method to the use of experts. *Management Science,* 9(3): 458–67.	Method.

Daniels, L. M.	(1976/ 1993)	*Business information sources.* (3rd ed.). Berkeley, California. University of California Press.	7.1
Darwin, C.	(1859/ 1869)	*The origin of species: By means of natural selection, or the preservation of favoured races in the struggle for life.* 5th ed. London. Murray. (Original work published 1859). <Downloaded 8 January 2010 from http://darwin-online.org.uk/content/frame set?viewtype=side&itemID=F387&pageseq=121>.	Dim. Two
Date, C. J.	(1975/ 1999)	*An introduction to data base systems.* (7th ed.). Reading, Massachusetts. Addison-Wesley Longman. (Original work published 1975).	8.4, 17.3.2
Davenport, T., & Prusak, L.	(1998/ 2000)	*Working knowledge: How organisations manage what they know.* (Originally published 1998). New preface edition. Boston, Massachusetts. Harvard Business School Press.	Dim. Three
Davis, C.	(2009)	*Eyewitness: The rise and fall of Dorling Kindersley.* Petersfield, England. Harriman House.	12.2
Davis, P., & Stern, D.	(1980)	Adaptation, survival, and growth of the family business: An integrated systems perspective. *Human Relations, 34*(4): 207–24.	1.2
Dawes, R., & Hastie, R.	(2001)	*Rational choice in an uncertain world: The psychology of judgement and decision-making.* Thousand Oaks, California. Sage.	14.0, 14.1
De Bono, E	(1986/ 1999)	*Six thinking hats.* (Revised and updated ed.) NY. Back Bay Books (Hachette).	7.0
DeMarco, T.	(2001)	*Slack: Getting past burnout, busywork and the myth of total efficiency.* New York. Broadway Books/Dorset House.	8.5, 14.4
DeMarco, T.	(1978/ 1979)	*Structured systems analysis and system specification.* New York. Prentice Hall. (Original work published 1975).	6.2, 17.4
De Vries, M. F. R.	(2009)	*Action and reflection: The emotional distance between consultant and client.* INSEAD Working Paper Series. *<Downloaded from http://insead.edu/facultyresearch/research/details_papers. cfm?id=25943 on 13 November 2009>*	14.4
Deming, W. E.	(1982/ 1986)	*Quality, productivity, and competitive position.* Cambridge, Massachusetts. Massachusetts Institute of Technology, Centre for Advanced Engineering. Reissued as: *Out of the crisis: Quality, productivity, and competitive position.* Cambridge, Massachusetts. MIT.	1.1, Dim. Two, 12.1, 14.4
Dervin, B.	(1992)	From the mind's eye of the user: The sense-making qualitative-quantitative methodology. In J. Glazier & R. Powell (Eds.) *Qualitative research in information management* (pp 61–84). Englewood, Colorado. Libraries Unlimited. Reprinted in (Eds.) Dervin, B & Foreman-Wernet (2003): *Sense-making methodology reader: Selected writings of Brenda Dervin.* (pp 269–92). Cresskill, New Jersey. Hampton Press.	7.0
Dewey, J.	1933/ 1986	How we think. In Volume 8, 1933 *Essays and how we think.* Carbondale, Illinois. Southern Illinois University Press.	Intro.
Dhalla, N. K., & Yuspeh, S.	(1976)	Forget the product life cycle concept! *Harvard Business Review,* 54(1): 102–12.	1.1
Dickson, A. L.	(1913/ 1918)	*Accounting: Practice and procedure.* New York. Ronald Press.	13.2
Dixon, N.	(1994/ 1999)	*The organisation learning cycle: How we can learn collectively.* (2nd ed.). London. Gower. (Original work published 1994).	12.2

Donalson, G.	(1969)	Strategy for financial emergencies. *Harvard Business Review,* 47(6): 67–80.	10.2
Donaldson, T., & Preston, L. E.	(1995)	The stakeholder theory of the corporation. *Academy of Management Review,* 20(1): 65–91.	2.4
Dörner, D., & Schölkopf, J.	(1991)	Controlling complex systems; or expertise as 'grandmother's know-how'. In K. A. Ericsson & J. Smith (Eds.): *Toward a general theory of expertise: Prospects and limits* (pp 218–39). Cambridge, England. Cambridge University Press.	14.5
Dosi, G., Malerba, F., & Teece, D.	(2003)	Twenty years after Nelson and Winter's An evolutionary theory of economic change: A preface on knowledge, the nature of organisations and the patterns of organisational changes. *Industrial and Corporate Change,* 12(2): 147–48.	Dim. Two
Drucker, P. F.	(2001/ 2005)	*The essential Drucker: The best of sixty years of Peter Drucker's essential writings on management.* New York. HarperCollins. (Original work published 2001).	6.4, 7.1, 11.1
Drucker, P. F.	(1994)	The theory of the business. *Harvard Business Review,* 72(5): 95–107.	2.7, 7.1
Drucker, P. F.	(1993)	*Knowledge: Its economics; its productivity.* Chapter 10: Post-Capitalist Society. London. Butterworth-Heinemann: 165–76.	19.5
Drucker, P. F.	(1985/ 1994)	*Innovation and entrepreneurship: Practice and principles.* (2nd ed.). London. Butterworth-Heinemann. (Original work published 1994).	10.4
Drucker, P. F.	(1974/ 1993)	*Management: Tasks, responsibilities, practices.* London. Heinemann. (Original work published 1974).	Intro., 11.1
Drucker, P. F.	(1964)	*Managing for results: Economic tasks and risk-taking decisions.* London. Heinemann.	6.4
Drucker, P F	(1946/ 1972)	*The concept of the corporation.* With new introduction by the author. New York. Transaction Publishers. (Original work published 1943).	6.2
Dutton, K.	(2009)	*Flipnosis: The art of split-second persuasion.* London. William Heinemann.	14.5
Dyer, J. H., & Singh, H.	(1990)	The relational view: Cooperative strategy and sources of interorganisational competitive advantage. *Academy of Management Review,* 23(4): 660–79.	Dim. Three
Dyregrov, A.	(1989)	Caring for helpers in disaster situations: Psychological debriefing. *Disaster Management,* 2(1): 25–30.	4.5
Edvinsson, L., & Malone, M. S.	(1997)	*Intellectual capital.* New York. Harper Collins.	Dim. Three
Eisenhardt, K.	(1989)	Agency theory: An assessment and review, *Academy of Management Review,* 14(1): 57–54.	3.5
Etzioni, A.	(1988)	*The moral dimension: Toward a new economics.* New York. Free Press.	13.1
Evans, P., & Wurster, T. S.	(1999)	Getting real about virtual commerce. *Harvard Business Review,* 77(6): 84–94.	2.0
Fayol, H.	(1916/ 1949)	*General and industrial management.* (C. Storrs, Trans.). London. Pitman. (Original work published in French 1913).	Intro., 6.4

Feigenbaum, A. V.	(1951/ 2004)	*Quality control: Principles, practice, and administration.* New York. McGraw-Hill. (Original work published 1951).	12.1
Fermi, E.	(1965)	*The man and his theories.* London. Souvenir.	11.2, 11.5
Fermi, L.	(1995)	*Atoms in the family: My life with Enrico Fermi.* Chicago. University of Chicago Press.	11.2, 11.5
Feil, M.	(2010)	*The failure of free-market economics.* Melbourne, Victoria. Scribe Publications.	Intro.
Fischer, R. G.	(1978)	The Delphi method: A description, review, and criticism. *The Journal of Academic Librarianship,* 4(2): 64–70.	Method.
Fisher, A. G. B.	(1935)	*The clash of progress and society.* London. Macmillan.	2.1
Fisher, I	(1978)	What is capital? *The Economic Journal,* 6(24): 509–34	3.2
Fisher, P. A.	(1996)	*Common stocks and uncommon profits and other writings.* New York. Wiley. (Original work published 1958).	Dim. Three
Fischoff, B.	(1982)	For those condemned to study the past: Heuristics and biases in hindsight. In D. Kahneman, P. Slovic & A. Tversky (Eds.), *Judgement under uncertainty: Heuristics and biases* (pp 497–502). Cambridge, England. Cambridge University Press.	14.5
Florence, P. S.	(1933)	*The logic of industrial organisation.* London. Kegan, Paul, Trench, Truber.	Intro., 2.1
Follett, M. P.	(1941)	*Dynamic administration.* H. C. Metcalf & L. F. Urwick (Eds.). London. Pitman.	Intro., 6.4
Forrester, J. W.		Counterintuitive behavior of social systems. *Technological Forecasting and Social Change,* 3(1): 1–22. (Testimony for the Subcommittee on Urban Growth of the Committee on Banking and Currency, U. S. House of Representatives, on October 7, 1970).	7.1
Forrester, J. W.	(1958)	Industrial dynamics A major breakthrough for decision makers. *Harvard Business Review,* 36(4): 37–66. Also see Forrester, J. (1961): *Industrial dynamics.* Cambridge, Massachusetts. MIT.	4.2, 8.5
Fortune, J., & Peters, G.	(1995)	*Learning from failure: The systems approach.* Chichester, England. John Wiley.	10.3
Foster, T. R.	(1993)	*One hundred and one great mission statements.* London. Kogan Page.	2.1
Foucault, M.	(1977/ 1980)	*Power/knowledge: Selected interviews and other writings 1972– 1974.* (Ed.). C. Gordon. New York. Pantheon.	6.3, 9.0
Frank, R. H.	(1988)	*Passions within reason: The strategic role of the emotions.* New York. Norton.	14.0
Frank, R. H.	(2011)	*The Darwin economy: Liberty, competition, and the common good.* Princeton, New Jersey. Princeton University Press.	Intro.
Franzese, M.	(2009)	*I'll make you an offer you can't refuse: Insider business tips from a former mob boss.* Nashville, Tennessee. Thomas Nelson.	2.0
Freeman, R. E.	(1984)	*Strategic management: A stakeholder approach.* Boston, Massachusetts. Pitman.	2.4
French, J. R. P., & Raven, B.	(1959)	The bases of social power. In D. Cartwright (ed.) *Studies in social power.* Ann Arbor, Michigan. University of Michigan Press.	9.0
Frumkin, N.	(1955/ 2005)	*Guide to economic indicators.* (4th ed.). Armonk, New York. M E Sharp. (Original work published 1958).	7.1

Fursten, S.	(1999)	*Popular management books: How they are made and what they mean for organisations.* London. Routledge.	8.5
Galbraith, J. K.	(1983a)	*The anatomy of power.* Boston. Houghton Mifflin.	9.1
Galbraith, J. K.	(1983b)	*Interview by Richard D Bartel editor of Challenge: John Kenneth Galbraith The Anatomy of Power.*	9.1
Galbraith, J. R., & Kazanjian, R. K.	(1987)	*Strategy implementation: Structure, systems and processes.* Minneapolis, Minnesota. West Publishing.	2.1
Garvin, D. A.	(1988)	*Managing quality: The strategic and competitive edge.* New York. Free Press.	12.1
Geis, G.	(1976)	The heavy electrical equipment antitrust cases of 1961. In (Eds.) *Criminal behaviour systems.* (pp 139–50). New York. Holt Rinehart & Winston.	Intro. 12.5
Giddens, A.	(1979)	*Central problems in social theory: Action, structure, and the contradiction in social analysis.* London. Macmillan.	6.3
Giddens, A.	(1984)	*The constitution of society: Outline of the theory of structuration.* Cambridge, England. Polity Press.	6.3
Gilovich, T.	(1993)	*How we know what isn't so: The fallibility of human reason in everyday life.* New York. Free Press.	14.5
Gilovich, T., & Medvec, V. H.	(1995)	The experience of regret: What, when and why. *Psychological Review*, 102(2): 379–98.	14.1
Gilovich, T., Vallone, R., & Tversky, A.	(1985)	The hot hand in baseball: On the misperception of random sequences. *Cognitive Psychology*, 17(3): 295–317.	14.5
Girard, J.	(1977)	*How to sell anything to anybody.* New York. Warner Books.	2.3
Girard, J.	(1979)	*How to sell yourself.* New York. Warner Books.	2.3
Gladwell, M.	(2000/ 2001)	*The tipping point: How little things can make a big difference.* London. Abacus. (Original work published 2000).	4.0
Goldmann, H. M.	(1958/ 1971)	*How to win customers.* (Rev. ed.). London. Pan Books. (Original work published 1955).	2.3
Goldratt, E. M.	(1999)	*Theory of constraints.* Great Barrington, Massachusetts. North River Press Publishing.	4.0, 8.5
Goldratt, E. M., & Cox, J.	(1984/ 2004)	*The goal: A process of ongoing improvement.* (3rd ed.). Great Barrington, Massachusetts. The North River Press. (Original work published 1984 as *The goal: Excellence in manufacturing*).	4.0, 8.5
Gordon, M. J., & Shillinglaw, G.	(1951/ 1964)	*Accounting: A management approach.* (3rd ed.). Homewood, Illinois. Richard D Irwin. (Original work published 1951).	10.2
Gowers, E.	(1948/ 1986)	*The complete plain words.* (3rd ed.). London. Penguin. (Originally published as a pamphlet first published 1948).	8.4
Grafton, A.	(1997)	*The footnote: A curious history.* London. Faber & Faber.	Intro.
Graham, B., & Dodd, D.	(1951)	*Security analysis.* New York. McGraw-Hill	Dim. Three
Gramsci, A.	(1971)	*Selections from the prison notebooks.* (Q. Hoare and G. Nowell, Ed. & Trans.). New York. International Publishers.	9.0

Granovetter, M.	(1978)	Threshold models of collective behaviour. *American Journal of Sociology,* 83(6): 1420–443.	4.0, 18.2
Grant, R. M.	(1996)	Toward a knowledge-based theory of the firm. *Strategic Management Journal,* 17(Special issue): 109–22.	19.5
Halberstam, D.	(1986)	*The reckoning.* New York. Morrow.	2.3
Hall, B. H. & van Reenen, J.	(2000)	How effective are fiscal incentives for R&D? A review of the evidence. *Research Policy,* 29(4–5): 449–69.	11.4
Halle, B. von	(2002)	*Business rules applied: Building better systems using the business rules approach.* New York. John Wiley.	17.3.1
Halpin, J. F.	(1966)	*Zero defects.* New York. McGraw-Hill.	12.1
Hamel, G., & Prahalad, C. K.	(1996)	*Competing for the future.* Boston, Massachusetts. Harvard Business School Press.	3.1
Hamel, G., & Prahalad, C. K.	(1989)	Strategic intent. *Harvard Business Review,* 67(3): 63–73.	11.2
Hamilton, D. L.	(1976)	Cognitive biases in the perception of social groups. (Eds.) J S Carroll & J W Payne: *Cognition and social behaviour.* (pp 81–93). Hillsdale, New Jersey. Erlbaum.	14.5
Hammer, M.	(1990)	Reengineering work: Don't automate, obliterate. *Harvard Business Review,* 68(4): 104–12.	11.3, 12.1
Hammer, M., & Champy, J.	(1993/ 2001)	*Reengineering the corporation: A manifesto for business revolution.* (Rev. Ed.). New York. Harper Business. (Original work published 1996).	11.3 12.1
Hansen, M. T., Nohria, N., & Tierney, T.	(1999)	What's your strategy for managing knowledge? *Harvard Business Review,* 77(2): 106–16.	19.5
Hansmann, H. B.	(1980)	The role of nonprofit enterprise. *The Yale Law Journal,* 89(5): 835–901.	Intro.
Harding, S., & Long, T.	(1998)	*MBA management models.* London. Gower.	Intro.
Hare, R.	(1999)	*Without conscience: The disturbing world of the psychopaths among us.* New York. Guilford Press	9.1
Harley-Davidson	-	*www.harleydavidson.com*	2.1, 5.0
Haugaard, M	(1997)	*The constitution of power: A theoretical analysis of power, knowledge and structure.* Manchester. England. University Press.	6.3
Hayes, R., & Abernathy, W.	(1980)	Managing our way to economic decline. *Harvard Business Review,* 58(4): 67–77. Reprinted with a retrospective by R. H. Hayes: *Harvard Business Review,* 85(7–8): 138–49.	15.5
Hayes, R. H., & Garvin, D. A.	(1982)	Managing as if tomorrow mattered. *Harvard Business Review,* 60(3): 71–79.	15.5
Hayward, M. L. A., & Boeker, W.	(1998)	Power and conflicts of interest in professional firms: Evidence from investment banking. *Administrative Science Quarterly,* 43(1): 1–22.	3.4

Heath, C.	(1995)	Escalation and de-escalation of commitment: The role of budgeting in mental accounting. *Organisational Behaviour & Human Decision Processes,* 62(1): 38–57.	14.2
Henderson, B. D.	(1984)	*The logic of business strategy.* New York. Ballinger Publishing.	3.4
Heraclitus	(1979)	*The art and thought of Heraclitus: An edition of the fragments with translation and commentary.* (C. H. Kahn, Ed. & Trans.). Cambridge, England. Cambridge University Press.	Dim. Two
Herzberg, F.	(1968)	One more time: How do you motivate employees? *Harvard Business Review,* 46(1): 53–62.	14.4
Hickie, D.	(1985)	*The prince and the premier. The story of Perc Galea, Bob Askin and the others who gave organised crime its start in Australia.* Sydney. Angus and Robertson.	9.2
Hilmer, F. G.	(1985)	*When the luck runs out: The future for Australian at work.* Sydney, Australia. Harper & Row.	Acknowl.
Hippel, E. von	(1998)	The economics of product development by users: The impact of 'sticky' local information. *Management Science,* 44(5): 629–44.	10.4
Hippel, E. von	(1994)	*Sources of innovation.* New York. Oxford University Press	10.4
Hiromoto, T.	(1988)	Another hidden edge: Japanese management accounting. *Harvard Business Review,* 66(4): 22–26.	7.3
Hofer, C. W.	(1988)	Turnaround strategies. *Journal of Business Strategy,* 1(1): 19–31.	5.1
Hofstede, G. H.	(1968/ 2003)	*The game of budget control.* London. Routledge. (Original work published 1968).	11.2
Holland, J. H.	(1998)	*Emergence from chaos to order.* Oxford, England. Oxford University Press.	Dim. Two
Hollander, A. S., Denna, E. L., & Cherrington, J. O.	(2000)	*Accounting information technology, and business solutions.* (2nd ed.). New York. McGraw-Hill Education.	17.2
Hope, J., & Fraser, R.	(2003)	Who needs budgets? *Harvard Business Review,* 81(2): 108–18.	6.4
Hopkins, C. C.	(1923/ 1966)	Scientific advertising. Collected in: *My life in advertising and scientific advertising.* New York. McGraw-Hill. (Original work published 1926).	2.3
Hsee, C. K., Blount, S., Lowenstein, G. F., & Bazerman, M. H.	(1999)	Preference reversals between joint and separate evaluations of options: A review and theoretical analysis. *Psychological Bulletin,* 125(5): 576–90.	14.2
Hubbard, D. W.	(2007)	*How to measure anything: Finding the value of intangibles in business.* Hoboken, New Jersey. John Wiley.	3.4, 11.1
Huczynski, A. A.	(1996/ 2007)	*Management gurus.* (Rev. ed.). New York. Routledge. (Original work published 1993).	8.5
Hume, D.	(1777/ 1975)	*Enquiries concerning human understanding and concerning the principles of morals.* (3rd ed.). Oxford, England. Clarendon Press. (Original work published 1774).	13.1

Independent Commission Against Corruption	(2009)	*Investigation into the misuse of Sydney Ferries Corporate Cards.* Sydney, NSW. November, 2009. Independent Commission Against Corruption. <Downloaded from icac.nsw.gov.au on 9 November 2009>.	13.5
Institute of Management Accountants, USA.	(2005)	*Statement of ethical professional practice.* <Retrieved 27 October 2009 from http://www.imanet.org/about_ethics_statement.asp>	13.4
International Institute of Business Analysis & Brennan, K	(2006/ 2009)	*A guide to the business analysis body of knowledge® (BABOK Guide). (v2.0 and 2nd ed.).* Toronto, Ontario. International Institute of Business Analysis. (Original release v1.6 published 2006).	Intro.
International Organisation for Standardisation	(2000)	*ISO 9000 Quality management.* Geneva, Switzerland. International Organisation for Standardisation.	Intro, 12.1
ISO		See **International Organisation for Standardisation**.	
Jackson, H. J.	(2005)	Marginal frivolities: Readers' notes as evidence for the history of reading. In R. Myers, M. Harris & G. Mandelbrote (Eds.): *Owners, annotators and the signs of reading.* (pp 137–51. London. British Library.	11.0
Jamieson, B.	(1995)	*The accounting jungle.* Elsternwick, Victoria. Wrightbooks.	15.4
Janis, I. L.	(1972/ 1982)	*Groupthink: Psychological studies of policy decisions and fiascos.* (2nd ed.). Boston, Massachusetts. Houghton Mifflin. (Original work published 1972).	14.5
Jaques, E.	(1989/ 1998)	*Requisite organization: A total system for effective managerial organization and managerial leadership for the 21st Century.* (2nd ed. amended). Arlington, Virginia. Cason Hall.	6.5
Jaques, E.	(1976)	*A general theory of bureaucracy.* London. Heinemann.	6.5
Jay, A., & Lynn, J.	(1981)	*The compassionate society.* Episode 1 series 2. Yes Minister. Yes minister: The complete series 1–6. London. BBC DVD Video.	8.4
Jiggens, J.	(2009)	*The killer cop and the murder of Donald Mackay.* West End, Qld. Network to Investigate the Mackay Murder.	9.2
Johnson, G., Scholes, K., & Whittington, R.	(1984/ 2005)	*Exploring corporate strategy: Text and cases.* (7th ed.). London. Financial Times Prentice Hall. (Original work published 1987).	2.1
Juglar, B.	(1862/ 1989)	*A history of panics and their periodical occurrence in the United States.* (Ed.). D. W. Thom (Ed.). (2nd ed.). New York. Kelly. (Original work published in French 1862).	1.1
Juran, J. M.	(1964/ 1995)	*Managerial breakthrough.* (30th anniversary revised edition). New York. McGraw-Hill. (Original work published 1967).	12.1
Kahneman, D.	(2000)	Preface. In D. Kahneman and A. Tversky (Eds.), *Choices, values, and frames* (pp ix-xvii). Cambridge, England. Cambridge University Press.	14.1
Kahneman, D., Slovic, P., & Tversky, A.	(1982)	*Judgement under uncertainty: Heuristics and biases.* Cambridge, England. Cambridge University Press.	14.5

Kahneman, D., & Tversky, A.	(1979)	Prospect theory: An analysis of decision under risk. *Econometrica*, 47(2): 263–91.	14.1, 14.5
Kant, I.	(1948/ 2005)	*The moral law: Groundwork of the metaphysic of morals.* (H. J. Paton Trans.). London. Routledge Classics. (Original work published in English 1945).	13.1
Kaplan, R. S., & Norton, D. P.	(2004)	*Strategy maps: Converting intangible assets into tangible outcomes.* Boston, Massachusetts. Harvard Business School Press.	8.4, 11.1
Kaplan R. S., & Norton, D. P.	(1996)	*Balanced scorecard: Translating strategy into action.* Boston, Massachusetts. Harvard Business School Press.	6.4
Kaplan R. S., & Norton, D. P.	(1992)	The balanced scorecard: Measures that drive performance. *Harvard Business Review*, 70(1): 71–80.	6.4
Katona, G.	(1967)	On the function of behavioural theory and behavioural research in economics. *American Economic Review*, 58(1): 146–49.	4.5
Katz, F. E.	(1965)	Explaining informal work groups in complex organisations: The case for autonomy in structure. *Administrative Science Quarterly*, 10 (2): 204–26.	11.5
Kawakita, J.	(1975)	*The Original KJ Method* (Rev. ed.) (Originally published 1975). [Pamphlet]. Meguro, Tokyo: Kawakita Research Institute.	
Kelly, K. K.	(1997/ 1999)	*New rules for the new economy: 10 Ways the economy is changing everything.* (Alternate subtitle: *10 Radical Strategies for a Connected World*). London. Fourth Estate.	2.0
Kepner, C. H., & Tregoe, B. B.	(1965)	*The rational manager: A systematic approach to problem solving and decision-making.* Princeton, New Jersey. Kepner-Tregoe. (2nd ed. 1976; titled *The new rational manager*, 1981).	8.5, 10.5, 14.0
Kester, R. B.	(1917/ 1939)	*Principles of accounting.* (4th ed.). New York. Ronald Press. (Original work published 1914).	10.2
Kildall, G.	(1993)	*Computer connections: People, places, and events in the evolution of the personal computer industry.* Privately Published. Limited to 50 copies.	13.5
Kitchin, J.	(1923)	Cycles and trends in economic factors. *Review of Economics and Statistics*, 5(1): 10–16.	1.1
Knight, F. H.	(1957/ 2006)	*Risk, uncertainty and profit.* (4th ed.). New York. Dover Publications. (First published 1921.)	8.2, 8.5
Kobielus, J. G.	(1997)	*Workflow strategies.* New York. John Wiley.	17.3.1
Koehler, J. J.	(1996)	The base rate fallacy reconsidered: Descriptive, normative and methodological challenges. *Behavioural & Brain Sciences*, 19(1): 1–17.	14.5
Kondratieff, N. D., & Stolper, W. F.	(1935)	The long waves in economic life. *Review of Economics and Statistics*, 17(6): 105–15.	1.1
Kramer, R. C.	(1992)	The space shuttle *Challenger* explosion: A case study of state-corporate crime. In (Eds.) K. Schlegel & D. Weisburd: *White collar crime reconsidered.* (pp 214–43). Boston, Massachusetts. Northwestern University Press.	13.2

Kranz, G.	(2000/ 2001)	*Failure is not an option: Mission control from Mercury to Apollo 13 and beyond.* New York. Berkley.	10.4
Krosnick, J. A., & Fabrigar, L. R.	(1997)	*Designing rating scales for effective measurement in surveys.* In L. Lyberg, P. Biemer, M. Collins, L. Decker, E. DeLeeuw & C. Dippo *et al.* (Eds.), *Survey measurement and process quality* (pp 141–64). New York. John Wiley.	2.3
Kuznets, S.	(1930)	*Secular movements in production and prices: Their nature and their bearing upon cyclical fluctuations.* Boston, Massachusetts. Houghton Mifflin.	1.1
Lai, D.	(2004)	*Learning from the stones: A go approach to mastering China's strategic concept, Shi.* Carlisle, Pennsylvania. Strategic Studies Institute. <Downloaded from publication http://www.carlisle. army.mil/ssi on 26 February 2009>.	3.1
Langford-Smith, K., Smith, D., & Stringer, C.	(2000)	*Managing the outsourcing relationship.* Sydney, NSW. The University of New South Wales Press.	8.5
Law Society of New South Wales	(2009)	*Statement of ethics.* <Retrieved from http://www.lawsociety.com. au/ForSolictors/professionalstandards/Ethics/statement_of_ ethics/index.htm on 4 November 2009>	13.4
Levitt, T.	(1965)	Exploit the product life cycle. *Harvard Business Review,* 43(6): 81–94.	1.1
Levitt, T.	(1960)	Marketing myopia. *Harvard Business Review,* 38(4): 45–53.	2.3, 4.0, 7.3
Lewin, K.	(1947)	Frontiers in group dynamics 1: concept, method and reality in social science; social equilibria and social change. *Human Relations,* 1(1): 5–41.	17.5
Lewis, J	(2003/ 2007)	The perfect money machine(s): George Lucas, Steven Spielberg and auteurism in the new Hollywood. *Film International, 1 (1):* 12–26. Reprinted in J. Lewis & E. Smoodin (Eds.) *Looking past the screen: Case studies in American film history and method.* (pp 61–86). Durham, North Carolina. Duke University Press.	10.4
Library of Economics and Liberty		www.econlib.org	Refs.
Livermore, J.	(1940)	*How to trade in stocks The Livermore formula for combining time element and price.* NY. Duell, Sloan and Pearce.	7.1
Loan Council	(1993)	*Future arrangements for loan council monitoring and reporting.* Canberra, Australia. Australian Government.	3.2
Lomas, R.	(2002/ 2009)	*The invisible college: The secret history of how the Freemasons founded the Royal Society.* (Revised ed.). First published 2002. London. Headline.	6.5
Longman, H. H.	(1967)	*How to cut office costs.* London. Anbar Publications.	8.4
Lovell, J., & Kluger, J.	(1994/ 2000)	*Apollo 13.* New York. Houghton Mifflin. (Original work published 1994 as Lost Moon).	10.4
Lowenstein, G. L., & Prelec, D.	(1993)	Preferences for sequences of outcomes. *Psychological Review,* 100(1): 91–105.	14.2

Luftman, J. N. (Ed.).	(1996)	*Competing in the information age: Strategic alignment in practice.* Oxford University Press.	Dim. Two
Lukes, S.	(1974)	*Power: A radical view.* London. Macmillan Press.	9.0
Lynch, P. & Rothchild, J.	(1989/ 2000)	*One up on wall street: How to use what you already know to make money in the market.* Millennium ed. New York. Fireside.	11.1
Lynn, M.	(1991)	*The billion dollar battle: Merck versus Glaxo.* London. Heinemann.	10.4
Machiavelli, N.	(1958/ 1989)	*Machiavelli: The chief works and others.* (Ed.) A. H. Gilbert. (3 vols.). Durham. Duke University Press.	9.0
Macintyre, A.	(1991)	*Three rival versions of moral enquiry: Encyclopaedia, genealogy, and tradition.* (Gifford lectures delivered in the University of Edinburgh in 1988). London. Duckworth.	13.1
Mackay, C.	(1841/ 1980)	*Extraordinary popular delusions and the madness of crowds.* New York. Harmony Books. (Original work published 1841).	4.1
Malone, T. W., Laubacher, R., & Dellarocas, C.	(2009)	*Harnessing crowds: Mapping the genome of collective intelligence.* MIT Centre for Collective Intelligence Working Paper, January 2009. <*Downloaded from http://cci.mit.edu/publications/ CCIwp2009-01.pdf on 9 November 2009*>	6.2
Malone, T. W.	(1989)	*The logic of electronic markets. Harvard Business Review,* 67(3): 166–71.	2.0
Mandelbrot, B.	(2004)	*The misbehaviour of markets: A fractal view of financial turbulence.* New York. Basic Books.	9.5
Marcus, M. L., Tanis, C., & van Fenema, P. C.	(2000)	Enterprise resource planning: Multisite ERP implementations. *Communications of the ACM,* 43(4): 42–43.	Intro.
Marciniak, J. J., & Reifer, D. J.	(1990)	*Software acquisition management: Managing the acquisition of custom software systems.* New York. Wiley.	17.5
Marsden, S. J.	(2006/ 2008)	*Australian master bookkeeper's guide 2008/2009.* (2nd ed.). Sydney, Australia. CCH Australia. (Original work published 2006).	Intro., 10.2
Marshall, A.	(1890/ 1920)	*Principles of economics.* (8th ed.). London. Macmillan. (Original work published 1890).	4.5
Martin, B.	(1999)	*The whistleblower's handbook: How to be an effective resister.* Charlbury, UK. Jon Carpenter.	9.5
Marx, G. T.	(1974)	Thoughts on a neglected category of social movement participant The agent provocateur and the informant. *American Journal of Sociology,* 80(2): 402–42.	9.2
Machlup, F.	(1967)	Theories of the firm: Marginalist, behavioural, managerial. *American Economic Review,* 57(1): 1–33.	4.5
Machlup, F	(1962)	*The production and distribution of knowledge in the United States.* Princeton: Princeton University Press.	19.5
Mayo, E.	(1945/ 1975)	*The social problems of an industrial civilisation.* With a foreword by Prof Smith on the significance of Elton Mayo. (Originally published 1945). London. Routledge & Kegan Paul.	9.5
McCoy, A. W.	(1980)	*Drug traffic: Narcotics and organised crime in Australia.* Sydney, NSW. Harper & Row.	9.2

McDonald, L.	(2009)	*A colossal failure of common sense: The incredible inside story of the collapse of Lehman Brothers*. London. Ebury Press.	9.2
McGregor, D.	(1960)	*The human side of the enterprise*. New York. McGraw-Hill.	6.5
McKenzie, N.	(2012)	*The sting: Australia's plot to crack a global drug empire*. Carlton, Vic.: Victory Books	9.2
McKinsey Consulting Organisation	(1968/ 1971)	The 1968 McKinsey report on computing utilisation. Reprinted in T. W. McRae (Ed.), *Management information systems* (pp 94–122). Harmondsworth, England. Penguin Books.	17.4
McMillan, E.	(2006)	*Policies and procedures to prevent fraud and embezzlement: Guidance, internal controls and investigation*. New York. John Wiley.	8.2
McNeely, I. F., & Wolverton, L.	(2008)	*Reinventing knowledge: From Alexandria to the internet*. New York. Norton.	12.2
Meehl, P. E.	(1954)	*Clinical versus statistical prediction: A theoretical analysis and a review of the evidence*. Minneapolis. University of Minnesota Press.	14.2
Merton, R.	(1942/ 1973)	The normative structure of science. In *Sociology of science: Theoretical and empirical investigations*. (pp 267–80). Chicago: University of Chicago. (Originally published in 1942 as A note on science and democracy, In *Journal of Legal and Political Sociology*, 1(1–2): 115–26).	10.4
Milgrom, P., & Roberts, J.	(1990)	The economics of modern manufacturing: Technology, strategy, and organization. *American Economic Review*, 80(3): 511–28.	4.1
Miller, D.	(1992)	*The icarus paradox: How exceptional companies bring about their own downfall*. New York. Harper Collins.	3.1
Miller, G.	(2009)	*Spent: Sex, evolution and consumer behaviour*. New York. Viking.	2.3
Miller, G.	(1956)	The magical number seven, plus or minus two: Some limits on our capacity for processing information. *Psychological Review*, 63(2): 81–94.	11.2
Mills, C. W.	(1956)	The structure of power in American society. *British Journal of Sociology*, 9(1): 29–41.	9.1
Mintzberg, H., & Quinn, J. B.	(1991)	*The strategy process*. Englewood Cliffs, New Jersey. Prentice Hall.	2.1
Mintzberg, H., & Waters, J. A.	(1985)	Of strategies, deliberate and emergent. *Strategic Management Journal*, 6(3): 257–72.	3.1
Mitchell, J. T.	(1983)	When disaster strikes: The critical incident stress debriefing process. *Journal of Emergency Medical Services*, 8: 36–39	4.5
Mlodinow, L.	(2009)	*The drunkard's walk: How randomness rules our lives*. London. Allen Lane.	9.5
Mokyr, J.	(2009)	*The enlightened economy: An economic history of Britain, 1700–1850*. (New Economic History of Britain). New Haven, Connecticut. Yale University Press.	2.2
Moore, G. A.	(1991/ 2002)	*Crossing the chasm: Marketing and selling high-tech products to mainstream customers*. New York. Harper Business.	2.2
Moore, G. E.	(1965)	Cramming more components onto integrated circuits. *Electronics*, 38(8): 114–17.	17.4

Moore, P. G., & Hodges, S. D.	(1970)	*Programming for optimal decisions.* Harmondsworth, England. Penguin Books.	17.4
Morgan, N. & Saxton, J.	(1994/ 2006)	*Asking better questions.* (2nd ed.). (Originally published 1994). Markham, Ontario. Pembroke Publishers.	Intro.
Morgan, T.	(2002)	*Business rules and information systems: Aligning IT with business goals.* Indianapolis, Indiana. Addison-Wesley.	17.3.1
Napoleoni, L.	(2010)	*Terrorism and the economy: How the war on terror is bankrupting the world.* New York. Seven Stories Press.	3.1
Nelson, P.	(1974)	Advertising as information. *Journal of Political Economy,* 82(4): 729–57.	12.2
Nelson, P.	(1970)	Information and consumer behaviour. *The Journal of Political Economy,* 78(2): 311–29.	12.2
Nelson, R. R., & Winter, S. G.	(1982)	*An evolutionary theory of economic change.* Cambridge, Massachusetts. Belknap Press.	1.2, Dim. Two
Neumann, J. von, & Morgenstern, O.	(1944/ 2004)	*Theory of games and economic behaviour* (60th anniversary ed.). Princeton, New Jersey. Princeton University Press. (Original work published 1944).	14.1
Niskansen, W. A. Jr.	(1968)	The peculiar economics of bureaucracy. *American Economic Review,* 58(2): 293–305.	8.4
Niskansen, W. A. Jr.	(1970)	*Bureaucracy and representative government.* Chicago. Aldine.	8.4
Nonaka, I., & Takeuchi, H.	(1995)	*The knowledge creating company: How Japanese companies create the dynamics of innovation.* New York. Oxford university Press.	18.1
O'Byrne, S., & Young, D.	(2000)	*EVA and value-based management: A practical guide to implementation.* New York. John Wiley.	15.4.2.1
OECD	(1995)	*The life cycle approach: An overview of product/process analysis.* Paris. OECD.	1.2
OECD	(2002)	*Measuring the non-observed economy: A handbook.* Paris. OECD.	9.2
Ogburn, C. Jr.	(1957)	Merrill's marauders: The truth about an incredible adventure. *Harper's Magazine,* January: 29–44. (Expanded as a book: *The marauders* (1959) in chapter 2, p. 60).	Dim. Two
Ogilvy, D.	(1983)	*Ogilvy on advertising.* New York. Vintage Books.	2.3
Ohmae, K.	(1982)	*The mind of the strategist: The art of Japanese business.* Maidenhead. McGraw-Hill.	3.1
Ohno, T.	(1988)	*The Toyota production system: Beyond large-scale production.* New York. Productivity Press.	6.2, 8.5
Oliver, G. R.	(2010)	Sharing an assumed business body of knowledge: An evaluation using critical management theory. *Proceedings of the 11th European Conference on Knowledge Management, 2–3 September 2010.* Universidade Lusiada de Vila Nova de Famalicao, Portugal.	Method.
Oliver, G. R., & Snowden, D. J.	(2005)	Patterns of narrative in organisational knowledge sharing: Refolding the envelope of art-luddism and techno-fabulism. In G. Schreyögg & J. Koch (Eds.), *Knowledge management and narratives: Organisational effectiveness through storytelling* (pp 15–71). Berlin, Germany: Erich Schmidt Verlag.	4, 7.0, 10.5, 12.2

Oliver, G. R., & Walker, R. J.	(2006)	Reporting on software development projects to senior managers and the board. *Abacus*, 42(1): 43–67.	17.4
Olsen, J. E.	(2003)	*Data quality: The accuracy dimension.* San Francisco. Morgan Kaufmann.	11.2
Olson, M. S., & van Bever, D.	(2008)	*Stall points: Most companies stop growing – yours doesn't have to.* New Haven, Connecticut. Yale University Press.	5.1
Owen, G.	(2011)	*The rise and fall of great companies: Courtaulds and the reshaping of the man-made fibres industry (Pasold Studies in Textile History).* Oxford. Oxford University Press/Pasold Research Fund.	9.1
Packard, D.	(1995)	*The HP way: How Bill Hewlett and I built our company.* New York. Harper Collins.	2.1
Page, S. E	(2007)	*The difference: How the power of diversity creates better groups, firms, schools, and societies.* Princeton, New Jersey. Princeton University Press.	10.5
Panko, R.	(1998/ 2008)	What we know about spreadsheet errors. Originally published in *Journal of End User Computing*, 10(2): 15–21. <Downloaded froPagem http://panko.shidler.hawaii.edu/SSR/Mypapers/whatknow.htm on 10 February 2010>	7.2
Pareto, V. F. D	(1909/ 1971)	*Manual of political economy.* (A. S. Schwier & A. N. Page Trans.). Fairfield, New Jersey. Augustus M. Kelley. (Original work published in Italian 1906).	14.3
Parkinson, C. N.	(1958)	*Parkinson's law: The pursuit of progress.* London. John Murray.	8.4
Parkinson, F.	(1997)	*Critical incident debriefing: Understanding and dealing with trauma.* London. Souvenir Press.	4.5
Parmenter, D.	(2007)	*Pareto's 80/20 rule for corporate accountants.* New York. John Wiley.	14.3
Payne, J. W.	(1976)	Task complexity and contingent processing in decision-making: An information search and protocol analysis. *Organisational Behaviour and Human Performance*, 16(2): 366–84.	14.1
Payne, J. W.	(1988)	*The psychology of attention.* Cambridge, Massachusetts. MIT Press.	14.1
Perkin, H. J.	(1970)	*The age of the railway.* London. Panther.	Dim. One
Perrow, C.	(1986)	*Complex organisations: A critical essay.* New York. Random House.	8.5
Peters, T., & Waterman, R. H. Jr.	(1982)	*In search of excellence: Lessons from America's best run companies.* New York. Harper & Row.	3.1, 4.1
Petrarch (Petrarca, F.)	(1366/ 1991)	*The remedies of both kinds of fortune.* (C. H. Rawski, Trans). 5 vols. Bloomington, Indiana. Indiana University Press.	10.3
Pfeffer, J., & Salancik, G. R.	(1978)	*The external control of organisations: A resource dependence perspective.* New York. Harper & Row.	3.4, 6.3
Piaget, J., & Inhelder, B.	(1966/ 1969)	*The psychology of the child.* (H. Weaver, Trans). New York. Basic Books. (Original work published in French, 1966).	7.0
Pigou, A. C.	(1927)	*Industrial fluctuations.* London. Macmillan.	1.1

Pigou, A. C.	(1920)	*Economics of welfare*. London. Macmillan.	8.4
Plous, S.	(1993)	*The psychology of judgement and decision-making*. New York. McGraw-Hill.	14.1
Polanyi, M.	(1966/1983)	*The tacit dimension*. London. Routledge & Kegan Paul. (Original work published 1963).	12.2
Ponzi, C.	(1937/2001)	*The rise of Mr Ponzi*. Naples, Florida. Inkwell Publishers. (Original work published 1934).	2.0
Porter, M. E.	(1990)	*The competitive advantage of nations*. New York. Free Press.	3.1
Porter, M. E.	(1987)	From competitive advantage to corporate strategy. *Harvard Business Review*, 65(3): 43–59.	3.8, 11.3
Porter, M. E.	(1985/1998)	*Competitive advantage: Creating and sustaining superior performance*. New York. Free Press.	1.4, 2.1, 11.3, 12.0, 16.0, 16.2, 16.3, , 16.4, 16.5
Porter, M. E.	(1980)	*Competitive strategy: techniques for analysing industries and competitors*. New York. Free Press.	Intro, 2.1, 7.1, 16.1, 16.3
Porter, M. E.	(1979/2008)	*The five competitive forces that shape strategy*. In *On competition* (pp 3–38). (Updated and expanded ed.). Boston, Massachusetts. Harvard Business Review. (Original work published 1979 as How competitive forces shape strategy in *Harvard Business Review*, 57(2): 137–48).	2.1, 4.1
Porter, M. E., & Millar, V.	(1985)	How information gives you competitive advantage. *Harvard Business Review*, 63(4): 149–60.	7.3, 16.4
Porter, M. E., & Siggelkow, N.	(2008)	Contextuality within activity systems and sustainability of competitive advantage. *Academy of Management Perspectives*, 22(2): 34–56.	2.1, 4.1
Prahalad, C. K., & Hamel, G.	(1991)	The core competence of the corporation. *Harvard Business Review*, 68(3): 79–91. Reprinted in (Ed.) M. H. Zack (1999): *Knowledge and strategy* (pp 41–59). Woburn, Massachusetts. Butterworth-Heinemann.	1.2, 2.4, Dim. Three
Pratt, S. P.	(2003)	*Business valuation body of knowledge*. New York. John Wiley. (Original work published in 1981 as *Valuing a Business*).	Intro.
Price, D. J. de Solla	(1963/1986)	*Little science, big science- and beyond*. Foreword by Robert Merton. New York. Columbia University Press. (Originally published 1963).	6.5
Project Management Institute	(2000)	*A guide to the project management body of knowledge (PMBOK Guide)* (2000 ed.). Newtown Square, Pennsylvania. Project Management Institute.	Intro.
Prusak, L., & Cohen, D.	(1997/1998)	*Knowledge buyers, sellers, and brokers: the political economy of knowledge*. Ernst and Young Centre for Innovation Working Paper. (Reprinted in (Eds.) D. Neef, A. Siesfeld & J. Cefola (1998): *The economic impact of knowledge: Resources for the knowledge based economy* (pp 137–59). Woburn, Massachusetts. Butterworth-Heinemann.	12.2
RAND Organisation		*www.rand.org*	Method.
Rappaport, A.	(1999)	New thinking on how to link executive pay with performance. *Harvard Business Review*, 77(2): 99–101.	15.4.3

Reddin, W. J.	(1971)	*Effective management by objectives: The 3-D method of MBO.* New York. McGraw-Hill.	6.4
Redman, T. C.	(1996)	*Data quality for the information age.* Norwood, Massachusetts. Artech House.	11.2
Repo, A. J.	(1989)	The value of information: Approaches in economics, accounting, and management science. *Journal of the American Society for Information Science,* 40(2): 68–98.	11.0
Rezaee, Z.	(2002)	*Financial statement fraud: Prevention and detection.* New York. John Wiley.	6.1
Reis, A. & Reis, L.	(2009)	*War in the boardroom: Why left-brain management and right brain marketing don't see eye-to-eye and what to do about it.* New York. Harper Business.	2.3
Rich, B. R., & Janos, L.	(1994)	*Skunk works: A personal memoir of my years at Lockheed.* New York. Back Bay Books.	10.4
Ricardo, D.	(1817)	*On the principles of economy and taxation.* London. John Murray.	3.1
Ridgway, V. F.	(1956)	Dysfunctional consequences of performance measurements. *Administrative Science Quarterly,* 1(2): 240–47	8.3, 11.2
Robertson, S. I.	(2001)	*Problem solving.* Hove, England. Psychology Press.	10.5
Robock, S. H., & Simmonds, K.	(1977/ 1989)	*International business and multinational enterprise.* (4th ed.). Homewood, Illinois. Richard D Irwin. (Original work published 1974).	3.1
Roethlis-berger, F. J., & Dickson, W. J.	(1939)	*Management and the worker.* Cambridge, Massachusetts. Harvard University Press.	8.3
Rogers, E.	(1962/ 2003)	*Diffusion of innovations.* (5th ed.). New York. Free Press. (Original work published 1962).	10.4
Romer, P.	(1990)	Endogenous technical change. *Journal of Political Economy,* 98(5) (Pt. 2): S71–S102.	10.4
Romney, M. B., & Steinbart, P. J.	(2009)	*Accounting information systems.* (11th ed.). Upper Saddle River, New Jersey. Pearson/Prentice Hall.	17.0
Rosenberg, M.	(1968)	*The logic of survey analysis.* New York. Basic Books.	11.5
Royce, W.	(1970)	*Managing the development of large systems. Proceedings of IEEE WESCON,* 26 (August): 1-9. <Downloaded 6 January 2010 from http://leadinganswers.typepad.com/leading_answers/files/ original_waterfall_paper_winston_royce.pdf>.	1.1, 17.5
Russo, J. E., & Shoemaker, P. J. H.	(1989/ 1990)	*Decision traps: The ten barriers to brilliant decision-making and how to overcome them.* New York. Fireside. (Original work published 1989).	14.1
Ryan, B., & Gross, N.	(1943)	The diffusion of hybrid seed corn in two Iowa communities. *Rural Sociology,* 8: 15–24.	10.4
Sackman, H.	(1974)	*Delphi assessment: Expert opinion, forecasting, and group process.* Santa Monica. The Rand Corporation, R-1283-PR.	Method.

Salancik, J. R., Wenger, W., & Helfer, E.	(1972)	The construction of Delphi event statements. *Technological Forecasting and Social Change*, 3(1): 65–73	Method.
Salter, M. S.	(2008)	*Innovation corrupted: The origins and legacy of Enron's collapse.* Cambridge, Massachusetts. Harvard University Press.	5.1, 11.0, 13.0
Salter, M. S., & Weinhold, W. A.	(1979)	*Diversification through acquisition: Strategies for creating economic value.* New York. Free Press.	3.3
Sarbin, T. R.	(1944)	The logic of prediction in psychology. *Psychological Review,* 51(4): 210–25.	14.2
Schaeffer, M. S.	(2006)	*Accounts payable and Sarbanes-Oxley: Strengthening your internal controls.* New York. John Wiley.	8.2
Schein, E. H., Schneier, I., & Barker, C. H.	(1961	*Coercive persuasion: A socio-psychological analysis of the 'Brainwashing' of American civilian Prisoners by the Chinese communists.* New York. Norton	17.5
Schelling, T.	(1971)	Dynamic models of segregation. *Journal of Mathematical Sociology,* 1(2): 143–86.	4.0
Schendel, D. G., Ratton, G. R., & Riggs, J.	(1976)	Corporate turnaround strategies: A study of profit decline and recovery. *Journal of General Management,* 3(3): 3–11.	5.1
Schnaars, S. P.	(1989)	*Megamistakes: Forecasting and the myth of rapid technological change.* New York. Free Press.	7.1, 14.2
Schon, D.	(1983)	*The reflective practitioner.* New York. Basic Books.	8.5
Schumpeter, J.	(1954)	*A history of economic analysis.* London. Allen & Unwin.	6.8
Schweiter, L. O., & Douma, B.	(2002)	The dark side of goal setting: The role of goals in motivating unethical decision-making. *Academy of Management Proceedings.* <Downloaded 8 October 2009 from http://opim. wharton.upenn.edu/~schweitz/papers/AoM_Proceedings_ Goal_setting.pdf>	13.0
Seligman, J.	(1982/ 2003)	*The transformation of Wall street. A history of the securities and exchange commission and modern corporate finance.* (3ʳᵈ ed.). New York. Aspen Publishers.	4.0
Selznick, P.	(1948)	Foundations of the theory of organisations. *American Sociological Review,* 13(1): 25–35.	3.4
Shank, J., & Govindara- jan, K. V.	(1993)	*Strategic cost management.* New York. Free Press.	7.3
Shapiro, C., & Varian, H. R.	(1998)	*Information rules: A strategic guide to the network economy.* Cambridge, Massachusetts. Harvard Business Press.	2.2
Sharp, A., & P. McDermott	(2001)	*Workflow modelling: Tools for process improvement and application development.* Norwood, Massachusetts. Artech House.	17.3.1

Sherif, M., Harvey, O. J., White, B. J., Hood, W. R., & Sherif, C. W.	(1954/ 1961)	*Intergroup conflict and cooperation: The Robbers Cave experiment.* Norman, Oklahoma. University of Oklahoma Book Exchange.	9.5
Shewhart, W. A.	(1939/ 1986)	*Statistical method from the viewpoint of quality control.* New York. Dover Publications.	1.1
Simmel, G.	(1904)	The sociology of conflict, Part 1. *American Journal of Sociology,* 9(4): 490–525.	9.4
Simon, H. A.	(1991)	Bounded rationality and organisational learning. *Organization Science,* 2(1): 125–34.	14.0
Simon, H. A.	(1987)	Making management decisions The role of intuition and emotion. *Academy of Management Executive,* 1(1): 57–64.	14.0
Simon, H. A.	(1955)	A behavioural model of rational choice. *Quarterly Journal of Economics,* 69(1): 99–118.	14.1
Simon, H. A.	(1945/ 1997)	*Administrative behaviour: A study of decision-making processes in administrative organisations.* (4th ed.). New York. Free Press. (Original work published 1945).	14.1, 15.1
Simons, R.	(1995)	*Levers of control: How managers use innovative control systems to drive strategic renewal.* Boston, Massachusetts. Harvard Business School Press.	8.3
Sinclair, D.	(2003/ 2004)	*The land that never was: Sir Gregor MacGregor and the most audacious fraud in history.* New York. Da Capo Press. (Original work published 2003).	3.2
Sinclair, I.	(1988)	*Filofax facts.* London. David Fulton Publishers.	2.2
Slater, J., & Haywood, K.	(2009)	GE capital paves the way with $545M Islamic bond. *The Weekend Australian* Business section 21-22 November 2009, page 31. Reprinted from the Wall Street Journal.	3.2
Sloan, A. P.	(1963/ 1990)	*My years with General Motors.* (New ed.). With forward by Peter Drucker 'Why my years with GM is must reading.' New York. Currency/Doubleday. (Original work published 1963).	6.2
Smith, A.	(1759/ 2010)	*The theory of moral sentiments.* London. Penguin Books.	8.4
Smith, A.	(1776/ 1999)	*An inquiry into the nature and causes of the wealth of nations.* Two volumes. London. Penguin Books.	Intro., Dim. Three
Southall, B., & Perry, R.	(2006)	*Northern songs: The true story of the Beatles song publishing empire.* London. Omnibus Press.	3.2, 10.4
Speedy, B.	(2009)	Foster's hives off 13 wines to Vok. *The Weekend Australian.* Business section. 24–25 October 2009. Page 23.	5.0
Spencer, H.	(1864)	*Principles of biology.* London. Williams & Norgate.	Dim. Two
Stack, J.	(1994)	*The great game of business.* (Paperback ed. with new introduction). New York. Currency Paperback. (Original work published 1992).	10.2
Staw, B.	(1976)	Knee-deep in the big muddy: A study of escalating commitment to a chosen course of action. *Organisational Behaviour and Human Performance,*16(1): 27–44.	17.5

Stein, J., Shiely, J., & Ross, I.	(2001)	*The EVA challenge: Implementing value added change in an organisation.* New York. John Wiley.	15.4.2.1
Sterne, J.	(1997)	*What makes people click: Advertising on the web.* Indiana, Indianapolis. Que.	Dim. Two
Stevenson, W.	(1953)	*The Study of behaviour: Q-technique and its methodology.* Chicago. University of Chicago Press.	Method.
Stewart, M.	(2009)	*The management myth: Management consulting, past, present, and largely bogus.* New York. Norton.	Intro.
Stone, J.	(2011)	A master lesson in tackling the boom, 1980 cabinet papers. *The Australian* 1 January 2011	7.1
Strauss, H. J., & Zeigler, L. H.	(1975)	The Delphi technique and its uses in social science research. *Journal of Creative Behaviour,* 9(4): 253–59.	Method.
Strunk, W., & White, E. B.	(1918/ 1999)	*The elements of style: A style guide for writers.* (4th ed.). London. Longman. (Original work published 1918).	8.4
Sun, T.	(6BC/ 1996)	*The complete art of war.* (R. D. Sawyer, Trans.). Boulder, Colorado. Westview Press. (Original work published in English 1905).	3.1
Surowiecki, J.	(2004)	*The wisdom of crowds: Why the many are smarter than the few and how collective wisdom shapes business, economies, societies and nations.* New York. Doubleday.	4.0
Sutter, J., & Spenser, J.	(2006)	*747: Creating the world's first jumbo jet and other adventures from a life of aviation.* New York. Smithsonian Books.	10.4
Sutherland, S.	(1992/ 2007)	*Irrationality.* (2nd ed.). London. Pinter & Martin. (Original work published 1992).	2.0
Tainer, E	(1993/ 2006)	*Using economic indicators to improve investment analysis.* (3rd ed.). New York. John Wiley. (Original work published 1996).	7.1
Taleb, N. N.	(2007)	*The black swan: The impact of the highly probable.* New York. Random House.	8.5
Tan, H.-T., & Yates, J. F.	(1995)	Sunk cost effects: The influences of instruction and future return estimates. *Organisational Behaviour and Human Decision Processes,* 63(3): 311–19.	14.2
Taylor, F. W.	(1911)	*Principles of scientific management.* New York. Harper Brothers.	8.5
Taylor, R. S.	(1982)	Value-added processes in the information life cycle. *Journal for the American Society for Information Science,* 33(5): 341–43.	6.2
Templeton, L.	(2008)	*Investing the Templeton way: The market-beating strategies of value investing's legendary bargain hunter.* New York. McGraw-Hill.	Dim. Three
Tenbrunsel, A. E., & Messick, D. M.	(2001)	Power asymmetries and the ethical atmosphere in negotiations. In J. M. Darley & D. M. Messick (Eds.) *Social influences on ethical behaviour in organisations* (pp 201–13). Hillsdale, New Jersey. Erlbaum.	13.3
Thompson, J. D.	(1967/ 2003)	*Organisations in action: Social science bases of administrative theory.* (With a new preface by M. N. Zald and a new introduction by W. R. Scott ed.). New Brunswick, New Jersey. Transaction Publishers.	6.3
Thompson, M.	(1979)	*Rubbish theory: The creation and destruction of value.* Oxford, England. Oxford University Press.	1.1

Toffler, A.	(1982)	*The adaptive corporation*. New York. McGraw-Hill.	1.2, 8.1
Toffler, A.	(1970)	*Future shock*. New York. Bantam Books.	2.1
Tornborgh, B. V.	(1943)	Principles of system designing: Fundamentals of preparatory work (Chapter 3). In J. Lasser (Ed.) *Handbook of accounting methods* (pp 26–51). New York. Van Nostrand.	10.2
Townsend, R.	(1970/ 2007)	*Up the organisation: How to stop the corporation from stifling people and strangling profits*. (Commemorative ed.). San Francisco. Jossey-Bass. (Original work published 1970).	8.4
Tufte, E.	(1983/ 2001)	*The visual display of quantitative information* (2nd ed.). (Originally published 1983). Graphics Press. Cheshire, Connecticut.	11.5
Tversky, A.	(1972)	Elimination by aspects: A theory of choice. *Psychological Review*, 79(4): 281–99.	14.1
Tversky, A., & Kahneman, D.	(1981)	The framing of decisions and the psychology of choice. *Science*, 211(4481): 453–55.	14.2, 14.3
Tversky, A., & Kahneman, D.	(1992)	Advances in prospect theory cumulative representation of uncertainty. *Journal of Risk and Uncertainty*, 5(4): 297–326.	14.1
United States Congress	(2011)	*Final Report of the National Commission on the Causes of the Financial and Economic Crisis in the United States*.	4.0 Dim. Four
United States Senate	(1961)	United States Senate Committee on the Judiciary Subcommittee on Antitrust and Monopoly Hearings on Administered Prices (1961): *Price Fixing and Bid Rigging in the Electrical Manufacturing Industry*. 87th Congress. 1st Session. Parts 27–28.	Intro.
UNSW World	(2009)	*UNSW world special anniversary issue: 60 alumni over 60 great years*. Kensington, Australia. University of New South Wales. Issue 11 December 2009.	Concl.
Vernon Inquiry	(1965)	*Report of the committee of economic inquiry*. Canberra, ACT. Australian Government Publishing Service.	14.4
Walker, R. G.	(2011)	Issues in the preparation of public sector consolidated statements. *Abacus*, 47(4): 477–500	10.2
Walker, R. G.	(2009a)	Public sector consolidated statements: An assessment. *Abacus*, 45(2): 171–220.	3.2, 7.3
Walker, R. G.	(2009b)	Discussion of Lev, Radhakrishnan and Zhang. *Abacus*, 45(3): 299–311.	11.1
Walker, R. G., & Oliver, G. R.	(2005)	Accounting expenditure on software development for internal use. *Abacus*, 41(1): 66–91	13.0
Walker, B., & Walker, B. C.	(2002/ 2006)	*Privatisation: Sell off or sell out. The Australian experience*. Sydney, NSW. ABC Books. (Original work published 2000).	4.3
Waterman, R. H. Jr.	(1990/ 1992)	*Adhocracy: The power to challenge change*. New York. Norton. (Original work published 1990).	10.4
Weber, M.	(1956/ 1968)	*Economy and society: An outline of interpretive sociology*. G. Roth & C. Wittich (Eds.). First published 1922. Berkeley, California. University of California Press.	Intro., 9.0, 9.1
Wechsberg, J.	(1968)	*The merchant bankers*. New York. Simon and Schuster.	4.4

Weick, K.	(1995)	*Sensemaking in organisations.* Thousand Oaks, California. Sage.	7.0
Weick, K.	(1988)	Enacted sensemaking in crisis situations. *Journal of Management Studies,* 25(4): 305–17. Reprinted in Weick, K (2001): *Making sense of the organisation* (pp 100–24). Oxford, England. Basil Blackwell.	7.0
Weill, P., & Ross, J. W.	(2004)	*IT governance: How top performers manage it decision rights for superior results.* Boston, Massachusetts. Harvard Business School Press.	17.1
Weill, P., & Vitale, M.	(2001)	*Place to space: Migrating to ebusiness models.* Boston, Massachusetts. Harvard Business School Press.	2.0, 16.1
Weinberg, G.	(1975)	*An introduction to general systems thinking.* (30th anniversary ed.). New York. Dorset House.	17.0
Weinberger, D.	(2007/ 2008)	*Everything is miscellaneous: The power of the new digital disorder.* New York. Holt.	5.5
Weiner, N.	(1948)	*Cybernetics or control and communication in the animal and the machine.* New York. John Wiley.	8.3
Weinstein, L., & Adam, J. A.	(2008)	*Guesstimation: Solving the world's problems on the back of a cocktail napkin.* Princeton, New Jersey. Princeton University Press.	11.2, 11.5
Wernerfelt, B.	(1984)	A resource-based view of the firm. *Strategic Management Journal,* 5(2): 171–80.	1.2
Whiteley, R.	(1984)	The scientific status of management research as a practically oriented social science. *Journal of Management Studies,* 21(4): 369–90.	8.5
Whitton, E.	(1985)	*Can of worms: A citizen's reference book to crime and the administration of justice.* Sydney. Fairfax.	9.2
Wilcox, J. W.	(1976)	A gambler's ruin approach to business risk. *Sloan Management Review,* 18(1): 33–46.	4.3
Wickelgren, W. A.	(1974)	*How to solve problems: Elements of a theory of problems and problem solving.* New York. W H Freeman.	14.1
Wiener, M. J.	(2004)	*A English culture and the decline of the industrial spirit, 1850-1980.* (2nd ed.). (Originally published 1981). Cambridge, England. Cambridge University Press.	2.2
Williamson, O. E.	(1981)	The economics of organisation: The transaction cost approach. *The American Journal of Sociology,* 87(3): 548–77.	3.4
Williamson, O. E.	(1964)	*The economics of discretionary behaviour: Managerial objectives in a theory of the firm.* Englewood Cliffs, New Jersey. Prentice Hall.	Intro.
Womack, J. P., & Jones, D. T.	(2003)	*Lean thinking: Banish waste and create wealth in your corporation.* (Revised and updated ed.). New York. Free Press. (Original work published 1996).	8.4
Womack, J. P., Jones, D. T., & Roos, D.	(2007)	*The machine that changed the world: The story of lean production – Toyota's secret weapon in the global car wars that is revolutionising world industry.* (Rev. ed.). New York. Free Press. (Original work published 1990).	7.5
Wright, O.	(1977/ 2005)	*The Oliver Wright class A checklist for business excellence.* (6th ed.). New York. John Wiley. (Original work titled *Oliver Wright ABCD checklist for operational excellence* published 1977).	Intro.

Wright, R. V. L.	(1974)	*A system of managing diversity.* Cambridge, Massachusetts. A D Little.	7.3
Yamarone, R.	(2004/ 2007)	*The trader's guide to key economic indicators.* (Revised & expanded ed.). New York. Bloomberg Press.	7.1
Yuen, A.	(2007)	*Bill & Dave's memos.* Palo Alto, California. 2DaysOfSummer Books. (Original work published 2006).	2.1
Yunus, M.	(1999/ 2007)	*Banker to the poor: Micro-lending and the battle against world poverty.* (Revised ed.). New York. Public Affairs.	3.2
Zeisel, H.	(1985)	*Say it with figures.* (6th ed.). New York. Harper Collins.	11.5
Zuboff, S.	(1988)	*In the age of the intelligent machine: the future of work and power.* New York. Basic Books.	11.0
Zwiers, J. & Crawford, M.	(1988)	*Academic conversations: Classroom talk that fosters critical thinking and content understanding.* Portland, Maine. Stenhouse Publishers.	Intro.

Acknowledgements

There are three immediate and several long-term acknowledgements:

Graeme Dean offered advice on the initial 30 page outline and then read through the first draft giving detailed and valuable comments particularly concerning risk, audit, fraud, and the role of directors. Several intermediate drafts were edited by Carl Harrison-Ford who reshaped the preface and introduction to enable the author's voice to emerge. The final draft was edited by Susan Murray-Smith who meticulously pinpointed omissions and obscurities in both the points and the footnotes eliminating some potential embarrassments. It was a pleasure receiving the benefit of their considerable expertise. When I started at HM Customs Jack McLean and Jack Eriksson revealed the public service body of assumed business knowledge.

During my years with the quickly evolving Metal Manufactures Limited many of the assumptions documented here were discussed both with the corporate staff and with divisional managers. The description of their goal and role by Fred Hilmer in *When the luck runs out* (pages 89, 115, 120–21) was both strategy and rationale: 'Their work is to do these tasks at least as well as outside firms … provid[ing] advice … on a regular basis … and concentrat[ing] on the main areas of general management, setting direction, allocating money, or deciding about people and organisation. … Once this … is recognised, creation of a small headquarters follows naturally.' (p 115). I gratefully acknowledge the wholehearted support from the Finance Director at the time, John Allen.

The Australian Graduate School of Management, whilst I was its Chief Information Officer provided many scholarly insights into business practices. The formidable writings of Adam Smith on *The Wealth of Nations* had a central place in its ethos and informed many aspects of the BOSBOK.

A sabbatical from The University of Sydney in 2009 enabled completion of the first draft. Research supported by grants from the Faculty of Economics and Business at The University of Sydney (now The University of Sydney Business School) is drawn on to illustrate many of the assumptions.

I gratefully acknowledge the superb research training and mentoring from Professor Marcus O'Connor who emphasised finding the knowledge gap in the literature and formulating a research agenda with significant research contributions and Professor Michael Lawrence who emphasised a rigorous theoretical foundation with a robust methodology. My interest in research was informed by a discussion with Professor Steve Elliot who advised me to speak with Marcus. I thank him for that advice which began my research career.

Without wishing to offload any of the responsibilities that as author are solely mine, I heartily thank them all for what has now become known as mentoring.

Index of brands, businesses, companies, and organisations

Index of topics

www.ingramcontent.com/pod-product-compliance
Lightning Source LLC
Chambersburg PA
CBHW061744210326
41599CB00034B/6787